'WHY IS YOUR AXE BLOODY?'

'WHY IS YOUR AXE BLOODY?'

A READING OF *NJÁLS SAGA*

WILLIAM IAN MILLER

OXFORD
UNIVERSITY PRESS

OXFORD
UNIVERSITY PRESS

Great Clarendon Street, Oxford, OX2 6DP,
United Kingdom

Oxford University Press is a department of the University of Oxford.
It furthers the University's objective of excellence in research, scholarship,
and education by publishing worldwide. Oxford is a registered trade mark of
Oxford University Press in the UK and in certain other countries

First Edition published in 2014
Impression: 1

Published in the United States of America by Oxford University Press
198 Madison Avenue, New York, NY 10016, United States of America

British Library Cataloguing in Publication Data
Data available

Library of Congress Control Number: 2014932445

ISBN 978-0-19-870484-3

Printed and bound by
CPI Group (UK) Ltd, Croydon, CR0 4YY

For Ginger: Jan. 1, 2000–Aug. 7, 2012

'Sárt ertú leikinn, Sámr fóstri, ok búð svá sé til ætlat at skammt skuli okkar í meðal.'

Foreword

Heather O'Donoghue

Medieval Icelandic family sagas—the Sagas of Icelanders—are a unique
literary genre: never before or since, anywhere in the world, have texts like
them been composed. They are long, naturalistic prose narratives, poised
somewhere between history and fiction, which offer a vivid, detailed,
and uncannily believable picture of the everyday life of the first settlers
in Iceland. These settlers created a self-governing republic with its own
complex legal systems and a precocious parliament which lasted for four
centuries after the settlement in the year AD 870.

Njáls saga is widely recognized as one of the finest examples of the genre,
not only because of its length and breadth, and huge narrative sweep, but
also because of its wide range of forceful individual characters—women as
well as men—and the depth and naturalism with which they are depicted.
This calls for some special explanation. For unlike traditional novelists,
saga authors hardly ever reveal (that is, of course, create) the inner life of
their characters; we are very rarely told what these people are thinking, and
thus what motivates their actions, or lies behind their responses. Traditional
literary criticism has always taken a dim view of readers taking it upon
themselves to re-create backstories, or invent inner lives, for fictional characters (even, or especially, those based on historical figures). But William
I. Miller's *A Reading of Njáls Saga* does just this. 'Ferreting out motive', to
use Miller's own terms, is what this book is about.

William I. Miller has two impressive qualifications for writing the kind
of reading which flies in the face of time-honoured literary convention.
First, he is the world's leading expert on medieval Icelandic law, and the
sagas, in their depiction of the social lives of the settlers, take lawsuits as
one of their primary subjects and continually concern themselves with
legally regulated social interactions: marriage, theft, recompense, or slander. Although we cannot measure the plausibility of the action of *Njáls saga*
against any historical record (for the sagas themselves, in a frustratingly

closed circle, constitute virtually the only evidence for the workings of medieval Icelandic society), Miller can cite the medieval Icelandic law-codes in crucial and authoritative defence of his explanations of how and why characters are shown to act as they do. But Miller is also himself a lawyer—trained in the practice of law. He knows how to put together a case, to adduce (in this case, textual) evidence, to infer motive, to offer balances of probabilities, and call for reasonable assumptions. The book is a brilliant example of the forensic lawyer as literary critic.

But Miller is also a teacher—of both law and literature. He has taught *Njáls saga* to generations of students, collecting over the years their inter-pretations of motives and emotions—left largely unstated by saga authors—and weaving them into his own developing theories of what is going on beneath the surface of these narratives. The critic W. P. Ker, whom Miller cites more than once in this book, famously suggested a luminous meta-phor to explain the relationship between surface narrative and inner life in a saga: 'The brevity and externality of the saga method might easily pro-voke from admirers of Richardson a condemnation like that of Dr. Johnson on those who know the dial plate only, and not the works. The psychology of the sagas, however, brief and superficial as it may be, is yet of the sort that may be tested; the dials keep time, although the works are not exposed.' In the process of teaching *Njáls saga*, Miller has tried and tested his theories, and now exposes the works, and the dials do indeed run like clockwork. But then Miller parts company with Ker, for he shows that the psychology of saga narrative, especially *Njáls saga*, is not brief and superficial at all, even if its surface is laconic, but on the contrary, startlingly subtle and com-plex. Many of even the saga's most ardent admirers will be surprised by the psychological depth and literary artistry which Miller's interpretations of motive forces reveal the author of *Njáls saga* to have been a master of.

Some readers, perhaps, will wonder if Miller's method is a legitimate one. It does, for instance, assume a sort of timelessness for the psychology of the saga characters, and does not allow for (arguable) changes in essen-tial human character and its representation over the intervening centuries. But we can appeal once again to the uniqueness—the exceptionalism—of Icelandic sagas, and particularly their distinctive scarcity of authorial com-ment or depiction of inner life. It might be argued that in paring down to a minimum his own judgment and analysis of character and action, the saga author was in fact purposefully providing a text designed to provoke debate, discussion, disagreement amongst its original audience (and of course, not everyone will agree with all of Miller's explications).

A Reading of Njáls Saga is wonderfully unconventional literary criticism, but then the Icelandic saga is wonderfully unconventional narrative. Miller's reading of *Njáls saga* is compelling, absorbing, witty, learned, insightful, and illuminating. Afficionados of the saga will love it, and so too will academics who are willing to loosen up a bit. Readers who do not (yet) know saga literature first-hand will be astonished and delighted. And all three groups will be irresistibly drawn to read or reread the text itself. I'm sure that Miller would and could ask for nothing more.

Preface

I have been blessed to teach annually a course called Bloodfeuds to law students in which we spend more than six weeks on *Njáls saga*. It captures their souls. They buy copies for their parents and siblings; they force their friends to read it. Within five weeks they are talking saga-talk to each other, mimicking its laconic, cool style. The women in the class (and more than a few men) admire variously Gunnhild, Hildigunn, Bergthora, and even the much-maligned Hallgerd. The men predictably cast themselves in their daydreams as skilled warriors like Gunnar or Kari, or even as Njal, the intelligent, non-martial counselor and lawman, and, of course, as the unmatchable Skarphedin. Even in late age, I confess, Skarphedin owns much of my fantasy life.

Given its powerful appeal, it is strange that *Njáls saga* has generated so few books, four in the last fifty years. Perhaps it is the saga's sheer richness and length that have deterred scholars from full monographs. Articles and book chapters are much more numerous. I published one of these articles some thirty years ago: 'Justifying Skarpheðinn.' I have discussed various incidents in the saga in my book on feud and law in the sagas, *Bloodtaking and Peacemaking,* in other articles on saga topics, and in some of my non-Norse books, most recently in *Losing It.* The ideas in some of this earlier material will make an encore here, but not without changes of emphasis and even changes of mind. Except for some sentences here and there, this book is new.

My imagined audience for this study is one that includes students of history, literature, and law, graduate students first, some undergrads, saga scholars and other medievalists, and those interested in political and social theory. The professionals might find space devoted to matters that they would think obvious; the students might find some of the discussions presuming too much background. One never is quite sure one has struck the right balance.

As is my wont, I will be more concerned with the politics and law, the sociology and psychology, of the action and of the characters than with matters that have occupied most saga scholarship for the past century: issues of origins, sources, influences, form, and structure. No proper reading of this saga can dispense with its sociology, the politics of feuding, or its law; there can be no separating the literary from the social and political, unless by some perverse desire we refuse to give the subtle psychological and political intelligence of the author its due. Except for the mainly German-speaking legal historians of the nineteenth and early twentieth centuries (the *Rechtsschule*), work on the sagas concerned itself mostly with how such excellence could have arisen *when* and especially *where* it did. The ever-perspicacious W. P. Ker captured the sentiment more than a hundred years ago: 'there is little in the art of the Sagas that is of doubtful import, however great may be the lasting miracle that such things, of such excellence, should have been written *there* and *then*' (my italics).[1]

The bulk of family-saga scholarship thus became a battle between those who supposed largely oral origins for them, arrayed against those who argued for more literary origins, the literary influences then being disputed as to whether they were native Icelandic and lost, or continental and borrowed, whether vaguely imitated or slavishly followed, whether mainly clerical or secular. The disputes still continue, with some tours de force backing various theories.[2] Often lost in these scholarly wars, which have only abated somewhat, if at all, was the substance of the actual stories except as it related to the consuming issues of origins, influences, and

1. Ker, 236. [References are to author and page number; date of publication is added when more than one work by an author is listed in the Works Cited section at the end of this book, where full entries can be found.]
2. See Andersson 1964, 2012*a*, and Clover 1982, 1985*b*, for ably-argued opposing theories. For overviews see Andersson 2012*a*: 1–8; Allen, 1–56; Clover 1985; and also Cormack; Grønlie 2012; and the general introductions cited in Introduction, n. 2; see also the recent production in the oralist camp of Gísli Sigurðsson. Perhaps the most imaginative and convincing argument on behalf of the oralists was recently made by Andersson 2012*b*, matching the mentions of landing-spots and harbors in the sagas against what recent archaeological evidence tells us were the landing-spots actually in use when the sagas were written. The Icelandic school, following Sigurður Nordal, on the other hand, claims that the sagas are works of creative genius written in much the manner, say, that Dostoyevsky wrote a novel. I remain mostly agnostic on issues of origins as regards *Njáls saga*, assuming some regional traditions that lay behind an actual historical burning, but by the time our author gets his hands on the story, writing toward the end of nearly a century of saga writing, we have all the elements of a self-conscious literary production. When I refer to the writer of this saga as an 'author', I think I am largely justified, even if I do not mean to import all the modern baggage that comes with that term.

formal structure. The *Rechtsschule* scholars, as I said, were notable exceptions, mining the sagas for whatever information they might contain about
early Germanic social and legal forms. By far the best of these for students
of the sagas was the Swiss Andreas Heusler, who was no less sophisticated
on literary matters than he was on legal ones.[3] He and W. P. Ker are the
giants on whose shoulders we pygmies in later generations try to stand, but
we often do not make it beyond their laps, or if we get to their shoulders we
stumble and smash our skulls on the floor.

Wm. I. Miller

3. Heusler's book (1911) on feud and law in the sagas is still the single best work on saga substance as well as being a significant contribution to legal history; he also remains the starting
   point on issues of saga form and structure. The best book on the literary aspects of *Njáls saga*
   is, in my opinion, Allen's. But the single best reading of it may still be Maxwell's article,
   more than fifty years old. KJJ's relatively recent book, except for its strange central thesis
   (see Ch. 3, n. 30), is filled with perceptive observations. It should be translated into English.

Acknowledgements

I owe more than I can properly express to the law students I teach. They write papers based on English translations of the sagas, but every year some three or four of them make a point or come up with an interpretation that teaches me something, that pulls me out of the ruts my own views have gotten me into. I have footnoted some of these papers when I feel it would be grand theft not to give the student credit. I have them on file.

Six people read complete drafts of this book and made valuable suggestions. They will recognize their contributions should they ever undertake to read this final version: John Hudson, Helle Vogt, Ingrid Hedström, Don Herzog, Kathy Koehler, Jordan Corrente Beck, and two anonymous readers for the press, both of whom went beyond the call of duty, one of them even sacrificing anonymity and more time to agree to write a foreword to this book. Svanhildur Óskarsdóttir is to be thanked for answers to specific queries. My general debt over the years to Ted Andersson and Carol Clover should be apparent in the footnotes, even if we ride very different hobbyhorses. Thanks too to Laura Harlow, secretary to ten of us, to Bess and Eva Miller, and to the University of Michigan Law School where for some thirty years I have been more than merely tolerated, but actually encouraged to go wherever my interests led me. Or did I miss their hints?

Contents

Abbreviations

BP	Miller, William Ian (1990), *Bloodtaking and Peacemaking: Feud, Law, and Society in Saga Iceland.* Chicago: University of Chicago Press
CSI	*The Complete Sagas of Icelanders including 49 tales.* Edited by Viðar Hreinsson, 5 vols. (1997), various translators. Reykjavík. I will on occasion list other translations, still readily accessible
DGL	*Danmarks gamle Landskabslove med Kirkelovene*, vols. 1–8 (1932–51), ed. Johs. Brøndum-Nielsen. Copenhagen: Gyldendal
EÓS	Einar Ól. Sveinsson
Grágás	*The Laws of the Icelandic Commonwealth*; see entry in Works Cited
ÍF	Íslenzk Fornrit. Various editors (1933–present). Reykjavík: Hið Íslenzka Fornritafélag
JD	Juris Doctor
JEGP	*Journal of English and Germanic Philology*
KJJ	Kristján Jóhann Jónsson (1998), *Lykillinn að Njálu.* Reykjavík: Vaka-Helgafell
Lehmann	Lehmann, Karl, and Hans Schnorr von Carolsfeld (1883), *Die Njálssage insbesondere in ihren juristischen Bestandtheilen: ein kritischer Beitrag zur altnordischen Rechts- und Literaturgeschichte.* Berlin: R. L. Prager
ModI	Modern Icelandic
MT	*Sturlunga saga*, trans. Julia H. McGrew and R. George Thomas, 2 vols. (1970–4). New York: Twayne
NGL	*Norges gamle Love*, vol. 1 of 5 (1846), ed. R. Keyser and P. A. Munch. Oslo
ON	Old Norse
SS	*Scandinavian Studies*
ST	*Sturlunga saga*, ed. Jón Jóhannesson, Magnús Finnbogason, and Kristján Eldjárn, 2 vols. (1946). Reykjavík: Sturlunguútgáfan. For translation see MT

Note to Readers

Since I mean to include non-specialists in my intended audience I have anglicized Norse names in the text and partly too in the footnotes by rendering thorn (þ) and eth (ð), as th and d, hooked o as o, and by omitting diacritics and dropping the nominative inflection of proper names, thus Skarphedin, not Skarpheðinn, Thorhall, not Þórhallr. I have also taken the liberty of doing the same with quotes from other scholars. Bibliographical references retain Icelandic characters and diacritics. I cite Icelandic scholars under their given name as in Icelandic style. I have used Einar Ól. Sveinsson's standard excellent edition in the Íslenzk fornrit series and I generally adopt the Magnusson/Pálsson translation, but I make occasional changes in the direction of literalness, which I will not burden the reader to note. I prefer their translation to any other because of its liveliness and enviable ability to capture the wit, irony, and most of the 'feel' of the original. It has been criticized for being rather free at times, but it makes the legal aspects of the saga intelligible to an Anglo-American audience much better than other translations.[4]

A caveat. Certain observations made in earlier chapters will be recalled or briefly recapitulated at times in later chapters. This is advertent and I hope that I have avoided seeming repetitive. It is a concession to how

4. Cook's translation, the one presently available in Penguin, is mostly very literal, with random deviations from literalism when the literal rendering would be better; his version does not quite read like modern English. Cook (2002) presents his translation theory; Andersson (2003) is sharply, but not unjustly, critical of Cook's text. Bayerschmidt/Hollander is a little too stiff for my tastes, but superior to Cook. The 19th-century Dasent translation, despite the initial annoyance one must overcome because of its archaisms, captures the saga's power nonetheless. On Dasent and his translation, see Wawn, 142–82; Cook 1998; on the history and politics of translations of *Njáls saga*, see Jón Karl.

I imagine this book will often be used, and offered up as a favor to those who might have trouble keeping the saga's mass of detail fresh in mind.

Citations to *Njáls saga* are to chapter since chapters are short and all translations except Dasent's maintain the same chapter division and his deviates only slightly after chapter 57. Other sagas will also be cited to chapter.

Introduction

No one is all that surprised when first reading Shakespeare, Milton, the *Iliad*, Austen, or Dostoyevsky to discover that they are even better than promised. We have come to expect that from Greece, England, and Russian novelists. No one, however, expects such greatness from a barely-populated volcanic excrescence, hauntingly beautiful as it is, in the middle of nowhere. Had *Njáls saga* been produced by an ancient Greek, a biblical Hebrew, a Russian, Italian, Frenchman, Spaniard, German, or Englishman, it would be very well known indeed. Those who do know it count it among the greatest works of literature.[1] But it happened to be the work of an Icelander, a medieval one at that, who wrote his saga *c.*1280.

Compare, as a thought experiment, ancient Israel to Iceland. If the land that produced the Hebrew Bible seems rather bleak, parched, and very small to the modern visitor, and its people neither powerful nor numerous, they were situated in a place where armies of empires clashed for 4,000 years, halfway between Egypt and Babylon, Egypt and Assyria, Egypt and the Hittite Empire, halfway between Persia and Greece, Rome and Persia, and very near to where our alphabet achieved its first form, the navel of the world. Things were and are still happening there that would make the Book of an insignificant people get itself read outside the group that produced it. The fortuities of location (among other things) made what they thought mattered enough to write down, matter.

Yet, strangely, the Icelandic Althing—the polity's annual two-week midsummer meeting where lawsuits were heard, laws were promulgated, and the law recited—can, if we shift the plane, match Jerusalem for symbolic possibility. The Althing is situated at the very place where the Eurasian and North American tectonic plates are at war, pulling apart, mimicking the polity's division at the time of the Conversion or the Battle

---

1. 'One of the great prose works of the world': Ker, 61.

at the Althing in *Njáls saga*. The location itself offers a performance of the first ten verses of Genesis. Visit the site. You can see the fissures and cracks that mark the boundary between the plates; you witness Creation.

Like the ancient Israelites, the authors of the family sagas (*Íslendingasögur*) thought things worth writing down had happened and were happening in their land too.[2] One might even discern in these texts a sense of election in their exodus to Iceland, though whether there was much divinity in that election is barely hinted at, if hinted at at all. God (and gods) are quite reticent in this saga, and leave it open to scholars to argue whether the spirits they think they have seen are really there.[3] As with the Lord, so too with lords. The family sagas are not tales of princes or kings (except when an Icelander travels abroad). They are tales of the disputes and feuds of what we might think of as the better-off sheep- and cattle-ranchers jockeying for position among others like themselves. And except for some strange occurrences now and then, the saga-writers mostly share a commitment to plausibility, none more so than the author of *Njáls saga*.[4]

Njála (the Icelandic nickname for the saga) represents the apotheosis of what is sometimes called the mature or classical saga style; it is indisputably the greatest saga of them all.[5] If the number of preserved manuscripts

2. The sagas are prose narratives. Scholars have divided the sagas into several genres, only two of which figure in this book: the family sagas, also called the 'sagas of the Icelanders' (*Íslendingasögur*), and the so-called contemporary sagas (*samtíðarsögur*), which are further divided into secular sagas and bishops' sagas. The family sagas are about events set in the Saga Age (930–1030). *Njáls saga* is thus a family saga. The contemporary sagas describe events that took place in the 12th and 13th centuries, within a century of their being written. The contemporary secular sagas, with two exceptions, are collected in a single compilation known as *Sturlunga saga, c.*1300, although the sagas making it up were composed at various times earlier in the previous century. When Icelanders wanted to write about kings, they knew how to do it; thus the so-called 'kings' sagas', largely about the Norwegian kings, but often interleaved with short stories of various Icelanders' adventures with Norwegian or Danish royalty (see most recently Andersson 2012a: ch. 3). Most of these sagas, of whatever type, were probably written between the late 12th and early 14th centuries. Dating the composition of individual sagas is problematic, though *Njáls saga* can be dated fairly confidently to *c.*1280. Several good introductions to the sagas are available, a spate of them appearing in the last decade, most recently by Clunies Ross, and also the book-length chapter by Vésteinn and Sverrir (2006); O'Donoghue (2004) covers much ground very readably. The comprehensive critical bibliographies in Clover and Lindow, somewhat dated now, are still excellent regarding the genres of Old Norse literature and the various critical stances taken toward them; see also the collection of essays on Icelandic literature and society in McTurk (ed.) 2007.
3. God does intervene at times via the miraculous in some sagas more than others. Scholars have identified instances of family-saga authors borrowing from saints' lives and other Christian writings, but the extent of these borrowings, or whether in fact they are even borrowings, is still contested; see Grønlie 2012.
4. Allen, 5.
5. Let Ker, 191, stand for the general opinion: 'the greatest of all the Sagas.'

is a good proxy, it was also the most popular in its own time.[6] Given that twenty-one vellum manuscripts survive from 1300–1600, and many later paper ones, the textual variation is not as great as one would expect. *Njála* presents nothing like the problems facing an editor of *Hamlet*.

Word on the sagas, however, is getting out, assisted in some small measure by the sexiness of Vikings in video games, the pretense of Viking-like settings for popular television programs, and by Iceland serving as the ignominious emblem of the financial excesses that brought the world to its knees in 2008—its banks acting as if they were American or British banks. Then, too, its volcanoes disrupt transatlantic air traffic, and have rendered the Great Circle from Chicago to London not as attractive as the longer route several hundred miles south of Iceland. But mostly it is the agreed excellence of these texts that is finally getting them assigned in college literature and history courses.

Some Social Background

Because much of the crucial action of *Njála* takes place at 'Things', and because this book is meant to reach more than those schooled in the Icelandic sagas, I offer a brief account of some of the social and legal givens of the saga. In the ancient and medieval Nordic world—not just Iceland— 'Things' were assemblies where lawsuits were heard, laws laid down, and other business relevant to the community discussed. The settlers of Iceland continued the custom. Juridical freedom was generally the only necessary qualification for attendance, though certain property qualifications might be imposed for membership on jury panels or panels of judges, as at one point becomes relevant in the saga (ch. 142). The Things met at fixed times and fixed locations. In 930, at the conclusion of what is known as the Age of Settlement (870–930), a Thing for all of Iceland, the Althing, was established at Thingvellir—Thingfields—to be held annually for two weeks at midsummer. Given the latitude, there would be abundant light even at midnight, 'so that if a person wanted to work or pick lice out of a shirt he could'. Those words come from the earliest source (late eighth century)

---

6. See EÓS 1971: 47–8, and EÓS 1953 (19 vellum mss. to 1550); http://www.arnastofnun.is/ page/breytileiki_njalu_manuscripts.

irrefutably referencing what would become known as Iceland. It records the observations of seamen who made it there and back to tell their tale to an Irish monk, who wrote it down nearly a century before the permanent Norse settlement of Iceland began in 870.[7]

There were also local Things. According to the laws of the commonwealth (930–1262/4), collectively known as *Grágás*,[8] there were ideally three local Things per quarter, except for the North Quarter, which was to have four.[9] *Njála* pays lip-service to this ideal arrangement in chapter 97, but the neatness of three chieftains per local Thing, and twelve plus one local Things, is largely a creature of rationalizing provisions in the laws. The reality was messier. In *Njáls saga* it is not clear who the three chieftains are that were supposed to inaugurate each spring the Thingskalar Thing, the local Thing for the Rangriver district in which most of the saga takes place. Though the saga does not conform in every detail with the idealized account in the laws, very little hinges on the deviations.[10]

The English word *thing*, not surprisingly, is cognate with the Norse word. In Old English, as in more than a few of the old Germanic languages, *thing*'s core sense indicated a matter in dispute requiring a determination and/or the place at which such determinations were to be made. The word was thus tied up with law, contention, dispute-resolution, and governance.[11] Strangely, similar semantic developments took place in other languages, where the word for 'contention' also ended up becoming the bland word for 'thing'. Thus German *Sache,* originally a dispute or legal claim, came to mean 'thing' and Latin *causa,* a lawsuit, yields French *chose* (thing)

---

7. Dicuil (fl. late 8th and early 9th centuries), *Liber de Mensura Orbis Terrae* 7.2.6, http://penelope. uchicago.edu/Thayer/L/Roman/Texts/Dicuil/De_mensura_orbis_terrae/text*.html.

8. The two chief codices composing *Grágás* date to roughly 1260 and 1280 respectively. *Grágás* exists in a splendid English translation, which I use when quoting the laws. The translation provides the pagination of Finsen's classic 19th-century edition, which, following the usual practice, I cite to; see Works Cited, s.v. *Grágás*. Andrew Dennis's inexplicably unpublished 1973 Cambridge dissertation is indispensable for a proper understanding of the very difficult procedure section.

9. The country was divided into quarters *c.*965, the most important consequence of which was to determine the proper venue for lawsuits, and to allocate some kind of representative equality at the Althing for the main regions of the country. Recent scholarship, based partly on archaeological findings made in the past twenty years, has done much to undermine the classic account of Things and chieftaincies, which at times even *Grágás* itself admits is an idealized construct (*Grágás* Ia 38); see Orri 2007: 117–22 and cf. Jón Viðar.

10. On some of the deviations, see pp. 127ff, 265ff.

11. See *OED* s.v. 'thing' n. 1 for the sense development.

and English *cause* of action or *chose* in action. One is tempted to imagine that what gives substance to 'something' is its being worth fighting over.[12]

Outside of these local Things and the Althing (and a small administrative unit, the *hreppr*,[13] which was in charge of local indigents) there were no formal governing institutions. The enforcement of rights and duties fell to the wronged parties who, as much of this saga will show, needed to gather support from kin, friends, and chieftains to help plead their cases at the Things, but also to enforce any judgment they got from the courts there.

There were three main types of relief obtainable by suing in the courts held at the Things. For any serious offense the penalty was full outlawry, which was pretty much a death sentence. The outlaw's property was forfeit as per the recitation given by Mord in chapter 142. Anyone could kill a full outlaw with impunity, and the person who got him outlawed was obliged to kill him, with some small exceptions that need not concern us. No one could aid the outlaw or assist him in any way, not even to transport him out of Iceland, unless his outlawry had been formally mitigated to allow for passage abroad. The laws also provide for a lesser outlawry, which involved property forfeiture and a three-year exile. The sagas never show this lesser outlawry imposed by a court, but we do see something like it announced fairly frequently by arbitration panels, such as the settlement Gunnar violates.[14] There were also lesser actions involving three-mark fines, a number of which appear in the saga, and judgments providing relief for what we would call contract and tort claims, where damages and rights of possession and title were determined and something resembling injunctions issued.

A person who had suffered a wrong had basically four choices: he could lump it, either because he was too weak to do anything else or because he did not think it wise or worth it to sue. He could settle with the offending party, either by first going to law and then having the case removed from the judges and submitted to arbitrators chosen by the parties; or he could settle without going to law, as Gunnar and Njal do for each of the killings that their wives encompass. Yet even between these friends, their

---

12. Notice a similar sense development for 'matter' and Hamlet's punning on it to mean trouble or a bone of contention, as in 'what's the matter', as well as 'matter' meaning substance, and then among us, solid stuff itself. Polonius (as Hamlet reads): 'What's the matter, my lord?' H: '*Between* who?' P: 'I mean the matter that you read, my lord.' (II. ii).

13. A unit of at least twenty households whose householders are wealthy enough to pay the Thing attendance tax; see n. 20 and *Grágás* Ib 171–80.

14. See Heusler 1911: 137–9, 167.

settlements were concluded by a formal arbitration, with one party conferring the power on the other to decide the amount of compensation due, a procedure known as 'self-judgment'. Third, one could take the law to its conclusion and obtain an outlawry judgment, and then be put to the dangerous duty of hunting the outlaw down. Thus it is that arbitration produced a settlement (*sætt*); a court issued a judgment (*dómr*). Finally, the wronged party could take blood revenge, and raise the justifiability of his revenge as a defense to an action for homicide brought by his victim's kin. (The laws provided a right to avenge certain serious wrongs for a limited length of time, after which one was required to get an outlawry judgment first.)[15] In either case—revenge or going to law—corpses were contemplated, but in fact settlements often substituted exile or property transfers for blood. Which method one employed would depend on several variables, and *Njáls saga* is rich in illustrating the deliberations and considerations that informed these choices. Serious feuds, such as the one in this saga, are more than legal and moral matters; they are also political contests over power and dominance.

The polity had only one paid official: the Lawspeaker, whose duty it was to recite the laws at the Althing, a third of them each year, with the procedure section recited annually. He was paid 240 ells of woolen cloth (*vaðmál*), which also served as the chief money substance; he also received half of the fines imposed at the Althing.[16] Two Lawspeakers play a substantial role in the saga: Skapti Thoroddsson (term 1004–30), the Lawspeaker for much of the post-Conversion portion of *Njála*; and the remarkable Thorgeir of Ljosavatn (985–1001), who formulated the compromise by which the polity peacefully accepted Christianity (ch. 105).

In addition to the courts which were held at the Althing there was also a Court of Legislature, the *Lögrétta*. Each chieftaincy (*goðorð*) held a right to a seat in the *Lögrétta*, and the chieftain (*goði*)[17] was to appoint two of his thingmen as advisers to sit with him (the saga describes fairly accurately the

---

15. See e.g. *Grágás* Ia 147 and also Ch. 2, n. 39.
16. See more fully *Grágás* Ia 208–10.
17. 'Chieftain' is a term that most English translators apply both for *goði* and *höfðingi*, though the former is frequently rendered 'priest' (not a Christian one), as in the Magnusson/Pálsson translation, on the not clearly warranted assumption that *goðar* (pl.) had cultic functions in the tenth century. The sagas themselves do not always maintain the *höfðingi*/*goði* distinction with great precision. A *höfðingi* might be a *goði* or hold part of a *goðorð*, but he might simply be a big man, a leader, the head of a large kin-group. The imprecision runs mostly in one direction; a leader of a group without a *goðorð* will not be called a *goði*, but someone who is a *goði* might only be referred to as a *höfðingi* if he has real power. Not every *goði* was a *höfðingi*; some might be mere title-holders and have little power beyond the right to sit in the Court

Lögrétta in ch. 97). It is probably as one of these thingmen-advisors that Njal proposes his Fifth-Court reform. The Lawspeaker and eventually the two bishops also had a seat. This body made and altered law and decided what the law was if there was disagreement.

The law knew only two statuses of person: slave and free, with some small taint that endured one generation for a freedman.[18] To be sure, there were informal status rankings, the ordering of these being perhaps the most important matter in the social world of the sagas. These rankings were the measure of one's honor. There was no set formula for the content of honor. Courage, intelligence, learning, wealth, birth, generosity, good looks, good will were part of it, as was—importantly, and circularly—the reputation for having it. Honor was also partly reflected in the price arbitrators put on the corpse of a man to settle the claim against his killers. *Njála* sets the price of a slave at 12 ounces of silver, a freedman of modest standing at 100 ounces, and at 200 ounces for a member of the established classes. Such man-prices are not found in the laws, where the infringement of serious rights of any free man or woman, including freedmen, all carried the same price: 48 ounces, a sum called *réttr*. Some people are deemed worthless, as when arbitrators conclude that it was good riddance, in effect rating the person as an outlaw or no man. Thus Skammkel (ch. 56). Even an outlaw had a kind of value, for there was a price on his head of three marks if he were outlawed for any of four specifically enumerated offenses, one of which is burning a man inside his house; otherwise his head was worth one mark.[19]

A chieftaincy, a *goðorð*, could be bought, sold, inherited, shared, or split into shares. According to the classical view derived from the laws, every free man had to announce himself the thingman of a chieftain (*goði*) in his district for purposes of Thing attendance, both at the local Things and at the Althing. Thingmen who met certain wealth requirements were obliged to pay a tax as a penalty if they did not attend the Althing with their chieftain, the proceeds of which were used to defray the expenses of those who attended in their place.[20]

---

of Legislature. In any instance where it matters I will clarify the usage; see Jón Viðar, 48–50; Orri 2007: 118–22.

18. For example, if a freedman died childless his manumitter inherited ahead of the freedman's more distant kin; see e.g. *Grágás* Ia 227.

19. *Grágás* Ia 178. Despite my using numerals for 100, 200, these represent mostly long hundreds of 120, 240, etc. Consider the numerals a shorthand to translate the native commitment to roundedness.

20. Those required to pay the tax were 'those who for each household member who is a charge on them own a debt-free cow or its price or a net or a boat and all the things which the household may [not] be without'; *Grágás* Ia 159; II 320.

Njáls saga is less than clear about how important the chieftain–thingman bond was, it having ceased to be operative when the saga was written. For instance, as we shall see later, it is never indicated who either Njal's or Gunnar's chieftain was, yet the number of chieftaincies prior to the reform that instituted the Fifth Court, *c.*1004, matters greatly to the plot. Indeed, the saga explains the institution of that court as a 'plot' of Njal's to increase the number of chieftaincies so that his foster-son Hoskuld could obtain one.

The Story in a Nutshell

I have assumed that the examples that I included from the saga in the preceding section helped clarify the overview, but I will add this summary to refresh the reader's memory of the broad outline of this complicated tale. The task is not an easy one. The saga names 649 people, half of whom play a role in the action (the rest are genealogical). Some 170 of those have speaking-parts, to which we can add another twenty or so unnamed speakers.[21] Add what the estimable commentator Andreas Heusler called the author's *Stofffreude* ('"Stuff"-delight'), by which he meant to capture the density of the saga's rich and apt detail, providing contextual nuance to motive and action, and you might understand why I preface this summary with some equivocation.[22] I hope to have kept the interpretive tendentiousness any summary must indulge to a fair minimum, and if the saga is fresh in your mind you are invited to skip the section.

The saga's first thirty-four chapters treat of marriage and marriage termination. There are nine marriages. Two end by divorce and two more by death, not from old age but by axe-blows. Several betrothals are dealt

---

21. These genealogies are important for they allow us to grid kinship connections. A significant number of these twenty anonymous speakers' words are of vital (or lethal) importance. There are also 99 named women, twenty of whom speak, to whom we must add six of the most crucial of the unnamed speakers. Again, roughly half of the named women (52) are genealogical. Female presence in the genealogies indicates that the Icelanders computed kinship bilaterally, i.e. through people of both sexes. That leaves some 27 without speaking-parts who are alive and part of the array, some ten of whom are present onstage, either acting or being acted upon. The mere numbers underestimate the importance of the women to the action. See Hallberg (1966), who provides these numbers, though my own count differs by one or so.
22. Heusler 1922: 4, 14. The extraordinary detail of *Njála* is frequently noted; Dronke, 3–5; Ker, 190.

with in detail, as are the property transfers that are a good portion of marriage's motive. Property is also at issue when the marriages terminate. That is the story of the saga's first marriage, also its first of several bad marriages. Hrut is betrothed to Unn, but the wedding is postponed so that Hrut can go to Norway to claim an inheritance there. In exchange for Hrut's sexual services, Gunnhild, the Norwegian king's mother, undertakes the work of recovering Hrut's inheritance, but when Hrut leaves Gunnhild to return to Iceland she curses his marriage, rather effectively, since Hrut is unable to consummate it, try though he and Unn may. After three years Unn divorces him and returns to her father, Mord Fiddle, who then sues to recover her marital property. He loses the case when he, an old man, refuses Hrut's challenge to a duel.

The saga then deals with the first two marriages of Hallgerd, daughter of Hoskuld, Hrut's half-brother. These marriages both end when her foster-father, Thjostolf, kills her husbands. He was doing her bidding in the first instance, and acting against her orders when he dispatched the second, after which she sends her foster-father to his death.

Later, Unn seeks out her kinsman Gunnar to help recover her property from Hrut. Gunnar goes to his friend Njal for legal advice as to how to proceed with the claim. With some poetic justice, Gunnar recovers Unn's property when Hrut refuses Gunnar's offer to duel. Property back in hand, Unn marries Valgard the Gray; they have a son named Mord. He is painted as a malicious fomenter of strife, who plots against Gunnar and is later complicit in the death of Hoskuld, Njal's foster-son.

Njal's sons, Skarphedin and his brothers, are introduced and married off, but all of them still reside together at the farm of their father and mother, Bergthora. Two of the marriages bring property into the family, the third adds prestige, as Helgi Njalsson is married up into the prominent family of Asgrim Ellida-Grimsson, who will later serve as one of the chief opponents of the Burners of Njal and his sons.

Gunnar goes abroad to have great success raiding and hobnobbing with Scandinavian royalty, and returns with his already good reputation greatly enhanced. Njal warns him to beware of provoking people's envy. Though Gunnar means to take the advice to heart, he is not all that successful implementing it over the remaining forty-seven chapters of his life. At the Althing that Njal advised him not to attend, he meets Hallgerd and is smitten. Hrut, holding no grudge against Gunnar over Unn's dowry recovery, tries to warn him off marriage, but to no avail. Njal predicts she will be nothing but trouble. The wedding is held at Gunnar's farm, Hlidarend, and soon turns into a double wedding, as Gunnar's maternal uncle Thrain divorces his wife at the festivities and immediately seeks the hand of Hallgerd's 14-year-old daughter, Thorgerd.

Strife begins soon thereafter when Njal's wife, Bergthora, and Hallgerd argue over seating arrangements at a feast. These two women begin exchanging annual killings of each other's household members while the men are attending the Althing. Their husbands settle each killing, but the women keep raising the stakes by involving ever-higher-ranking members of their households in the lethal action. Bergthora makes the crucial escalatory move by recruiting her sons' foster-father, Thord Freedmansson, to the feud, to which Hallgerd adds more fuel by coining insulting nicknames for Njal—Old Beardless—and for his sons—Little Dungbeards—which are then versified at her suggestion by Sigmund, a kinsman of Gunnar. It is their foster-father's death that ensures that the enmity between the sons of Njal and the kin of Gunnar—the Sigfussons—will never be fully resolved, though hostility will remain repressed as long as Gunnar is alive, for the friendship of Gunnar and Njal survives their wives' hostility.

The women finally cease their killing and the saga shifts to depict the troubles that Gunnar begins to have in the district. He becomes the object of enmities that will eventually lead to his death. The first dispute begins when Gunnar attempts to buy provisions during a period of local shortages from a well-connected farmer, Otkel. Otkel refuses to sell food and instead offers to sell Gunnar a worthless slave, who Gunnar buys, apparently to make the best of an already awkward encounter. Hallgerd, to avenge the insult to her husband of Otkel's refusal, orders that slave to steal food from Otkel's storehouse and to burn it down to cover his tracks. The crime is discovered and Gunnar, furious that Hallgerd would stoop to theft, slaps her in front of company. Hallgerd's two prior husbands had also slapped her, and met their maker the day they did. Not Gunnar. He must wait.

Otkel, following the bad advice of his friend Skammkel, summons Gunnar for receiving stolen goods. Attempts to settle the trouble only lead to more of it, when the very nearsighted Otkel loses control of his horse on his way to visit a friend and rides Gunnar down; Skammkel makes insulting remarks, which Otkel does not disown. Shortly thereafter Gunnar and his brother Kolskegg kill Otkel and seven others in Otkel's party. A settlement is concluded with Gizur the White and Geir the Priest, the big men in Otkel's kin-group. Gunnar emerges with honor enhanced, but Njal counsels him not to kill twice in the same lineage, and to make sure he honors any settlement resolving matters should he violate the first of these admonitions.

More trouble arises when Thorgeir Starkadarson and his kinsmen challenge Gunnar to a horsefight. Not untypical of saga horsefights, this one ends in a brawl, with Gunnar knocking out Thorgeir and his cousin Kol. Thorgeir promises revenge, and a year later he, Kol, and their brothers and fathers assemble a group of thirty to ambush Gunnar. The result is that fourteen of the thirty attackers die, and Thorgeir and his father Starkad are each wounded, while Gunnar loses his brother Hjort. Njal devises complex plans for the lawsuits that follow, which end in an arbitrated settlement. Again Gunnar wins all the honor. But his list of enemies is growing.

Gunnar's enemies seek counsel from Mord, a chieftain and kinsman of Gunnar, who is deeply envious of him and makes no secret of his loathing. With Mord's facilitation, Gunnar's enemies unite. More attacks on Gunnar follow, from which Gunnar emerges with great honor thanks largely to the skillful counsel and strategizing of Njal. But when Gunnar kills Otkel's son, also named Thorgeir, in one of these attacks—thus killing twice in the same lineage—he remains in Iceland contrary to the terms of the settlement which stipulated that he leave for three years. He is justly killed by a posse led by Gizur the White, but not before Hallgerd makes his last stand especially memorable when she denies his request for some of her hair to replace his slashed bowstring. She had not forgotten the slap.

The saga takes a respite for trips abroad by Thrain, Gunnar's uncle, and by two of the lesser Njalssons, Grim and Helgi. These latter return with a gripe against Thrain, who refuses to show any gratitude for the injuries they suffered when they refused to betray him to jarl Hakon, when Thrain was concealing Hakon's outlaw, the irrepressible rogue Hrapp. The Njalssons also bring home a person who will come to play a key role in the last quarter of the saga, Kari. Thrain returns with Hrapp, who, it is rumored, becomes Hallgerd's lover. Kari marries a daughter of Njal.

Pursuant to Njal's advice, the Njalssons provoke Hallgerd and Thrain's followers into uttering the insulting epithets Hallgerd had coined earlier. Skarphedin, in a feat of extraordinary athleticism, kills Thrain. A settlement follows, after which Njal arranges to foster Thrain's son, Hoskuld. After some years Njal negotiates a prestigious marriage for Hoskuld to Hildigunn, niece of Flosi, a prominent East Quarter chieftain. In order to meet Hildigunn's demand that she will only marry a person who holds a chieftaincy, Njal engineers a constitutional reform to make one available for Hoskuld.

A short time after Hoskuld obtains his chieftaincy a certain Lyting, Thrain's brother-in-law, kills Njal's illegitimate son, also named Hoskuld. A settlement is concluded over the killing between Njal and his foster-son, Hoskuld, but it is this incident which opens an irremediable breach between Njal and his sons.

The saga pauses to tell of Iceland's conversion to Christianity. Immediately after the Conversion the dead Hoskuld Njalsson's son, Amundi the Blind, is miraculously granted his sight long enough to embed his axe in Lyting's skull. Now the saga moves quickly to its core tragic events. Following his father's advice, Mord convinces the Njalssons and Kari to kill Njal's beloved foster-son, Hoskuld, who forgives his killers as he dies beneath their blows.

Flosi, father-in-law of the victim Hoskuld Thrainsson, emerges as the leader of the Sigfusson group. He is gruesomely charged to take revenge by his niece Hildigunn, Hoskuld's widow. And though he agrees to accept a delicately negotiated settlement at the Althing, her demand for blood carries the day. He rejects the settlement with a flurry of insults he rather strangely directs at Njal, who grieves the death of his foster-son more deeply than anyone, grief Flosi fully knows is sincere. This is the Althing dominated by Skarphedin, who with great panache insults everyone from whom his faction is seeking support.

Later that summer Flosi leads a group that burns Njal, his wife, sons, a grandson who is the son of Kari, and some servants in their farmhouse. The scene is powerfully realized and raises doubts as to Njal's motives for advising—contrary to the more astute advice of Skarphedin—that they defend from inside the farmhouse. Kari escapes the flames.

The mutability of alliances in saga feud and politics is pointedly and realistically illustrated in the make-up of the group that emerges to take up the cause of the burned Njal. Gizur the White and Mord, Gizur's son-in-law, the enemies of Gunnar, are now on the side of the angels. But the case against the Burners collapses when Mord makes a fatal procedural error. A battle ensues, started by the great lawyer Thorhall Asgrimsson, another foster-son of Njal, who rises from his sickbed to spear the first Burner he sees. Peace is made, largely by the good offices of Hall of Sida, Flosi's father-in-law, but Kari and Njal's nephew, Thorgeir Skorargeir, refuse to be a party to it.

Kari and Thorgeir soon ambush members of the Sigfusson clan, killing five. At Kari's urging, Thorgeir reluctantly makes peace. Kari's blood-urge remains unsated, however; he accepts that he and Thorgeir have avenged the Burning, but his son who died in the fire, he claims, has not yet been avenged. After seeking the help of the comical braggart Bjorn of Mork, Kari kills ten more, travelling to Orkney and Wales to get his last two victims, while fifteen other Burners are killed at the Battle of Clontarf in Ireland. Flosi and Kari each make a pilgrimage to Rome. Sometime later Kari and Flosi reconcile, Flosi giving him Hildigunn in marriage.

This book's organization largely follows the plotline, with certain chapter groupings offering the opportunity for different general thematic discussions.

Saga Narrative and the Motives of Characters

The classic saga style is remarkably sophisticated in how it deals with motive, demanding similar sophistication from its readers. The best of the sagas are written in chiseled prose, perfectly controlled, capable of generating the subtlest ironies, both comic and tragic; characters are deeply drawn. But the authors, as Heather O'Donoghue notes in her Foreword, seldom chooses to give their narrators, and hence us, privileged access to the internal mental states of their characters, but relegate us to the same techniques we use to discern motive in our own lives. When I try to figure you out, or what drives your behaviors, I make inferences based on your reputation, what you say, what you actually do, the setting in which you are doing and saying this, and certain conventional understandings about what the usual forms of action in such a setting are, what facial expressions and bodily postures should accompany those actions, and more. Were your actions not quite proper, I would sift for what would most likely account for your failures of propriety. In other words, I make 'sense' of your behavior if proper, or search for excuses or explanations if improper, and that involves imputing to you certain mental states. That is exactly how we must make sense of saga action and deal with saga characters.

The saga way of dealing with motive is thus more realistic than that of the classical nineteenth-century novel, in which an omniscient narrator has magical access to the thoughts of his characters, who thereby seem more in touch with their own motives than they themselves, or any party dealing with them, could ever be in the so-called real world. No wonder we know fictional characters from these novels better than we know our friends or ourselves.

I will thus unashamedly attempt to ferret out the motives that drive the action, because deep saga realism forces that task upon us. Certain characters may behave without good sense, but they never behave without something 'sensible' driving them. When Flosi, in a flux of fury, kicks over a pile of silver stacked up to buy placidity from him he may be behaving irrationally, but we can make very good guesses as to what the roil of emotions is that makes placidity impossible for him at that moment. His actions make very good psychological sense; and so too those of minor characters such as Otkel and Thjostolf, supporting ones such as Thorhall Asgrimsson and Bjorn of Mork, and major ones, such as Gunnar, Njal, Bergthora, and Hallgerd.

I

Njála's Unity Problem and the Very Beginning: Chapter 1

The saga's first chapter raises vividly what has been the core critical problem of the saga: how does its mass of detail, its complex plot, cohere? How does the beginning properly start a story that ends where it does? Or, for that matter, how does the beginning lead to more than a few points in-between? If, as its full title indicates—*Burnt-Njáls saga*—this is a story primarily about how a man named Njal comes to be burned with his family in his farmhouse, then the author's route to that event seems at times strange, as also do some parts of the aftermath of the burning. Readers, whether trained in the sagas or not, can be troubled, though few put the book down, or fail to recognize its greatness.[1]

The standard allegations are that *Njála* seems to be compounded of two earlier texts (no longer extant): a hypothetical **Gunnars saga*[2] that makes up roughly our saga's first half and a shorter **Njáls saga* that occupies most of its second half, these two hypothetical sagas being pasted together by the convergence of trips abroad by Thrain (Gunnar's uncle) and Grim and Helgi (Njal's lesser sons) and by giving Njal a secondary role in Gunnar's story. The shorter **Njáls saga* is in turn interrupted by a six-chapter account of Iceland's conversion to Christianity. Some would even add a third hypothetical source, a **Kára saga*, starting when Kari escapes from the Burning, which then follows his vengeance-taking missions until the saga ends, that narrative too enduring an interruption by what is sometimes called **Brjáns saga*, recounting the Battle of Clontarf in 1014 in which Brian Boru, first high king of Ireland, meets his maker.

---

1. See the discussion in Clover 1982: 19–41.
2. The asterisks indicate these are hypothetical.

Mostly the problem for critics has been the large, even leading, role played by Gunnar in the first half of the saga. With Gunnar (ch. 19) comes Njal (ch. 20), a non-warrior, whose skill is as an advisor, strategist, and lawyer. But there is nothing more appropriate than to see Njal in that role, whether he is advising Gunnar in the so-called *Gunnars saga* or advising his own sons or foster-son in the putative *Njáls saga*. He is an advisor from his first appearance until his last. The anxieties about Gunnar's prominence are simply misplaced. Njal plays the same role throughout the saga.

A more difficult structural problem, though, resides rather in the efforts to explain the length of what are deemed to be purely introductory portions of the saga. Why so much time spent on Hrut, Hallgerd's half-uncle, who plays no role after chapter 33 except for one brief mention? Why so much time devoted to Hallgerd's first two marriages? Commentators do not agree on what counts as the introduction to the story proper either, whatever that is. No one puts it at less than the first eighteen chapters, a prelude to Gunnar's first appearance in chapter 19; some declare the first thirty-four chapters to be introductory, ending when Hallgerd marries Gunnar, and one eminent critic even considers the first forty-five chapters to be mere introduction, the story proper, to his mind, starting only once the Bergthora–Hallgerd dispute is concluded.[3] But not unlike Shakespeare's own problems with certain aspects of narrative unity, the warts seem less to detract than to attract, to add to the aesthetic experience, as well as to the richness of the saga's social and psychological acuity.

W. P. Ker finessed the unity problem by basing this and other sagas' unity on a different principle than the aesthetic unity of plot, character, and time: 'The best of [the sagas] have that sort of unity which can hardly be described, except as a unity of life—the organic unity that is felt in every particular detail.'[4] Others claim unity by fiat, as does the nineteenth-century Swedish poet and translator of *Njála* A. U. Bååth: '[the author] had the last line firmly in mind when writing the first.'[5] Still others argue that saga composition has its own rules, rules which *Njála* meets,

---

3. EÓS (first 18 chapters), Allen (first 34), likewise Maxwell; Andersson 1967 (first 46); see Allen, 120. For the tripartite division with a final third devoted to Kari, see EÓS 1954: cxxv; and also Guðrún Nordal, 189.
4. Ker, 235. Writes Maxwell, 'why then does this impression of unity evaporate as soon as critics. . . examine it?' but then he too resolves his doubts, finding that 'unity is confirmed with deeper power [by] the reconciliation of Flosi and Kari' (21–2). As will become evident, I have problems with the terms of that reconciliation.
5. Bååth, 159, quoted from Clover 1982: 22.

constructing a whole from smaller units of 'scenes' or with complex inter-lacing of multiplex action in the manner of those gripping-beasts and ten-drils which adorn the margins of medieval manuscripts.[6] One might mix fiat with finessing the issue by seeking the unity of *Njála* on a different plane, a conceptual plane, as I am inclined to do. This is a saga about politi-cal and social competition, about tactic and strategy, almost Thucydidean in its intelligent social and political analysis, though why that should confer narrative unity, any more than having the last word in mind when writing the first, should not be pressed too hard. The saga's unity remains a prob-lem, but mostly because the particular blood-feud which is the subject of the saga is true to the real-world complexities of actual feud, of how enmi-ties arise and continue beneath the surface only to re-emerge with previ-ous alignments having shifted. Boundaries that separate opposing hostile groups are porous and unstable; people switch sides. I guess that puts me somewhat with Ker, though the unity conferred is not a unity of life, but a unity of death in what starts as a small localized feud, that eventually spreads until it comes to engulf half the country.

The unity problem has never troubled me, but I concede that those who are troubled are not merely succumbing to over-learned reflection. The author fully means to press the limits of what still might count as a single story, and not have it become merely a chronicle of one damned thing after another. He may even have exceeded his own considerable abilities to rope everything together, as we shall see when we discuss the difficulties he has ending his saga, for it is the ending, not the beginning, that troubles me.

The first word of the saga is a man's name: *Mörðr* (Mord).[7] This is not the Mord who will figure centrally as the saga's villain in just about everyone's estimation, to the extent our notions of Iago-like villainy are applicable to this saga (they are not).[8] This Mord is the source of the name that will be given to his grandson, the child of his daughter Unn, who is intro-duced two sentences later as the best marriage match in her region. This first Mord is a lawyer, apparently the most important of his generation, for it is said that unless he were present no judgment could be assured to be properly in accord with the law. His cognomen is *gígja*, or fiddle. We are not told how he got his nickname but it has been suggested that it might be

6. Cf. Clover 1982, 1986*b*, with Allen, 67–78; Clover 1974; Lönnroth, 43–55.
7. *Mörðr hét maðr*: 'There was a man named Mord.'
8. I examine the issue of Mord's and Hallgerd's 'villainy' in the Conclusion (Ch. 22).

a reference to his lawyerly facility with words. This particular Mord will
not do very well in the four chapters in which he figures actively; he never
appears onstage again after chapter 8. We only hear of him once more when
his death notice is given ten chapters after that, and a little later when brief
mention is made of the discomfiture that befell him in chapter 8.

With hindsight mobilized, we can see what the author has already
accomplished. For those who were familiar with some version of this story
in which they knew a Mord figured prominently, the tone borne by the
saga's first word is ominous. He has reminded his listener, or reader, that
this will not be a happy tale. He also indicates that law and legal abilities
will feature prominently in what follows;[9] and he gets down to the business
of marriage, the chief subject of the first thirty-four chapters, all in a mere
three sentences.

The author ostentatiously marked these sentences to be paragraphed in
future editions and translations, even if the author or his scribe would have
written the chapter as continuous text. Two English translators felt compelled to insert an empty line,[10] an entire break of white space, between this
first paragraph and the next, because the transition to the next paragraph
could not be clumsier: 'The saga now moves west to the Breidafjord Dales,
where a man called Hoskuld Dala-Kolsson. . . lived at Hoskuldstead in
Laxriverdale.' The awkwardness has been noted before. How could it not
be?[11] Why pack up the saga and send it on a troublesome journey west when
it could have started there? Mord Fiddle is not needed until chapter 2, when
this Hoskuld will seek him out to negotiate a match with Mord's daughter
on behalf of his half-brother Hrut. It is as if after the first paragraph was
written down the author got an idea for a vignette to offer a more ominous
beginning than the mere name Mord could achieve, and so rather than
waste vellum by starting over, he moved his saga west to begin anew.

I suspect this was no mistake. If the first word 'Mord' was to remind us
of a later Mord then why not immediately juxtapose this first Mord with a
Hoskuld who would in fact provide the name of a later Hoskuld, just as 110

---

9. Wolf, 64; Fox, 296. Some might wish to give significance to the near rhyme of *mörðr*, m.,
   a marten, which yields the personal name, as animals frequently do, and *morð*, n., murder,
   which in Icelandic law is a secret killing; see Ch. 2, n. 50.
10. Cook 2001, Bayerschmidt and Hollander.
11. Clover (1982: 77) calls it flamboyant, citing Finnur Jónsson regarding the strangeness of the
    beginning, not paralleled in any other saga. Maxwell, 26, sees the 'unusual break' as linking
    within a short space both Unn and Hallgerd and thus preparing the reader for the advent in
    ch. 19 of Gunnar, who will champion one and marry the other.

chapters and two generations later a Mord will stand over a Hoskuld whom he has stabbed. Right at the start he brings the names of the fomenter and his victim together—one positioned immediately above the other, so to speak—in case you forgot where this story is heading.[12] What the 'clumsiness' achieves is to have a Hoskuld appear in the wrong place at the wrong time, just as another Hoskuld would later. And what better way to bring them together than have one father–daughter pair—Mord and Unn—suggest another—Hoskuld and Hallgerd, she too, but in a rather different way, out of place in this first chapter?[13]

So understood, this awkward transition is not a sign of incompetence, but of self-confidence. No false start at all. This is a highly self-conscious writer calling attention to himself as one who will not quite play by the rules. It is as if he is letting us peek behind his curtain. Despite how many other sagas or versions of this saga his listeners might have heard or read, his saga, he intimates, will be unlike any saga they know.[14]

Having thus transported the saga west in a sentence, Hoskuld and Hrut are now introduced. They are given longer genealogies than Mord, whose father alone is mentioned. Only Hrut merits a character description. In Mord's case it is sufficient to establish his legal credentials and suggest that he is somewhat given to litigation; for Hoskuld his bloodlines are sufficient. But for Hrut we are told of his handsome appearance, his size, his martial skills, and of his key dispositional and moral attributes—he is intelligent, even-tempered, and good to have with you rather than against you. That Hrut's introduction goes deeper indicates he will play a somewhat larger role than the other two men, but not a larger role than the second female we meet.

No sooner are the Laxriver men introduced than we are invited to a feast at Hoskuld's farm. Hrut sits next to him. We are told Hoskuld has a daughter, Hallgerd, and then we see her, a young girl, just 8 or 9, playing on the floor with other girls. She is a beautiful child, tall for her age, 'with long silken hair that hung down to her waist'.[15] Hoskuld calls her over to him, lifts her chin to kiss her, and she goes back to play.

12. On the author's employment of prolepsis, see p. 179.
13. Thanks to Alex Conway JD 2014 for this observation.
14. Allen concurs: 'By calling attention to itself [the clumsy move of the saga], it also calls attention to the man controlling the saga' (78). See Andersson's gloomy view of the writer's playing with prior saga conventions (2006: 184).
15. Hallgerd is unlikely to be more than 15 at the time of her first marriage, for reasons to be discussed, thus putting her at 8 or 9 here, though time in the saga does not often add up, just as it famously does not in *Hamlet*. And the time is not quite right for her to be eroticized so young.

Then Hoskuld asked Hrut: 'What do you think of her? Do you not think she is beautiful?'

Hrut made no reply. Hoskuld repeated the question. Then Hrut said, 'The child is beautiful enough, and many will suffer for her beauty; but I cannot imagine how thief's eyes have come into our kin.'

Hoskuld was furious; and for a time there was coldness between them.

When a parent asks a rhetorical question about his child's beauty, you have no choice how to respond and maintain politeness, let alone a friendship. The requested compliment is less fished for than it is an innocent expression of the parent's own overflowing love, with the hope that you might confirm the irresistibility of it and even share it. But this innocent offer of communion is often felt as a burden as you gaze at your friend's grotesque newborn. Hrut is suffering from one of those moments in which the demands of ordinary politeness are oppressive. He attempts to avoid the obligatory performance demanded of him by making no response. If his silence were meant to hint to Hoskuld to be tactful enough to let the silence stand for agreement and let the matter drop, that hint is lost on Hoskuld who, as we shall see, was not the subtlest of men. He wants to hear answers to his questions, rhetorical as they may be, so he repeats them. How recognizably wearisome this is, no different then than now.

Hrut admits her beauty. No one disagrees with that; nor is Hoskuld likely to take offense at the anodyne prediction that many will suffer for her beauty. I can attest to readers of the saga longing for Hallgerd, her long legs, her long hair. But Hrut's forced concession as to her beauty serves only to augment the force of the insult it introduces: her beautiful eyes—they have to be beautiful—are morally ugly. She has the eyes of a thief.[16] Thievery is about as low as you can go in the Icelandic moral order, this among a people who, when abroad, took great delight in raiding others and alleviating them of their goods and lives. But a Viking raid is against people who do not quite count as people; and a raid is open, a theft secretive, and its victims in small, close-knit societies are mostly neighbors and kin; it is thus a violation of a trust. So opprobrious is an accusation of theft that if you sue a person for theft and do not succeed in proving your claim the

---

16. For feminist defenses of Hallgerd, see Heinrichs, who chastises Hrut for saying such things about a child which Heinrichs supposes was in her hearing (336), but the saga takes care to send Hallgerd back to play before Hrut makes his hostile judgment. See also Helga Kress 1977; Dronke. EÓS (1971: 49) rightly points out that the author includes enough material to construct a differently valenced account of Hallgerd.

defendant has a defamation action against you with lesser outlawry as the penalty.[17] Summon someone for receiving stolen goods and you might die (see ch. 50). No wonder Hoskuld is angry.[18]

This introduction of Hallgerd is unsettling. Somehow our author thinks that the complex tale he is about to tell can only properly start with this vignette, with a little girl whose uncle does not like her. He draws even more attention to her by the clumsy shift of the saga, the motive of which seems only to taint this little girl. Part of the undercurrent of eeriness that tinges the scene can be attributed to the false start: Dear reader, something is happening out west this very instant, and we must relocate immediately lest we miss it. Remarkably, nothing is happening. We must wait for a feast some unspecified time later as children play innocently on the floor; a proud father dotes on his beautiful child. The father, again innocently, lets the effusiveness of his pride (and love) annoy his brother. Hrut then turns the scene into an early instance of what would become a standard trope that begins horror films in which changelings or bad seeds figure. No one would decide it worthy to move the saga west after one paragraph in order to show a perfectly innocuous family feast.

The start of this saga never ceases to feel a bit strange, most everything in it just a little out of place, as suggested earlier. The story is not going to be easy on Hallgerd. One might wonder even after she has played her part whether she should bear the weight of badness that is already attributed to her as she plays like a normal child with other little girls. Though she will leave a string of dead husbands in her wake, it is no less her problems with women than with men, and particularly at feasts, that fuel the saga. Once she grows up, gets off the floor, and must be seated at a table, problems, to put it mildly, will arise. Yet she is rather similar to some other women we shall meet who are quite as good at generating corpses; in them it will be a sign of formidable character and they are respected for it. But then husbands were not among their victims. And Hrut is only half right; there is some small defense for what turns out to be Hallgerd's act of thievery, when in chapter 48 she orders a slave to steal foodstuffs from a man who had treated her husband with contempt.

---

17. *Grágás* Ib 162–3; see p. 115.
18. Hoskuld and Hrut share a mother but have different fathers. Hoskuld could read Hrut's remark as insulting to Hoskuld's father or Hoskuld's wife. Once Svan and Brynjolf, maternal kin of Hallgerd, enter the saga, the latter is more likely. But Hallgerd bears, it seems, the full force of the insult.

The beginning will become even stranger once you have read the whole saga, for why the tale should start here remains a mystery. Hindsight only makes it more puzzling. The first chapter forces upon us the recognition that hindsight is not much more likely to provide answers than foresight, that the causal chains we construct after the fact to explain the present put us to guessing, no less than predicting the future puts us to guessing. Both looking forward and looking back require better evidence than is to be had, and both require interpretation of the evidence that can be had. Such reminders of the limits of human knowledge would be merely trite if this were not a work in which its eponymous hero is claimed to be prescient. Some of the most difficult interpretive cruces raised by the saga will center on defining the limits of, or recognizing the failures in, Njal's prescience. That other characters have the habit of speaking Delphicly at times, as Hrut does here, is a saga convention, but to employ it before the story even gets going is unconventional. I am not sure the author could have conceived a better beginning, and yet it remains rather inexplicable.

If the clumsy shift of saga location turned out to have its subtlety despite itself, that kind of move can only be played rarely before ineptitude becomes its most plausible explanation. But the author makes other moves in this short chapter that reveal the subtlest artistry. Observe his manipulation of the conventions governing the introduction of saga characters. Hrut was the only one of the three adult males in the chapter to have a conventional three-part introduction giving genealogy, physical appearance, and moral attributes, though his genealogy is truncated somewhat. But what of Hallgerd? The narrator gives us a description of her looks, but not her character traits. Nonetheless she gets the fullest tripartite introduction of anyone in the chapter. No need for a separate genealogy. She gets the benefit of her father's very full one, and hers is longer by one generation because she can count him in hers. To Hrut falls the task of providing her character. Three men, Hoskuld, Hrut, and the narrator, combine to give her a classic commonplace saga introduction accorded a character of any consequence. It took three men to do it, turning two brothers against each other in the process.[19] Wait for the discord her introduction to the South Quarter will generate when Gunnar brings her there to live.

The conventions governing saga beginnings and character introductions are given one more playful push in the chapter's last sentence: 'Hallgerd's

---

19. She will also get a brief reintroduction when she is of marriageable age in ch. 9.

brothers were Thorleik (father of Bolli), Olaf the Peacock (father of Kjartan), and Bard.' Five male names are thrown at us as afterthoughts, thereby extending Hallgerd's genealogy. Only Olaf will play any part in this saga, mostly as the source of a more important character: the dog Sam; and Thorleik is named once more as attending Hallgerd and Gunnar's wedding. Two of these *mere* names are the central male characters of *Laxdæla saga*, who here merit nothing more than being introduced and dismissed in the same breath. Their naming is their exit, but being named is an honor of sorts, because in this case the names are meant to register with the reader. What goes around comes around though, for that is how the author of *Laxdæla saga* treated Hallgerd where all she got was this single mention: '[Hoskuld and his wife] had a daughter, Hallgerd, who was later known as Long-Legs.'[20] That line in *Laxdæla saga* gives everyone who reads it a small frisson, even though *Njála* was still some forty years away from being written.

---

20. *Laxdæla saga*, ch. 9; on 'Long-legs', see Ch. 16, n. 20.

2

Marriage Formation and Dissolution: Chapters 2–34

This block of chapters has something of the look of a casebook on family law. We see seven marriages established and four terminated, each
raising slightly different legal issues. Some are first marriages, some second
and third. Two terminate with the violent deaths of the husband, two end
by divorce: one of husband by wife, the other of wife by husband (though
we do not see that marriage arranged).

Among medieval Icelanders of wealth, as is mostly the case in
pre-industrial societies, death and marriage were the two points in the
life-cycle of both men and women when substantial amounts of property
would acquire new owners. Marriage and death were of much greater economic and political significance for them than they are for us. Since my
focus, and the saga's, in these chapters is on marriage I will be very spare
about the trips abroad taken by Hrut and Gunnar, especially since these
conventional saga travel interludes have produced very good discussions by
others.[1]

Case 1: Hrut and Unn

The saga moves to the Althing, where it will spend a considerable amount
of its most intense time. The Althing is not just the location for lawmaking
and trying of lawsuits, it also serves as a two-week midsummer gathering at
which acquaintances are renewed and made, and what we see in chapter 2

---

1. See Hieatt; Clover 1982: 28–34; Andersson 2006: 187–9.

(and again in chapter 33) is that it also serves as an occasion for matchmaking. Marriageable girls are on display there, and an occasional lusty widow too. Hoskuld wants his brother Hrut to fix himself permanently in Iceland. Though the saga does not explicitly say so, it suggests that Hrut is recently settled in Iceland. Hence the lack of knowledge Mord Fiddle has of him, and the need for Hoskuld to endow Hrut and to vouch for his brother's separate property.[2]

Hoskuld has selected Unn for Hrut, because she is the wealthy Mord's heir, she having no brothers to inherit ahead of her.[3] Even though this marriage is mostly about securing wealth for Hrut, the woman must pass a certain attractiveness test. Hoskuld has Hrut eye Unn as she sits on display outside the Rangriver booth; she meets merchantable standards. As it turns out, Hrut does find her sexually attractive enough once they marry to have no problems getting erections when they engage in foreplay. The problem though is that foreplay is where it ends, for reasons that could hardly escape the reader's attention. Hrut, again in Delphic mode, predicts if not doom for the marriage, then gloom.

The marriage contract negotiated by Mord and Hoskuld on behalf of Hrut and Unn contemplates, eventually, a marital property arrangement called a *helmingarfélag*, a kind of community property, the Icelandic word meaning 'fifty-fifty partnership'. The separate property each spouse brings to the marriage becomes joint marital property, to the advantage of the spouse who brings in less separate property. We need to know how this particular contract works to explain several things: why Unn is so reticent about giving particulars when she first goes to the Althing to complain to her father; why Mord wants to terminate the marriage as soon as he finds out it will be sterile; why Mord does not negotiate a better deal for himself upfront, instead of postponing the *helmingarfélag* until the couple has 'heirs'.[4]

---

2. For a different account of the dealings of Hrut and Hoskuld when Hrut relocates from his natal Norway to Iceland, see *Laxdæla saga*, ch. 19. On Hoskuld vouching for Hrut, see Ch. 3, n. 10.

3. On the ordering of inheritance, see *Grágás* Ia 218. A girl with brothers got her share of the family property as a marriage portion, the portion not to exceed the share her brothers would take by inheritance (II 64).

4. I am oversimplifying the complexities of Icelandic marital property law, but the general statement more than serves our present purposes. For a discussion of *helmingarfélag* compared with other marital property arrangements, see Agnes, 299–307 and *passim*.

The contract provides that Mord will endow Unn with 60 hundreds, to which Hrut will add 30 hundreds. That 90 hundreds is Unn's separate property. Except for the 30 hundreds Hrut pays Unn, his separate property remains his until they have heirs, which can only mean children in this context. That is the effect of the dual plural used in Mord's stipulation: 'if you (two) have heirs then you will have a *helmingarfélag.*' A child would be an heir of both of them.

Now we can see why Mord is willing to postpone the marriage for three years for Hrut to augment his separate estate, especially since the value of that inheritance is more than will fall to Unn at Mord's death. It means that Hrut will be making a bigger contribution to their joint property, once children are born, than she will. It is a riskier proposition for the father of the bride than for the groom to agree to hold a betrothal agreement binding for this long without a wedding. A girl has fewer marketable years before her stock begins to fall than a male of the same age.[5] To ask Unn to relinquish three years of marriageability and fertility should Hrut get shipwrecked or not return is a real risk. This is not only why Hrut needs to get Mord to agree to postpone the wedding, but why Mord questions closely regarding the value of Hrut's Norwegian inheritance. Mord has to do a cost–benefit analysis of sorts: is the amount of Hrut's Norwegian inheritance discounted by the probability of his dying or not returning worth postponing the wedding for three years? Mord judges yes. He turns out to be wrong, but how could he (or Hrut) have guessed the physiological consequences to Hrut of leaving Gunnhild before she had tired of his sexual services?[6]

Because Hrut's property will remain entirely his until the couple has a child, we can see why Mord would want out and advise Unn to divorce once it becomes apparent that there will be no children. Unn's reticence in the first year is explained by it being too early to back out; who would believe such a story? Not enough time has passed for infertility to be proven to a wider public.[7] From the wedding to the following Althing not much

---

5. This is true as a general matter, but if the woman has sufficient property the husband could often care less how old she was or whether she was fertile.
6. At the time Mord names his terms he is not anticipating any augmentation of Hrut's property via inheritance since both Hrut's parents are dead. That is why Mord demands that Hoskuld bulk up Hrut's property. Hrut's Norwegian inheritance is a pleasant windfall which, to Mord's mind, makes it worth postponing the wedding.
7. O'Donoghue (1992: 85), showing that imputing psychology to characters is less unusual among saga critics than she supposes in her Foreword, believes Unn is silent the first year because she 'is intimidated by the men who have arranged the marriage'; that hardly deters

more than nine months have passed. After another year and still no baby, sexual failure looks more credible. She can then tell her father graphically what is wrong (could you, women or men, imagine speaking so frankly and explicitly to your father about your sexual troubles, your arousal and frustration?).

If Mord is supposed to be such a clever lawyer and Unn, as an only child, has enormous market potential as his sole heir, then why isn't his bargaining advantage better reflected in the marriage contract for which he unilaterally set the terms? We will soon see how fathers with marketable daughters fleece suitors when we turn to Hallgerd's first marriage. In the case of Mord negotiating with Hoskuld and Hrut, one does not take unseemly advantage of men of standing, of the same social rank as oneself. Plundering is what you do to would-bes and wannabes, and though Mord does not know much about the recently arrived Hrut, he knows Hoskuld, a chieftain, and marrying his daughter into such a family on reasonable terms is a sensible move for him. The old Mord is more likely to die, making Unn a whole lot richer, before Hrut is likely to get a whole lot richer. Mord is thus in no rush to want a *helmingarfélag* by which more of Unn's property would pass to Hrut than his to her. Until such time as children are born he means to secure Unn's property to her and not give her husband title to half of it until they have children. When Mord stipulates the terms neither he nor Hrut knew of Hrut's prospects in Norway, nor that during his three-year absence Hoskuld would so well manage Hrut's property that it would greatly increase in value (ch. 6). Mord has to be chagrined once he learns that a *helmingarfélag* with the greatly enriched Hrut would not be possible.

Hrut sets off for Norway for an interlude with Queen Gunnhild, whose dangerous delightfulness needs no explication. She figures as something of a bogeywoman in the saga world, especially in *Egils saga*. She has a special fondness for male Icelanders. More than a few saga authors indulge the fantasy that Icelandic men are irresistible to continental Scandinavian noblewomen, especially ones as expert in the 'olde daunce' as the nearly insatiable Gunnhild; only an Icelander can satisfy her. Hrut, whose name means 'ram', delivered the goods. Even an enterprising Icelandic lowlife like Hrapp will be irresistible to a Norwegian nobleman's daughter, and

---

her from a graphic discussion the next year; Allen, 86, thinks it is because she is too embarrassed to discuss the details, though she is hardly too embarrassed the next year.

Gunnar would have been given jarl Hakon's kinswoman if he had thought to ask (ch. 31). British women too: even the Burner, Kol Thorsteinsson—dispatched by Kari as he counts silver—had won the heart of a rich Welsh woman (ch. 158). In any event, Gunnhild makes Hrut's trip economically worthwhile. She secures his inheritance, provides him with ships to raid and acquire loot, and dresses him up in fine style. She seems actually to have acquired genuine feelings for Hrut, and does not take it lightly that she cannot make him happy enough to stay.[8]

Unn divorces Hrut (ch. 7) using a procedure believed by some to reflect an ancient ritual but nowhere else attested. The procedure—witnessed declarations at the bedstead and the threshold—is mentioned again when Gunnar forgets to plead that these steps had been taken when he sues Hrut on behalf of Unn later (ch. 24); but they apparently are no longer necessary by the time the saga allows Thrain, some years later, to use a divorce procedure about as summary as imaginable (ch. 34). The more formal ritual looked like genuine ancient history to *Rechtsschule* scholars;[9] we just do not know, despite its aura of authenticity.

Hrut kept his counsel the whole year after Unn left him, but when the next Althing came around he and his brother attended with a large following, a clear indication that though Hrut may have 'discussed the matter with no one', he surely discussed the need to show up in strength with Hoskuld, who no doubt could discern why, without much needing to be said. Those men making up the force could also be expected to deduce exactly why there were more of them than usual. Hrut was planning for the worst.

On the day suits were to be published for prosecution Mord goes to the Law Rock[10] and sues for Unn's dowry,[11] which he puts at 90 hundreds. Hrut responds aggressively to what he perceives to be an aggressive lawsuit. He accuses Mord of pressing the claim with 'greed and aggression' rather than with 'decency and fairness'. Hrut challenges Mord to a duel for the 90 hundreds, Hrut to put up an equal amount, 'winner take all'. A challenge to a

---

8. Cf. Norma Desmond in *Sunset Boulevard* (1950): 'No one leaves a star.'
9. Lehmann, 37.
10. The exact rock cannot be presently ascertained. The Law Rock was the location where suits at the Althing were formally commenced and important announcements were made.
11. The author incorrectly uses the word *mundr*, the husband's contribution, in this case 30 hundreds, to refer to the entire amount, when Mord is more properly suing for the *heimanfylgja*, the dowry, plus the *mundr*; Lehmann, 23.

duel was a valid legal defense until 1005, and these events are taking place in the saga's chronology in about 968.[12] Mord consults with his friends as to how to respond. With typical saga gallows humor, Jorund tells him what is obvious to all: that if he fights Hrut he will lose his 'life *and* the money'. We can guess that Mord is an old man, and this fact is explicitly confirmed later (ch. 21). Mord announces he will not fight; there is loud jeering, and he gains nothing but 'the greatest dishonor'.

How are we to understand Mord's expertise as a lawyer? It would have been easy enough to have planned around the possibility of a duel. Icelandic legal claims for both plaintiff and defendant are assignable. All Mord needed to do was what Unn did later: find someone as tough as Gunnar to take up the case. Mord's blunder is not, however, a mistake of law, but a serious mistake of judgment in more ways than one. Mord did not anticipate being called out for a duel. He was an old man. He thought that age would protect him. He was relying on Hrut's sense of propriety; what kind of honorable warrior would bully or mock an old man for property he knew was certainly two-thirds and probably entirely Unn's? As Skarphedin reminds Flosi later: 'it is wrong to mock [a man] in his old age' (ch. 123). Yet if there was such a reliably powerful norm against beating up an old man, why then the derisive reaction of the crowd when Mord formally declined to fight?[13]

The reasons are right in the text. Mord has already offended community norms in at least two ways. The first was to have taken his claim to law in the first place. This was the kind of claim people expected to be settled privately. The author cares to record this governing norm in a brief notice before Mord had formally initiated the lawsuit: 'Everyone expected that [Hrut] and Mord would discuss their differences, but this did not happen.' Also to be considered is Hrut's intimation that he would have paid over Unn's share if the claim had been made in a more amicable fashion: 'You are pressing your daughter's claim with greed and aggression rather than decency and fairness, *and because of that* I will respond this way. . .'[14] Had

---

12. See EÓS 1954: lxi. On duels, see Ciklamini; Heusler 1911: 35–6.

13. On the immunity for old men, see *BP* 209–10. Even Helgi Droplaugarson, who comes close to being a sociopath, reprimanded his men for throwing snowballs at an old woman for fun; *Droplaugarsona saga*, ch. 10. Old age is also what allows Thorbjorn not to fear riding up to Hrafnkel's farm to ask him for compensation for his son and also stupidly to refuse Hrafnkel's generous offer; see further Miller 2006: 61–2.

14. *enda mun ek hér lata nökkut í móti koma*: the conjunction *enda*, rather than the more non-committal *ok*, indicates causation.

Mord gone to Hrut and merely asked that they set the clock back and restore everything to the status quo ante, Hrut keeping his 30 hundreds and Unn getting her dowry back, Hrut would have looked as bad as Mord ended up looking if he did not agree to the offer. To ask for Unn's 60 hundreds back instead of 90 would take care of the accusation of greed, and settling the claim privately, the charge of aggression. In any case, Hrut had absolutely no right to that 60 hundreds.[15]

There is another problem with publicizing this case and it further helps explain why the assembled people are hostile to Mord. To publish and plead his complaint, Mord had to allege the grounds. We know this is so because that is how the children who act out the events a few days later would have come to know that Hrut 'couldn't have intercourse with [Unn]'.[16] Mord did not have to be more specific than that. He did not need to, nor apparently did he in fact, give the particulars regarding Hrut's inability to consummate the marriage: no one knew that he was too big to fit, and not just forever limp. Gunnhild was not *that* cruel. If there was a cruel joke in her curse, it was directed more at Unn than at Hrut: that no little Icelandic girl was woman enough to take on Hrut like she could.

To state his claim, Mord insults Hrut sexually. This is perilously close to a *níð*, a sexual defamation, in this case of an honorable man.[17] Had Hrut not responded aggressively to such an insult, people might chortle at his expense; they are doing that anyway, as again the children's theatrical proves. The case is too delightfully salacious not to amuse the average soul.

Yet we know that some people felt otherwise about Hrut's response, for the saga-writer forces some poetic justice on Hrut when he makes him endure the same humiliation he visited upon Mord when a young Gunnar, suing to recover Unn's property, forces Hrut to back down from a challenge to a duel (ch. 24). The balancing of accounts, the meting out of justice both poetic and pragmatic, suggests that Hrut's moral position in the dispute with Mord was not unambivalently pure. But Hrut lost no face when he declined to accept Gunnar's invitation. There was no jeering at the Law Rock, as there was when Mord backed down. This lack of

---

15. *Grágás* Ib 43.
16. The term the boys use for intercourse, *serða*, is one of the three words that give the right to kill the person who says it, if it is used with a male as its object, hence in the sense of bugger. See *Grágás* II 392; cf. *Grágás* Ib 184 which gives only two of the words. But *serða* is not used here in its lethal sense.
17. On *níð*, see Clover 1993; Gade; Meulengracht Sørensen; Sayers 1997*b*.

derision confirms the reasons why Mord was greeted with scorn. Hrut is not the moving party offending others by pursuing an insulting claim with aggression. Nothing in Hrut's backing down provokes derision because he did not seek the quarrel; it is Gunnar who came looking for him. No one faults Hrut for prudently avoiding certain death. Mord, on the contrary, had already lost the excuse of prudence by imprudently publicizing such a claim.

Yet it is from Hrut himself that we learn that the moral balance-sheet between him and Mord was not as clear as the crowd at the Law Rock would have it. Hrut and Hoskuld witness a children's game at a farm they stop at on their way home from the Althing. Two young boys and a girl were playing on the floor in front of them:

> One of the boys said, 'I'll be Mord and divorce you from your wife on the grounds that you couldn't have intercourse with her.'
> The other boy replied: 'Then I'll be Hrut and invalidate your dowry-claim if you don't dare fight me.'
> They repeated this several times, and the household burst out laughing. Hoskuld was furious, and hit the boy who was calling himself Mord with a stick. It struck him on the face and drew blood.
> 'Get outside,' said Hoskuld, 'and don't try to ridicule us.'
> 'Come over here to me,' said Hrut. The boy did so. Hrut drew a gold ring from his finger and gave it to him.
> 'Go away now,' he said, 'and never provoke anyone again.'
> The boy went away, saying, 'I shall always remember your noble-mindedness.' Hrut was highly praised for this. (ch. 8)

This brief episode can tell us something about the violence children could look forward to. Not all children: these children were not the host's. They were pauper children, or at least the boys were, *veizlusveinar*, boys imposed on the householder by the poor laws. Such children were circulated among the farms in the *hreppr*, an administrative unit whose main responsibility, as mentioned above, was poor-relief.[18] These waifs were not as immune to being beaten by a guest as would be the householder's own children. These were children who were raised by the community and could expect disciplining, it seems, from any adult minded to cane them.

In remarkably efficient fashion, the episode also tells us as much about violence to old people, and even more about delicacy, reticence, and

---

18. See Introduction, n. 13.

conscience. When the saga-writer decided to produce this play within a play, he had the choice of having either Hoskuld or Hrut strike a child. He also had the choice of having the child struck be either the boy playing Hrut or the boy playing Mord, or even, for that matter, the girl playing Unn. The scene shows Hrut making amends to a surrogate Mord. The surrogate is like the real Mord in several ways: both Mords make foolish errors of judgment, both are beaten for it, and, most importantly, both are inappropriate targets for warrior-age men. The author could as easily have had the actors be servants rather than children; in fact, it is the servants and other household members who laugh at the children's performance. The servants, too, could have been struck for laughing, but then the symbolism regarding the age-appropriateness of targets for violence would have been lost.

The author constructed the scene to allow Hrut to make amends to a Mord, even if not the real one. In the admonishment Hrut gives to the boy who played Mord, 'never provoke anyone again', we hear advice that was equally serviceable to the real Mord. The scene is a triumph of unobtrusive saga symbolism, subtle and utterly natural. It reveals, without interior monologue and without narratorial omniscience, Hrut's qualms about challenging an old man to a duel. It displays Hrut's bad conscience and his way of salving it.[19] Writing does not get much better than this scene, nor more sophisticated. *Njála* has much such subtle symbolism which in more than a few instances has never been noted, and it is easy to see why. It is because this author seldom makes anything *merely* symbolic; his efforts in this mode are so natural that they fly right by. They look like nothing more than mere description, than flat facts. Little kids are putting on a play. Note too how the scene resonates with an earlier one that plays in the symbolic register. This is the second time Hoskuld and Hrut have dealt with children playing on the floor, the second time a child is called over, but this time, unlike chapter 1, it is Hrut who makes all the generous gestures, Hoskuld the hostile ones.

Two more matters. First: law is so much a part of this culture that children's games and theatricals re-enact lawsuits. They thus learn to plead, learn to be the sophisticated observers that find so much pleasure in

---

19. Some scholars are reluctant to concede our fully-developed conscience, to the extent we have one, to many people before Abelard, with a rare Augustine counted as a freak of nature. I am very sceptical of this school; for a fuller justification, see Miller 1995.

watching the courtroom dramas that are the stuff of Thing-life, and surely of the life of this saga.[20]

Second: Mord actually has a better claim for the full 90 hundreds than Hrut allows him.[21] View his claim in light of the observation made earlier about the costs to Mord of delaying the marriage for three years while Hrut goes to Norway, and you will see why Mord might feel that suing for the full 90 hundreds is not greed, but a fair valuation of the costs to him and his daughter of the failed marriage. Hrut simply wants to restore both parties to the status quo ante and forget it ever happened; it was all a mistake. Unn, however, has in the meantime lost seven years of marriageability and fertility: the three-year wait and the four-year marriage. Hrut lost little if anything during those years, collecting as he did his Norwegian inheritance and doing rather well with plunder and gifts from royalty (less the gifts paid out to Gunnhild and King Harald as a return on their investment for providing him with ships and muscle). Are not Mord's losses worth about 30 hundreds? Still, the way to have made that claim would have been by negotiating with Hrut privately, as Mord found out. Hrut was right about the 'aggression' part, not so clearly right about the 'greed' part of Mord's claim.

Case 2: Hallgerd and Thorvald, with Cameos by Skarphedin and Thorhild, Grim and Astrid, and Helgi and Thorhalla

Marriage has the capacity to produce heirs or, more darkly, to disinherit people who otherwise would be heirs. For that reason not every legitimate baby is a joyous event: not for older siblings, for uncles, and, in the next marriage we will examine, for its mother and maternal grandfather. Where in Hallgerd's first marriage is that an issue? Not explicitly, but with a little help from *Laxdæla saga*, we will see why Hoskuld, the doting father, 'is anxious[22]

---

20. Andersson and Miller, 150 n. 51.
21. If the man is at fault the laws provide that Unn would get her 90 hundreds; *Grágás* Ib 42–3. This also helps explain why Mord would need to be explicit when publishing the case. But *Grágás*'s rules, under some Christian influence, have made divorce harder than what it may have been in the time the saga was set.
22. *hugr á*: 'anxious' in Magnusson/Pálsson might be a bit strong, but it does not misrepresent his desire to get her married as soon as possible.

to marry [his beloved Hallgerd] off' against her will, and in a marriage
rather beneath her, to boot. How do we square his rush to get her out of the
house with the pride and love he exhibited for her in the saga's first chapter? How do Hoskuld's marriage plans for his daughter make sense, when
surely, beauty that she is, with family connections to make her attractive
even were she not, she would be able to command a more prestigious marriage partner than Thorvald? The author, we shall see, was not nodding.

Not infrequently, the sagas mention women married somewhat beneath
their station for money, *gefin til fjár* ('married for money') in the well-known
saga trope, the husbands often being much older.[23] The same goes for men
too, who in the style that became a feature of nineteenth-century novels go heiress-hunting, or marry down in social standing because the prospective wife has substantial property, though men are not said to be *gefin*
('given,' 'married') for money; the participle *gefin* is appropriate only to
marriage from the woman's position. These marriages of men for money
are more frequent than are directly indicated, for men were always on
the lookout for rich wives for their sons. Njal is no different (ch. 25): 'Njal
asked Skarphedin, the eldest, if he wanted to marry; he asked his father
to decide. Njal asked for the hand of Thorhild daughter of Hrafn from
Thorolfsfell, and that is how he got a second farm there. For Grim he asked
for Astrid of Deepriverbank; she was a rich widow.' These marriages are
not about setting up new households, but augmenting the existing one at
Bergthorsknoll, for the sons bring their wives back to their parents' farm,
it becoming sufficiently populous to qualify as almost a small village.[24]
If these are not quite disparaging marriages, they are not about making
political connections, for these women seem to have no connections worth
making. What they have to recommend them is property.

Njal and his sons aspire to higher standing, but first they need the property to fund such aspirations. *Njáls saga* is in part the story of a *novus homo*
in the Roman style; Njal is on the make, or if that sounds too vulgar, he is
a man looking to rise.[25] Njal himself is asking nothing more from his first
two sons than he apparently was willing to ask of himself. He married

---

23. For a list of those women in the family sagas *gefin til fjár*, see Jochens, 191–216.
24. On Icelandic household formation, see *BP*, ch. 4; Njal's household is at the larger end of the
distribution but it is not the largest of households mentioned in the sagas.
25. He is already described as wealthy when we are first introduced to him, but he is still in the
accruing stage, or the reference is to be taken as what he will be when he begins to act in
the saga.

property too, for his chief residence has his wife Bergthora's signature on it. The farm's name—Bergthorsknoll—bears the masculine form of her name, probably borne by her grandfather. Njal married her neither for her beauty, which is impliedly disclaimed, nor her kin connections, which are never mentioned. Nor are his daughters considered great prizes; one, Thorgerd, marries a good farmer, Ketil Sigfusson of Mork, fairly early (ch. 34)—we are not told when; the other, Helga, is given to Kari apparently to secure his muscle (ch. 90), for Kari had no Icelandic connections or property.[26] Even by that late date a daughter of Njal was apparently not drawing suitors from more established families.

The marriages of the first two sons are to be contrasted with the one Njal arranges for his third son, Helgi, which is described in some detail (chs. 26–7), and takes place perhaps a couple of years after the marriages of the first two sons. This marriage is of an altogether different sort. It merits two chapters rather than the one sentence allotted to the marriages of his older brothers. Njal seeks the hand of Thorhalla Asgrimsdottir. Her father, Asgrim, is a powerful player in the more westerly part of the South Quarter. Njal is looking for a marriage with more symbolic capital than the ones he has arranged so far, no doubt because he is now of sufficiently high standing to dare to ask the established Asgrim for his daughter. No property is mentioned coming with Thorhalla, and indeed it seems from that standpoint Thorhalla was not going to bring much property beyond her lofty social standing into Njal's house. This marriage alliance turns out to have been a long-term political success. Track Asgrim after the killing of Hoskuld Hvitanesspriest and after the Burning.

Some part of the price Njal offered for the marriage includes undertaking to foster Asgrim's son, Thorhall, a name, whether in masculine or feminine form, Asgrim or his wife was intent on making sure got through to the next generation: '[Asgrim] had two sons both named Thorhall. . . and also a daughter named Thorhalla' (ch. 26).[27] Njal would bear the costs of raising presumably the smarter of the two Thorhalls, of training the precocious lad to be his successor as the best lawyer in Iceland. To request to act as a foster-father bears a symbolic load of submission, for as the proverb has

---

26. A third, unnamed daughter is mentioned (ch. 20), but the author forgets her. Kari's grandfather was outlawed from Iceland (*Grettis saga*, ch. 10, *Landnámabók*, S 381, H 336) and Kari and his father lived abroad until Kari's return in this saga.

27. One would expect that Thorhall(a) was the name of some valued ancestor, yet neither in Asgrim's nor his wife's genealogy do we find one; see EÓS 1954: 73 n. 1.

it: 'he who fosters another's child is always considered the lesser man.'[28] Njal is marrying his son up, Asgrim his daughter down.[29] Moreover, to confirm the point, Thorhalla is singled out in the household at Bergthorsknoll for special treatment. She is given the woman's seat of honor in the house-hold as hers by right. Woe to anyone else who should presume to occupy that seat.

Njal's marriage strategy for his sons in a nutshell: look for moneyed spouses first, then look for one that brings status, since you can now afford her. An enterprising father with several children wants to think in terms of a portfolio of marriages. There is no particular ideal marriage type. The best is what fits with the present state of your political and social aspirations and the number of sons and daughters you have to play with.[30] The older sons in this case subordinate whatever desires for independence they might have had to a joint family project. At this stage in the saga they are more than willing to submit to their father. He alone decides whom they are to marry.

Now, if we examine Gudrun Osvifrsdottir's first marriage in *Laxdœla saga*, the account being more detailed, we will be better able to understand Hoskuld's reasons for hastily marrying off Hallgerd to Thorvald, marry-ing her *down*. We might call this kind of marriage a plundering marriage.[31] Such marriages only make sense if the girl's guardian, in these cases her father, understands that the girl will be married more than once. A mar-riage of this sort is a high-risk game whose success or failure depends on the vagaries of fertility and mortality. And one variable without as much vagary: divorce.

28. *Laxdœla saga*, ch. 27. These meanings could be played with; see pp. 165-6, but the fosterer at least assumed the symbolic and official posture of being lower than the biological father, even when he was not, thus allowing fostering to serve as a gesture of abnegation when that was called for to mend some fences.

29. The invitation to foster Thorhall takes place at the conclusion of the wedding feast, but it is all roughly contemporaneous (ch. 27).

30. KJJ's central interpretive thesis rests on his view that Skarphedin and Bergthora, whose favorite he claims Skarphedin is, never forgive Njal for getting Helgi the most prestig-ious marriage. The text simply provides no proof and, as I have suggested, someone of Thorhalla's status would not have yet been available for a son of Njal until he had acquired more wealth and built up his legal reputation.

31. EÓS (1933: §15, 107) and others have seen the similarity of Gudrun's and Hallgerd's first marriage as evidence that the *Njála*-writer borrowed the account in *Laxdœla saga*. Andersson refutes that claim definitively (1964: 96–103). As is evident, I think a perfectly sensible type of marriage strategy is being described because the authors are drawing on social practice.

Gudrun's first marriage, like Hallgerd's, is to a man named Thorvald.[32] 'Thorvald was rich and not much of a warrior', says the saga. He sought to marry Gudrun when she was 15 years old. The proposal was not dismissed out of hand, but Osvifr, Gudrun's father, said the marriage terms would reveal that Gudrun and Thorvald were not of equal rank.[33] Thorvald replied that that was fine with him, since it was 'a wife he was looking for, not money'. Osvifr then states the terms of the contract; he takes full advantage of his bargaining power. Gudrun was to have complete control of their joint property as soon as she entered his bed; they were to hold the property as *helming* (marital property each with a half share) 'no matter how long or short their marriage' (*hvárt er samfarar þeirra væru lengri eða skemmri*). He was to buy her jewelry so that no woman of equivalent standing should own better, except that her demands were not to make it impossible to maintain the household.[34]

This is rather extraordinary: Osvifr, Gudrun's father, hardly plays down the risks the groom is running, given the ready availability of divorce: 'no matter *how long or short*' the marriage.[35] Here the *helmingarfélag* negotiated is funded completely with the husband's property, half of which goes to Gudrun immediately, and she is also given the power within very generous limits to invade her husband's share of the marital property, without diminishing her own.

Gudrun takes full advantage and demands Thorvald buy her everything she desires (and she desires everything) from his share. He finally remonstrates after she heaps insults on him, and slaps her. The marriage ends shortly thereafter in divorce. Gudrun walks away rich in her own right at 17 years of age. Osvifr knew exactly what he was doing. He and his daughter were intent on plundering Thorvald to make sure that Gudrun had her own property to fund her subsequent marriages. No need for those marriages to be a drain on her parents' estate. The divorce was pretty much

---

32. The father of Gudrun and the father of the Thorvald in *Njáls saga* share a name too: Osvifr. The r that ends Osvifr is not the nominative masculine inflection but is part of the root, so it must by my principles remain; see *Note to Readers*.
33. Still not so unequal as to invalidate the marriage; see p. 40.
34. *Laxdæla saga*, ch. 34.
35. A Jewish traveler to what appears to be 10th-century Jutland noted that 'women take the initiative in divorce proceedings. They can separate from their husbands whenever they choose'; Ibrahim ibn Ya'qub (Abraham ben Jacob, c.965), in *Ibn Fadlān and the Land of Darkness*, 163.

planned from the start, the first marriage arranged with an eye to other ones down the line.

Why in the world, though, would anyone be stupid enough, with all the red flags waving as to the risks, to agree to such a contract? It is not as if Thorvald was besotted with love for Gudrun. He had never exchanged words with her before the marriage, though he may have seen her at the Althing or heard tell of her beauty. It must be this: he figures, if he is thinking at all, that though risky, there is a chance things could work out in ways that, if not perfect, might still be worth it. First, if Gudrun and he should have children, then the marital property would pass to the children, who were his children even should she divorce him. He will have succeeded in advancing these children's cause by supplying them with the high-status blood of their mother, which would then accrue to the benefit of his other kin. Second, and a corollary to the first, he gets credit at least among the people at his own social level for having bedded a real catch, and for having connected himself with an important family, even if from that family's point of view they were slumming it. Third, Gudrun may come to love him despite herself, and settle into the marriage.[36] He was not so lucky; she made clear from the start that she loathed him, and in a short time was having an affair with the man who was to become her second husband.

So the risks were not all Thorvald's. The point for Gudrun's father was to have Gudrun get into the marriage and then get out quickly, and he is explicit about that: thus the 'no matter how long or *short*' their union. The marital property arrangement put nearly all Thorvald's property at risk right from the start, no children necessary or wanted in this marriage by the girl's side.[37]

Why would Osvifr take the risk, though, of losing some of the benefits of the contract upon the birth of a child? No doubt he is fully aware of the condition of Gudrun's sexual maturity. We have no idea of the distribution of the ages of menarche back then but it undoubtedly occurred later than it does today, though presumably rich girls, because of better diet, would be fertile earlier on average than their poorer neighbors. Nonetheless, that this marriage was childless for two years, and that she was soon pregnant by her

36. This appears to be the case with the marriage underlying the famous inheritance dispute, Deildartungamál, *Sturlu saga*, chs. 30–4; see Miller 2010.
37. The risk of fertility that the fathers of Gudrun and Hallgerd wished to avoid Mord embraces for Unn. Mord does not have to get Unn independently funded so that he can maintain his estate for other children. Unn is his only child.

second husband, suggests she was not sexually mature when she married Thorvald. That was part of the risk someone in Osvifr's shoes would have put into his calculations, and Thorvald too. She could not deny Thorvald her bed at the beginning; no doubt she did her best to kill desire in him by the time she had begun having her periods, which even then often means another year until ovulation kicks in. By then she had started her affair with Thord on the neighboring farm and any baby born to her would have its paternity and hereditability cast into doubt. Gudrun's father wanted early in, early out, for good reasons.

I have spent this much time away from *Njála* because *Laxdæla*'s account gives more details, but they so nicely map on to Hallgerd's marriage that I know of no better way of explicating that marriage convincingly.[38] Hallgerd's unfortunate Thorvald pays an even stiffer price for marrying up than his namesake in *Laxdæla saga* did. The first lost his property and his self-respect; this one loses his life. As with Gudrun's first marriage, the groom gives the father of the girl the right to name the terms. Hoskuld is not as aggressively harsh as Gudrun's father was; Hallgerd does bring some property with her to her new home, which, it is said, Hoskuld paid out promptly at the wedding: presumably her clothing, some horses (chs. 11–12) for her small entourage, and not much more. If we accept that this is a plundering marriage, not designed to last but entered into by the girl's father to pay for the girl's future marriages, we can account for why Hoskuld is eager to marry her off. Her maturity clock is running and some wealthy aspiring male must show up soon, for in neither Gudrun's nor Hallgerd's case do their fathers initiate the process. We do not see fathers seeking out prospective plunderees, but if some gull happened to show up at the right time, then pluck him they would. I suspect that Hallgerd is still quite young, 15 or so, not fertile yet, and Hoskuld knows this marriage needs to end before she becomes so. This is just business, a kind of rite of passage for certain girls who can command the highest of prices on the marriage market and be expected to be sought after by a variety of suitors. Though she cannot be

---

38. This marriage is often discussed by writers concerned with female marital consent. See Agnes and especially Bandlien, 151–88. Canon-law consent, like incest rules, might have been more of a boon to inheritance-hunters looking to find grounds for raising doubts about the legitimacy of a marriage and hence of the legitimacy of those who stood in their way of collecting, than of expanding women's agency. Boys had not much more say than girls as to their marital partners, as witness the marriages of Skarphedin, Grim, and Hoskuld Thrainsson. The consent issue is less about men controlling women than about mostly older men controlling the younger generation of both sexes.

expected to like it, it is in her interests as well as that of her family, because
she will end up rich in her own right if all goes well. It doesn't matter if she
complains about it. It is only a step in her career.

Others more than understand the point of this marriage. Says Hallgerd's
foster-father, Thjostolf, as he attempts to mollify the angry girl: 'Cheer up,
you will be married a second time.' He knows that this is meant to be a
temporary arrangement; indeed, he will make sure it is. What precisely
is Thjostolf's job, by the way? Not to mince words, he is Hallgerd's bodyguard.[39] Before her marriage he was something of a chaperon. Now his
responsibilities shift. A father who sends his young daughter into a household in which all know that she is there to plunder them, that she is looking for an excuse to cart off half that household's property, is sending her
into a hostile environment. Husbands might take to slapping their very
demanding and expensive young wives, who they know are there to clean
them out. That is what happens to both Gudrun and Hallgerd when their
plundering becomes unbearable. A loving father, or a father wishing to
preserve his investment, will make sure to send some protection for his
daughter. Hallgerd may anger her husband but she is very popular with the
household servants, feeding them well and giving them gifts: this gives us a
nice glimpse of the tactics a young wife might employ for self-protection in
a hostile domain. She also comes with more muscle than her foster-father's;
she brings a certain Ljot the Black from home too. She comes with servants
of her own, all the better to impose costs on her in-laws.

There was a special legal limitation that might have interfered with such
plundering marriages. The law required marriages to be *jafnræði*, that is, the
marriage had to be what qualified as an 'equal match',[40] but money made
up for a lot of status difference, as it must have in Hallgerd's and Gudrun's
cases. Even a grandson of a manumitted slave could still validly be married to a first cousin of Gunnar, if he had enough property, as in the case
of Bjorn of Mork (ch. 148). Just as Bjorn escaped humiliation on his forays
with Kari and proved himself a little less the coward than we expected him

---

39. Dronke, 17, finds Hallgerd to be the only woman outside the legendary sagas said to have
   been fostered by a man, but see *BP* 124, for a more mixed view. To be noted is that a
   foster-daughter is one of the six women whose rape or attempted rape gives a man the right
   to kill, indicating perhaps that fostering girls is less rare than the sagas suggest; see *Grágás* Ia
   164; the others are one's wife, mother, daughter, sister, and foster-mother.
40. *Grágás* Ib 29, 241 (a woman gets to marry herself to third *jafnræði* if the man who controls her
   marriage refuses two previous qualified matches); also II 156, 162; see Jochens, 21.

to be, so too he managed to save himself from being fleeced because, as the saga notes, though Valgerd 'did not have much love for him, *they nonetheless had children together*'.[41] Even should Valgerd divorce Bjorn and claim the marital property, at her death that property would pass to the children she had by Bjorn. Like Gudrun, Hallgerd's marriage is childless, and again one wonders if she was sexually mature.

We cannot leave Hallgerd's first marriage yet; the mess she made needs to be cleaned up.[42] We first met Hrut angering his brother because he could not manage to say an innocuously nice thing about his niece; in chapter 12 Hrut again angers Hoskuld, turning him red as blood. Ostensibly what gets Hoskuld angry is yet another unkind word of uncle for niece, this time, however, not gratuitous. Hrut convinces Hoskuld to pay Osvifr, the father of the dead Thorvald, compensation for his son. Hoskuld agrees but then, taking advantage of his greater power, asks Hrut to determine the sum to be paid over. Hrut warns Hoskuld that if he thinks this is going to be a sweetheart deal he should think again:

> 'Will you act as arbitrator then?' asked Hoskuld.
> 'Certainly,' said Hrut, 'but I shall not be lenient with you, because, if the truth be told, it was your daughter who was responsible for his death.'

This is the remark that turns Hoskuld blood-red. Hrut judges Hoskuld liable to pay a full compensation, to be paid 'promptly and in full', a stipulation that should alert us to the difficulties the recipient of compensation might realistically have trying to collect the sum. There are more than a few indications of such realism throughout the saga. The concern with actually collecting the adjudged compensation accounts for the arbitrators contributing substantially to the amount they award Flosi (ch. 123), and also explains the stipulation that Thorgeir Skorargeir imposes later before finally agreeing to settle with Flosi: 'I do not want to have to collect the compensation from you all one by one: I want you, Flosi, to be responsible to me for it and collect it from your followers yourself' (ch. 147).

---

41. Sometimes the woman declared herself divorced ill-advisedly without taking care to have her kin come and collect her property first; see *Laxdæla saga*, ch. 16. Sometimes the bride's family figured they would not have to worry about their daughter divorcing the wealthy husband because they made sure he was advanced in years: old enough in pre-Viagra days to make him incapable of fathering children and to let mortality do the work of divorce; see *Droplaugarsona saga*, ch. 6.
42. For a fuller treatment of Hrut's decision in this case, see Miller 1984.

Osvifr notices that a rift has opened up between Hoskuld and Hrut, and tries to turn it to his advantage. This is why he addresses the brothers separately, first chiding Hoskuld for appropriating to himself the substance of self-judgment, if not the form—'It cannot be an impartial settlement. . . if your brother arbitrates'—then praising Hrut's conciliatoriness and moderation—'but your attitude has been so fair, Hrut'. Hrut wants to give his brother two messages, one explicit, the other implicit. Hrut is explicit about one thing—paying full compensation for Hallgerd's wrongs is purely rational: 'we must disarm criticism by paying this man compensation for his son. In that way we can improve your daughter's prospects.' If Hallgerd's family shows they will indemnify those harmed by her, she remains marriageable for her kinship connections alone.

The implicit message, if I may put it in direct quotes, is this: 'Don't you dare, Hoskuld, ever again make decisions that affect your kin without first consulting them.' Hoskuld consulted neither Hallgerd nor Hrut when he arranged this marriage. Hoskuld even knows it was wrong to have done so, for he admitted as much when he invited Hrut to the wedding: 'I hope you're not offended, kinsman, that I did not send you word while the deal was being arranged' (ch. 10).

The duty to consult about important matters is a given in the world of the sagas, where kin bear much of the liability for each other's actions. This time it only cost Hrut a cloak, which he gave as a gift to Osvifr. Kin owe it to kin to seek their input and consent for actions that they might end up having to pay for. The rules of feud provide that the actual wrongdoer need not be the one who expiates the wrong; kinsmen or in-laws were at risk for each other's misdeeds, and if the wronged party did not take revenge but accepted compensation, it would be the kin who would have to help pay it. They are thus owed and demand their say in important matters. This saga almost fetishizes the issue of consulting, taking counsel, and advising. It goes out of its way to note that uncounseled marriages lead to bad results and very costly spillover effects, costs, that is, borne by others: Unn marries Valgard 'without consulting any of her kinsmen' (ch. 25).[43] The result is Mord. Gunnar marries Hallgerd on his own motion (ch. 33). The result is *Njáls saga*. So, in one way, not all the spillover effects

---

43. *Grágás* does not back Unn's right to marry without her *fastnandi*, the man who controls her marriage, handling the matter. Likewise Hallgerd (ch. 13), though the Norwegian code that superseded *Grágás* would grant a widow that power; e.g. *Jónsbók* 5.1.

are negative. This saga also is one in which counselors figure greatly. It is named after one. And thus these pairings of counselors good and bad, with their advisees fortunate and less so: Hrut/Hoskuld, Njal/Gunnar, Skammkel/Otkel, Mord/the Thrihyrning folks, Njal/his sons, Hall of Sida/Flosi, and for a short time Gizur/Kari.[44]

Hoskuld gets the message. Never again does he venture to make a decision without asking Hrut's opinion. When Hallgerd's next suitors come calling, Hoskuld sends for Hrut and asks him: 'what do you advise?' (ch. 13). He again sends for Hrut when Thorarin comes calling after the death of his brother Glum (ch. 17). When Gunnar asks for Hallgerd's hand (ch. 33), Hoskuld turns to Hrut: 'what do you think about it, kinsman?' And the same when Thrain proposes (ch. 34): 'what do you advise, kinsman?'

This conclusion of Hallgerd's first marriage makes for an explicit comparison with Unn's divorce from Hrut. When we compare the rigmarole Gunnar must go through to reopen Unn's dowry claim (chs. 22–3), we see how astutely Hrut manages this fiasco so that Hallgerd can get her property back in the cheapest way possible. By forcing Hoskuld to pay the fullest value for Thorvald's corpse they gain more than Hallgerd cost them: 'Later Hrut and Hoskuld went to see [Osvifr] about the division of property and reached a satisfactory agreement. They went back home with their share and Osvifr is now out of the saga . . .'

Gudrun in *Laxdæla* ends her marriage by divorce, Hallgerd ends hers by having her bodyguard kill her husband. We can figure that the reason Hrut would not have agreed to this plundering marriage had he been consulted in advance is that, given his low estimation of Hallgerd's character, she was unlikely to make the marriage worth its costs. Gudrun was much better at keeping them low. Yet Hrut's intelligence in placating the dead man's father gained a good deal of the ends Hoskuld had anticipated. Even subtracting the cost of the corpse, Hoskuld and Hrut do quite well when it comes to retrieving Hallgerd's marital property: 'Hallgerd's property grew and became quite substantial.' Not only is Hallgerd beautiful, but her kin will back her, and she is also well endowed with her own property, no longer a drain on paternal resources.

44. Ármann, 192 n. 8 and *passim*, would eroticize many of the male pairings.

Case 3: Hallgerd and Glum (chapters 13–17)

What can we say about a good marriage? Hallgerd and her second husband, Glum, had one, but not all happy families are alike in their luck. We
learn that Hallgerd can love and feel pain. Glum qualifies by status, the
Lawspeaker's brother no less, to be within the class of those eligible to be
loved. That evenness of rank is reflected in their marital property arrangement, in which each contributes an equal amount to their joint property.

A matter of special interest arises in this marriage negotiation. This is not
a plundering marriage and so no bodyguard is needed. Hrut insists this stipulation be made part of the marriage deal: 'Thjostolf must not be allowed
to go south with her, and he should never stay there longer than three days
without Glum's permission; if he does, Glum should have the right to kill
him as an outlaw.'[45] Imagine Thjostolf hearing this stipulation. Can Hrut
and Glum contract away Thjostolf's life? Not directly. What Hrut is stipu-
lating is that they (Hoskuld, Hrut, Hallgerd) will waive any right to sue on
behalf of Thjostolf should Glum kill him in accordance with this agreement.
It is their own rights they are waiving, not Thjostolf's. They are condition-
ally repudiating him, conditional on staying longer than the three-day win-
dow period without Glum's permission—repudiation of an erstwhile group
member being roughly the same as disowning him. Thjostolf is a foreigner
from the Hebrides, without kin in Iceland. So if his head of household,
Hoskuld, refuses to stand behind him—refuses, that is, to sue on his behalf or
take revenge for him should Glum kill him—Glum is effectively being given
a carte blanche to kill.[46]

---

45. Dasent, Magnusson/Pálsson, and Cook render 'to fall *óheilagr fyrir*' as to kill him 'as an out-
    law'. That is not strictly accurate. On *óhelgi*, see *BP* 352–3, 351 n. 16; Heusler 1911: 114–15.
    The difference between falling *óheilagr*, or being in a state of *óhelgi* on the one hand, and full
    outlawry on the other (*skóggangr*), is that *anyone* can kill an outlaw with impunity, but *óhelgi*
    means the no-harm principle is forfeited only as against particular people. If, for example,
    you kill someone trying unjustly to kill you he falls *óheilagr* as to you or anyone trying to aid
    you but not as to any random person.
46. *Grágás* Ia 173, II 339–40, provides that a foreigner lodged in Iceland should not be quite so
    vulnerable. If he was killed while lodged with a householder, the householder had the right
    to prosecute. If he was killed by the householder, the case belonged to the householder's
    chieftain; if these two were the same person, as they are here, the case belonged to the
    other chieftains of the local Thing. The realities of the matter, however, were that no
    other chieftains were going to risk confrontation with Hrut and Hoskuld over someone as
    unpopular as Thjostolf.

Thjostolf suspects he is being sold out (thus his answer to Hallgerd when she advises him to go to Hrut: 'I don't know whether this is good advice'; and why, after knocking on Hrut's door, he goes around to the north side of the house, readying himself for a fight); but what can he do? He has no place left to go. His former protector Svan was lost at sea (ch. 14); Hoskuld has kicked him out for good for beating a servant (ch. 15); Hrut is all that is left. It is a tribute to how smart the characters are at reading the meaning of certain actions that Hrut can immediately discern that Hallgerd has had enough of her foster-father, for Hrut is the one who insisted that Thjostolf's repudiation be made part of the marriage contract. 'Why did you come here?' asks Hrut the moment Thjostolf informed him of the killing. 'Hallgerd sent me to you. . .' 'Then she had nothing to do with it', said Hrut correctly and drew his sword and killed him. When Hallgerd dispatches her foster-father to Hrut to be dispatched, she has fully repudiated him, we might say, with a vengeance.

This is as about as irreversible as repudiation can get. You kill your own trouble-making group member. That still might not be an answer to Thorarin, Glum's brother, who, like Thorvald's father, comes looking for compensation from Hoskuld. In this case his claim is considerably weaker than the one for the killing of Hallgerd's first husband because Glum was partly responsible for his own death. He gave Thjostolf permission to stay longer than the three days for which Hoskuld and Hrut agreed to remain liable. Had there been no stipulation accepted by Glum on how to deal with Thjostolf the compensation claim for Glum is unlikely to have been completely obviated by Hrut's having killed Thjostolf. There is a world of difference between the value of Glum and the value of Thjostolf, which, had Glum not ignored the terms of the prearranged deal, would have to be accounted for with some compensation to make up the difference.

The wedding feasts of Unn and Hallgerd are given brief descriptions, but they too display the author's gift for unobtrusive symbolism, some of which provides useful interpretive keys to the ensuing action.

1. Unn's wedding (ch. 6): 'The men were seated down the length of the hall, and the women sat on a dais at one end. The bride was rather downcast. The feasting and drinking began, and everything went off well.'

2. Hallgerd's first (ch. 10): 'Now the guests arrived for the wedding. Hallgerd sat on the dais, and was a hilariously cheerful bride. Thjostolf kept going over to talk to her, and at other times he talked to Svan; and people were disturbed at this. But the wedding feast went off well.'

3. Hallgerd's second (ch. 14): 'Glum and his brother gathered a large and select company. They all rode west to the Dales and came to Hoskuldstead... Hoskuld and Hrut occupied one bench, and the bridegroom the other. Hallgerd sat on the dais, and was properly behaved. Thjostolf stalked about brandishing his axe in a sinister way, but no one paid any attention.'

4–5. For Hallgerd's third wedding, which turns into a double wedding as her daughter becomes a sudden bride, the author gives us a fairly detailed seating chart, a tableau vivant of what will be the Sigfusson–Bergthorsknoll feud, the central feud of the saga. Arrayed on a single bench is one group on Gunnar's right, the other on his left (ch. 34), an image of convivial division, enjoying the feast before they begin their course of mutual extermination.[47] I will postpone discussing the double wedding until the next chapter.

Just quoting these 'mere' descriptions shows that they are more than that. They are also renderings of how each marriage will play out. The tableaux for Hallgerd quite clearly reveal the complicity of Hallgerd, Thjostolf, and Svan in the killing of Thorvald, and equally clearly excuse her of culpability in the killing of Glum. Thjostolf is acting on his own desires, not on Hallgerd's in that case. The weddings are not meant to predict the future; they are meant to interpret it. The author revels in showing how many games he can play with the saga topoi of portentousness, some of it spoken by characters as self-conscious prophecy, some of it voiced as misgivings or uneasiness, some of it spoken without a clue of how significant the remarks will turn out to be, and some of it, as here, provided by the narrator as mere description of present mundane facts. The author—nor his narrator—does not bang your head with an eclipse of the sun or moon, or a comet. And when his hand gets heavy at the very end and blood rains from the sky, he

47. Maxwell, 29: 'Gunnar is sitting between the house of Njal and its inveterate enemies to be'; also Allen, 216 n. 12.

shifts genres and location, moving the story to Ireland, where plausibility plays by less restrictive rules.

No chapter on marriage in *Njála* would be complete without comment on the Great Divorcer, Thjostolf. He is darkly comic; at least he sees himself that way. He is one of several examples where the author displays his knack for creating deeply-realized minor characters with admirable efficiency. Too gloweringly ominous to be charming, Thjostolf is, nonetheless, witty.[48] He and the narrator join to turn the killing of Thorvald into farce, partly by comprehending the scene through the uncomprehending eyes of Thorvald's companions, who are reduced to shouting curses at Thjostolf as he rows away after he had scuttled their skiff along with Thorvald's body (ch. 12).[49] His way of satisfying the law that requires a killer to announce his killing or have it be deemed a murder[50] elicits a smile of admiration:

> Hallgerd said, 'Your axe is bloody; what have you done?'
> 'I have now arranged that you can be married a second time.'

It is as if he were continuing the conversation from months earlier, when he told her that this marriage was fully intended to be of short duration.

We may not like to think that thugs can have high IQs, but why should an intelligent person not like his violence as well as the next man or woman? In this saga alone, in addition to Thjostolf, we have Skarphedin, Hrapp, and perhaps Kari. *Egils saga* provides an extended portrait in the example of its eponymous hero. Thjostolf is not without his share of resentment and bitterness at his lot; he is a 'foreigner', with no kin, assigned to tasks beneath his station. Do not ask him to round up sheep.

People have found the relationship between Hallgerd and Thjostolf troubling, for obvious reasons. He took his chaperoning responsibilities very seriously indeed, allowing not much more sexual access to her husbands than to any random local Lotharios. When he dispatches her husbands it is with references to their doing 'it' with her. The remark about Thorvald's general ineptitude is veiled but suggests impotence: 'You are both inept and clumsy (*lítilvirkr ok óhagvirkr*)' (ch. 11); the one to Glum is direct and vulgar: 'Thjostolf said that Glum had not the strength for anything except for romping on Hallgerd's belly' (ch. 17). Thjostolf was not

---

48. Cf. Bandle, 6; Heusler 1922: 12.
49. See KJJ 31, on the comedy of the account.
50. *Grágás* Ia 153–4, II 313. Both murder and a killing are punishable by full outlawry, but the murderer is denied the right to raise any defenses of excuse or justification.

about to allow himself the forbidden fruit either. That does not mean he has to like others rightfully getting what has been denied him. But it would be a mistake to see him as tormented by the prohibition he feels obliged to enforce. Enforcing it is a purely pleasurable act, with her sexuality no less on his mind than it is on ours. The displaced and not quite normal eroticism would be no less apparent to them than it is to us in a post-Freudian age.

3
Making a Scene:
Chapters 34–5, 48

This chapter is not about the formal construction of scenes in saga com-position.[1] It is about 'making a scene' in the contemporary English sense of disrupting a reasonably routine social interaction, thus generat-ing mounds of embarrassment. Scene-making tests our capacity for poise and tact. If, following the best theorist of face-to-face interaction, Erving Goffman, we think of poise as maintaining one's cool in difficult circum-stances, we can think of tact as the capacity to spare others having to mobi-lize their poise. The most extraordinary feats of poise are readily available in the sagas, poise being at the heart of so much of what we think of as heroic cool. Tact is a bit harder to find. The sagas often go out of their way to depict scenes in which the willful avoidance of tactfulness is pre-cisely what makes for a great scene in every possible sense of making a scene: think of Hrut and Hoskuld in chapter 1, think of Skarphedin at the Althing insulting everyone who asks who he might be (chs. 119–20). But tact is not absent from *Njála*, as will be adduced in time.[2] For now, note the practice that when people visit another person of the same status to pro-pose a marriage alliance, the matter is not raised until the next day. That Thorvald and his father immediately raise their proposal upon arriving at Hoskuldstead (ch. 9) is not so much a sign of their vulgarity[3] as of recog-nizing that, given the difference in status, they are not willing to impose

1. The submerged reference is to Clover 1974.
2. For a tale in which tactfulness is much of the key to its interpretation, see the story of Audun and the polar bear; Miller 2008.
3. Thus Allen, 75; the custom of waiting to state one's business is made the substance of *Ófeigs þáttr* in *Ljósvetninga saga*, chs. 6–7 (Andersson and Miller, 139–44).

themselves on Hoskuld for a night before raising the proposal. They are actually being deferential by getting to the point.

First, some small groundwork for the courtships preceding the wedding feast at Hlidarend, Gunnar's farm. Compare the courtships of Gunnar and his uncle Thrain. Both are rather hasty. Gunnar falls for Hallgerd in the meant-for-each-other way that makes movie stars marry movie stars and celebrities celebrities of the same rank. The anachronism is not quite inapt here. Gunnar comes back a star from abroad, and has the looks to match. He is as much a challenge for Hallgerd as she makes him think she is for him. Gunnar has ignored Njal's advice not to attend the Althing (ch. 32),[4] to be careful about managing the envy he was likely to arouse, but Gunnar seems never quite to have understood envy management very well. One might say he lacks, in that particular respect, tact. He dies as a result, but more of that later. Both are dressed to the nines. Hallgerd is a brilliant flirt as she coyly hints that he might not be man enough to dare marrying her; she knows just how to appeal to and challenge a man for whom any suggestion of fear, of women no less than of men, is not to be borne.[5] She is not only beautiful, but also intelligently artful, confident, and witty:

> They talked aloud for a long time, until finally he asked if she were unmarried.
> 'Yes,' she replied, 'and there is little risk of anyone changing that.'
> 'Do you think no one good enough for you?' he asked.
> 'Not at all,' said Hallgerd. 'But I may be a little particular about husbands.' (ch. 33)

No sooner is the conversation completed than Gunnar is seeking out her father to ask for her hand. Gunnar is besotted and Hrut says as much.[6] One does not marry on the basis of something as shallow as sexual desire generated by one good conversation and beautiful looks, especially in a culture in which marriage was too important a political matter for someone of Gunnar's promise to waste. Gunnar could perhaps rationalize his desires, supplying good reasons for making it a sensible marriage. Marrying her would make amends to her family for discomfiting Hrut over Unn's dowry claim; nor is it stupid to marry into a prominent West Quarter

---

4. Wolf, 67, notes the irony that Gunnar attends despite Njal's advice because he always liked 'the company of good men', but meets Hallgerd, a bad woman, instead.

5. For a useful discussion of this scene, see Sayers 1994: 12–13.

6. Hrut says both Gunnar and Hallgerd are *girndarráð*, 'ruled by lust', but also with a possible double-entendre playing on *ráð* when it means 'marriage'.

family. Gunnar, however, is not thinking along such lines, as Hrut makes clear. Hrut tries his best to talk Gunnar out of the marriage, saying things about Hallgerd nearly as slanderous as in chapter 1, almost crueler because the tone is not one of portentousness but of objective evaluation. A marriage of Hallgerd and Gunnar, he says, would not be *jafnræði*:[7] Gunnar is so much her better that the marriage would fail the test of legality if morality rather than social status and wealth were the criteria. For she is *blandin mjök*, 'much mixed', the idea being not that she is both good and bad by turns, but that the bad has polluted the good. Hrut comes very close to dissuading Gunnar, which is the author's own subtle way of equating Hallgerd with doom itself, because she was the evil so nearly avoided, the opportunity to do so frustratingly missed, as in the standard tragic trope.[8]

Thrain

Remember that the seating arrangements for this wedding feast are specified with some care. Seated next to Gunnar on one side is his uncle Thrain Sigfusson. He is married to Thorhild the Poetess (*skáldkona*), who is described as 'a sharp-tongued woman given to lampooning in verse, and he had little love for her'. Thrain finds himself staring at Hallgerd's 14-year-old daughter, Thorgerd. Thorhild notices Thrain's obvious desire and composes a couplet about it which she recites to the company. Thrain immediately jumps over the table onto the main floor, 'names witnesses, and declares himself divorced'. Thrain threatens to leave the feast unless Thorhild is driven out. Says the saga laconically: 'the outcome was that she had to leave.'

First a general question: where is the embarrassment one would expect when the general assumptions of conviviality in which the controlled contentiousness of banter and teasing, the very stuff of a good time, breaks down because someone makes a scene? If the saga does not formally indicate general feelings of embarrassment are we to imply them anyway, or do we have to imagine an emotional world that does not allow much room

7. 'An equal match'; see p. 40.
8. See Miller 2011: 200–9 on the sense of 'what-if'.

for embarrassment in settings in which we would expect it to be elicited almost reflexively?

Is there the least indication of discomfort among the assembled guests? Not so that it is worth mentioning explicitly, for as soon as Thorhild is driven away, 'the guests stayed in their seats, each in his place, drinking and being merry'. There may be, however, a subtle hint of some discomfort in the saga's insistence that *nú sátu menn hverr í sínu rúmi* ('now people sat each in his place'), with its suggestion that for a brief moment everyone sat frozen, at a loss for what to do. That might be foisting the discomfort you and I would feel upon the scene; perhaps their world was closer to a Dostoyevskian one where such 'scenes' were so frequent as to be the norm.

Imagine if at your wedding your uncle got into a fight with his wife, your aunt, announced a divorce, and then demanded, angrily and peremptorily, that everyone join in expelling her from the festivities; if they did not, he would leave instead. Maybe in Thrain's case his leaving would be even more embarrassing than their driving Thorhild out; or make for greater awkwardness for the host because Thrain is an honored guest of high rank, assigned the seat next to Gunnar, whom no one wishes to see offended, and she, his now ex, is merely a sharp-tongued former wife, whom no one seems to care to defend.

Her couplet, though not easy to parse,[9] hardly comes close to breaking the very generous rules for such edgy, insulting poetizing that is a standard Icelandic party game. Given her nickname, does Thorhild the Poetess have no right to utter verses, or is it that she is not to utter verses that embarrass her husband and thus embarrass the company? It cannot be because female skalds are discriminated against, for Steinunn is generously allowed to embarrass Thangbrand the missionary with her unanswered verses against Christ (ch. 102). Maybe propriety requires that she ignore Thrain's ogling and take him to task later when they are back home—that it is, in other words, she who makes the scene, she who made all hell break loose. Not that a wife could not go after her husband before others, but maybe not on these grounds; if he is cowardly, OK, but if he merely has a roving eye? Is not eye-roving as important to the success of a feast as the food and drink?

---

9. One of the main alliterative words in this two-line, eight-word verse only appears here (*gapriplar*, generally understood to indicate gaping), and another key word (*gægr*, understood to be 'agog') is not quite clear as to its sense either. The gist of the couplet nonetheless is fairly clear. It blames Thrain for eying the girl.

Given that in the sagas women's tongues are so commonly in cheek, and not much in check, it has to be the lovelessness of the marriage—whatever the probable monetary basis for it had once been, it is now no longer worth the price—and the allure of younger flesh that moves Thrain.

People really must not have liked Thorhild; perhaps they too had feared or felt the force of her tongue. Did they jeer at her as she was shown the door? Did she make a scene by resisting? Was it the duty of the host, in this case Gunnar, to escort his uncle's former wife from the hall with some accompanying explanation and apologies, or was she to find her own way out, with a servant perhaps unlatching the door? Did no one feel sorry for her, or ashamed for ganging up on her? It is painful enough just to read these questions, is it not?

Might it be that the unlikelihood of embarrassing himself or others makes Thrain's move possible? Can he count on not ruining the party by making a scene, because he can count on no one being very upset except Thorhild, and she was forgotten as soon as the door was closed behind her? She did not even merit the trope: 'and she is now out of the saga.' Yet, I strongly suspect that the guests and host think his behavior makes a scene and that that is why it is sagaworthy.

Thrain is not finished. Now that he has center-stage he makes another scene by immediately asking for the hand of the young Thorgerd, addressing the request to Hoskuld, the girl's maternal grandfather, she being fatherless for some years now. Hoskuld hesitates as to how to answer: 'I'm not so sure about that. It seems to me that you have taken scant leave of the wife you had already. But what kind of man is he, Gunnar?' Hoskuld's chariness about Thrain's proposal reveals some awkwardness, as well as uncertainty as to how to answer. He explicitly notes the unusualness of the request, given the timing of it. And he does register some embarrassment, though that seems more immediately prompted by how to answer the marriage proposal made before so many people, with no prior sounding-out as to its acceptability, a proposal that apparently violates no fewer rules of how a proposal ought to be made than the divorce violated those of how a divorce should be made. Some small, tactful remonstrance seems to lurk in Hoskuld's remark that is directed to driving Thorhild out, but it may well be that the new cause of embarrassment—the proposal—blocks out whatever discomfort had been generated by driving her out, much in the way a new pain blocks one that had heretofore been plaguing you.

Gunnar declines to evaluate Thrain, saying Thrain is his kinsman, and asks Njal to give an unbiased assessment of Thrain's character. Normally kinship would be no barrier to Gunnar's signing on to Thrain's proposal. Kin were expected to have their say on the quality and advisability of the marriage of their close kinsmen, as we have seen; they were also supposed to vouch for their kinsmen, as Hoskuld was eager to do for Hrut in the marriage negotiations for Unn (ch. 2).[10] If Gunnar's refusal to warrant Thrain's character is a tactful remonstrance directed to Thrain's unacceptable behavior, as indeed it appears to be, it is too subtle for the socially-obtuse Thrain to notice. Thorhild was right: Thrain is consumed with sexual desire, and as such is not even thinking as much, be it ever so little, as he normally thinks. Otherwise we would have to attribute to Thrain a tactical cunning he gives no evidence of elsewhere. In other words, Thrain did not plan to make a scene so as to put Hoskuld into a situation where he would have to accede to the proposal in the interest of tact, in the interest of sparing everyone else excruciating awkwardness.

It is left to Njal to overcome the suspect impression Thrain has made with information that works to Thrain's benefit: he is wealthy, Njal says, an accomplished man of standing, which is sufficient to make him an acceptable match. Hoskuld's brother Hrut is in accord, declaring the match to be appropriate. Wealth and kin connections more than make up for tactless misbehavior. Seating arrangements are then altered at the bride's end of the table to make space for another bride. The feast now proceeds uneventfully, apparently without much of a damper thrown on the festivities. The occasion has merely doubled the fun, two marriages based on lust rather than one.[11] One of them seems to have worked out rather well.

---

10. In only one instance in this saga does a man propose without a prominent male kinsman or other prominent person present to aid the suit and vouch for the prospective groom: Gunnar's proposal for Hallgerd. And though Unn marries Valgard the Gray without consulting her kin, Valgard's brother was present to support the proposal (ch. 25). Here Hrut and Njal make up for Gunnar's unwillingness to warrant Thrain.

11. The wedding of Hallgerd and her daughter bears comparing with the wedding at Reykjahólar in 1119 (*Þorgils saga ok Hafliða*, ch. 10). At each wedding an ultimatum is issued by a prominent guest that he will leave unless another less-favored person is driven out. In our saga she is driven out, in the other the less-favored man stays, forcing the ultimatum-giver out. The depiction of that feast shows considerable embarrassment on the part of the hostess.

Seating Arrangements

We do not have to wait long for another incident which we would call an embarrassing scene. It occurs in the chapter following the double wedding.

> Because of their close friendship, Gunnar and Njal used to take turns at inviting one another to an autumn feast. This time it was Gunnar's turn to attend Njal's feast and so he and Hallgerd went to Bergthorsknoll.
>
> Njal gave them a warm welcome. Helgi [Njalsson] and his wife Thorhalla were out when they arrived, but returned after a little while. Bergthora went over to the dais with Thorhalla and said to Hallgerd, 'Move down for this woman.'
>
> Hallgerd said, 'I'm not moving down for anyone, like some outcast hag.'
>
> 'I am in charge here,' said Bergthora; and Thorhalla took her seat. (ch. 35)

That is just the beginning. When Bergthora comes to the table with washing water, Hallgerd 'seized hold of her hand and said, "There's not much to choose between you and Njal; you have scaly nails on every finger, and Njal is beardless." '[12]

Bergthora responds by reminding Hallgerd that she at least did not have her husband killed, as Hallgerd did her first husband. Hallgerd demands that Gunnar avenge the slander, and then, like his uncle Thrain, Gunnar vaults the table and makes an announcement: 'I am going home. You would be better off squabbling with your own household, Hallgerd, and not in other people's homes. I am too deeply in debt for all the honor Njal has done me to be "your egging-fool" (*eggjanarfífl*).'[13] Gunnar and his company leave, but not before Hallgerd and Bergthora indicate to each other that business between them is not finished.

More table-vaulting and festivity-disruption. Consider Thorhalla. She rates special treatment, not just in Bergthora's eyes but in her own. Among us the tactful thing to do, were we Thorhalla, would have been to give up our claim to the seat. But Thorhalla makes no statement like, 'Oh, that's all right, Hallgerd, I'll sit over here.' Such a statement could have been made in their world, even if not in quite as casual a manner as we would make

---

12. In other Norse sources beardlessness does not prompt ridicule; see Dronke, 11, for examples, but compare Falk.
13. A colorful term best translated literally. Note that not all goading by women worked; the concept of the egging-fool shows that the object of a taunt was supposed to exercise judgment as to the advisability of the action being urged.

it now. At Gunnar's wedding, when the narrator lists the people's seats in declining order, from the most honored center seat on down to the one at the end of the bench, he notes that Njal's brother, Holta-Thorir, 'insisted on sitting farthest out of all the honored guests, for that made the others feel satisfied with their places'. A lot of strategy lies behind Holta-Thorir's move. He displays tact, and he also finesses the issue of his own not being seated as high up as he might have wished by volunteering to sit way lower than anyone would dare seat him. He thereby pre-empts the grounds for complaint of any others who by general estimation are below Holta-Thorir in status, since they now are, by virtue of his move, seated higher than he is.

We might call this tactical tact, or even graciousness, though the former better captures the strategic aspects of Thorir's face-saving move. Whatever Thorir's motives, his behavior shows that giving up on a prerogative in matters of seating was more than thinkable, it was also doable.[14] Not in Thorhalla's estimation.

Thorhalla has special privileges. She married down for Helgi, and her recompense is constant deference. Thorhalla does not serve guests as other honorable women do, wives of big men, like Thorhild, or Bergthora, mistress of the house, but instead gets served by them. She has by custom the most-honored seat on the Bergthorsknoll dais. In the wedding at Hlidarend, while Hallgerd was still the sole bride, it was she who occupied the center, the seat of honor. She is flanked by her daughter Thorgerd and Thorhalla, who even at Gunnar's farm is given the next best seat. Once the wedding goes double, however, it is explicitly noted that the seating was reordered: 'The women were reseated; Thorhalla was then positioned between the two brides.'

Hallgerd gives up the seat of honor to Thorhalla with nary a fuss. But that involves no dishonor. She moves in the interests of treating her daughter to a dignity equal to her own by allowing, necessarily, Thorhalla to occupy the center. It is a matter of achieving symmetry in the seating. So we know Hallgerd can move down, for symmetry's sake, for her daughter's sake, in her own house where from that day forward she will be mistress. Yet in that case she was not moving *down* for Thorhalla; she was moving *over* for the sake of her daughter on her own turf. Thorhalla is a necessary

---

14. When Gunnhild insists Hrut occupy her seat (ch. 3), a different set of meanings are in play; she is not conceding a place to another woman, and she is clearly exercising authority over the man whom she is doing a 'favor'.

placeholder, a highly honored one to be sure, since not just anyone would be allowed to hold that place without too many undesired ironies arising.

But at this routine feast at Bergthorsknoll no ready excuse can cover for Hallgerd not being honored with the center seat, unless it be that, as against Thorhalla, she is not special enough to be worthy of it. One suspects Hallgerd must know that this is Thorhalla's regular seat. Yet she also feels a sense of her own importance, not unjustly; she is a guest and she too is the daughter of a big man and married to an even bigger one. It surely is not impossible that she would be assigned that seat, and since Thorhalla was nowhere to be seen, Hallgerd can almost convince herself that commandeering the special seat was not really commandeering at all. It could even be vaguely innocent, to the extent, that is, that anyone in that society, no matter how complacent their sense of privilege, could claim innocence in taking the seat of honor without being formally shown to it.

Thorhalla is of such social and political importance to Njal's household that Bergthora is not about to play gracious hostess to Hallgerd to defuse a tense situation. No Holta-Thorir she, nor is Thorhalla either. Bergthora seats the people; as she says, she is in charge. Hallgerd was thus assuming a privilege that she had no right to. The saga suggested earlier another method employed to lower the risk of giving offense. At Hallgerd's second wedding the hosts, Hoskuld and Hrut, were seated on one bench, while the groom's company occupy the facing bench, and it is implied that the risks of getting it wrong were borne by the persons most likely to get things right—that is, Hrut and Hoskuld arranged their people, Glum his.[15] That made perfect sense, for the hosts would be unlikely to know many of the people in the groom's party. But there are two benches where the men sit, one running down each side of the hall, each with its own seat of honor; the risk is more easily shared. There is, however, only one dais and Bergthora knows all the invitees.

Bergthora may also be caught in a zero-sum game. If she does not ask Hallgerd to move down, Thorhalla could be displeased in a way that she will make felt later, if not in a temper-tantrum now. But that lets the

15. It is explicit that Gunnar (ch. 34) appointed the seats for his party at his wedding, though that is at his farm. The difference between explicitness and suggestion in Glum's case (ch. 14) is that the verb *skipa* (to appoint, array, order) has an accusative rather than a dative complement as in Gunnar's, the dative registering more active ordering.

pugnacious Bergthora off the hook too easily. Perhaps we should accept the standard reading and admit that Bergthora *means* to insult Hallgerd and she now has an opportunity to do so under the very thin cover of giving to Thorhalla what is by custom Thorhalla's anyway. Thorhalla knows better than to offer to give up her seat graciously in the interests of peace, since she can see her mother-in-law will brook no peace. Strange, is it not, that something about Hallgerd (or about Thorhalla) could provoke Bergthora in this way, when she is graciousness itself when she concedes her husband to the grieving Hrodny the night Hrodny's son by Njal is killed (ch. 98)?

Here we have three women, all of whom might have saved matters by employing a little tact—Bergthora could have left Hallgerd undisturbed, Thorhalla could have graciously acceded to such a move by Bergthora or insisted on giving up her seat on this occasion to Hallgerd, or Hallgerd could have said, 'Oh sorry, I'll move down.' Gunnar surely supplies the relevant norm: such squabbling is best done at home with your servants (a gem of information about day-to-day life in a well-off household), not as a guest in another's home, or probably not in your own home with guests present either. But none of the women take the opportunity to ease the tension. Quite the contrary.

When Hallgerd demands that Gunnar avenge her insult, what could she have meant him to do? He is not about to slap Bergthora, challenge Njal to a duel, or come up with a witty poem—none of these are remotely plausible. It must be at this moment that the thought occurs to Hallgerd, barely formed, to force a break between her husband and Njal, so that she never again has to be at a feast with Bergthora. Nothing grander or deeper than that. Gunnar storms out, taking his wife with him, apparently conceding that the present situation is already beyond remedy. But what did the people who remained feel? Did they keep their places and merrily continue the festivities?

To be fair, Hallgerd is no more culpable than the other two. A good thing none of these women was moved to graciousness. Any one of them could have prevented the saga from happening. I am not forgetting that these scenes and the characters in them are also authorial creations doing work to advance a story, such as, in this case, constructing Bergthora's character to match the fullness of Hallgerd's. But they are so well constructed as characters that serious criticism must delve into mental states that allow us to make sense of their actions.

Wife-beating in Company

Some seven or eight years later, while Gunnar was away at the Althing (ch. 48), Hallgerd, fulfilling the ominous prediction of the first chapter, ordered a slave to steal some food from a wealthy farmer, Otkel. Otkel had earlier treated Gunnar contemptibly when Gunnar had sought to buy some hay and food from him during a period of local food shortages. Nonetheless, as was rehearsed in the Introduction, he does offer to sell Gunnar a worthless slave, who Gunnar buys (ch. 47). Gunnar returns from the Althing and invites a large number of people to lodge with him on their way back to their homes further east. Hallgerd serves them butter and cheese which Gunnar knows they did not have in stock and he asks Hallgerd how she came by them:

> 'From a source that should not spoil your appetite,' said Hallgerd. 'And besides, it's not a man's business to bother about kitchen matters.'
> Gunnar grew angry. 'It will be an evil day when I become a thief's accomplice,' he said, and slapped her on the face.
> Hallgerd said that she would remember that slap and pay him back if she could. She left the room and he went with her. The tables were cleared and meat was brought in instead. Everyone thought that this was because the meat was considered to have been more honestly obtained. After that, the thingmen went on their way. (ch. 48)

Thrain divorces his wife at a feast; Gunnar slaps his in front of a large number of guests and calls her a thief. No table-vaulting this time. That gesture seems to be a preliminary move to parting, but Gunnar is in his own home. Two points to note: husband and wife leave the room and then come back in. Are there to be further words between husband and wife, and both feel that it is best not to continue their fight before the company? Are they thus revealing a sense of decorum that in the heat of the moment was forgotten? Was it to compose themselves? Or did he try to make up to her for losing his temper? Did they mean to give the guests time to restore their own sense of equanimity? Whatever happens offstage (interesting that the narrator does not follow them out of the room but stays seated with the guests; is he too embarrassed to move?), it seems to be merely a prelude to clearing the tables and finding substitute food that is theirs to give.

The guests? The narrator shows some small concern to record a wisp of awkwardness, but it is subtle. Though wife-beating may be standard fare in many cultures in the Amazon basin, the Mediterranean littoral, the Middle East, and Micronesia, it is not standard fare in the sagas, as a first-time reader of *Njáls saga* finds out in no uncertain terms. Slap Hallgerd, as three husbands can testify from their graves, you die. The guests' awkwardness, if any, is hinted at by their response to the meat replacing the dairy dinner— 'everyone thought that this was because the meat was considered to have been more honestly obtained'. There is a small indication that they needed a justificatory account for the violence that they had witnessed and they find it by joining Gunnar in blaming the suspect title of the original food. But that is guessing. Are we really to believe that eating stolen food is more immediately upsetting than watching a husband slap his wife across the face at a convivial gathering, even if, by law, eating such food would turn the guests into receivers of stolen goods, and thus punishable as thieves themselves?[16] The better explanation seems to be that the anxiety about eating stolen food is mostly a displacement of the discomfort the slap generated. That this embarrassing scene is somehow different from the two previous ones should be obvious, however. Not the least bit of comedy informs the account, outside of Hallgerd's failed attempt at humor directed at her husband for concerning himself with kitchen matters, and no one there thought it was funny; nor does the reader of the saga.

What would surely be embarrassing scenes for us, scenes in which it would be the experience of embarrassment that would become the focal point of the narration, are not treated the same way by this writer.[17] Yet the author thinks these vignettes make for good stories. Why? Is it that he finds these incidents noteworthy, but for reasons other than that they generate embarrassment or some form of social awkwardness? But what could that be? It might be that he expects his audience to be tickled by their own lack of civility, which would mean they have a fairly good sense of what it is they lack, or what it is that *some* of them are lacking. I prefer that explanation, for it makes these 'scenes' embarrassing scenes for them too. Why else tell the tale? Such social glitches are the very stuff of comedies of manners. It might be that the comedy of them is exactly what proves how embarrassing they are. But why only the subtlest hints of any awkwardness felt by the guests?

---

16. *Grágás* Ib 163. Cf. *Morkinskinna*, ch. 81 (Andersson/Gade, ch. 74) where King Sigurd slaps his wife in public and throws a bible in the fire, which, along with other behaviors, are taken as signs of madness; a commoner rescues the bible and admonishes the king to make up to his wife.
17. But cf. this chapter, n. 11.

A lot of saga feasts, indeed the great majority of them, pass without note-worthy incident, and instead of getting a chapter they merit only a sentence or two. It is not unlikely that someone like Holta-Thorir would lower the tension by volunteering to take a seat beneath the status he was entitled to, thereby undoing the moral basis of anyone else's complaint. Or that the people invited were old friends who might tease each other but it all stayed well to the side of the line declared to qualify as good-natured. Then again, being old friends, like Njal and Gunnar, did not seem to bind their wives, who were not old friends, not to ruin a feast.

Civility—in the sense of our anxious concern not to give offense, to maintain distancing norms of politeness—was not absent among them. Tact is surely present in the saga world, but it plays in a rougher terrain than in, say, a nineteenth-century novel of manners. Could there be anything more subtly decorous than the mature saga style itself, a model of reserve, with its edginess so finely tuned, its insistent irony so sophisticated, that propriety is created and honored in the process? Could there have been anything more tactful than Hrut's masterful handling of an embarrass-ing scene in chapter 8 generated by the children and his brother? And yet that was the same Hrut who could not muster the tact to suppress his feel-ings about Hallgerd in the saga's opening scene. Even those blessed with a capacity for tact are not always able to summon it on every occasion when it might do some good work.[18]

---

18. I am not trying to make these people into paragons of middle-class civility, but neither do I want them reduced to barely socialized barbarians awaiting Norbert Elias to civilize them.

4

Looking Forward: Njal's Prescience: Chapters 22–3

The most dedicated worshipers of *Njála* find chapter 22, and its real-world replay in chapter 23, embarrassing; critics no less than legal historians. It is here that Njal provides Gunnar with the charade for reopening Unn's dowry suit in which Gunnar is to pose as an ill-mannered peddler. Are we to believe that Njal did not know the summoning formula and could not teach it to Gunnar himself, but had to trick Hrut into teaching it to him? And why must the case be initiated by summons at Hrut's domicile when the author had earlier shown that dowry cases could be initiated by publication at the Law Rock, as Mord Fiddle had done?[1] Heusler called the chapter 'that masque, for whom anyone would be better cast than Gunnar', and then simply '*das Monstrum*' ('the monstrosity'); for Lehmann it is a 'caprice. . . a strange mummer's play'.[2]

I am not about to disagree, but even when the author does not please, he is too smart not to instruct. His purpose, for which he could have chosen a better means, is to dazzle us with Njal's prescience and intelligence. It is his intelligence and prescience, along with his inability to grow a beard, that present him in his introduction (ch. 20) as a liminal and ambiguous sort, his Celtic name enhancing the effect. The beardlessness will inspire insults directed his way, and the mere mention of it will inevitably prompt violent responses. But if he is meant to be marked as uncanny it is a pretty mundane

---

1. There were two ways a legal action could be commenced: (1) by summoning at the domicile of the defendant, or (2) by publishing the case at the Thing for prosecution. In the former instance the panel of neighbors was recruited from those neighbors who happened to be at the Thing; in the latter, the neighbors were called locally to attend the Thing before the publication. Cases specified as summoning cases had to be commenced by summons, but publishing cases could be initiated by either means (*Grágás* Ia 178–9, II 359).
2. Heusler 1922: 14–15; Lehmann, 48.

uncanniness right from the start, mobilized not to work magic, but to gain pragmatic ends in law and politics via astute practical means. He is also said to be 'gentle, of great integrity', and then, in an expansion of his being prescient (*forspár*), he is also described as *langsýnn ok langminnigr*, as 'discern[ing] the future and remember[ing] the past'. *Langsýnn* is not a synonym of *forspár*. The latter suggests the gift of prophecy; *langsýnn* is less magical, indicating, rather, that kind of rationality that does not sacrifice the long-term for the temptations of the short-term; again, the stuff of intelligent pragmatism.

Disenchantment

Even a cursory look at chapter 22 shows nothing very magical about Njal's ability to discern the future. Here and elsewhere what his 'prescience' reveals is his excellent capacity to predict the consequences of actions— actions, moreover, that he puts into motion. He has the skills of a good strategist and tactician, skills a good lawyer, which he is, must have. These abilities allow him also to be a good advisor; it would be impossible to be a good advisor without them. Like the good lawyer, but not always the ethical one, he can help make sure his predictions come true by creating the necessary facts, sometimes by rigging the game (to chapter 22 add chapter 97), sometimes by feeding his clients the lines that they should say.

I can find only one occasion in which Njal's so-called prescience operates in a way that could not be better explained naturalistically.[3] That occurs one night, when Njal finds himself suffering from insomnia while at his farm at Thorolfsfell (ch. 69); he sees the fetches (guardian spirits or doubles) of Gunnar's enemies before his eyes.[4] Yet he does absolutely nothing in response to this vision. It is not until the shepherd-boy hastens home to report that a band of two-dozen men lurked in the woods that Njal moves into action. As an aside: on this occasion we hear the only direct speech granted to Thorhild, Skarphedin's wife, who has something more urgent

---

3. See McTurk's article (1992) on the supernatural in *Njála*; he rightly discounts most of the foreseeing as educated and intelligent prediction. On the other hand, Njal's son Helgi's display of prescience in ch. 85 is better accounted for non-naturalistically.
4. Clover (2012: 123–6) discusses this scene as an example of how legal facts, in this case for conspiracy, are 'cognized' by the saga-writer, as he engages in making proof of his own narrative facts.

to ask the shepherd-boy that could not more vividly remind us of what concerns most people most of the time: 'Did you find the sheep?' (ch. 69), which adds a subtle mock-heroic blush to the scene. Another example of the author's mastery.

Even in a culture in which people believe in the prophetic value of dreams and visions, not many will act on them without ancillary and confirming factual evidence. People in cultures that set great store by dreams and prophecy also are acutely aware that there are false dreams and visions, false omens, no less than false prophets. Even true dreams do not yield their truth without interpretation. Njal is not about to waste time mustering a force of men or warn Gunnar because he has a case of the heebie-jeebies.[5]

That people attribute causal powers to Fate (I employ the upper case without wishing to vest it with much meaning) and that some claim they have prophetic access to it are social facts; but belief in Fate and prophets is not always intense, nor does it operate on all occasions. Invoking Fate can be a mere fashion of speaking, or a simple statement of boredom at the low end, or it could be a heartfelt prayer at a higher end; a person given to talking prophetically may only be giving advice, or he may really believe he is seeing the future. This saga, more than most, is itself remarkably agnostic on the extent of supernatural intrusion into human affairs. The hedges and ironies of the author and his characters regarding beliefs in an enchanted world that I point out will be their hedges and ironies, not mine.[6]

It is an often unexamined scholarly view that Fate is some controlling force in *Njála* and other sagas. People do indeed talk fate-talk in the sagas, but they show very different levels of belief in it. Of course, the author must accept that the outcome of his history is determined: a historical man named Njal was burned in his house. But with one small exception to be noted later, none of the characters in this saga act as if they do not have options. They do not act as if they are merely playing parts in a done deal, though occasionally they may talk that way, such talk being mostly a sign of the saga's preference for understatement and its commitment to the wit of pessimism. Njal believes, like Beowulf, that Fate helps those who help themselves, when Fate is not taking one of its many naps.[7]

---

5. Note too that though Hrut (ch. 2) doubts when first seeing Unn that they will be happy together he still marries her.
6. See Bartlett 2008: 108–10; Reynolds.
7. One modern Icelander with philosophical credentials is among the few to point out how little fate has anything to do with *Njáls saga*; see Thorstein Gylfason; also Wolf, 68, who emphasizes the free will that sustains the action; but cf. Vilhjálmur, 230.

Let me sketch a few of these matters now, before revisiting them in particular scenes, especially in the aftermath of the Burning. When Njal has a vision of the gable walls collapsed and blood on the table, he is seeing his fetch. This is little different from how Thord Freedmansson sees his, and Thord is not considered prescient (chs. 41, 127). Though Thord does predict that Skarphedin will avenge him, that prediction hardly requires prophetic powers. Seeing fetches is not a special feature of Njal's prescience. When Njal sees the gable walls down, he seems more surprised than informed by the vision. When he states that Gunnar will live to old age if he does not kill twice in the same lineage,[8] but then if he should do that, to make sure to abide fully by any settlement reached over the killings, Njal is merely stating a legal and social truth (ch. 55), though perhaps not a medical one. This is manifestly not a prophecy of the ilk of telling Gunnar he will kill his father and marry his mother; it is not even of the sort that tells Macbeth not to worry about anything 'until | Great Birnam wood to high Dunsinane hill | Shall come against him'. Njal's prediction is only slightly less certain than prophesying that Gunnar is mortal. Mord does use the verb *spá*, 'to prophesy', when he refers to Njal's prediction about Gunnar later, but he has tactical reasons for describing the prediction as a prophecy to his interlocutors (ch. 67). When Njal makes that 'prophecy' Gunnar had not asked that Njal prophesy (*spá*) his future, as Kari would do later (ch. 111), but only that Njal give him *heilræði*, 'good advice'. The famed prophecy is just some good advice: 'Look Gunnar, here is some *heilræði* for you: if you kill twice in the same lineage and don't honor settlements you'll be killed.'

The author uses premonition, prediction, and prophecy as so many saga authors do to carry out various literary tasks: to give the reader a heads-up as to what is likely to happen (most, but not all, of these dire predictions come true), and to indicate the risk level of certain enterprises, among other things. But this author has much of this fate-and-doom talk play a social function in the world the characters inhabit. It is a widespread belief that prophecies formally designated as such have a way of bearing a causal connection to what they predict, which is why a prophecy of doom can get the prophet bearing it killed, just as a prophecy proclaiming a bright future can get its prophet rewarded. The truly wise person would be wise to be more suspicious of a good prophecy than a bad one, because good

8. Magnusson/Pálsson render *knérunnr* as 'family' which is too inexact; Dasent gets it better by rendering 'stock', as does Cook by 'bloodline'.

prophecies were more likely to be infected by the prophet's interest in a reward—or interest in not getting killed for delivering a bad one—as well as by his hearer's wishful thinking. The prophet Jeremiah actually elevated this to an interpretive principle: if a prophet is predicting good news then he is most likely a false prophet.[9] This is why Ospak, who knows he is about to give an unfavorable prophecy to Brodir, waits until night to announce it, because he knew 'Brodir would never kill at night' (ch. 156). And this explains why Kari, after Njal had just predicted the death of himself and his wife and sons, can pretty safely ask, since Njal had not included him in the list of the doomed, what he 'prophesies' (spá) for him (ch. 111). Kari gets to hear exactly what he wants to hear, and had already been cued to hear: that his luck will be hard to beat.

To give some idea of the author's agnosticism on saga characters' portentous talk, consider this one of many examples. Hrut and Ulf the Unwashed are in the heat of battle against the Viking Atli. Hrut deftly dispatches Asolf, Atli's prowman. Ulf then makes this quip: 'That was a strong blow Hrut: you have much to thank Gunnhild for.' Hrut answers in the ill-boding style he used in his first speech of the saga: 'I have the feeling you speak as a man fated to die.' At that same moment Atli hurls a spear that transits Ulf's body, killing him (ch. 5). Prophetic powers? I doubt it. Hrut resents being teased about his relationship with Gunnhild. I am hardly sure why; he might have thought that it suggested his battle-skills were a function of her magic, otherwise teasing of this sort between two warriors in the heat of battle, even in the saga world, could not justify such touchiness.[10] Hrut, nonetheless, is annoyed enough to resort to cold prophecy-talk as he sees a spear headed for Ulf, rather than finding it in his heart to shout: 'Hit the deck, Ulf!' or 'Duck!' Or interposing his shield. The link between prophecy and causation in this case is rather unmagical.

Nothing better captures the author's agnosticism regarding the other-worldly than his account of the death of Svan, though in this case prophecy is not his subject so much as other aspects of the supernatural and the

9. Jer. 28: 1–17, esp. v. 8: a bearer of good news is not to be treated as a prophet; his advice is not to be acted on, until the events prove him a true prophet. The Babylonian Talmud tells of Bar Hedya, an interpreter of dreams: 'To one who paid him he used to give a favorable interpretation and to one who did not pay him he gave an unfavorable interpretation'; Berakoth, f56a–b: http://www.come-and-hear.com/berakoth/berakoth_56.html.

10. Dronke, 7, suggests Gunnhild's magic might be responsible for the stone that hits the sword-hand of a Viking about to slash Hrut.

ranges of credulity or scepticism among the people. Svan, the sorcerer who sheltered Thjostolf after he killed Hallgerd's first husband, had gone out fishing and the boat was lost in a fierce gale, no survivors: 'Some fishermen at Kaldbak thought they had seen Svan being warmly welcomed into the innermost depths of Kaldbakhorn Mountain; other people denied this and said that it was all lies. But no one could deny that no trace of Svan was ever seen again, either living or dead' (ch. 14). As the author knows, some people are more credulous than others, more willing to leap to supernatural explanations. Others think such easy believers fools and the tales they tell hogwash, given that they never have come close to seeing such phenomena themselves. Svan, though, was just the sort of weird soul whom one would expect to be an afterwalker (*aptrgangr*), given that he was a sorcerer and magic man. This is the expectation that the author is having fun with. The credulous explain the non-zombification of Svan by his having found a happy home inside a mountain with the other strange creatures dwelling there. The more sceptical simply reject that story. As for the final verdict? Who cares? The practical matter, whether he is at the bottom of the sea or eaten by fish, or inside the mountain with the otherworldly, is that he never reappeared, living or dead. And that is all that matters. That is agnosticism as a cultivated and witty position. It refuses to commit to anything except to verifiable consequences, and dismisses any attempt to provide a story of causation for an effect you do not see—Svan afterwalking—as a waste of time.

On other matters regarding Svan, the author is more generous. Svan does appear to have some ability to bring on fogs and quick changes in the weather, but every time I have been in Iceland I seem to be cursed with similar abilities, except Svan, unlike me, can bring on fogs that he desires. What the author and I both readily concede is that Svan holds himself out as a sorcerer, a professional of sorts, and that people vary in their views as to his powers, his magic working better for those who are inclined to believe in his skillfulness in black arts, and who are of his ilk.

One more example. In this one, not the author but one of his characters shows how manipulable prophecies and beliefs in them are. When Atli—not the Viking but one of the hitmen employed in the feud that embroils Hallgerd and Bergthora—asks to have his employment contract at Bergthorsknoll renewed for another year, despite Njal suggesting that he go back to the Eastfjords before Hallgerd has him killed, Atli answers thus:

> 'I would rather die as your servant than change my master. But I want to
> ask you that if I am killed not to accept slave-payment for me.'
> 'You shall have a freeman's compensation,' said Njal, 'and Bergthora will
> promise—and no doubt provide—blood-revenge for you as well.' (ch. 38)

Atli, a character I treat more fully later, as predicted, is done in by
Hallgerd. Njal keeps his promise and does not accept the 12 ounces that
he and Gunnar have exchanged over the previous two killings in the feud.
Njal demands a full 100 ounces for Atli. When he returns from the Althing
and Bergthora sees the money, she says to her husband:

> 'You will be thinking that you have kept your promise to Atli; but my
> promise has still to be fulfilled.'
> 'There is no necessity for you to keep it,' said Njal.
> 'But you have already guessed otherwise,' said Bergthora, 'and so it shall be.'

Njal has made a prediction as to his wife's future behavior. Bergthora, as
his loving wife, will make sure that she does nothing to undo his reputation for prescience. Since he is Njal, after all, what he predicts should come
true. She will make him look good as the prophet that he likes to posture
as—and he does posture in this way in more than a few places, as when he
manages his silences to help confirm his reputation for uncanniness (chs.
21, 64). Bergthora uses Njal's prophecy-talk against him, and as a warrant to carry out her own freely willed actions. Bergthora has her promise
forced upon her, she claims, with more than enough tongue-in-cheek, by
Njal's prediction that she would make the promise. This is one of many
instances where the author is able to make his characters show intelligent
and self-consciously ironical ways of shifting or avoiding responsibility. She
also cleverly parries her husband's statement, 'There is no necessity for you
to keep it.' He is now trying to claim that his early prediction was 'merely'
a prediction, not binding in the way a prophecy is. She will have none of it.

The author spared himself explaining how Bergthora came to know
of Njal's prediction as to how she would deal with Atli's death. She was
not mentioned as present, but that hardly bothers us. Bergthora benefits
by what the critic Maynard Mack called 'umbrella speeches', speeches that
are understood to be heard by more than the people onstage to whom they
were directed. They are frequent in Jacobean drama, and we seldom find
ourselves even noting the violation of realism.[11]

---

11. See Mack, 26–7. For other examples in *Njála*, see the use of scoundrel, *illmenni*, in chs.
    36–7, where it seems both Hallgerd and Atli have read the author's description of Kol; see

Das Monstrum **and the Future Tense**

Now let us confront chapter 22, *das Monstrum*. Njal is playing author to his own saga here. In chapter 22 he writes the script for chapter 23. Part of what is monstrous about chapter 22 is that narration is not supposed to take place in the future tense. Standard narration of stories—indeed, what makes them stories—employs the past or present tense. In modern English we use both, as Old Icelandic used both. Old Icelandic tends to use the present more than standard English narrative would (the proportion of present-tense to past-tense narration changes from saga to saga). Within sagas, narrative tense-shifts sometimes work to heighten effect; sometimes the shifts do not bear much weight at all.[12]

But you cannot narrate in the future tense, as Njal is doing here, without engaging in a genre-shift. What is told in the present or the past tense makes it a tale; if told in the future tense it turns into prophecy, or into something more mundane and practical, like planning a course of action, which necessarily involves prediction.[13] Planning, and the advising of those who will carry out the plans, will employ the future tense, the imperative mood and conditional tenses too: how else are we to counsel, advise, command, and, as a corollary, to threaten?

Nothing in this chapter depends on seeing into the future, any more than we are manifesting prescience when we plan to teach a class or have a dinner party. We, no less than Njal, can predict what Hrut or his equivalent will say in response to speeches designed to elicit the predicted response. Njal need only know the rules of hospitality in his culture, how people treat obnoxious traveling salesmen, the styles and subjects of entertaining repartee (which turn on recognizing how universally entertaining it is to hear your peers mocked and ridiculed). He then can write his script and make his predictions, which by now are not even predictions, but a

---

Hallgerd's 'now they will find out whether Gunnar will run away weeping' when she was not present when the shepherd told Gunnar that insult a few lines earlier (ch. 54).

12. On tense-shifts in saga narration, see Andersson 1964: 54.

13. Much less obviously than the *Njála*-author collapsing the future into the present, modern TV and film often show someone setting forth a plan with the plan's execution occupying the same space in the story; one can see it as a modification of Mack's umbrella speech. See e.g. http://tvtropes.org/pmwiki/pmwiki.php/Main/IKnowWhatWeCanDoCut.

connived lock-in of the future, because one of the characters—Gunnar as Hawker-Hedin—is not playing fair.

The advice Njal gives Gunnar is designed to make the future accord with the substance of the advice, no differently than when Mord Fiddle advised Unn as to how to go about divorcing Hrut (ch. 7). This is a cunning way for the author to let us know that Njal is not a magic man, but that he can certainly be a manipulative one.[14] No wonder his opponents can read his hand in certain strategies: 'Gunnar would not have thought this up by himself. Njal must have been behind this plan, for no one can match Njal for cleverness' (ch. 23); 'Valgard said that it sounded like Njal's idea, and that it would not be the last of the schemes that Njal had planned for Gunnar' (ch. 65).

To be seen as manipulating or manipulative has a pejorative cast for us, but our author is subtler. An advisor—and that is what Njal also is to his sons, as well as to the polity assembled at the Althing—must engage in manipulative actions because that is what it means to argue persuasively. That is what the science of rhetoric is about, persuasion depending in great part on manipulation: of emotions, of facts, of reasons, of agendas. It can be put to good, bad, or neutral uses, but the burden on the advisor is the same whether his advice is good or bad: he must persuade, cajole, threaten, command, beg, nag, flatter, and employ a host of other means of selling his case, and a lot of it will be presented in the future tense.[15] Njal does engage in some kinds of manipulation that make one wonder how he maintains a reputation for being good-willed, though more of that later, when we address certain inertias in honor and reputation.

Poor Hrut, smart himself, was caught unawares by a smarter man. One wonders if the saga-writer also wanted to play up Njal's cunning by having him outsmart the smartest character he had introduced up until then, a man who we are told on the first page is 'most wise' or 'very clever' (*vitrastr*), as well as have Gunnar intimidate the best warrior to grace the saga before his appearance; but that can hardly be an adequate explanation for why Hrut occupies as much space as he does. Not that the reader minds, but the

---

14. The over-elaboration of the plan, such as taking two horses, one fat, one lean, shows Njal playing as if he were doing a bit of magic, for that particular advice seems pointless unless to imbue his advice with hocus-pocus, perhaps to burnish his own reputation for uncanniness.

15. Other information more mundane is worth gleaning from ch. 22. We get some sense of the trade in small goods by peddlers, and Hawker-Hedin, no less than Hen-Thorir in his saga, shows that these types were not especially well thought of.

critic is at a loss. In any event, Njal did not play fair beating Hrut; he took advantage of his hospitality, of his trying to have an entertaining evening with a stranger he took in, who is a stranger only under false pretenses. But Hrut committed a sin that the wisdom literature always tells the wise man to avoid: he talked too much. As *Hávamál* has it: 'the ready tongue, if it's not restrained | will do you damage.'[16] Even otherwise intelligent people can have bad days. The noble Hrut, however, does not harbor a grudge for long. He tried to dissuade the infatuated Gunnar from marrying Hallgerd—or maybe it is that he gets more pleasure out of trying to deny his unloved niece what she desires than doing Gunnar any particular favor (ch. 33).

There lurks another message in Njal writing Gunnar's lines. We do not see much evidence that Gunnar is blessed with wit. Of the many virtues listed in his lengthy introduction (ch. 19), most go to his superior athleticism and his good looks, some to his basic decency of character, one to his wealth, but none to his intelligence. The sagas generally take care to indicate when a man (or woman) is *vitr* (smart), or when he has a way with words. Gunnar did not need much wit to charm Hallgerd. It was enough that he looked the perfect match for her, and had been places, and was now by all estimation the best catch in Iceland. On their first meeting Gunnar had adventures to tell; he hardly needed to display any rhetorical virtues to play them up. The hard facts spoke for themselves. Not too many years into their marriage Hallgerd will find it more entertaining to converse with a man clever with words, Gunnar's cousin, the poet Sigmund Lambason (chs. 41, 44).[17]

Prescient Coda

One of the author's better moves is to make his main character prescient and then critique that very notion, by showing that even if we presuppose prescience, it is not capable of achieving certain knowledge. As with physics—at least, the physics I last knew anything about—ultimate certainty is not possible, and if not in physics then how could we expect to have certain

---

16. *Hávamál*, st. 29.
17. In the saga's genealogies Sigmund and Gunnar are first cousins once removed; Sigmund's grandfather is Gunnar's great-grandfather.

knowledge in the mutable world of politics and human affairs? We satisfice; we make judgment-calls.

If the author wanted us to understand Njal's prescience as some seamless uncanny ability to see the future, he would have given us less mundane examples of its range and accuracy. The author must want us to subject Njal's prescience to the same kind of inquiries a wise person like Njal would make about a dream, a prophecy, or a prediction that was told to him. He would evaluate its source, what the source stood to gain or lose by speaking thus. He would classify it. Was it a prediction, a prophecy, a curse, a hope, or mere wishful thinking? If it had all the marks of a prophecy from a serious source he would then subject it to interpretation, and apply some discount as to whether it was a true or false prophecy. Mostly, it seems, the author means to create interpretative puzzles for us about Njal's motives: what role, if any, did Njal's prescience play in placing the cloak and boots on top of the pile of silver, a cloak that seemed to provoke Flosi into refusing the settlement he had previously agreed to (ch. 123), or in counseling his sons to defend against Flosi from inside the farmhouse, which ensured the death of himself and his family (ch. 128)? If the author did not mean to generate such puzzles, he nonetheless succeeded in doing so, because he made sure to suggest that Njal's prescience also had to be subjected to a discount rate. His prescience is not foolproof, nor does it operate in all domains with equal perspicuity, nor is it constant over time. One part of Njal's story is to suggest that his remarkable astuteness grows less certain as he ages, as it moves from legal and bargaining situations to more martial ones, where he has not much competence at all.

5
Bergthora vs. Hallgerd, Part I.
The Theory: Chapters 35–45

These chapters are among the most important in all the sagas. Surely they are some of the most stunningly crafted. The fast-paced action advances masterfully almost entirely by dialogue, with the dialogue skill-fully attuned to conveying a rich variety of intentional and emotional states. At the micro-level of face-to-face interaction, they reward close explication. At the level of plot, they are crucial to understanding why the Sigfusson–Bergthorsknoll feud is not going to be easily suppressed and why its various eruptions will in fact become the plot of the saga. Perhaps the most important violent death in the saga other than that of Hoskuld Hvitanesspriest is that of Thord Freedmansson, which is presented merely as one of the repeat plays in this women's tiff.[1] Or if we want to push that death back one step earlier: no tactical decision in the saga is more conse-quential than Bergthora's callous (it was not thoughtless) decision to involve Thord in the assassination cycle that she and Hallgerd were engaged in.[2]

At the macro-level these chapters present a model of the feud that deeply informs the native ideology of justice and revenge. The author then subjects the model to a substantial critique, showing that in many ways the model is incoherent.[3] That the author means to present the native model is part of the reason the events in these chapters are so structured and predictable, so

---

1. Maxwell, 30: 'It is the killing of Thord that divides the sons of Sigfus and of Njal. . . This is the essential connexion between Parts I and II.'
2. See further for the equally important, but critically underestimated, killing of Hoskuld Njalsson by Lyting (chs. 98–9).
3. For a fuller discussion of some of these themes, see Miller 2006; I treat the balanced-exchange model in *BP*, ch. 6, but the account I give here modifies and clarifies it in some key respects. Certain scholars have mistaken my explication of this *model* of the feud as if it were a *descrip-tion* of the actual Icelandic feud. *BP*, after presenting the model, then undertakes to show the reality; see e.g. the otherwise interesting piece by Firth, 140–1.

stylized.[4] The author of *Njála* needs to be taken seriously as a political and social theorist, for he is one of consummate ability. His saga does not make sense unless we see that the very legal and political culture of the saga is as important to his story as are Njal, Gunnar, Flosi, Hallgerd, Mord, and Skarphedin.[5]

Once I set forth the model I will go small and show how subtly the author handles certain aspects of this dispute, how complexly he deals with the psychology of the actors, how nuanced the dialogue and action is. The model of the feud that the author will critique is one that, in a moment of utter failure of inspiration, I called 'the balanced-exchange model'. It was an attempt to account for the 'getting even' aspect of feud ideology that required (ideally) that each hostile move that resulted in wounds or death, or an actionable insult, or even an attempt, be paid back with an equivalent return. The feud not only balanced corpse against corpse or wound against wound, insulting poetic verses against insulting poetic verses,[6] but money or deportation against all these. Just what was held to balance against what was itself often a source of dispute, but 'balancing', 'evening', was what people understood the process was. This is hardly unique to Iceland, as the balance-beam scales in the hand of iconic Lady Justice indicate.

The theory of balanced exchange was given real-world application in the awards arbitrators announced. It was not mere ideology. Thus, arbitrated settlements took the form of balancing the wound on X against the wound on Y, the corpse of a Skarphedin against the corpse of a Hoskuld Hvitanesspriest. These awards assigned values in order to justify putting an equals-sign between them so as to create an emblem of closure, a symbol of fair requital. They called these balancing acts 'man-evening', *mannjafnaðr*. So rich a concept was 'man-evening' that the same word—*mannjafnaðr*—was applied not only to the equivalences declared by arbitrators when they balanced one dead man against another, but also to a party game that could end up leading to corpses needing to be balanced, a game in which the goal was not equivalence, but rather precedence. The game was to compare the men of the district and determine who was in first place, who was the better man; or two men themselves could argue why the one should be deemed

---

4. Cf. Andersson (2006: 191–2), who has a very different view of the 'elaborate and symmetrical detail', finding it 'parodic'.
5. By 'political' I mean the competition for power and dominance.
6. *Bjarnar saga Hítdœlakappa*, ch. 29, similar to Aristophanes, *The Frogs*.

greater than the other.[7] The very term *mannjafnaðr* captures exactly a necessary equivocation in the balanced-exchange model in which the quest for precedence and the demand for equivalence were conceptually and practically part of the same problem of pricing, of measuring, of ranking, of evaluating: man-evening required man-comparing. And this tension is only one of several that will permeate the model with contradictions.

That goes to the 'balance' of balanced exchange; 'exchange' accounts for the predominance of the metaphors of gift exchange, repayment, and debt that inform feud, revenge, and justice. The author gives Bergthora the honor of stating the governing principle (ch. 44): 'Gifts have been given to you, father and sons alike; and you would scarcely be men if you did not repay them.' The feud is about one 'good' turn deserving another, of paying back what you owe, of giving as good as you get. The chief attribute of a gift, as Odin insists, is the repayment obligation that comes with it. Bergthora also borrows from Odin the idea that gifts have positive and negative value: you would not be a man if you did not make return to someone who made a gift to you of a horse or a shield, nor would you be a man if you did not make a proper return to someone who lamed your horse, or killed your father, gifts of negative value. It is the basic principle of any theory of justice worthy the name: 'Repay a gift with a gift, a falsehood with a lie'—

> *Gjalda gjöf við gjöf. . . lausung við lygi.*
> (*Hávamál*, st. 42)[8]

The Balanced-Exchange Model and its Contradictions

Let the following table serve as the briefest of plot summaries, with each man killing the man one lower in the numbering; thus Kol kills Svart, Atli kills Kol, and so on. Each killing except that of 6 by 7 takes place annually while the husbands and sons of Bergthora and Hallgerd are at the Althing.

---

7. See Miller 2006: 174–6; *BP* 301–2; also *Magnússona saga*, ch. 21.
8. See also *Hávamál*, st. 45.

Bergthora	Hallgerd	Price
1. Svart (slave)	2. Kol (slave)	12 oz.
3. Atli (freedman?)	4. Brynjolf (free kin of Hallgerd)	100 oz.
5. Thord Freedmansson	6. Sigmund (free kin of Gunnar)	200 oz.
7. Skarphedin kills Sigmund but not technically in revenge for Thord, but for Sigmund's verses.		

We have 12-ounce, 100-ounce, and 200-ounce corpses. Each row pays homage to the balancing principle: 12 ounces requites 12 ounces, a man named Kol ('black') kills and is balanced against a man named Svart ('black'); 100 ounces balances against the same; and so on. It is all very simple, except some disconcerting problems appear right on its face. Why are there three rows rather than just one? Isn't everything back to equal when Kol and Svart are balanced off? Why do things continue? That they do is the first substantive critique the author levels against the balanced-exchange model. Whatever balanced exchange is supposed to mean, supposed to do, it does not necessarily wrap things up.

These chapters also show that the model contains within it, or cannot keep out of it, a principle of escalation. We thus move from 12- to 100- to 200-ounce men. With the escalation in price comes an escalation in each victim's juridical and social status, which is what one would expect, the price of a person bearing an inevitable relation to his status. In the Bergthora column we move from slave, to the ambiguous Atli (who at least in death is manumitted to a free man worth 100 ounces), to Thord, a freedman's son. In the Hallgerd column we move from slave, to her free kinsman, to her husband's first cousin. Forcing balance into a pas-de-deux with escalation is a contradiction so fundamental as to incline one to shrug and say, oh well, it must be that one man's balance is another man's imbalance; that is surely what Bergthora and Hallgerd think each time their husbands strike a balance. This is the identical contradiction present in the double sense that 'getting even' bears in our folk theory of corrective justice. 'I will get even with you' hardly means climbing back to the same level with you, but rather being able to stand over you and glory in your defeat.

Not only is there escalation, there is also an imbalance by which the author reveals his partiality to the Bergthora party. In each row a balance is struck by declaring a Hallgerd-column person of higher formal status to be equal to a lower-status person in the Bergthora column. Svart, a servant (*húskarl*), thus balances against Kol, an overseer (*verkstjóri*).[9] Brynjolf, a free kinsman of Hallgerd, balances against Atli, a posthumously-manumitted slave; and Sigmund, Gunnar's cousin once removed, a man of some accomplishment, having returned from a successful venture abroad, is balanced against a manumitted slave's son, Thord. Hallgerd cannot be pleased that her husband (and the author) are willing to allow the moral quality of Njal's servants to make up for their lack of social or juridical standing. Svart was well liked, while Kol was a scoundrel. Atli, a real man, no matter what misfortunes may have placed him so low, thus balances against the cowardly Brynjolf, a free man, who axes him in the back. So too the decent freedman's son Thord, loved by his foster-sons, equals the price of the enterprising poet Sigmund, who turned out to be unwise in his choice of people to calumniate. The good men who die in the left column, Bergthora's people, always give their victims a fighting chance; those on Hallgerd's side sneak up from behind or take advantage of numbers.

Putting a price on men takes into account more than social and juridical rank; moral quality figures too. But how is that priced, there being no fixed schedule? Bergthora might not mind that her lower-status men equal Hallgerd's higher-status men, but Hallgerd scarcely thinks that the balance has been restored when 100 ounces is paid for Atli or 200 for Thord.

The ideology, the model, requires balance, but it does not, or rather it *cannot*, specify what is to be balanced against what. There are at least two sides that have very different views of what it means to get even. That is why third parties, arbitrators, often have to set the price and hope that both parties can accept not only the exchange-rate they articulate when they issue the terms of the settlement, but also the kinds of specie they put in

---

9. Though Svart and Kol are priced as slaves in death, it is not clear that they were in fact slaves. Svart is thus called *húskarl* ('housecarl') by the narrator, and a *heimamaðr* ('homeman') by Njal; they are compensated for with 'thrall payment' (*þrælsgjöld*) perhaps because Gunnar and Njal are trying to play the matter down by pricing them below their true value. Skarphedin refers to them generally as slaves, though he too could merely be making light of the killings. They may be debt slaves; we might read Hallgerd's remark to Kol about 'all the things [she has] done for [him]', for which the Icelandic has a term that implies pursuing legal claims (*mæla eptir*), that Kol is working off some debts Hallgerd has paid for him: *þar sem ek hefi mælt hvern hlut eptir þér.*

the scales to get the pans of the balance back to even. Will it be the moral quality of the corpse, its age, its rank, its sex; will it be land or animals, will it be exile?

The author also makes clear that the last row is not a strictly accurate statement of what the 200 ounces paid over for Sigmund is accounting for. Skarphedin promised his father not to break the settlement that Njal made in his and his brothers' absence for the corpse of Thord Freedmansson, but warned that 'if something else happens' they would remember the prior wrong. Sigmund immediately gives independent grounds for getting killed: the insulting verses. As a legal matter, the 200 ounces are not the same 200 that paid for Thord; the money paid for Sigmund has a different lineage. Skarphedin, unlike his mother and Hallgerd, breaks no settlement when he kills Sigmund. When he cuts off Sigmund's head and hands it to Hallgerd's terrorized shepherd-boy he orders him to ask Hallgerd 'whether it was the head that had *made the lampoons*' (ch. 45). He is not avenging Thord, but the lampoons. The model, in other words, achieves balance in its third row, by fiat, because the killing of Sigmund does not quite belong in the matrix.

There is still another twist. As we know, it is not easy to get a fix on what our own motives are. What we think moved us in the heat of the moment will not always be what, upon reflection later that evening, we decide truly motivated us earlier—to say nothing of what some therapist will suggest many years later. Many chapters (and years) later, when the Njalssons and Kari are heading out to kill Thrain, who was present at the killing of Thord Freedmansson and also in the room when Sigmund composed those lampoons, Kari asks the meaning of a little in-joke that Skarphedin and Njal made back then about looking for sheep, a joke that father and son have just repeated. Asks Kari:

> 'When was the other time you said that?'
> 'When I killed Sigmund the White, Gunnar's kinsman,' replied Skarphedin.
> 'What for?' asked Kari.
> 'He had killed Thord Freedmansson, my foster-father.' (ch. 92)

Add now to these contradictions of the model this: even if an agreed balance is struck in the present, it could be reconceived over time. What you believed to have been your motive for killing the poet who insulted you when you killed him, would not be what you believed your motive was when asked about it fifteen years later. Both beliefs are held in good faith.

Both are true, though one is more durable and deeper than the other. The very moment Skarphedin chops off Sigmund's head and hands it over to the shepherd, he is thinking about the verses and of his having avenged them. His invoking the insulting verses as the grounds for killing Sigmund is not a sham; it is the reason he kills him. Skarphedin honored his father's settlement over Thord Freedmansson in letter, and somewhat in spirit too, the letter being the spirit.

But time passes and understandings undergo revision. Skarphedin now completes the idealized model on its own proper terms. Fifteen years later he sees the 200 ounces paid for Sigmund as the same that they had accepted for Thord Freedmansson. With Gunnar long since dead, they have no worry now that the reformulation of motive means that they violated the settlement that Njal and Gunnar negotiated, for they did not violate it. Such is the implicit legalism that governs everyone's view of the matter.

The author understands how self-destructing the balanced-exchange model is. The core commitment to balance is subverted by a competing structural principle of escalation that is incorrigibly part of the model, because each side has a different narrative of the events, a different view of what it means to get even. Add to that the problems of pricing and determining exchange-rates across an array of qualities from economic to juridical and to quality of character. Throw in how to price years of exile, or a marriage, in units of cloth, in units of corpses, in units of silver or cows, and you end up having to doff your hat to the arbitrators who at times do indeed convince the opposing parties that an acceptable balance has been struck, everyone in the interests of peace accepting that a certain Thorgrim equals a random Bjorn who happened to fall on the other side.

Compensation and its Contradictions

But the cleverest and most devastating critique the author makes is one that reveals the conflicting incentives generated by paying compensation, rather than taking blood revenge instead. He severely undermines the idea that a feud can be settled with money or property rather than blood. He shows that compensation, unless the specie is blood or exile, is at its core self-contradicting. This knowledge is available to the smarter characters.

Skarphedin and Njal are even willing to joke about it, eliciting in the process Skarphedin's first grin:

> One day Njal produced a purse of money.
> 'What money is that, father?' asked Skarphedin.
> 'This is the money that Gunnar paid me last summer for our servant,' said Njal.
> 'That will come in handy,' said Skarphedin, and grinned.

Then, at the Althing, Gunnar prices his dead servant the same as Njal had priced his the year before.

> 'I put an equal price on the two men, Svart and Kol: you are to pay me 12 ounces of silver.'
> Njal took the purse and handed it to Gunnar, who recognized it as being the money that he himself had given Njal. (chs. 36–7)

Compensation, a money or property transfer, paid by the wrongdoer to the victim or his representatives, is meant to settle the victim's claim by buying from him his right to take revenge in blood.[10] An untenable, but still not-quite-dead, view claimed by certain legal theorists, and silently subscribed to by literary critics, and some historians who should know better, holds that humanity evolved from a pure blood-revenge system to a system in which blood revenge could be substituted for by compensation payments. Some of the earliest laws thus contain price schedules for injuries, death, and other losses, as in Hammurabi, Exodus, the Hittite laws, and the laws of King Æthelberht of Kent. But compensation was unthinkable unless revenge in blood remained something more than a remote possibility. What would be the inducement to pay silver or sheep, were not the avenger's axe poised to crease your skull if you did not, unless we supply, by cost-free magic, state enforcement institutions which would have to exist before revenge could 'give way' to compensation?[11]

---

10. This statement simplifies a more complicated reality. Sometimes the compensation comes from third parties who are not kin of the wrongdoer. Mostly this did not seem to matter to the victim; as long as he got paid he did not care where the money came from. At other times it mattered greatly; in this saga Grim and Helgi cared that Thrain pay them; they were not going to excuse him by having already been compensated by Eirik Hakonarson (ch. 89); see *BP* 370 n. 32.

11. Getting paid for dead kin also created an incentive to set them up and then collect. The Gulathing Law in Norway thus declared that a person who made a habit of taking compensation for slain kin was presumed to have been improperly motivated: 'No one, either man or woman, has a right to claim atonement more than three times, unless he has taken revenge in the meantime'; *NGL* 1: 68, §186 (tr. Larson, 140). These Norwegians were clearly aware of the incentive to set up and sell out kin that compensation generated; see also Ch. 12, n. 4.

Look closely at this transaction and observe the knowledge that informs Skarphedin's grin. Kol kills Svart. Gunnar pays the price for Svart that he had granted Njal the right to determine in order to settle the matter. Njal self-judges a 'slave-payment' of 12 ounces and Gunnar hands over a purse with the sum. End of the matter? Not according to Bergthora. Moreover, it will cost her nothing to break her husband's settlement, for Gunnar has already financed the breach of the very peace he bought. That is the incentive problem that paying compensation generates. Compensation gives the recipient the financing to violate the settlement, if not quite for free then not from his own hoard. The 12 ounces is kept fully segregated from the family's other property.

Njal and Skarphedin are both here making an in-the-know joke, registering their knowledge of the paradox of buying peace. That is part of the reason why the culture works so hard to shame and blame those who break settlements: because the temptation to violate comes so attractively priced. Violators are thus cursed with the name *griðníðingr*, an opprobrious term, one Kolskegg is not willing to endure (ch. 75); and he tries to convince his brother Gunnar not to let himself be branded one either in that most famous of saga scenes where Gunnar refuses to leave Iceland as he was obliged to do. Not even Mord is willing to take on being called a *griðníðingr* or advise someone else to risk being labeled one (ch. 67).

Reconsider the purse. What is it doing as it sits for a year, from one Althing to the next? It is not invested, it is not earning interest. It simply stands in the place of the dead Svart; it is his replacement. One could go buy another slave with it. In the Hittite laws the killer was required in fact to hand over a replacement slave.[12] That the purse is meant as a replacement or substitution is more than borne out later in this saga, and in other sagas, when a person pays himself over to replace the person lost in the victim's household. Thus *Thorstein the Staffstruck*, in which one man, said to be worth three men, replaces the three servants he killed; or *Thorstein the White's saga*, in which a man replaces another's son whom his brothers killed.[13] In our saga Flosi substitutes for Helgi Njalsson, whom he killed, in jarl Sigurd's band of retainers (ch. 153). We might even see the final marriage of this saga, Kari married to Hildigunn, as Kari substituting for the man he helped kill, Hoskuld Hvitanesspriest.

---

12. Roth, 217 §§1, 3.
13. *Þorsteins saga hvíta*, ch. 7; also *Vápnfirðinga saga*, ch. 18. See Miller 2006: 32.

Or you could use the 12 ounces to buy Kol's life. A dead Kol replaces a
dead Svart as you exchange the 12 ounces in silver for the blood of another
12-ounce man. The 12 ounces, in other words, just buys time, but time
is often worth buying. A modern economist would call this irrational.
Why waste the 12 ounces by buying a dead slave with it? What is the
incentive to buy a dead one when you could more rationally substitute a
live one, paying for him with the 12 ounces? But there was no active slave
market in Iceland, and no one wanted to accept Kol into their household
to replace Svart. So the silver stays in the purse because Bergthora will
make the spending decision; as far as she is concerned the family will be
out no silver at all, it being good for nothing else than buying corpses. So
much for silver being an impersonal medium of exchange in purely market
transactions.

The author is not just making literary jokes here. In higher-stakes situations much of what Njal does as Gunnar's *consigliere* is to be his banker
and investment counselor as much as his lawyer. The substantial sum
paid to Gunnar for the abortive attack on him, unlike the purse of 12
ounces, the smallish sum not being worth it, is indeed invested (and also
kept out of Gunnar's estate should he be outlawed, legal title to it resid-
ing in Njal).

> 'The compensation for this conspiracy against your life shall be no less,
> since so many of them are involved, than it would be for the killing of
> either of the Thorgeirs, if that ever happens. I shall look after the money
> for you and make sure that it is available to you when needed.' (ch. 69)

And then later:

> Gunnar gave no sign that he was dissatisfied with this settlement. He asked
> Njal for the money he had entrusted to him: Njal had accumulated inter-
> est on it, and now paid over the entire sum. It turned out to be the exact
> amount that Gunnar was to pay as compensation. (ch. 74)

What of the coincidence that the money Njal has accumulated on
Gunnar's previous compensation award, principle and interest, turns out
to be the exact amount that Gunnar had been adjudged to owe for the
corpses he piled up? The stuff of saga magic, a sign of the literariness of
the account, continental influences? Hardly. Any lawyer today knows
that a case will tend to settle for the defendant's insurance limits, and that
might very well be what is happening here. The arbitrators put the award
at exactly what they knew Gunnar had insured against. The reason why

this writer is such a literary genius is that he understands the economic and tactical aspects of his world cold.[14] That he masks the hard and the real so it can 'pass' as mere literary commonplace shows how skillful he is at his craft; he is indeed crafty. Moreover, he does not hide the deck in this instance. There is no joking; no grins accompany the transactions. The money is specifically invested to pay for future corpses.

Return to the 12-ounce purse to see how the theme raised there about compensation financing the next round—thereby accounting for how the model integrates the principle of escalation with the principle of balance— describes a reality borne out in the rest of the saga. It shows that the smarter actors in their world understood the opposing forces at work in their way of buying peace. Do not think that all people are locked inside their 'epis- teme', unable to get a purchase on their own social models and metaphors, that they cannot joke about them, and play with them. Some can; some can't. Njal and Skarphedin can, and surely this author can.

By one account of balance, things are balanced when Njal accepts the slave-payment from Gunnar. That is supposed to end it. But to Bergthora's mind, a view strongly held in the culture, getting paid in sheep, wool, cloth, silver, though acceptable and often forced upon the victim or the victim's group, is a second-rate form of compensation. Bergthora is among those who prefer not to 'carry their kin in their purse', as the sneering expression employed on occasion suggests. Some kinds of money are worth more than others, some kinds are cleaner than others, and, though not impossible, it is very difficult to set exchange-rates among or between them. In a time when it was hard to be sure of the purity or quality of the silver you were accepting, or the quality of the sheep or the measure of the cloth you were paid, you could be sure if a Kol, a Brynjolf, or a Sigmund was dead. And by killing him you were declaring and accepting the equivalence between the blood of victim and expiator.

Blood was thus itself a kind of money, a form of compensation, but more honorable, so the incentive to get paid in it worked against making peace via the receipt of conventional money substances. When the argument was over blood or money, it was an argument over the means of payment, not over payment itself. One way or another, in the terms of the model, you

14. See also ch. 80, where the compensation adjudged against Mord is fixed to the amount adjudged for the victims of Skarphedin's and Hogni's revenge for Gunnar. The same Norse idiom is used in both cases—*á endum standask*—for which see Miller 2008: 26, 43.

were going to have to pay, and it is the payment metaphor, the gift metaphor, hence the exchange part of the balanced-exchange model, that controlled. Both Bergthora and Hallgerd felt that blood was a more accurate measure of the debts needing requiting than the number of silver ounces their husbands felt settled the matter. One might conceptualize this as a problem of imperfectly calibrated exchange-rates or of the imperfect fungibility of the various money substances. There was also an obvious practical side to taking blood every now and then. It meant people would think harder about harming you and, if they did, you were likely to receive more compensation than you would if no one feared blood revenge from such as you.

The saga shows the same kinds of dispute arising over the types of property paid in conventional compensation. This might explain something of a minor crux in the saga. It goes to the issue of how secure settlements were and what kinds of actions could be seen to be breaches of them. On one occasion it involves a preference for land as against movables. A settlement is reached after the battle at Knafahills in which Gunnar and his two brothers kill fourteen, injure many others, and suffer the loss of their brother Hjort (ch. 63). In this settlement too Njal is Gunnar's banker; he has money and chattels out on loan to Gunnar's enemies, which debts he assigns to Gunnar so that Gunnar can waive them in favor of his victims. Njal bears no loss of status, nor Hrut either (chs. 6–7), for being lenders, regular lenders it appears, which was an important aspect of the relations most substantial farmers would have with others less substantial.[15] Sometime later, after the settlement for the battle at Knafahills, Thorgeir Starkadarson, a party to the settlement, is looking for a way to reopen hostilities. He seeks Mord's advice on the matter. Mord said it would be difficult to do so without being called a *griðníðingr*, but suggests they might be able to show that Gunnar's party had breached the settlement already, entitling them to declare themselves no longer bound by it:

> 'I have heard that Kolskegg is planning to go to law in order to regain the fourth of Moeidarknoll which your father was given as compensation for one of your brothers. Kolskegg is bringing the action on behalf of his mother, but it was Gunnar's idea to pay with movables and not lose the land. We shall wait until they carry out his plan, and then accuse him of breaking the settlement he made with you.' (ch. 67)

15. Thus the Sigfussons have property out on loan, as do Flosi and Hrut; see Orri (2007: 131) re livestock rental.

Problems like this must be quite frequent when there is no money substance working *only* as money. Cows, cloth, sheep, land can be money, but
they also have use values independent of being money. Not enough silver
was available in Iceland to have it pay all debts; and surely Gunnar does
not have access to enough silver to pay for all the corpses he generates.
Recourse must be had to other money substances, but since these kinds
of currency also have use values this makes for something of a problem of
valuing each piece of 'money'. Though all these money substances—land,
silver, sheep, assignments of debts, cloth—are in theory exchangeable and
fungible, in practice there is a lot of friction. For a stunning example, consult the law I have relegated to this footnote.[16]

In the case at issue in chapter 67 it seems that Gunnar and Kolskegg
paid over some of their mother's land, and now, apparently, Gunnar has
obtained other assets, probably on loan, to redeem the land, and substitute
cows, sheep, or cloth to repay the loan of land he obtained from his mother.
The land apparently means something special to Rannveig, his mother,
and she wants to redeem it for an equivalent in a different specie. The compensation awarded to Thorgeir's father would still be paid in full. Mord is
playing on the idea that the settlement meant designating specific assets
as payment, that by being so designated are no longer deemed fungible or
exchangeable. The kind of claim he is making is much more likely to fly
in an economy in which no single ready means of payment exists, and the

---

16. *Njála* shows silver passing hands in considerable amounts for bodies and not much else.
The laws and apparently the author shared the belief that silver at the time the saga was
set was plentiful. Says *Grágás* Ib 192, 'at the time when Christianity came here to Iceland,
silver was the currency in all major debts'. But the later world reflected in the laws is one in
which silver does not figure as a frequent means of payment. Thus the laws purport to set
exchange-rates or price-lists for commodities any of which could also fill various money
functions, as measures of value, means of payment, sometimes as units of account and as
stores of value (Ia 192–5). I quote one small section to provide an idea of the pressure on
transaction costs that could accompany the simplest purchases or loan repayments: 'a standard value of an ounce-unit' equals 'six ells of valid homespun, new and unused. . .' The
following are all declared to be worth one ounce-unit: two skins of old tomcats, three skins
from cats one summer old, six fox skins. A cow between three and ten years old is a standard
value: 'she is a valid form of payment.' Surely a cow ten years old would have to be depre-
ciated to account for her expected useful life. Anyway, a three-year-old ox equals a cow,
two two-year-old oxen equals a cow. A four-year-old ox, castrated or not, equals a cow, a
seven-year-old ox is worth two cows and so too 'any ox older than that. An old plough-ox
in the spring has a value subject to assessment.' It would seem that the problem of assessment
would not be limited to the last old plow-ox in the spring but exist for every item listed. And
so it does, for another provision requires 'lawful viewers' (*lögsjándi*, sg.) to assay the quality
of the means of payment (Ib 141).

various money substances are only imperfectly working as money. One wonders if all these problems in valuation do not work as an incentive to prefer blood. One can imagine someone like Bergthora, saying: 'To hell with pricing all these means of payment, let's just kill one of them.' But that only postpones the pricing problem, which would eventually have to be faced, unless the quality of corpses balanced out perfectly on each side. And what went into determining that was hardly set in stone.

Part of the joke Njal and Skarphedin share must be the anticipation of the look on Gunnar's face when he is paid back with his own purse with the same silver still in it, the joke being at his expense in more than one way. Except the purse is not quite the same purse. When it was first handed over it was a mummy of Svart, now it is one of Kol. Skarphedin's first grin detaches itself and seems to hover above the action, finding grimly comical the paradox that both he and his father understand to be at the heart of the peaceful resolution of killing.

The Model's Simplifications

The model clearly raises these issues, the author and his brighter characters are totally aware of them. Three other aspects of the ideology of balanced exchange, which reveal even more inadequacies and contradictions, the author develops later. One: in the Bergthora–Hallgerd feud only the person who killed the previous year gets killed the following year. The model simplifies reality greatly, as models must do to remain models. But in actual feuding practice one need not go after the killer. The model avoids the issue of the more expansive rules of liability that we will see can be used to justify killing Thrain or, in other sagas, the wrongdoer's nephews, brothers who were non-complicit, even out of the country when the events occurred, as in *Hrafnkels saga*. Such unlucky souls can serve as *legitimate* targets of revenge within the norms of the feud, though not always within the rules of the law. Two: the model cannot account for the timing of each turn or, importantly, what counts as a turn. In these chapters each turn is indisputably a turn, and each turn takes place exactly a year apart when the household heads are away at the Althing. Reality is messier. And third—and to which the author devotes the Lyting and Amundi episodes—is that the model simply ignores the crucial issue of who has to be paid; how many people have an interest in the corpse who need to be bought out? Let Amundi capture the sentiment of those who fall on the wrong side of the line that gets drawn between those getting paid compensation and those not: 'I know that you came to terms with *them*. I am asking what compensation you are prepared to pay *me*' (ch. 106).

In the real feud, timing is subject to much variation and depends some-times on well-wrought plans (the Burning), at other times on mere con-venience (a Hoskuld Njalsson happens to ride by your farm). Timing is something for the person whose turn it is to put to good use, for he can impose the costs of playing defense on his enemies, by forcing them to have to take constant precautions against attack. And as against the fashionable (and idiotic) claim that revenge is just hardwired and an instinctual response programmed into our genes and neuro-structures, actual Icelandic feuding and the model made it preferable for revenge to be served up cold; take your time and *think*. Only the stupid hit back right away, governed by anger; the wise avenger takes his time, as do Bergthora and Hallgerd, each coolly waiting a year.[17]

But what counts as a turn? Turn-taking is an active principle in the feud and is subject to dispute and manipulation. A turn is pretty clear in games like chess and tennis, but not in life or in a lot of other games. Remember your childhood games in which half the time was taken up arguing whether a turn counted (because you weren't ready, because you flubbed it too badly to have it really count). When Njal intercepts a planned attack on Gunnar and the attack is thus aborted (chs. 71–2), does that failed attempt count as a turn, even though a botched one, or as no turn at all, thus warranting a do-over? 'Attempts' are not always clearly turns, but in this case it counted, because Njal sued on it and collected compensation. That meant, though, that Njal and Gunnar had taken their turn, and now it was the Thorgeirs' turn again to move, which they do.

One needs really to acknowledge the sophistication of the author's cri-tique of the culture's dominant model of getting even, or of justice. I have seen few that can match it in any anthropological, social, literary, historical, or legal theoretical writing on revenge.

---

17. 'Only a slave avenges himself immediately' (*Grettis saga*, ch. 15), i.e. only a stupid person forgoes the opportunity to make his enemy stew in fear, making him wait perhaps several years for the hit to come. For a compelling critique of those medievalists who think revenge just a hardwired response and who therefore cannot account for the delay, coldness, and the politics of so much of it, among a host of other problems, see White 2013.

6

Bergthora vs. Hallgerd, Part II: Some Facts

Start first with the pure naturalism of this depiction of untranquil domesticity:

> Gunnar rode to the Althing. Before he left home, he said to Hallgerd, 'Be good while I am away, and don't make trouble if you have to deal with my friends.'
>
> 'The trolls take your friends,' she replied.
>
> Gunnar rode away; he realized that it was no use trying to talk to her. (ch. 36)

This brief exchange reveals rather starkly the difference in dealing with Old Icelandic texts and many Latin texts of the same period in which the author feels obliged to attempt high Latin style. This scene could be a recording of my wife and me, were she not significantly better disposed towards the few friends I have than Hallgerd is toward Gunnar's.

Nor does the stylized plotting of this female feud destroy the conditions for creating sophisticated social interactions, nor for painting in rapid strokes characters you care for. One of them is Atli.

Atli's Story (chapters 36–8)

Some months after Kol had killed Svart, the first killing in the cycle, Bergthora is outside the farmhouse while Njal and her sons are up at their other farm that came with Skarphedin's wife. She sees a man ride up on a black horse.

> She waited for him instead of going inside. She did not recognize him. He was carrying a spear, with a short-sword at his belt.
>
> She asked him his name.

'My name is Atli,' he replied.

She asked where he came from.

'I am from the Eastfjords,' he replied.

'Where are you going?' she asked.

'I am unemployed,' he replied, 'and I was intending to see Njal and Skarphedin to find out if they would engage me.'

'What work are you best at?' she asked.

'I am a plowman,' he replied, 'and I can do many other things. But I won't try to conceal the fact that I am a quick-tempered man, and there are many who have had to bind up wounds because of me.'

'I don't blame you for not being a coward,' she said.

'Have you any say here?' asked Atli.

'I am Njal's wife,' replied Bergthora, 'and I have as much say in hiring servants as he.'

'Will you engage me, then?' he asked.

'Yes,' she replied, 'but only if you are prepared to do whatever I ask you to, even if I send you out to kill someone.'

'You have men enough for that kind of work without needing me,' said Atli.

'I make my own conditions,' said Bergthora.

'We'll settle on these terms, then,' said Atli, and so she engaged him.

A clearly 'bad' man rides up, heavily armed. He is alone, which is seldom a good recommendation; it mimics the condition forced on the outlaw and favored by the thief. He looks like he may be on the lam and does not say much to suggest otherwise.[1] Imagine a rough-looking stranger knocks at your door. You, a woman, are home alone, or your academic husband is there providing protection. The man at the door tells you basically that he is what he looks like, a killer. Would Bergthora's response have been yours? 'I don't blame you for not being a coward (bleyðimaðr).'[2] I do not pose that question lightly. She does not seem to find this encounter anxiety-provoking. We know that Bergthora has very little capacity for fear and that she is ruthless in defense of her own and her family's honor. We also know that a big farmhouse of a substantial farmer has more than a few folk of varying types of character living together under the same roof.

---

1. He says he is *vistlauss*, that is, he has not formally hired on for the year as a servant as the law requires him to do. If these are Moving Days, the four-day period at the end of May to negotiate a new annual term of lodging and employment (*Grágás* Ia 128–9), then he is still legal unless he is a runaway slave, which is also possible. He needs to hire on for a year soon, as we see him arrange to do a year later when Njal advises him to return to the Eastfjords.
2. Re *blauðr*, see Clover 1993: 353–4. The term does much of the work *ragr* does (see pp. 92, 105), indicating a not-very-manly male.

Those growing up with Hallgerd, for instance, had to get used to having the ominous Thjostolf around. He finally gets dismissed for beating a fellow servant, but Hoskuld and his wife apparently slept better rather than worse with him under the roof, though his co-workers may have felt otherwise. Bergthora might have had workmen in the fields, or inside, to back up their mistress. Then too there might not have been anyone, other than serving-women or children, within shouting distance.

She must know she has little to fear, that Atli puts her at no appreciable risk. We have a little data point here—and little is all it is without a whole lot more—that women of a certain class could feel reasonably secure without the leading men of the house around. The entire Bergthora–Hallgerd feud suggests as much. These two women order assassins about as if such orders contained no risk for them, no possibility of a servant uprising. A doting father may provide his willful adolescent daughter with a bodyguard of Atli's or Thjostolf's ilk, but it is rare to find the woman of the house at risk. Though we have examples from other sagas, they are remarkably few.[3] I only want to point this out, because the sagas, as they compress time from one violent or high-stakes episode to another, pass over months and sometimes years with little more than stating that the time had been uneventful.

Bergthora's power in the house, with typical Bergthorian bluntness, is made known to Atli: she has no less authority to hire servants than her husband. We also see that from an outsider's perspective Skarphedin is understood to have some management authority in the household, since Atli assumes Skarphedin as well as Njal can do the hiring. Njal, who firmly maintains his authority over his household's dealings with the outside world, may understand that he needs to cede some authority for running the economic unit to his eldest son, or risk fissure.[4] The fissure does eventually come anyway, largely because he was not willing to cede any of his authority over the household's 'foreign' or extra-household affairs. Yet even if he ceded some of the farm management to Skarphedin, it could not have been much, for the farm at Thorolfsfell, the dowry of Skarphedin's

---

3. See Þorgils saga ok Hafliða, ch. 6, where the would-be rapists were not pure strangers as Atli is here.
4. Given the law's restrictions on a married woman's rights to make contracts, Njal seems to have, as per the law, granted, or been forced to grant, Bergthora the power to hire and contract beyond what would be legal in the absence of such permission; see Grágás Ib 44–5.

wife Thorhild, is called Njal's and not Skarphedin's.[5] Atli might be making an unwarranted assumption.

The introduction of saga characters of some standing usually follows a conventional formula, as we saw in the discussion of chapter 1, in which a brief description is given of the person's looks and general temperament. People of high standing will get a genealogy, but unless they play a large part in the saga will not be described physically. Atli, whether criminal or runaway slave, is too briefly on the scene even to get a patronymic. It is Bergthora who introduces him to us, by asking him for a short biography. She likes both what she hears and sees. When her husband and sons return home and ask after the new household member, we get a dour statement from Njal that confirms that Atli looks the part he was hired for. Then, in a model of authorial economy, we get: 'Skarphedin liked Atli' (*Skarpheðinn var vel til Atla*).

To pay a character who will be dead in five pages an honor like that shows Atli is 'a man for a' that', that his self-description contains no puffery: 'I won't try to conceal the fact that. . . many a man has had to bind up wounds because of me.' Do we know enough of Skarphedin by this time to know all the work those few words are doing? If we do not, we are not reading very well, for that first grin calls all kinds of attention to itself for reasons that have already been noted. Skarphedin's introduction is not quite as conventional as other conventional ones either (ch. 25); it is one of the few things he shares with his father. Balanced against his father's noteworthy beardlessness is Skarphedin's ugly mouth, with teeth that seem naturally to be bared, calling attention to the pointed wit of the words that will issue from it, and to other traits that resemble those prominent teeth: his paleness and sharp features (*skarpleitr*), his very name being a partial pun on what he looks like: 'He was quick to speak and scathing in his words. . . His face was very pale and his features sharp. He had a crooked nose and prominent teeth, which made him ugly round the mouth' (ch. 25). Unlike Skarphedin, Atli is not lupine, but he is verbally clever, and a person to be reckoned with.

---

5. We might find one small sign of Skarphedin's interest in Thorolfsfell in ch. 69, when the shepherd-boy there is said to be the *sauðarmaðr þeira Þórhildar*, the plural pronoun indicating 'the shepherd of Thorhild and X'. One would normally expect X to be the husband but Skarphedin is not mentioned as present in the scene, while Njal is.

Atli is hired as an assassin and he does his assassinating with style. It is
Althing time again. Njal has left for it bearing the purse that Gunnar had
paid over the previous year. Atli asks Bergthora what his work for the day
was to be. She orders him to go kill Kol. Atli accepts the task without
demur: 'That is very fitting, for we are both of us scoundrels (*illmenni*).' He
sets out to look for Kol and meets some people who ask Atli where he is
heading:

> He replied that he was looking for an old cart-horse. They called that a
> petty task for a man like him—'but you had better ask those who have spent
> the night out of doors.'
> 'Who are they?' asked Atli.
> 'Killer-Kol, Hallgerd's servant, has just left the shieling[6]. . .' they replied.
> 'I'm not sure whether I dare go near him,' said Atli. 'He has a nasty temper
> and I might as well learn from another man's lesson.'
> 'You look anything but a coward (*ragr*),' they said and directed him to Kol.
> (ch. 37)

This short colloquy is packed with information. First we learn that tasks
are status-graded, and no one sends a man who looks like Atli, fully armed
to boot, to look for an old cart-horse. The people who direct him to Kol
understand that Atli is insulting him. Recall also why someone who looked
like Thjostolf so resented chasing sheep, even though the head of household
was forced to do the same. Kol, we notice, has acquired a nickname during the year. We can partly supply the collusive tone of the nameless men
who indicate where Kol can be found and the mockery in Atli's response.
We can hear him overacting with a feigned fearful voice of how risky it is
to have any dealing with a man like Killer-Kol. His interlocutors, no less
dark-humored than Atli, direct him right to his victim, knowing full well
what they are doing.[7] They even goad him on, implying that because he
does not look *ragr*—a word that can get you legitimately killed if you call
someone it—he should get on with his work. Kol is not a very popular man.

Atli kills Kol. In accordance with the law, he announces the killing to
the first people to whom he can safely do so. They are some of Hallgerd's
servants, whom he obviously does not fear:

> 'Go and see to that horse up there,' said Atli. 'Kol has fallen off its back and
> he's dead.'

---

6. An upland pasture with huts for the shepherds and dairy-maids.
7. See ch. 146 for another example of lethal direction-giving.

'Did you kill him?' they asked.

'Hallgerd will suspect that he hasn't died from natural causes,' said Atli, and rode back home. He told Bergthora, who thanked him for what he had done, and what he had said.

Equal to the killing is his wit, and he is equally thanked for both. 'Hallgerd was told of Kol's killing *and Atli's remarks*; she said that she would pay him back.' His words, obviously, get her goat. A dead Kol means nothing to her. And the words? For one, Atli directed them to Hallgerd: 'Hallgerd will suspect that he hasn't died from natural causes.' An insult also lurks in 'natural causes', rendering *sjálfdauðr*, literally self-dead, or dead on its own, not suicide. The word is applied to animals that are not slaughtered but drop dead of old age or disease or die by accident. They are not edible in the old Norwegian law,[8] just as they would not be kosher in biblical law. Atli is keeping up the joke about looking for an old cart-horse; Kol is not human, but edible because properly butchered, not inedible because dead by accident.

Bergthora's approval elicits from him some concern about how Njal will respond:

> 'Njal will not mind,' said Bergthora. 'As an indication, I can tell you that he took with him to the Althing the slave-payment we accepted last summer, and which will now be used to pay for Kol. But even though a settlement is made, you must be on your guard; for Hallgerd honors no settlements.'

The same might be said of Bergthora's respect for settlements. We have already seen, though, how much better Bergthora is at working around her husband than Hallgerd is at working around hers. Bergthora is able to take the air out of any remonstrance Njal will make to her, by citing his own predictions, as we discussed earlier, or here by taking his pre-cautionary preparations as another kind of prediction which she will do him the favor of proving true. When he takes the purse she reads it, if not as approval, then as a kind of acquiescence in what he expects her to do despite his wishes. It would be wrong, I think, to read Njal as signing on to what Bergthora wants to do. But she is delightfully clever in turning Njal's

---

8. *NGL* I: 18, but cf. *Grágás* Ia 34, which lets you eat animals as long as you know how they died, whether by landslide, avalanche, or storm, or whatever, but not if the cause of death is unknown. Icelanders, living closer to the margins than Norwegians, cast a wider net with the self-dead.

prudent planning for the worst into a partial warrant for accomplishing her goals, while deflecting some of her responsibility onto him for doing so. Njal has a wife whose IQ matches his own.

Economists invoke a concept called moral hazard. In simplest terms it supposes that carrying insurance will make people less careful than they would be without it. Because the insurance company or other insureds will bear most of the costs of the insured's risk-taking and not himself, the insured takes fewer precautions. Something like that is happening here. Njal plans for the worst, and those plans help in part to increase the risks that others will do exactly what he planned against, because (a) they see that the costs of doing so will be lower than they would have been without his having planned ahead, or (b) as here, they can use it as a kind of permission to engage in the risky behavior, because Njal is counting on some likelihood of it happening.

The men are not complicit in their wives' war. Their wives have wills and minds of their own. These women did not readily accept any supposed naturalism about gender hierarchies, as the broad comedy of Hallgerd's 'the trolls take your friends' should remind us.[9] The men are serious when they reproach their wives' settlement-breaking, when they ask them to refrain, or when they express genuine concern to each other that the stresses their wives are imposing on their friendship may be too much for it. Bergthora and Hallgerd only stop when they have basically gotten what they wanted: permanent hostility between the Sigfussons and Bergthorsknoll groups. (I use 'Sigfusson' broadly, applying it to that group that sees Thrain, later Hoskuld, as its leader, whether they are properly sons or grandsons or in-laws of their ancestor Sigfus.) Could the men have stopped the women if they had wanted to? I suppose so, but try to imagine how. Issue orders or make settlements? That did not work. Never leave their wives' sides? Divorce? Inform the servants that anyone obeying their wives to carry out a killing will be killed? Empty threat; after one year the servants already have factored that in.

Two more items should be mentioned before I conclude 'Atli's saga'. Good worker that he is, Atli is intently making charcoal in the same woods where Svart died. Byrnjolf, Hallgerd's kinsman, another *illmenni*, who needed some goading from Hallgerd to undertake the mission ('Thjostolf

---

9. See Herzog. Serving-women would throw the ideology of gender hierarchy in the face of their masters, as in *Þorsteins þáttr stangarhöggs*; see *BP* 59.

would have been less daunted'), sneaks up behind Atli under cover of the smoke and strikes him on the head with his axe. Atli turns around so fast that Brynjolf lets go of the axe. Atli still manages to throw his spear at Brynjolf, who hits the dirt to avoid the missile. Atli, though dying, and his skull no doubt badly smashed, has all his wits about him as he humiliates his killer: 'Hallgerd will be pleased when you report my death. But it is a consolation to me to know that you yourself will have the same fate soon. Come and get your axe you left here' (ch. 38). Brynjolf is in no rush to collect his axe, waiting until he is sure Atli is dead. Atli could hardly get in a better parting shot. One does not drop one's weapons, which from time immemorial marked the coward shedding weight for hasty flight. Atli's devastating parting sneer to his killer earns our respect.

Njal, as we saw, agreed not to accept a slave-payment for Atli. Atli has more than shown he deserves an honorable compensation. Njal feels, however, that he must give Gunnar warning. If Gunnar thinks he is about to pay over 12 ounces again—one wonders if Gunnar brought the same purse with him to the Althing that had been handed back to him the year before—he should know that the rules have changed. 'We have already agreed to let nothing come between our friendship, but I cannot put a slave's price on Atli,' says Njal. This is not just between Gunnar and Njal any longer. Njal admits to obligations to the dead servant, a worthy man. These settlements, even between such close friends, are not a charade; they are not taken lightly by either of them. Njal announces an award of 100 ounces, and 'many of those present called the figure high but Gunnar replied angrily that worse men than Atli had been paid for with full compensation' (ch. 38). Gunnar is tetchy, but adopts to his present purposes a locution Hallgerd had primed him with a year earlier when she registered her irritation that Gunnar had paid Njal for Svart—'better men than Svart [have] fallen without any compensation' (ch. 36). I think Gunnar may have been somewhat surprised by the tenfold increase (these are most likely long hundreds).[10]

As the rest of the account reveals, and as was noted in my preceding chapter, Atli's juridical status is hardly clear. But whatever it was when he

---

10. A long hundred is 120. Notice, too, the colloquy in ch. 36 after the first killing, when Njal tells Gunnar he cannot let Hallgerd have her way; Gunnar simply responds by giving Njal self-judgment, studiously saying nothing about his wife. There is some sense that he does not appreciate Njal lecturing him about how to handle his wife.

arrived at Bergthorsknoll, in death he unambivalently has been made a free man, manumitted if by nothing else than by Njal's ability to secure 100 ounces for his life.

The saga notes that Njal made no further additions to his household during Moving Days the next spring. If Njal means thus to put a brake on the killings by refusing to add obvious assassins and cannon-fodder to the household, this backfires and works instead to speed the escalation. Bergthora will now look to dearer household members, rather than to homeless toughs looking for a situation.[11] This is the first indication that Njal's prescience is not seamless and his strategic success-rate, though very good, is hardly perfect.

Njála and Independent People

It has recently been argued that the glorified democratic equality of saga Iceland that featured centrally in Icelandic nationalism and independence movements in the nineteenth and twentieth centuries is manifestly false, a romantic construction based on the immediate concerns of those political and cultural movements.[12] But let me split the difference between the now-dominant revisionists and that older Teutonic egalitarianism of the more romantically inclined. That there were big differences in wealth and power the family sagas hardly disguise (even if some earlier scholarship may have), the Sturlunga sagas even less so.[13] That there were little people who

---

11. Wolf, 70, notes the significance of not hiring on new servants.
12. In English there is no better example of this position than Lord Bryce's famous essay (1901), which can still be read fruitfully as something more than a primary source for the cultural history of the turn of the last century; he has general observations on the law that are worth attending to. He celebrates a 'republic' of 'independent people'. It is on this that the revisionists take issue. Poverty and differential access to resources reduced a good portion of the population to dependency, ever increasing, it seems, during the late 12th and early 13th centuries. See esp. Orri 2007; also Samson, Jón Viðar 1999.
13. Grágás, unlike the Anglo-Saxon laws, made no distinction among free men and women for the value of the no-harm principle. There was no scale of wergild by rank. A payment known as the réttr, as indicated in the Introduction, was also the same for all free men and women (for réttr, see Grágás trans, vol. 2: 391, s.v. personal compensation). Njála is exceptional in indicating a wergild of 100 ounces for a middling freeman and 200 ounces for a freeman apparently of some standing. The laws are committed to juridical equality similar to that which obtains in the laws of Exodus. But the laws hardly assumed economic equality. The most elaborate section of Grágás governs responsibility for poor dependents, Ómagabálkr, a section that makes one think that poverty rather than violence was by far the most pressing problem for the society.

did not matter greatly is not much of a revelation. Feud was a game that required some standing and fairly significant assets to play; it meant having connections, debts that could be called in.

But look at Atli, look at any number of nobodies in this saga. They are not merely cannon-fodder or message-bearers. In this saga the cannon-fodder is supplied mostly by farmers of some standing who make up the rather implausible body-counts generated by Gunnar and Kari, whereas some poor homeless people, like Atli, are given souls, grand ones. Skarphedin liked him. Very few men of the more substantial classes die as grandly as Atli. Our author evinces something of a commitment to an ideology, if not quite of independent people, then of non-deference of the little people toward their superiors.

Where, in this society with undeniable inequalities of wealth and power, is the deference that servants, male and female, are to give their masters? We see very little. They are cheeky and given to the same kind of tough talk as their bosses. They do not cringe. Thus Gunnar's reprimand to Hallgerd— 'you would be better off squabbling with your servants' (ch. 35)—suggests less-than-servile servants. When Kari and Thorgeir, two big men, meet a man leading a horse loaded down with peat, he addresses the chieftain Thorgeir with complete familiarity, though their social ranks could not be farther apart: 'There are not enough of you today Thorgeir, *my fellow*' (ch. 146). Beggarwomen are no more deferential, and they are the lowest of the low (chs. 44, 92, 127). Though it costs him his life, and his death ends up as one played for laughs, the author joins the sentiment expressed by Solvi, the barbecue man, who works the Althing each summer (ch. 145).[14] The reader is not meant to discount his view of the Eastfjord men fleeing before the enemy because he is of low status, even if there is something of the Thersites about him. The author does nothing to undermine the truth of his observation. Rather the contrary. And Hallbjorn the Strong, his killer, comes in for as many laughs as are meant for Solvi. For no sooner has Hallbjorn lobstered Solvi in his own pot than: 'Just then Hallbjorn was attacked, and he started fleeing.'

How do we account for the author taking such care to create characters like Atli, Thjostolf, Hrapp, Bjorn of Mork? The latter two own their farms, true, but Atli is at the very lowest rung of the society before he is made a

14. Cf. Helga Kress (1977: 298) asking us to compare the difference in treatment of Solvi with Ingjald of Keldur, both of whom insult Burners.

full household member. Atli and Bjorn are much more fully developed than
Hoskuld Hvitanesspriest, who barely descends from allegory. He was created to have his death matter, not his life. The household members whom the
two wives routinely send to kill and be killed are given their say, Bergthora's
more than Hallgerd's, but hers as well. They are treated as if they too had
their honor to defend. Hallgerd recognizes that Kol and Brynjolf, who are less
eager to carry out her commands than she would wish, will respond to insults
to their manhood. These men have a sense of shame that can be used against
them. They count themselves men.

The author shows respect for the unnamed beggars, the itinerant paupers,
mere laborers in the fields, who are given the important task of conveying
information from farm to farm in the saga.[15] Nor are they painted as mere
automatons when they do so, but are shown to have interests, even wit, as they
package their news so as to douse or fan the flames of feud of the big people, by
which they hope to cash in as messengers, and generate a little excitement in
their lives at the expense of their 'betters'. And though tasks are status-graded
so that Thjostolf thinks looking for sheep beneath him, and Atli is not the type
to be sent out looking for a cart-horse, the status differentiation is not such as
we see in richer continental Europe: Gunnar and Hoskuld Hvitanesspriest
do not think it beneath them to sow their own fields, even if they dress a little
ostentatiously to do so.

Undeniably great inequality, political and economic, does not undo our
author's commitment to a certain ideology of moral equality. This moral
equality manifests itself in the tough-talk familiarity that people assume
toward each other, that all parties, low and high, seem to enjoy as banter. Where we see more indirection, more formal politeness, is among the
better-off in their relations with each other. That said, the picture varies from
saga to saga. In *Laxdæla saga* the author is hardly generous to lesser souls, and
he is obsessed with birth and filiation to noble blood, which he seems to man-
ufacture for the occasion, turning slave-girls into princesses if need be. And
despite that author's somewhat ambivalent attitude to Kjartan, he does not
seem to be troubled by Kjartan's insufferable self-satisfaction, and his insatiable
demands for deference.[16]

---

15. For contrast compare *Gísla saga*, ch. 27, where the courageous risk-taking of a female slave
    on behalf of her master's kinsman is accompanied by an authorial snide remark about her
    sweat smelling from her efforts.
16. The family sagas have been noted to be either pro- or anti-chieftain in their biases, *Laxdæla
    saga* among the former, *Bandamanna saga* with the latter. *Njála* is more complex, but its con-
    ventional heroes—Gunnar, Njal, Kari—are not chieftains but big farmers, wealthy to be

Thord Freedmansson (chapters 39–43)

I have already scattered enough comments about Thord, foster-father to the Njalssons, to treat him fairly briefly. I said that he is one of the two or three most important victims in the saga, if we are thinking of causal inputs to the enmity that leads to the Burning. Thord was the son of Sigtrygg, a slave freed by Njal's mother. He gets a generalized patronymic geared to his father's juridical status rather than to his father's name. The reason he is known as Freedmansson is no doubt to fix in the community memory that Thord was born after Sigtrygg had been manumitted, otherwise, assuming his mother was free, Thord would have been born into slavery and if freed would be a freedman, not a freedman's son.[17]

If Thjostolf was a bodyguard what exactly is Thord's role as foster-father to the Njalssons? I assume that he was some kind of instructor. Even if he had never seen blood spilled, he may have been their trainer in martial arts, which hardly was a task their father could have undertaken. To Sigmund, his killer, he looks like someone who could more than hold his own; Thord is 'tall and strong'. Sigmund refuses to fight him in single combat; and he credits Thord with a quarter of Skarphedin's dauntingness (ch. 42). Thord is of the highest rank of the servant class or will soon be, for his 'significant other' occupies the highest female servant rank inside the house. We are told that 'he was in love with a kinswoman of Njal's who was housekeeper there, Gudfinna Thorolfsdottir. She was now pregnant' (ch. 39). Why that last superfluous detail, if not to humanize Thord even more, to make him an object of our solicitude? Thord was loved by his foster-sons, especially Skarphedin who, as Thord predicts, would avenge him (ch. 42); Thrain had already predicted such would be the outcome if they killed Thord (ch. 41).[18]

As soon as Thord kills Brynjolf the news, as usual, is sent to the Althing. Njal asks to be told it three times (ch. 40). He will ask the same when he hears that Gunnar was seen chanting from his grave-mound (ch. 78). Njal

---

sure. In any case, little people who can barely get a mention in *Íslendinga saga*, or the other *Sturlunga* sagas dealing with the last decades of the commonwealth, are much more of a presence in the family sagas written largely at the same time as most of the *Sturlunga* sagas.

17. See *Grágás* Ia 224; Karras, 51.
18. On the closeness of the fosterage bond, see Ch. 2, n. 39 and Ch. 9, n. 9. The love is indicated by Njal's admission that his sons would not accept compensation for Thord's death, but would insist on blood.

is manifesting disbelief, confessing limits to his prescience. (In Thord's case Njal's prescience fails more than once; he cannot, for instance, foresee when a river might be in spate so that it will prevent Thord from getting to the Althing the summer he is killed.) Njal's disbelief here, though, is less that Thord could kill, than that Bergthora would so escalate matters as to order him to do it and put her sons' foster-father in Hallgerd's sights. To ask three times is to make a feeble gesture of wishing it away, of trying to turn the clock back, a sort of apotropaic magic ritual. Within a sentence Skarphedin is wondering why he and his brothers are not yet involved; the escalation that Bergthora (and Hallgerd) clearly desire is reaching a point of no return.

When Bergthora ratchets up the seriousness of hostilities by enlisting Thord, Hallgerd tries to match her by recruiting Gunnar's cousin Sigmund, and her son-in-law Thrain. Now it is proper Sigfussons who will kill and die, not servants or remote kinsmen of Hallgerd's. The feud will now lock itself in until both sides are effectively exterminated. Thrain agrees to be present but not fight, when Sigmund and his unpleasant Swedish companion, Skjold, attack Thord. What does Hallgerd gain by Thrain just sitting and watching? The short answer is that she gets exactly what Bergthora got by recruiting Thord to the cycle of killing: escalation. After Gunnar, Thrain is the next leading man in the Sigfusson group. Thrain's presence at an attack on Thord means that he is in fact legally complicit in the killing. Outlawry liability attaches for riding out with the killers knowing what their mission is. That is enough to make Thrain an accomplice.[19] In this round we can discern that part of what may be driving the dispute is the wives' resentments at their husbands' setting more store in their relations to each other (hardly unwisely given their political ambitions) than to the narrower interests of their household members, who prefer competing, rather than allying, with the other group.

Hallgerd has Thrain hooked whether he fights or not. Later, when the Njalssons attack Sigmund and Skjold, Skarphedin tells his half-brother

---

19. On complicity, see *Grágás* Ia 145–6; Ia 183 (lesser outlawry for anyone who promises to go on an ambush), and Ia 184–5 (re promising to go burn a building with people or property in it). The rules regarding complicity, aiding and abetting, and helping an outlaw are quite strict, *Grágás* II 342–4; see also II 383–4 (on complicity in raiding, where receipt of any goods leads to full liability); see further *BP* 206. Notice that the lawyer Njal makes sure to inform Skarphedin that Thrain was present when Skarphedin asked his father who had killed Thord (ch. 43).

Hoskuld not to take part in the fighting, 'for you often have to travel by yourself without protection'. But Thrain is accompanying killers who do not have the legal right to kill. Thord's killing of Brynjolf has been settled. Killing Thord is a violation of that settlement. Though Hoskuld knowingly accompanies his brothers on their way to kill Sigmund, they are not violating a settlement to do so. Sigmund's verses are of the kind that give the insultees the right to kill,[20] and Hoskuld would possess that right, being one of the Dungbeards. Thrain thinks himself reasonably safe because some people would understand, despite the law, that watching was less culpable than actually doing the killing.

Why, though, would Thrain agree to go along and not fight? Because he is caught in the middle. He thinks he is making an acceptable compromise, splitting the difference between his obligations to his nephew Gunnar and to his mother-in-law, Hallgerd. He figures that it is probably best to placate her in some way because he could anticipate that she would make his life miserable were he not to appease her. Thrain is not very bright, as seems generally to be the case with most of the Sigfusson clan, including Gunnar, with the possible exception of the good man Ketil of Mork and the certain exception of the precocious Hoskuld Thrainsson.

The killing of Thord Freedmansson leads to a change in the routine of the previous settlements in this feud. Njal appears willing to settle without his sons present. Gunnar asks if they shouldn't be party to the settlement and Njal indicates that they would not settle if present, but that 'they will not break any settlement that I make'. His sons do not break it, as we discussed above.

Does a father's settlement bind his adult sons? A parent or guardian can bind his ward. Gudrun in *Laxdæla saga* evinces a belief in her power to bind her minor sons. That is why she refuses to settle for her dead husband Bolli. She wants her minor sons to avenge their father almost as a coming-of-age rite, and so she refuses to conclude a settlement that would interfere with the mission she intends to send them on once they reach puberty.[21] But such agreements on behalf of a minor had to be fragile. Hence Njal's careful questioning of the boy Hoskuld before taking him in (ch. 94).[22] As

20. *Grágás* Ib 183–4 (right to kill for *ragr*-type insults).
21. *Laxdæla saga*, ch. 56.
22. Hence too the nervous ending of *Thorstein the White's saga*, Sneglu-Halli's belief that for a minor to violate such a settlement would make him a *griðníðingr* notwithstanding; *Sneglu-Halla þáttr*, M and F versions, 278.

Gunnar's question whether the Njalssons should not be present indicates, the expectation would be that adult sons would be asked to agree to the settlement in person unless they had formally assigned that power to their father or some other adult. And, as Njal suggests, were his sons present and explicitly refused to be party to the settlement it would be much harder for Njal to oblige them not to break 'his' settlement.

The Lethal Insults (chapters 44–5)

An uneasy settlement is in place, the Njalssons bound indirectly to honor it as dutiful sons. Then enter people for whom feud is a source of sustenance: the beggarwomen. These poor women are an unnerving presence in the saga, not just for the information they bear and the deaths it leads to, but because they bespeak the desperate lot of a homeless segment of the population who either were unable, or for some reason preferred not, to hire on for a year's service as the law demanded. They distinctly do not have the look of mere plot devices, nor of those district dependents who are shunted from household to household but are entitled to a roof over their head the year round, such as the boy playing Mord that Hoskuld beat with a stick (ch. 8). These women look to be truly homeless, and one wonders at the surplus of women, and their age distribution.[23] The number of them included within the plural form can only be guessed at. They, however, are not unwelcome either at Bergthorsknoll or Hlidarend. Such visitors bear news, tell tales, and maybe exchange smallwares, and thus play their role in alleviating boredom. They also benefit from certain kinds of strife, playing one side off against the other, as these do here.

These women had been at Bergthorsknoll and then head to Hlidarend. Thrain and his wife Thorgerd, Hallgerd's daughter, are there too, their farm about two miles away. Hallgerd asks the women the news. They say they had nothing much to tell, evidently a typical understated way of

---

23. If old women servants did not have wealthier kin and their annual employment contracts were not renewed, was this their lot? Old Sæunn (ch. 124), a bit senile, is still a member of Njal's household, but his is a wealthy household, and she may have had a special privilege because she was Bergthora's foster-mother, or wet-nurse, making her very old indeed. On vagrants as saga plot devices, see Cochrane. He notes that beggarwomen in the sagas are always nameless and travel in groups, whereas male vagrants will not infrequently bear names (54 n. 38, discussing briefly this chapter in *Njála*).

setting up what news they do have to tell, or will invent.[24] But when they answer Hallgerd's question of where they had been and she finds that it was at Bergthora's, she cannot resist questioning them:

'What was Njal doing?' asked Hallgerd.
'He was busy sitting still,' they replied.
'What were Njal's sons doing?' asked Hallgerd. 'They at least think themselves men.'
'They look big enough, but they've never been put to any test,' they replied. 'Skarphedin was sharpening his axe, Grim was putting a shaft on his spear, Helgi was riveting the hilt of his sword, and Hoskuld was strengthening the handle of his shield.' (ch. 44)

It is the beggarwomen, not Hallgerd, who determine that the repartee will be one of edginess and insult. They are the first to go after Njal. They mock his unmartial cerebralism. These paupers are also playing to their audience, singing for their supper, so to speak. They can figure that this type of talk will not be displeasing to Hallgerd. Even the noble Hrut (chs. 22–3) delighted in what Ursula Dronke aptly calls 'the instinctive spite of local gossip'; nor did he have to be enemies with its objects to enjoy it.[25] In defense of such spiteful talk, it is crucial to monitoring and enforcing social norms, except the social norms against such spiteful talk. It exposes pretensions, and exerts a leveling force cutting people back down to their proper size. It is the mobilization of envy and *Schadenfreude* in the service of rough equality.

The beggarwomen consciously oppose Njal's inaction with a description of his sons' active martial preparation, their weapon work. That speech bears all the marks of a stylized composition, for composed it is, another tableau vivant, this time created not by the narrator but by the lowest of the author's characters, who are not without a talent for narrative artistry themselves. Even if they are not making the description up, they are ratcheting it up, cuing Hallgerd to keep the game going.

We find that Njal's servants are carting dung, which prompts Hallgerd, setting up the insult soon to follow, to ask what the point of that was. (Incredibly, it has been argued that Hallgerd was ignorant of manure's

fertile properties, and that the wise Njal was the first in Iceland to recognize its usefulness. Who in an agricultural community would not know
the value of dung?)[26] Then follow the well-known insults about Njal's inability to grow a beard. She had already called him Old Beardless—*karl
inn skegglausi*—three chapters earlier. Now she graces the sons with Little
Dungbeards (*taðskegglingar*).

It is rather remarkable, given the talent most saga characters have for
understated insult, that Hallgerd's humor here seems more at the level of
a squirting lapel-flower, about as witty as the universal insult when I was
a kid: fatso, which was hurled at the rail-thin as well as at the chubby.
Hallgerd is better than that. It has to be more than that they need to fertilize
their faces or else end up beardless like their father. Something has been
lost to us that was not lost on Njal or his sons, or anyone else in the saga
world. The saga informs us what that is, but it requires that we jump ahead
to one of its more memorable scenes: Skarphedin at the Althing as he, fifth
in line of the group seeking support to defend the case for killing Hoskuld
Hvitanesspriest, confronts Thorkel Hake (Braggart)[27] (chs. 119–20):

> Thorkel said, 'Who is that big baleful man, fifth in the line, the one with
> the pale, sharp, ill-starred, evil look?'
> 'I am called Skarphedin and you have no cause to pick on me, an innocent
> man, with your insults. I at least have never threatened my own father's life,
> as you once did, nor ever fought with him, as you once did. You have rarely
> attended the Althing or taken part in lawsuits, and you must feel more at
> home milking the cows at Oxarriver with your scanty household. You would
> be better employed picking out of your teeth the bits of mare's ass you ate
> before you came here—your shepherd saw you at it and was amazed at such
> disgusting behavior.'

Thorkel, like the others before him—Skapti, Snorri, Haf, Gudmund[28]—
cannot keep himself from asking after Skarphedin, whom 'everyone knew
at first sight' anyway. Somehow Skarphedin's mere presence suborns their

---

26. EÓS actually needs a footnote to dismiss politely a view asserted that Njal was the first in
    Iceland to discover the virtues of manure (1954: 112–13 n. 5).
27. Magnusson/Pálsson render *hákr* as braggart; *hákr* is probably hake, the fish, which has a very
    large and rather ugly mouth. But to translate 'braggart' is too tendentious. Exactly what
    feature of Thorkel's mouthiness is indicated is best left obscured. Thorkel gets no respect
    in *Njáls saga*, but Skarphedin would hardly get much credit humiliating a man of no con-
    sequence. *Ljósvetninga saga*, written before *Njála*, most likely known in some form by our
    author, presents a less easily-cowed Thorkel.
28. Notice that five characters ask after the fifth man.

will and makes them play a role, speaking lines that come out of them despite themselves. Thorkel cannot even help punning on his name: 'Who is. . . that man, fifth in the line, with the pale, sharp (*skarpleitr*), ill-starred, evil look?' The insults that Skarphedin rains down on Thorkel—the shabbiness of his gentility, his not having the grace to avoid the bad form of threatening and fighting his father, as is told at the beginning of *Ljósvetninga saga*, his lack of participation in litigation, that most chieftainly of activities, his being better off doing the women's work of milking cows—need little glossing. But eating mare's ass does, for in it lies the sting of 'Little Dungbeards'.

How do you get dung on your face? You engage in sloppily performed coprophagy, the sterilized Greek term for shit-eating. Or you can come by coprophagy and the face-smearing incidentically, as an inevitable side-effect of engaging in oral–anal sex with farm animals. How is this any better than fatso? Because Skarphedin makes it better by adding the shepherd's viewpoint, the point of which is: if something can disgust a shepherd, well, then that has to be really something. Shepherds, as the near universal joke has it, are known for indulgence in various forms of bestiality, they being far away from human companionship. They begin to fancy their sheep, cows, goats, and dogs. Evidently Thorkel goes further than shepherds, who would prefer genital penetration of farm animals; those who are Dungbeards are more orally inclined. The dungbeard insult, then, is part of the standard Norse repertoire of *ragr* accusations. These usually imply the anal penetration of males, but are also extended to any kind of sexual activity adjudged perverse, like bestiality, or as with Njal's beardlessness, to any effeminate trait.[29] Hallgerd is thus doing considerably better than fatso.

Hallgerd gets Sigmund to apply his poetic talents and versify these insults. Some manuscripts of the saga contain the verses, but these are generally agreed not to be original and in any event are not very good.[30] Gunnar overhears the poem, bursts in, and cows them into silence, except the beggarwomen, who have struck gold. They agree that Bergthora

---

29. Sayers (1994: 16) sees the dungbeard insult, rightly, to reference coprophagy, but does not link it to Skarphedin's insult of Thorkel. He makes it alimentary rather than sexual, citing Louis-Jensen, 106–7, on the rarity of insults of coprophagy. Laurence Sterne gestures in the same oral–anal direction as the *Njála* author: 'Did not Dr. Kunastrokius, that great man, at his leisure hours, take the greatest delight imaginable in combing of asses' tails, and plucking the dead hairs out with his teeth, though he had tweezers always in his pocket?' (*Tristram Shandy*, 1. 7).

30. See Guðrún Nordal.

would reward them for hearing what just got said. They head back down to Bergthorsknoll and tell her *ófregit*, unasked, which contrasts with the usual protocol we saw, as when Hallgerd first asked them the news. No time for niceties.

Bergthora confronts the men at table, saying the lines that I discussed as capturing in lapidary form the theory of feud as gift-exchange. She tells them of the gifts that they have been given and must repay if they are to be men. Says Skarphedin, 'We don't have women's dispositions, flying into a rage at everything.' When first introduced with his lupine features, it was said of Skarphedin that *þó löngum vel stilltr*, that he 'mostly kept himself well under control'. One can sense here that doing so did not always come easily, that it took fairly insistent self-monitoring, which, except for very few outbursts, he managed quite ably nonetheless.

His clever mother knows how to get them all going. Using Gunnar in the following passage to provoke them is a masterstroke, playing to their natural competitiveness with this paragon, while at the same time sneering at even-temperedness as a general principle:

> 'But Gunnar flew into a rage on your behalf and Gunnar is considered even-tempered. If you don't take vengeance for this you will never avenge any insult.'
> 'Our old mother is enjoying herself,' said Skarphedin, and grinned; but the sweat broke out on his forehead and two red spots flared in his cheeks, which had seldom happened before. Grim was silent and gnawed at his lip. Helgi did not change expression. Hoskuld left the room with Bergthora, but she came storming in again. (ch. 44)

Sweating and facial reddening are beyond conscious control. This flare of red spots on the cheek and sweat on the forehead are to Skarphedin what massive swellings, explosions of bodily fluids, and fainting are to Thorhall Asgrimsson. He does his best to keep his cool; but he is not keeping it coolly, for his body betrays how much effort it is taking him as his temperature rises. No amount of trying to feign nonchalance by downplaying his mother's comments with some tired commonplace about female emotionalism can cover for it. The psychological acuity of writing like this is hard to match. Even his grin this time fails him, for it does not have the same meaning. It is a false grin; this one has no wry or darkly comic aspect to it at all.

Notice too how the writer parodies the very scene the beggarwomen constructed for Hallgerd of the four sons working on their weapons a page

earlier, as each one is given his tableau-vivant response: sweat and red spots
for Skarphedin, lip-gnawing for Grim, sitting in silence for Helgi, and
Hoskuld leaving the room, to match with the earlier sharpening an axe,
putting a shaft on a spear, riveting a sword hilt, and strengthening a shield
handle.

Sigmund and Skjold will be dead in the next chapter, with the former
being forced to mimic some *ragr* sexual practice before he dies, and perhaps
in death too:

> Sigmund was pulled forward on to both knees, but jumped to his feet
> again at once.
> 'Now you have knelt before me,' said Skarphedin. 'But you will be flat on
> mother earth[31] before we part company.' (ch. 45)

Then follows the beheading of Sigmund, the handing of the head to the
shepherd-boy, who stands holding it but throws it down as soon as the
Njalssons leave, because 'he had not dared to do so while they were still
there'. The perfection of such a detail is that it gives an inner life to the
shepherd-boy. Where else do we see such generalized humanity, available
to shepherd-boys, beggarwomen, as well as to heroes, where the lowly are
not merely hauled onstage to play clowns or die in droves? This terrified
boy has his disgust briefly overwhelmed by his fear. How fully human.

As a legal matter, remember, Sigmund was killed for the insulting verses
he composed. Further to confirm that this killing is not a violation of Njal's
settlement with Gunnar, Njal, for the first time, is totally pleased with the
killings, indeed it is the only time in the entire saga when he unambivalently
praises any of his offspring. He is not about to activate the usual procedure
and offer Gunnar self-judgment. When Njal is the object of the insult, he is
not so blood-averse as he has appeared to be up until now. 'May your hands
prosper,' he says when his sons tell him that they took care of Sigmund, 'as
things now stand there is no question of granting self-judgment this time.'

Gunnar brings no action on behalf of his dead cousin, letting him lie
uncompensated for. Compare Gunnar's inaction here with his paying 100 ounces for Atli. In the latter case Atli's status is elevated in death,
in Sigmund's case it is lowered to an *óbótamaðr*, formally a person of no
price, for whom no compensation is due. After three years Njal eventually

---

31. *í móðurætt falla*, literally to fall into your maternal lineage, suggesting being buried in mother
earth, but also suggesting that he has been used as a woman.

offers to make it good to Gunnar, and does so in a way that incorporates Sigmund's death into the tit-for-tat that has governed until then. The 200 ounces received for Thord Freedmansson is at last handed back.

There are some legal issues to note. One: by not seeking compensation for Sigmund, Gunnar has in effect disowned him posthumously, analogous to how Thjostolf was repudiated by Hoskuld, Hrut, and Hallgerd. Gunnar's refusal to make any claim is fully appreciated and not forgotten, for Skarphedin some years later cites it as the reason he will help Hogni avenge his father, Gunnar: 'I have not forgotten how Gunnar behaved over the death of your kinsman, Sigmund' (ch. 78).

Second: when Gunnar and Njal finally settle, Gunnar announces it at the local Thing. He repeats the words which led to Sigmund's death and he declares that anyone who might say them could be killed without compensation. Why rehearse the insults in public? The law requires at least a half-stanza to be repeated when suing someone for a malicious verse, but that is not the case here. This is a settlement, not a lawsuit. The reason appears to be this: to kill gossip with the truth, to let everyone know that Skarphedin's killing of Sigmund was fully justified, and that Gunnar's refusal to respond was itself a proper response. This has to be the reason, since Gunnar is claiming nothing more by disallowing the repetition of these verses than the law already gives him. Full outlawry is the lot of anyone who composes a mere half-stanza of insulting verse, and the same for anyone who teaches it and for anyone who learns it or repeats it.[32] Sigmund's verses meet that test easily. What Gunnar has announced to the assembled community in effect is: now you all know that we have not behaved unreasonably—and if you say these words, we are warning you now that we will hunt you down and kill you.

32. *Grágás* Ib 183–4.

7

Otkel vs. Gunnar:
Chapters 46–56

An uneasy peace has been established between the two feuding households. Njal and Gunnar's friendship, their political alliance, has survived their wives' feud. As long as both of these men are alive they will
keep the hostility that now exists between other members of their kin and
households under wraps. The saga now moves to tell the story of how one
of these allies will be killed, and clearly marks its shift of focus by introduc-
ing an important new player, Gizur the White, who will lead the posse that
will kill Gunnar; Gizur is also one of the key players in the Christianizing
of Iceland and father of its first native bishop (chs. 46, 104). Mord is rein-
troduced, recalling his introduction in chapter 25, as someone who envies
Gunnar greatly and does not keep good kinship, especially with Gunnar.
Mord only comes alive when the saga shifts focus to Gunnar, where he
will figure as an advisor to Gunnar's various enemies. Brief as chapter 46
is, it has Gunnar's death written all over it and thereby indicates the plot's
trajectory. Once Gunnar is killed, the feud that Bergthora and Hallgerd
started will be seen to have only been in remission. The old enmity will
resurface not long after Gunnar dies. The women will have gotten what
they wanted.

The saga's lens now takes in a slightly wider view. The previous twelve
chapters focused on two households and their outlying properties where
killings took place, punctuated by the obligatory scenes at the Althing
where settlements for those killings were concluded. In these next
thirty-five chapters the Althing will feature yet again, but in between
Althings the action will expand beyond Fljotshlid and Landeyjar, Gunnar's
and Njal's local areas, to include the Rangriver plains a little to the west,
with visits further west, but still in the South Quarter, to Mosfell and Hlid,

homes to Gizur the White and Geir the Priest, who, along with Asgrim at Tongue, live west of the Thjors River. Eastwards it will now extend to Mork and Dale on the east bank of the Markar River, where Ketil and Runolf live (see maps). Hlidarend, Gunnar's farm, as before, will figure centrally.

The basic structure of these chapters is fairly straightforward. Gunnar's troubles with Otkel lead to Otkel's death, and then his troubles with the people of Thrihyrning lead to a host of deaths, including that of Gunnar's younger brother, Hjort. Gunnar turns out to be remarkably good at killing, clearing lavafields of men as he cleared pirate ships abroad (ch. 30). Eventually Gunnar's enemies unite to take him down, proving the wisdom of the adage: the enemies of my enemies are my friends. The narrator is quite partial to Gunnar and makes most of his enemies look like troublemakers or stupid or both. That is not the whole story. Good men oppose Gunnar too, not just envious ruffians like Thorgeir Starkadarson or ambitious dimwits like Otkel and his decent but none-too-bright son, Thorgeir, or troublemakers like Skammkel, or perhaps Mord. The author gives us enough information to construct a more nuanced account of what irritates people about Gunnar.

The 'Theft'

Problems with Otkel start during a localized famine. Gunnar shares out his stocks and needs to replenish his stores.[1] With his brother Kolskegg, his uncle Thrain, and one other kinsman, Gunnar rides to Kirkby,[2] the farm of Otkel Skarfsson, a wealthy man, to ask to buy hay and food. Otkel is well connected by kinship; he is second cousin to big men, Gizur the White and Geir the Priest. His grandfather is remembered for his success in a duel. He has two brothers; one, Hallbjorn, is portrayed as a well-intentioned, honorable man. Otkel, however, sets great store by his friend Skammkel, a person who delights in fomenting strife. He is the image of the bad counselor,

---

1. I deal with the Otkel episode at greater length in *BP* 84–93.
2. The farm name is probably an anachronism, having undergone a name-change after the Conversion. No one in Otkel's family tree is mentioned as having been Christian before the general Conversion.

a type who will be more fully developed with Mord; they are meant to provide a contrast with good counselors like Njal, Hall of Sida, and Gizur.

Otkel refuses requests to sell or give, and Gunnar nixes Thrain's suggestion that they just take what they want and leave behind the price, a forced sale that is called a *rán*.[3] We see a very consistent Thrain throughout the saga, impulsive and not very farseeing, shortcomings that will eventually get him killed. Though Otkel will not sell Gunnar food, he is more than willing to sell him another mouth to feed, a lazy Irish slave, Melkolf, whom Gunnar buys in an attempt to defuse a deteriorating interaction, an effort we might enlist among our earlier examples of mobilizing tact to save what has become an embarrassing situation.

Njal comes to hear of Gunnar's failed mission and laments. The dialogue is worth quoting because it again shows how intelligent the interactions between Njal and Bergthora are, this time Njal getting around Bergthora as cleverly as she has been able to get around him.

> 'It was a bad deed to refuse to sell to Gunnar. There is little hope for others there, when men like Gunnar cannot buy.'
>
> 'Why do you have to talk so much about it?' said Bergthora. 'It would be more generous just to give Gunnar the hay and food he needs since you are short of neither.'
>
> 'That is perfectly true,' said Njal. 'I shall provide him with something.' (ch. 47)

Only in an Icelandic saga could Njal be accused of talking too much for a sermon lasting two short sentences. We might ask why Gunnar sought out a stranger like Otkel, when his friend Njal was well stocked. The reason is that relations between the two households are very sensitive, and Bergthora has no love for the people of Hlidarend. That prevents Njal from offering, and Gunnar from asking. What Njal succeeds in doing in this colloquy is getting his wife's consent by annoying her into granting permission in order to shut him up. Just as she uses her husband's yen for talking portentously against him, he uses her hot temper against her. They, at some level, delight in each other, as they prove that even good marriages have some of the attributes of feud.

The thief's eyes of the first chapter at last catch sight of something to steal. Hallgerd sends the slave Melkolf to take the food that Otkel would

---

3. On the significance of the various types of exchange that feature in this abortive transaction—sale, gift, raid, ultimately theft—see *BP*, ch. 3.

not sell. Hallgerd's motives can be ascertained with reasonable confidence. She is trying to do right by her husband, who was humiliated by his fruitless expedition to Otkel's. She wants to even up the account on behalf of their household.[4] This is a strange kind of theft, because Hallgerd is inconsistent, and quite cavalier, about being secretive. She wants Melkolf to fire the buildings to hide the losses, but she pretty much confesses in front of a multitude of guests how she acquired the dairy products.[5] Hallgerd cannot understand what merited the slap we discussed earlier. What a nice touch, she must think, to have employed this worthless slave Otkel pawned off on her husband to carry out the property transfer. Serves Otkel right, with a poetic flourish too. She expects gratitude or a complicit wink for a job well done, and gets a humiliating reprimand instead. She now suffers the aching frustration and attendant rage of having one's good intentions misinterpreted. At another level, the author also makes use of this disreputable slave. He shows that fire can be borne to buildings, and by doing so (as well as by having Mord suggest doing so later in chapter 77) tars Flosi's defining deed, only a little less than he tars Hallgerd's, with the taint of slave morality.[6]

Hallgerd's good intentions seem to run afoul of some countering moral and social norms: theft is not an acceptable move in the get-even game, just as taking the best seat without being offered it was not acceptable either. She has a knack for not quite reading the norms governing competitiveness correctly. Yet in *Laxdæla saga* Gudrun Osvifrsdottir thieves, is not very concerned to hide her guilt, refuses to make restitution, and loses not a whit of honor.[7]

By one very compelling social norm—Njal invokes it to Bergthora's annoyance—Gunnar had a just claim that Otkel transfer food to him. Otkel was not quite as free as he thought to refuse to sell or give without some reprisal. We can imagine Gudrun making Otkel pay in quite the same way as Hallgerd did for having violated powerful norms of sharing

---

4. Heinrichs, 347, also sees Hallgerd to be protecting the honor of her household against Otkel's dishonoring of Gunnar.
5. The law provides that if someone takes property worth half an ounce-unit or more, and does not conceal it, he is liable for full outlawry but is to be summoned for 'taking of property to profit from it and not with a charge of theft'; *Grágás* Ib 162. He is to be spared being a thief, which means if outlawed he could kill three other outlaws and be in-lawed; that option was not available to an outlawed thief; Ia 87.
6. It is slaves, as part of a small slave revolt, who do the burning in *Landnámabók*, S 125, H 97.
7. Gudrun is responsible for the theft of a valuable headdress and is not shy about owning up to it; no blame comes her way; *Laxdæla saga*, ch. 46.

during hard times. One woman has everything interpreted in her favor, the other has everything interpreted against her.

Theft is distinguished from *rán* and other less culpable takings by its secrecy and the subsequent concealment of the goods. Like murder, the unannounced killing, theft is trying to get away with something for nothing. In a society without a police force or elaborate markets for insurance, theft is a famously big problem. Not petty thefts, but thefts of livestock, or as here, the produce of livestock. Unless the theft is actually witnessed or the thief caught red-handed, one must investigate and gather evidence. The thief and murderer, unlike the *ránsman* (the open-taker) and killer, do not leave their calling-card. Melkolf, though, inadvertently left his: his knife and belt, the attention to detail he manifested in killing the dog who welcomed him back to Kirkby eluding him here. Melkolf knows the dog's failure to bark would narrow considerably the list of possible perpetrators to Otkel's present or former household members.

The knife and belt are not sufficient evidence on which to incur the risks of a theft accusation. But they narrow the search and make it worth undertaking the extra work of gathering more and better evidence. Otkel and Skammkel seek out Mord and pay him to come up with proof.[8] Mord finds a way to get his hands on the stolen cheese by sending women around trading/begging smallwares on the belief that people holding stolen goods will try to unload them. The women Mord sends around the district might help fill out our vague picture of the groups of beggarwomen who trade in the smallwares of information and gossip. Mord's traders seem to be seen by the householders they deal with as beggarwomen of sorts, and perhaps we should think of those designated as beggarwomen as occupying the lowest end of a mercantile exchange system among farms. That would mean that no one expected the title to such goods as they bore could bear much inspection, but that the goods were too trivial in value to be worth investigating or to require assembling witnesses to the transaction.

Mord's investigation ignites community gossip, a nice side-benefit of gathering evidence, thus generating local knowledge, itself an important aspect of legal proof. Only then does Gunnar decide to go to Otkel to make

---

8. Presumably the guests at Gunnar's who witnessed the slap would also be a good source of proof. EÓS (1954: 125 n. 1) sensibly takes Mord's comment to Otkel and Skammkel (ch. 49), that he 'knows a thing or two about Gunnar's household that [they] do not know', as referring to information he got from those guests.

offers of reparation. He was willing to slap Hallgerd on a lower standard
of proof than it took him to admit liability and offer compensation.[9] He
assembles a group of twelve, large enough to provide protection, but also
to show he is behaving in a formal public manner. It indicates seriousness
of purpose. These negotiations, however, go no better than did the attempt
to buy hay and food. Otkel, following Skammkel's bad advice, refuses ever
more generous offers, taking up instead on Skammkel's suggestion to refer
the matter to the heads of Otkel's kin-group, Gizur and Geir. This is clearly
a stupid move, everyone in the saga saying so who gets a chance, but the
opportunity to humiliate Gunnar, or simply to say no to him, is something
certain would-bes cannot resist (ch. 49).

   In another effortless symbolic detail, Otkel turns out to have bad eyesight.[10] Everyone else can see merely by looking at Skammkel that he is
a bad man, but not Otkel. The same bad eyesight must also be partly the
cause of his riding down Gunnar later (ch. 53). Riding does not come easy
to him; this is why Skammkel offers to undertake the mission to Gizur and
Geir. These men can see Skammkel looks like a liar, and thus make him
repeat the whole tale twice, a kind of informal ordeal. Skammkel is able to
repeat the story; in fact he *is* telling the truth to them. It is to Otkel that he
will lie when he bears the return message that his powerful kinsmen advise
summoning Hallgerd for theft and Gunnar for receiving stolen goods.

   Skammkel's lies are revealed at the Althing, and another perfect detail
is tossed off. When Gizur asks where 'that lying wretch is', the answer is
that he is ill in his booth (ch. 51). If you have ever been caught up in a reasonably serious lie, you will recognize the sickness afflicting Skammkel.
Whatever could Skammkel have thought would have prevented this information from coming out? He made the trouble he desired to make, but for
the moment he is bearing some pain for his success.

   Gunnar is furious at having his generous offers of indemnity refused and
then to be summoned for theft and disgraced; he is in a killing mood. Njal
barely cools him down enough to get him to accept self-judgment. Gunnar
issues his decision 'without consulting anyone', an indication that his fury

---

9. We might explain Gunnar's behavior thus: the slap was in the heat of the moment, while he
   may be understood to be putting off the unpleasantness of further dealings with Otkel until
   it becomes unavoidable, partly procrastinating, partly because he, given Otkel's provocative refusal to sell that started all the trouble, would have good reason to believe that any
   conciliatory dealings with Otkel would be unlikely to prove fruitful.
10. Allen, 103.

has not abated an iota. Gunnar is more than capable of anger when crossed, and it may be that his reputation for being even-tempered was acquired before his patience was seriously tested. Now that he is every upstart's favorite target, the description of the Gunnar we first met is no longer quite apt. There is much more change, both in growth and deterioration, in saga characters than it has been usual to admit. We see here evidence that character might change under stress and over time or, more modestly, that behavior under stress might not always be consistent with character.

Arbitration awards abound in the sagas, but rarely are the reasons for their terms supplied. We usually only get the bottom line: X balances against Y, D against Q. Gunnar gives reasons:[11]

> 'This is my judgment,' he said. 'There is liability for the cost of the storehouse and the food it contained; but for the slave's actions I will pay you nothing, because you concealed his faults. Instead, I am going to hand him back to you, for the ears fit best where they grew. In addition, I find that you served summons on me with intent to disgrace me and for that I award myself damages to the exact value of the house and its contents destroyed in the fire.' (ch. 51)

Gunnar adjudges himself liable for zero damages. Absolving himself of liability for the slave's deeds hardly involves any overreaching. Otkel had a duty to inform him of the slave's defects, and the relief for such failure is simply to rescind the purchase of the slave. As to the liability for the storehouse and the food, he values that as equal to the disgrace of the summons for theft. Even here Gunnar is not overreaching. The laws provide, as was mentioned earlier, that a failed action for theft gives rise to a counteraction for slander; but it is also the case that the plaintiff must indicate in his summons that he believes the other has stolen and is not bringing the action 'in order to disgrace him'.[12] Gunnar seems to have more than enough evidence that slander was wholly Skammkel's and Otkel's motive, for he can show that he previously had made very generous offers of compensation that they had refused. It is even possible that, because Hallgerd was not very secretive about the 'theft', an action for theft was not the proper action, but one for 'taking for profit' was.[13] Gunnar's decision is well within the rules of the

---

11. See the fully reasoned self-judgments in *Hrafnkels saga*, ch. 19 (ÍF, ch. 9) and *Egils saga*, ch. 85.
12. *Grágás* Ib 162–3.
13. See this chapter, n. 5.

law. Still, one might have expected some indemnification of Otkel's losses, just as we shall see when Gunnar is required to pay some amount of compensation for the men he kills in self-defense.

Gunnar is in no mood for compromises. He tells his adversaries that should they not like his decision he has another plan ready, a clear threat. Gizur responds by asking if Gunnar will be Otkel's 'friend', a request the reader must find a *non sequitur* unless aware that the word 'friend' does not here mean friend in our sense: it means to be an ally. It has nothing to do with liking the other, but refers to a practical relationship in which one agrees to support the other politically. Gunnar refuses, making it clear he is itching to get Otkel: 'It would be more advisable for you to go and live with your kinsmen. But if you insist on staying on at Kirkby, take care not to interfere with me again.'

Gunnar's Lament

Before Gunnar issues his decision he advises Otkel 'not to give [him] any more trouble'. As with the case of Thord Freedmansson, we do not have to wait long for more trouble. In that case the actionable insulting verses were self-evidently a serious wrong. Had there been no prior history of enmity, the verses would have created it. But in Otkel's case the 'more trouble' looks like nothing more than an accident.

Otkel gets an invitation to visit Runolf of Dale. Otkel owns the fastest riding horses in the district, and he is not up to the demands they make on the skills of the rider.[14] On his way to Runolf's, Otkel's horses bolt off the track and he ends up spurring Gunnar, who was out sowing grain (chs. 52–3). Half-blind as he is, it is not even clear he saw Gunnar, but how Gunnar did not hear Otkel and avoid him is not told, nor, apparently, meant to be asked.

The event is described as an accident, and probably would have been understood as such by Gunnar had he been on good terms with Otkel, but as we know from our own experience, when a person we do not like

---

14. KJJ 97, aptly notes the near-timeless association of the all-too-recognizable type who seeks status via his wheels, usually with vehicles he cannot handle well or simply looks foolish driving.

stumbles clumsily into us by accident, we suspect it was not an accident. What Otkel needed to do to be able to claim this collision was an accident was immediately to have apologized and, in order to imbue the apology with sincerity, to have offered Gunnar compensation for the gash on his ear. Gunnar has already indicated that he is treating the spurring as intentional: 'this is a disgrace: first you summon me, and now you trample on me and ride me down.' But Skammkel answers before Otkel has a chance to speak, and his answer imputes post hoc intentionality to the incident by praising its results: 'hard riding, boys.'[15]

Intentionality after the fact might sound like an oxymoron, but it means to capture a couple of things that are hardly surprising. We often impute motive and intention to actions by how the agent reacts to their consequences. When Skammkel showed his delight in the injury, he ratified the consequences of Otkel's incompetent riding. At that moment, Otkel had to repudiate Skammkel. But he says nothing, offers nothing, and thereby ratifies Skammkel's pleasure in the events. These people are openly delighting in, and thus benefitting from, a harm one of their party caused Gunnar. Gunnar can now never understand this as an accident even if he had been inclined to let matters slide (which he wasn't), for none of the necessary remedial work—apologizing, offering compensation, repudiating Skammkel, disowning any pleasure or benefit from the incident—was attempted.

These are dead men walking. Kolskegg says as much when he advises Gunnar to make the incident known to many people, 'so that you are never accused of making charges against *dead men*'. As we shall see, you can make charges against dead men, but Kolskegg is nonetheless giving good legal advice. Gunnar needs to publicize the wound now if he is to raise it later in mitigation of any claims brought on behalf of these 'dead men'.

At Runolf's, Skammkel continues to display delight in the event. He claims Gunnar cried.[16] Within lines, at the start of the next chapter, Gunnar sees his shepherd-boy galloping up at full speed to the house (ch. 54). He asks the boy why he is riding so hard, apparently unable to get that phrase, 'hard riding', out of his head, it being the same phrase Skammkel used

15. I discuss accidents more fully in *BP* 61–8, and in Miller 2003: 77–95.
16. Men can shed tears without any dishonor if it is in sorrow, rather than out of fear or from physical pain; see e.g. *Laxdæla saga*, chs. 33, 76.

when Otkel rode him down.[17] The boy answers in something less than all innocence:

> 'I wanted to be loyal to you. I saw a group of eight men riding down along Markar River. Four of them were wearing brightly colored clothing.'
> 'That must be Otkel,' said Gunnar.
> The shepherd said, 'I have often heard their insults. Skammkel was saying, over at Dale, that you wept when they rode you down. I tell you this because I hate the bad talk of types like that.'
> 'We must not be over-sensitive,' said Gunnar. 'But from now on you need only do whatever work you wish.'

How the shepherd came to hear their insults we can construct from other sagas. We know shepherds would congregate in the highlands above their farms and socialize, exchanging gossip.[18] Again we have an unnamed person, a boy, assisting in local lethality. Unlike the nameless people who knowingly directed Atli to Kol, this shepherd can pretend to virtue. He alleges his loyalty, and his support of the norms against actionable insult.[19] He may have self-interested motives too. He has a stake in his master not being talked about that way, for it impinges on his own status relative to other shepherds; and, though he could hardly count on this, Gunnar rewards his service greatly. The boy gets a promotion, it being understood that shepherding was among the lowest of jobs available on the farm,[20] thus adding yet another layer to Skarphedin's insult of Thorkel Hake whose behavior managed to disgust someone as low as a shepherd. There is another aspect to rewarding the servant. Up until then Gunnar's grounds for killing Otkel on the basis of the spurring-wound alone are not as strong as they have just become when he hears about the insults. These qualify as *ragr* insults. Otkel will die for Skammkel's mouth, and his own bad eyes.

Says Gunnar: 'We must not be over-sensitive (*orðsjúkir*)', an evocative Norse word, literally 'word-sick, made sick by words'. Gunnar is in the midst of an adrenaline rush, and tells the boy to keep his cool as he strains to look as if he were maintaining his. The killing spirit is upon him; he is

---

17. Magnusson/Pálsson and Cook lose the look inside Gunnar's psyche here by varying the translation. They use 'hard' for the boy's riding, but 'good' for what Skammkel says about their riding. Dasent rightly maintains the original 'hard' in each instance.
18. E.g. *Laxdæla saga*, ch. 35.
19. On the philology of various ON terms for loyalty and similar concepts, and their development in Norwegian royal ideology, see Orning, 118–22.
20. *Hrafnkels saga*, ch. 4 (ÍF ch. 3) makes this explicit, as does *Grágás* Ia129.

elated at the chance to get Otkel and Skammkel, and of course angry too, all fueling ecstasy in the prospect of blood. Not even a wild man like Egil Skallagrimsson says he would accept odds of eight to one,[21] but Gunnar rides out alone to take on Otkel and his party.[22] Reminding a shepherd (and himself) not to be over-sensitive is not a prelude to prudent action on Gunnar's part, or to plausibility on the author's. This is about heroic style-points, and rather beggars belief. Kolskegg only gets to the battle once Gunnar has already killed four of the eight.[23]

Two matters of importance remain in this chapter. First: the battle is observed by women working at milking-pens nearby. One of them, a servant of Mord's, runs to urge him to separate the combatants. Not all nameless servants bearing messages mean ill. In fact, this woman is adhering to a powerful norm that one who witnesses an affray is supposed to attempt to break it up. The sagas are filled with examples of such obligatory intervention, one form of which we see repeatedly in this saga: those men of good will, like Hjalti Skeggjason and Hall of Sida, who make it a point to intervene in high-stakes lawsuits urging the parties to settle by arbitration. These kinds of intervention call less attention to themselves because they are devoid of the dark comedy that sustains the beggarwomen or that entertains the workers in the field who delight in directing Atli to Killer-Kol.

Mord refuses to get out of bed: 'They will only be people who are welcome to kill each other for all I care.' To which she incredulously responds: 'You can't mean that. Your kinsman Gunnar and your friend Otkel are there.' He just curses her. What this says about Mord hardly needs explication, except to emphasize that she thinks he is obliged to intervene, as she in fact is doing herself. She is right.[24]

Second: then follows one of several of Gunnar's famous speeches. In it he doubts his manliness, manifesting a kind of conscience in reverse: 'I wish I knew whether I am any the less manly than other men, for being so much more reluctant to kill than other men are' (ch. 54). Is the author being ironic? Compare Skarphedin in his attack on Thrain and seven other men,

---

21. Egil says he will go four on six, and eight on twelve, though within two chapters he undergoes considerably worse odds, but that is arguably in defense and forced upon him (*Egils saga*, ch. 74).
22. KJJ 98–9 finds the battle scenes in general comical in their exaggeration, this one especially because of the odds offered.
23. On Hallgerd knowing what the shepherd told Gunnar, see Ch. 4, n. 11.
24. On obligatory intervention, see *BP* 259–60.

in which the entire party attacked had uttered or signed on to the lethal banned words that Sigmund and Hallgerd composed. There it is five on eight (the saga says eight, but only seven are accounted for). The Njalssons have killed three:

> Skarphedin seized hold of Gunnar Lambason and Grani Gunnarsson. 'I have caught a couple of puppies,' he said. 'What shall I do with them?'
>
> 'You could choose to kill them both if you wanted them out of the way,' replied Helgi.
>
> 'I cannot bring myself to kill Grani and support his brother at the same time,' said Skarphedin.
>
> 'Some day you will wish you had killed him,' said Helgi. . .
>
> So they spared the lives of Grani Gunnarsson, Gunnar Lambason, Lambi Sigurdarson, and Lodin. (ch. 92)

Gunnar seems but slenderly to know himself. Unlike the people spared by Skarphedin and crew, the ones that Gunnar kills, except for Otkel and Skammkel, have done nothing that justifies killing them. No, they did not actively disassociate themselves from Skammkel's remarks, but we see no evidence they said offending words or actively signed on to them, which the author makes certain to indicate happened in the case of Thrain's men. The costs of Mord's failure to intervene with a group of his farmhands means four or five died who should not have died. It is hard to imagine after Gunnar killed the first three that the others did much of anything except try to get the hell out of there. Gunnar must have chased them down, as he does his fleeing attackers in chapter 63; and Kolskegg needed to add a few notches to his belt to save face. Presumably these last four whom the brothers dispatched were those in Otkel's company unable to afford brightly colored clothing to wear to Runolf's.

Skarphedin's attack on Thrain with his made-for-movies leap over the river, sliding on the ice and smashing Thrain's skull, turns out to be less subverted by literary exaggeration than Gunnar's dispatching of Otkel's party. The author strangely calls more attention to Skarphedin taking on Thrain five on eight by giving Thrain lines à propos:

> 'What can these men want? There are only five of them against the eight of us.'
>
> 'I believe they would risk an attack against even greater odds,' said Lambi Sigurdarson. (ch. 92)

Everything in the battle between Thrain and the Njalssons is plausible, both as to the extent of unfavorable odds offered and to the number of casualties before quarter is given. That is not so with Gunnar, and one suspects we are seeing the effects of the putative romance tradition commentators have linked to Gunnar and his style. He gets the benefit of romance odds and *chansons de geste* body-counts, while Skarphedin is a saga person all the way down and is restricted by the much homelier notions of saga plausibility.[25] Even Njal, manifestly of the saga world, thinks Gunnar has taken 'drastic action', but the *'mjök'*—that is, 'much, great, large'—that Magnusson/ Pálsson render as 'drastic' also suggests excessiveness.

'But,' says Njal, 'you had great provocation' (ch. 55). Njal's comment has the quality of a bland excuse, the blandness of which registers some disapproval and admonition, for Gunnar was only provoked by Otkel and Skammkel, not by the other six. For then follows in short order Njal's advice, which basically tells Gunnar to keep his killing under control: 'Don't kill twice in the same lineage. . .' The results of the arbitration also track what we have just adduced: Otkel's death is balanced against the spur-wound; Skammkel is priced at zero because everyone agrees that it is good riddance, and the other six are compensated according to worth (ch. 56). No fifty percent discount for these six, as there will be for those who Gunnar kills later in self-defense (see ch. 66).[26] They are paid for in full.

The author insists on making sure we do not give Gunnar a moral pass. The true heroic action in the encounter comes from Otkel's brother Hallbjorn, in every respect presented as a good man, a source of wise counsel to his brother that Otkel rejects. Gunnar knows he is a good man and warns him off, but Hallbjorn cannot stand by as Gunnar kills his brother. Are we to excuse Gunnar because he gave Hallbjorn a chance to save his own skin? Or is Hallbjorn there to taint our thrill with a sense of the tragic costs a certain style of the heroic entails? Perhaps, but when it comes to settling the matter at the Althing, Gunnar 'gained great credit from this', even though he had to reach pretty deep into his purse to pay for the six he had no right to kill.

Despite his foray into wistfulness and his inner states—'I wish I knew whether I am any the less manly than other men, for being so much more

---

25. See Heusler 1922: 8–9.
26. Gunnar must pay in full because he had no right to kill anyone other than Otkel, perhaps, and Skammkel, certainly. Although his other victims did not disassociate themselves from Skammkel's remarks, it is very hard for lower-status men, the four not in colored-clothing, to repudiate their household head for not repudiating Skammkel. Killing them is almost *déclassé* for such as Gunnar.

reluctant to kill than other men are'—Gunnar has released his inner killing machine, which is only constrainable by his remarkable ability to keep
count, add and subtract, and do basic cost accounting in the heat of battle:

> 'Let us pursue them,' said Kolskegg. 'Bring your bow and arrows, you can
> get within range of Thorgeir Starkadarson.'
> Gunnar said, 'Our purses will be empty enough by the time we have paid
> compensation for those who lie dead here already.' (ch. 72)

What reluctance to kill was Gunnar referring to in chapter 54? Ignore
clearing ships abroad; that game is played by different rules. But at home
he has killed all whom the saga has shown to have given him cause within
a short time of the cause having been given, and some who gave him no
cause. Angry as he is when he sets off to attack Otkel, Gunnar can distin-
guish levels of culpability in the members of the group he confronts; thus
his words to Hallbjorn. But he quickly loses that ability, as the four dead in
Otkel's party who could only dress drably attest. Perhaps his is a statement
of post-coital *tristesse*, post-adrenaline letdown; he now feels a little con-
fused by all the passion he had just shown—sticking it to these men turned
out not quite to entail the pleasure he anticipated or indeed felt it to be *in
medias res*.

8

Gunnar vs. the Thrihyrning
People: Chapters 57–66

Starkad and his sons, especially Thorgeir Starkadarson, of Thrihyrning, will play a key role in bringing about Gunnar's demise. They, along with their cousins, the Egilssons of Sandgil (Starkad's sister, Steinvor, is married to Egil), are described as unpleasant troublemakers. Each of these families has a daughter. Hildigunn the Healer Starkadardottir is another of those minor characters given depth with a couple of quick brushstrokes, enough to reveal her mordant intelligence and her irritation with the men in her family. The Egilssons' sister has no speaking lines and is little more than a piece of merchandise, but she bears such an enchanting nickname, Gudrun *náttsól*, Gudrun Night-Sun, that she sticks in one's mind. She is first attached to one amiable Norwegian merchant lodging at Egil's farm, Thorir. When he is killed, she is then transferred by her mother to his friend and business partner Thorgrim, another character whose brief role in the saga marks him as an attractive personality too.[1]

In his partiality to Gunnar, the narrator paints this bunch, except for their Norwegian guests and the daughters, quite unfavorably, Thorgeir Starkadarson especially and justly so. In the attacks on Gunnar he shows no compunction urging his brothers, or later his 'friend', Thorgeir Otkelsson, to bear the brunt of the fighting, while he stays safely to the rear and then runs when they get killed. But these families are not nobodies, for the author is conscientious about providing details that allow us to adjust for his or his narrator's biases. Though not having quite the kinship connections Otkel has, these families are members of the propertied class of householders; their genealogies in some lines go back considerably longer than Njal's

---

1. I draw on KJJ's discussion of Hildigunn; see too O'Donoghue, 90.

short one. They do not lack for allies and have no trouble recruiting people to attack Gunnar. They are among the class of better-off farmers. Mord, for instance, as part of the quid pro quo for agreeing to support them in their troubles with Gunnar, demands that Thorgeir Starkadarson accompany him when Mord asks for the hand of Gizur the White's daughter (ch. 65).[2] Mord obviously thinks that Thorgeir provides prestigious accompaniment. So complexly intermeshed are the relations among opposing groups in these troubles that we find that Njal has business dealings with the Thrihyrning and Sandgil people and has loaned them substantial amounts, debts he later assigns to Gunnar to help Gunnar defray some of his compensation liabilities (ch. 66). Already connected to the Thrihyrning people as their creditor, Njal is soon to share blood with them also, once his kinswomen Thorfinna gives birth to Thorgeir's baby (ch. 64).

The author hardly wants to keep the more complex truth from us; why else would he introduce the detail of the make-up of Mord's marriage expedition to Gizur? That Gunnar's enemies were of some standing is what we would expect anyway. Feuds and enduring quarrels of this sort are restricted to people of the wealthier classes who have the means to pursue costly activities such as cycles of killing, and pay for their consequences. These people, not without some justification, think of themselves as in the class that can worthily contend with Gunnar for status and pre-eminence. They turn out to be wrong about their own anticipated gains, but they do succeed in playing an integral role in bringing Gunnar down.

This feud starts as several saga disputes do, over incidents arising at the popular spectator sport, horsefighting. What starts out with horses fighting to the delight of a human audience ends up with the horses watching their handlers go at it.[3] One of the difficulties honor-based cultures have, especially among young males, is to keep 'stuff that happens' in games in the game. In this horsefight the stuff that happens will spill over, and many people will die as a result.

The author is again at his naturalistic best when he treats us to young peoples' talk at Thrihyrning, where the local young men are talking sports: who has the best horse, who would dare to take on whom, who

---

2. In ch. 67 Mord is referred to as Thorgeir Starkadarson's kin. The saga genealogies do not indicate the link, but that does not mean there is not one. More than sharing a common enemy might unite them.

3. For fuller horsefight descriptions, see *Víga-Glúms saga*, ch. 18 and *Þorsteins þáttr stangarhöggs*.

would be favored to win, and the like. In yet another indication that these
families are not without standing, it is noted that 'some of the men present, wanting to flatter [Thorgeir and his brothers],' said no one would dare
challenge Starkad's horse. Hildigunn the Healer finds this boy-talk, this
loud bragging buffoonery, tiresome, and so starts to needle them by talking
up Gunnar.[4] She, in effect, is goading them by refusing even to pretend to
accept their own self-estimation. Yet another reason why some men hate
Gunnar: he puts stars in the eyes of the women.

> 'You women all seem to think that there's no one like Gunnar. Just because
> Geir the Priest and Gizur the White were humiliated by Gunnar it doesn't
> follow that we would be, too.'
> 'You would come off even worse,' said Hildigunn. (ch. 58)

With Starkad's permission they seek out Gunnar to arrange a horsefight.
Gunnar is downright unneighborly dealing with the request, acting as if it
was the barest presumption for them to dare to ask. He does not bear his
sense of self as lightly as the narrator would sometimes like us to believe.
What are we to make of this?

> 'I make this request, that we fight our horses only to entertain others and not
> to make trouble for ourselves, and that you don't try to discredit me; for if you
> treat me in the way you treat others, I am likely to retaliate in a way you will
> find hard to bear. Whatever you do to me, I shall pay back in kind.'

Is this the same person who is more than once described as difficult to
provoke?

The horsefight turns out to be a disaster. Thorgeir pokes out Gunnar's
horse's eye. Gunnar knocks both Thorgeir and his cousin Kol unconscious and orders the injured horse to be put down.[5] No truce is concluded.
Thorgeir refuses to consider it, and manifests his own broken sense of
equivalence by saying he would see Gunnar dead before he would settle.
'And so a year passed', in a mere clause. The autumn after the following
Althing, Gunnar and his two brothers accept an invitation to visit Asgrim.
The Thrihyrning people plan an ambush in which they muster thirty
men and attack Gunnar at Knafahills, in which the attackers lose fourteen
people but Gunnar's brother Hjort is killed (chs. 61–3). The entire family

---

4. KJJ 104.
5. *Jónsbók* 7.39 sets the loss of a horse's eye at a quarter of its value.

from Sandgill—Egil and his sons—is wiped out, along with Thorir the Norwegian, who lived with them.[6]

Two details worth noting: a man name Sigurd Hoghead spies on Gunnar's movements on behalf of the Thrihyrning people (ch. 61). We meet him again when the attack on Gunnar begins. Sigurd, to his credit, is no slouch and is in the lead. One wonders why he takes it upon himself to be in the van, he having no particular claim against Gunnar that we know of, nor does it seem that he has any special relation with Starkad or his kin, other than neighborly relations. Sigurd is the first to die; the spy in him seems to cajole the heavens into determining his manner of death: Gunnar's first arrow pierces his eye and exits the back of his neck.[7] Poetic justice for a spy.

It is also clear in this battle, and his subsequent ones, that Gunnar goes into a killing zone and seems to enjoy the process. For someone who does not especially have any good one-liners, and seems to find such talk beneath him, we see him engage in it here (as well as when dead from his grave-mound); he cannot resist mocking Thorgeir and Starkad as they flee, and runs after them to give them wounds to show they actually had been in a battle in which they stayed well to the rear.[8] Hildigunn the Healer has some work to do patching up her father and brother when they come home; she cannot resist an 'I told you so' (ch. 63).

Njal as Banker and Lawyer

From now until Gunnar's death, Njal will figure importantly as lawyer and advisor, and the law begins to figure more centrally in the saga. Lehmann correctly pointed out long ago that the strictly legal forms and procedures in the saga do not always match up with *Grágás*. Some deviations from *Grágás* suggest that the author is quoting from various lawbooks or formularies

---

6. See Wolf, 74, who explicates the run-up to the battle (ch. 61) masterfully thus: Thorgeir brags he will kill Gunnar; Kol boasts he will take on Kolskegg. The name of the third of the brothers, Hjort, goes significantly unmentioned since the third of the enemy who speaks, Thorir, a Norwegian, is only taking part because of being goaded by his mother-in-law. He is not a braggart but an honorable man, and the only one to make a kill. He criticizes the cowardice of his companions and predicts his own death, not Hjort's, whom he will kill.

7. Noted both by Allen, 104, and KJJ 109.

8. See KJJ 108–11, for a consistently insightful description of the battle.

without attending to their pertinence to the exact saga situation. Many of these are fairly trivial.[9] Some of his deviations look wholly invented, his motive apparently being less to get the law right than to give the reader an impression of legal razzle-dazzle. These strike me as innocent enough, their literary purpose outweighing any legal-historical one.[10] Other errors no reader without the laws open before him would notice. *Njála* was written after the formal submission of Iceland to Norway in 1262, when *Grágás* was no longer the law but had been replaced by a Norwegian-imposed code called *Jónsbók* (1281), and some of that book's vocabulary and substance makes its way into *Njála*.[11]

Lehmann was often blind to how many of Njal's legal machinations make very good tactical and strategic sense, and especially monetary sense. To see this, one must look beyond the actual pleading and strictly legal claims to the inevitable arbitration proceedings that are in effect settlements 'out of court'. Lehmann failed to see, as Heusler did not fail, that law in action is often more complex than a mere matter of following *Grágás*.[12] Bear with me as I try to make the action as comprehensible as I can, and show how the details give us valuable information about the economic and financial side to law and feud as this astute writer depicts it.

---

9. E.g. when Geir (ch. 56) gives notice of the actions at the Law Rock against Gunnar for killing Otkel, he concludes with making a 'formal inquiry about the domicile and district of the defendants'. He is suing Gunnar of Hlidarend and his brother Kolskegg, two well-known people from an identifiable farm. The procedure is only applicable when the plaintiff is in doubt as to which court he should plead in because the defendant's official lodging for that year is unknown to him; Lehmann, 61. Lehmann, as far as I can discern, has assembled every mismatch between the saga and *Grágás*. Some are nitpicks that do not evince any authorial misunderstanding of law. For instance, that Geir is not the proper plaintiff for Otkel, but that his son Thorgeir is. Why not just assume, as we must, that the young Thorgeir assigned the claim to his chieftain kinsman Geir, once Geir drew the lot? It would be more surprising to see young Thorgeir bring the case when he had chieftain/lawmen as kin to whom he could assign it. Lehmann, a student of Maurer's, was much less critical of lawbooks than of sagas; see Heusler 1911: 4–5. It is certainly not the case that when the lawbooks oppose a saga the lawbook is necessarily right and the saga wrong; see this chapter, n. 12, Heusler 1911 generally, and *BP*, ch. 7.

10. The reopening of Unn's dowry claim is an obvious example, as is Thorhall's tricksterism invalidating the case against the Njalssons (ch. 121); see Ch. 16, n. 5.

11. On the complex story of Icelandic relations with and loss of independence to Norway, see the controversial but quite compelling arguments of Boulhosa, chs. 2–3; *Jónsbók* was preceded by another code, known as *Járnsíða* (1271–4), which *Jónsbók* replaced.

12. Another problem arises with the status of individual provisions in *Grágás*. There are more than a few internal inconsistencies; some provisions appear to have been repealed by subsequent legislation; other provisions have the look of laws that were proposed but never adopted; some look like school exercises; see *BP*, ch. 7.

After the battle Gunnar seeks out Njal, who advises as follows:

'Thorgeir has made my kinswomen Thorfinna pregnant; I am going to assign you my action against him for seduction. I am also going to assign to you an outlawry action against Starkad, for cutting wood on my property on Thrihyrning Ridges. Bring both these actions. You must go over to the place where you fought; dig up the bodies there, name witnesses to the fatal wound, and outlaw (*óhelga*) all the dead men for attacking you and your brothers with intent to wound and kill. . .'[13] You must also go to see Tyrfing of Berjaness; he will assign to you an action he has pending against Onund of Trollwood, whose duty it is to take action over the killing of his brother Egil.' (ch. 64)

Njal has causes of action that did not arise from the battle to bring against each of the main plaintiffs in the case. These are there to serve one main purpose. They are meant to be offsets in the arbitration he knows will be the likely outcome of the lawsuit. He can assure all the lawsuits against Gunnar will fail because he has a valid claim of self-defense which is raised procedurally by having Gunnar dig up the bodies and *óhelga* ('unhallow') the people who attacked him (that is, declare those corpses had forfeited the benefit of the no-harm principle vis-à-vis him). The detail about digging up the bodies and actually summoning them does not appear in *Grágás*, but it has the look of actual practice.[14]

Njal's strategy has less to do with legal skill than with positioning himself as a kind of clearing-house for unprosecuted claims. He either possesses claims in his own name or has access to people who have claims that he can acquire by assignment. There seems to be a fund of unprosecuted claims that probably are not worth taking to law but can yield some return in settlements and thus get cleared. I do not have enough evidence to flesh out the argument I am making, but something here strikes me as a genuine

13. The ellipsis is where Njal preserves Gunnar's right to attend the Althing by procedures undertaken at the local Thing. The sagas show virtually no evidence of the validity of the stricture in *Grágás* that denied Thing attendance to anyone who had a major wound published against him, Ia 174–5; see the full discussion in Heusler 1911: 109–13. On the technical aspects of chs. 64–6, see Lehmann, 64–76. Njal plays on words in the passage, 'it may be *objected* that you had previously *struck* Thorgeir a blow': *En ef þetta er prófat á þingi ok því sé við lostit at þú hafir áðr **lostit** Þorgeir: ljósta við*, to put forward as a proof, and *ljósta*, to strike, to hit.
14. Lehmann, 71, is willing to grant that digging up the bodies here to summon them might reflect actual practice; see also ibid. 54. On summoning a slain man to *óhelgi*, see *Grágás* Ia 181–2. For the formula for such summoning in cases where the dead man assaulted one of the six women on whose behalf one has the right to kill, see *Grágás* Ia 165, II 332–3 and Ch. 2, nn. 39, 45.

practice, and a pretty sophisticated one at that. In other sagas we see chieftains buying up unprosecuted claims at a low price which they would then use to harass people the chieftain had targeted for enmity, or who were already enemies.[15] Here we see unprosecuted lawsuits used as a sort of debt instrument; that they would be so mobilized makes perfect sense, given the shortage of silver and the practical absence of coinage. These dormant claims have value. Njal manages to get full value or even a premium for the woodcutting and seduction claims when they end up offsetting the compensation due on people Gunnar killed. Normally one would expect that these claims must trade at a substantial discount depending on the statute of limitations, many of these periods being quite short (some actions stay alive only until the next Althing or until the one the following year), but a substantial number of common claims have three-year limitation periods and some seem to be re-openable, as witness Unn's dowry claim.[16]

Because of their assignability, lawsuits in fact can function as a kind of money, though mostly as a limited-use money because they can only be assigned once or reassigned to the original holder; but they still have their full settlement value in the hands of the first assignee.[17] We do not see them signed over to pay for land, but we see something very close to that, as when Njal transfers to Gunnar the debts that the Thrihyrning people owe him to pay for the liability Gunnar generated in the affray at Knafahills (ch. 66). Njal's actions here, transferring debts and receivables (unprosecuted claims), comes pretty close to what it means to operate a bank. This is why Njal must be ever so knowledgeable about people's affairs in order to operate the way he does. He has a finger in a lot of pies.

It is a sign of the lack of liquidity and of the poverty of the society that very little money or money substances tend to exchange hands in arbitration awards, except among the very wealthy. What we see instead is the

---

15. *Þorgils saga ok Haflíða*, ch. 7. Buying up inheritance claims: *Guðmundar saga dýra*, chs. 1–2; *Sturlu saga*, chs. 15–7, 28.
16. On the limitations periods, see von Amira, 7 §61, pp. 590–3. Theft actions have no limitations until discovered, and then they have a three-year life; *Grágás* Ib 163. Many claims have a three-year period: those regarding land and fining cases involving major damage, II 506; adultery, intercourse, incest cases Ib 51, II 182, 184, 186; cases of insult if it was not said in the person's hearing, Ib 182; or for poetry about a person, whether defamatory or in praise, Ib 183, etc.
17. *Grágás* Ia 125. This limitation on assignability could be easily circumvented: suppose B, the assignee, wants to assign to C for a price. B simply need transfer back to the original plaintiff-assignor (A) and then have A make a new assignment to C. Indeed this very procedure is allowed in the case of a harpooner's action for payment; *Grágás* II 527–8.

use of offsets often arising from the same incident. That is hardly surprising. Probably the most common form of 'money' used in an arbitrated settlement after a battle is a corpse or a wound. Otkel's corpse pays for the blood his spur shed from Gunnar's ear; Gunnar's bloody ear pays for Otkel's corpse. But as Njal reveals here, the offsets could come from other, unrelated claims, bought, banked, or acquired in order to keep to manageable levels what someone actually had to pay out of pocket as a consequence of an arbitration award. Otherwise no one would have the large amounts necessary to buy peace. New disputes would arise over collecting the unpaid amounts from the settlement. When the saga mentions that the full amount was paid at the Althing, the author usually feels obliged to indicate how that was possible: the farmers attending the Thing with Hoskuld and Hrut contributed (ch. 24), Gunnar's friends helped pay (ch. 66), Njal had invested a prior award for that purpose (ch. 74), or the arbitrators themselves footed most of the bill (ch. 123). We must suppose that a good portion of these payments were via assignment of debts which accounts for part of the payment in this case (ch. 66), or more complex assignments of leases or entire conveyances of land, as discussed above.

Whereas Njal performs with genuine sophistication, we might chalk it up to an authorial stumble that he shows Mord's legal knowledge to be so incredibly under-informed.[18] It defies belief that Mord does not know the law of self-defense (ch. 66), nor the ins and outs of óhelgi proceedings, which is basic to the law of justification; nor should he be all that mystified that Kol was selected as the killer of Hjort even though the Norwegian, Thorir, killed him, for the laws allow one to name as the killer anyone who participated in the attack.[19] I will take this up later, but it seems that the author stacks the deck somewhat unfairly, not just against Hallgerd, but also against Mord, not that either of them do not leave themselves open to blame. For now, couple the rather cartoonish Mord of these Gunnar

18. Lehmann, 75–6, finds the entire colloquy in court in ch. 66 rather shocking: 'the unessential becomes essential, the obvious is handled with difficulty.'
19. See Grágás Ia 152; in keeping with the view that Njal is thinking ahead to the arbitration, he wants to make sure that Hjort is priced equal to the native Kol, rather than balanced against the Norwegian who, though not cost-free, being without kin in the country might not command as high a price as he would were he home. There is nothing unjust about the pleading rule that allows naming anyone who engaged in that attack as the killer; the rule makes a realistic concession to how hard it is to get the facts straight in the mayhem of a general affray when thirty-three men are fighting and, in any event, a person participating in the attack has already made himself subject to full outlawry. Naming him the killer adds no more liability to his account than he has already incurred.

chapters with the knowledge that Gizur, at the top of the pecking order in social status and portrayed as a man of intelligence and good-will, thinks Mord a worthy match for his daughter, not unwise to be allied to him, and competent enough as a pleader to select him to prosecute the case against Flosi (ch. 135).

Paying for Those You Have a Right to Kill

The question that frustrates many readers of this saga is why Gunnar should have to pay for the people whom he killed in self-defense. The question is raised even more vividly in chapter 74, when Njal has the same irrebuttable answer for Gunnar (which he raises employing a different procedure) that he employs in chapter 66,[20] and uses it, not to get Gunnar off the charges, but to force the opposition into an arbitrated settlement, the very settlement, it turns out, that Gunnar would violate. Again we see the naturalistic limits of Njal's prescience. There are two issues here: one is the preference for arbitrated settlements over legal judgments in certain cases; the other, and a corollary, is the expectation that a person attacked will have to pay some compensation for at least some of the people whom he had a perfect legal right to kill.[21]

Were these cases to go to judgment, Gunnar would win the legal action and have to pay nothing, but what would that gain him? The troubles that come Gunnar's way are not minor affairs. The men whom he kills are not insubstantial people. Nor are these lawsuits one-shot disputes, but evince deeper underlying problems that we shall postpone until later. If peace is going to have any chance at all, one side cannot be completely nonsuited in a legal action for dead loved ones and be expected to sit quietly. The parties have to come to some kind of settlement that lets both sides get something out of the arrangement, even if that something is quite modest. It is not only the people who had it coming that are harmed. They had kin and

20. You can raise self-defense, as we already have seen, either by summoning the men who attacked you to *óhelgi*, a suit that technically makes you the plaintiff and the men you killed defendants; or you can raise the same issue as a defense by asking for a clearing verdict (*bjarg-kviðr*) issued by a panel of five drawn from the plaintiff's panel of nine when he sues you for killing his kinsman; *Grágás* Ia 65.
21. See more fully *BP*, ch. 8.

spouses, who are now without the head of their household or a beloved member of it. These people did nothing wrong. Unless they are given some kind of stake in a peace, they will be newly aggrieved enemies of Gunnar, looking to make trouble. One must get some of these people to sign on to a formal agreement, at least so as to make them think twice about getting tainted as *griðníðingar* were they to resume hostilities.[22]

In some non-trivial way, it also makes sense to think that part of the work *some* compensation does is what life insurance does among us; it is meant to substitute partly for the economic value of the loved one lost: it is meant to ease the pain. But it would not be right to think that any Icelander who killed in self-defense would have to indemnify the family of the man whom he had a right to kill. Were this a one-on-one fight in which A killed B in self-defense, both men of modest standing with no prior complex history of enmity, A would assert his defense and that would most likely be an end of it, but then the dead man's family might end up on the rolls of the *hreppr* or the district anyway. In that sense we could see some of the compensation Gunnar is forced to pay as a form of social insurance meant to keep the farms the dead men came from viable economic units.[23]

But I also have a hunch that paying compensation in these instances where one has a right to do the thing one is paying for works partly in the way that a species of apology does, as when we apologize to someone who steps on *our* toe, for our having simply been there, for being sorry the whole thing happened. In Iceland, as I have written before, to say you are sorry means you have to buy the sincerity of your apology with paying something over.[24]

Do these settlements work? Yes and no. They buy time; they gain at least a semblance of peace 'for a while', in the saga's idiom; they function as the 'time out' that the modern western parent imposes on his child whom he no longer believes in spanking. One would have to be very naive to expect a settlement or peace treaty, which some of these settlements are, to be self-enforcing. No one should be so foolish as to trust fully the other side because they concluded a settlement with you. That is why in other settings

---

22. See e.g. the cases of Lyting and Amundi and Ch. 13, n. 10.
23. Such concerns are openly addressed in *Þorsteins þáttr stangarhöggs; BP* 69.
24. When it is our own toe that is stepped on, our 'Oh, I'm sorry' is also meant to prime the other to say the same; Miller 2003: 77–90, *BP* 61–8. Note that the law does not make killing in self-defense a matter of strict liability; it is the arbitrational system that thinks it wise for the self-defender to pay some compensation.

hostages are handed over, or marriages and fosterages are key terms in some of them, marriage and fosterage being a kind of hostage-taking. And that is why these settlements often enlist big power-brokers—the likes of Snorri and Gudmund—to put their honor on the line so that breaking the settlement is also an offense to them. Break the settlement and you incur their enmity.

Still, no one thought that because these arbitrated settlements did not or could not guarantee an end to hostilities their world would be better off without them. Sometimes they ended up working very well. Enough time was bought that the interests that drove the hostility simply no longer mattered; or people calmed down, or the hotheads on each side were replaced by cooler heads. Sometimes the settlement endured for a less happy reason: one side or both ceased to matter at all, or even to exist, as in *Njála*.

People also knew that outlawry had its costs. Legal judgment meant outlawry in big cases, and the saga is quite open about the risks of actually outlawing someone of the stature of a Gunnar, or even of an Otkel. He could ignore the ban, act above the law, as Gunnar did: 'It is said that Gunnar rode to all gatherings and assemblies, and his enemies never dared to attack him. And so, for a time, Gunnar went about as if he had never been outlawed' (ch. 75). Snorri thinks such would be the case if the Njalssons and Kari were to be outlawed for the killing of Hoskuld Hvitanesspriest:

> Gudmund asked, 'Is there any wish to impose either district outlawry or full exile?'
> 'No,' said Snorri, 'neither, for such sentences have often been disobeyed and thus given rise only to further killings and further enmities.' (ch. 123)

Yet Gunnar would have been wise to have adhered to the terms of the settlement. Kolskegg knows that defiance will mean his brother's death (ch. 75). Gunnar did not ignore the settlement with impunity. Nonetheless, it took quite a gathering, at some cost—several dead and wounded—to enforce a sentence of outlawry against such as Gunnar, but enforced it was.

9

The Two Thorgeirs and Death of Gunnar: Chapters 67–77

Nothing compels the author to name both Starkad's son and Otkel's son Thorgeir unless he drew from sources that are unavailable to us. Neither of these Thorgeirs is known outside *Njáls saga*. It is another of his barely noticeable symbolic moves, in which Gunnar's enemies are seen to unite not only out of shared interest but out of shared names, the shared name standing for the shared interest. Homophonic attraction and Gunnar bring the young men together.

The two Thorgeirs are quite distinguishable, however. Otkel's son is neither a troublemaker nor a bad man, rather the contrary: 'he was well-liked by people of most worth, and loved by all his kinsmen' (ch. 67). But he is 'rather easily led', and thus, like his father, not very good at seeing himself set up by his 'friends', namely Thorgeir Starkadarson, who, as we have seen, had no compunction in urging his brothers and cousins to their deaths and then fleeing the scene (ch. 63). He will do the same to his namesake.

As I indicated, Gunnar's enemies include all kinds of people, many of them without a streak of villainy. The author nicely makes the two Thorgeirs serve as emblems for the moral range of people who will kill Gunnar, from Mord to Gizur. It surely makes a difference to the fulfilling of Njal's 'prophecy' that this well-liked Thorgeir Otkelsson is the second to die in the same lineage, and is a kinsman of Gizur the White to boot. When Mord tells Thorgeir Starkadarson that Njal has 'prophesied' about Gunnar's future, they, like Bergthora, will undertake to make Njal look good as a prophet by taking their cue to action from the prediction, which Njal, recall, made sure not to make a prophecy but only 'good advice' (ch. 67).[1] Mord knows that killing any old father and son and then breaking the

---

1. On not wanting one's inklings or heebie-jeebies (*hugboð*) to be considered a prophecy (*spá*),

subsequent settlement would hardly motivate the gods to action. It matters greatly who the father and, in this case especially, who the son are. When Skarphedin and Hogni kill Thorgeir and his father Starkad, no scary music accompanies the action, just triumphal tones (ch. 79).[2]

Mord is not the one who pushes matters either. It is Thorgeir Starkadarson who seeks out Mord, as Otkel did before. Thorgeir wants Mord's help to find ways to get at Gunnar again, the disaster at Knafahills not deterring him but only aggravating his hatred. We have yet to see Mord invent trouble or volunteer himself to seek it, though he eventually will. In Gunnar's troubles he simply provides services for a fee. He gathers evidence to pin a theft claim against Hallgerd. He gives tactical and strategic advice, most of it ineffective, though he can hardly be blamed for not winning a lawsuit when his clients had no case. He does advise Thorgeir Otkelsson to seduce Ormhild, Gunnar's kinswoman (ch. 71), and that counts as adding fuel to the fire, but the flame is already burning out of control. Mord does not need to invent strife or even stir up strife that would not have been stirred up in his absence; Gunnar is more than obliging when it comes to generating energetic opposition.

Like the much more adept Snorri the Priest, Mord strives to gain from others' strife. He avoids taking positions of leadership that would make him a prime target of violent enmity. To anticipate something to be discussed more fully later, ask why Mord, who stabbed Hoskuld Hvitanesspriest, suffers no repercussions for that deed. He got away with murder. Valgard, his wily old father, understands why. What little justice Mord must suffer for his deeds is fairly small beer, as when Gizur makes him undertake the corvée of pleading the case against Flosi and, long before the killing of Hoskuld, when Skarphedin makes him fund Njal's revenge for Gunnar, both, however, getting Mord where it hurts: his love of money, and his desire not to front any dangerous action.

see *Laxdæla saga*, ch. 39; Miller 1986. How did Mord learn of Njal's advice to Gunnar? It could be that it was an umbrella speech, but I can see good reason why Njal and Gunnar would want it leaked. It functions as an announcement that Gunnar will keep his violence within limits and then abide by settlements: we can see it as an effort to issue a public statement of non-aggressiveness.
2. Later Skarphedin kills both a father and his son; the consequences are rather disastrous, but that, again, is because of who the son is.

The Two Prongs of the 'Prophecy'

More than a year passes before the bad Thorgeir befriends the good
Thorgeir. They join with more than twenty others in an abortive attempt
that Njal intercepts, he having been tipped off by his shepherd. The result,
as we have noted, is to fund Gunnar's liabilities for the next anticipated
round with the compensation they collect for the abortive attempt: 'I
shall. . . make sure that it is available to you when you need it' (ch. 69). It
is needed within a year. The Thorgeirs attack Gunnar and Gunnar kills
Thorgeir Otkelsson. I want to call special attention to the author's depiction of Thorgeir's death. The analysis works for both the original and the
translation, which maintains it with great accuracy.

With the death of Thorgeir Otkelsson, the first prong of Njal's prediction has been violated, if we allow for the violation of a figurative 'prong'.
To a person raised on the movies the cinematographic sensibility of this
author would not seem unusual, except that he pre-dated film by more
than six centuries:

> Thorgeir Otkelsson was now almost on him with his sword raised; Gunnar
> whirled on him in fury and drove the halberd right through him, hoisted
> him high in the air, and hurled him out into the river. The body drifted down
> to the ford, where it caught against a boulder; this place has been known as
> Thorgeir's Ford ever since.
> Thorgeir Starkadarson said, 'Let us run. . .' (ch. 72)

There is the noise of battle, clash of weapons, fast action, and then Gunnar
impales Thorgeir and hurls him in the air. We instantly leave the battle
and the noise, to watch the body float first through the air and then more
slowly down the river, the motion having been transformed into slow-mo.
All movement then comes to an abrupt halt when the drifting body strikes
a boulder. And that bump leads the author to transport us to a later time,
after the battle, when the place acquired the name which Thorgeir's dead
body would give it. The soundtrack is stopped, the action is slowed and
then halted. The paratactic style of the Icelandic makes the cinematography even more stunning.

Thorgeir Otkelsson is widely mourned; Gizur and Geir, his kinsmen,
begin preparing legal action. Njal reminds Gunnar that now that he has
killed twice in the same lineage he must make sure to honor the settlement.

As has been noted, Gunnar has a complete defense to the killing cases which Njal threatens to use if people do not agree to appoint arbitrators and settle the case. Compensation was awarded to be paid at once, and Gunnar and Kolskegg were to leave Iceland for three years, but if Gunnar failed to leave he could be killed by the kinsmen of the men he killed.

It is Rannveig, Gunnar's mother, who understands why the arbitrators 'punish' Gunnar with exile while his attackers get to stay home. 'She said that it was best to go abroad and leave them to find someone else to quarrel with' (ch. 74). It has become clear to everyone that Gunnar is a trouble-magnet. New enemies keep arising, old ones will not quit, and the only way peace stands a chance is for everyone to take a time out and remove the temptation. Neither Gunnar, Njal, nor Gunnar's mother thinks that the settlement is unfair. When Njal threatens to scuttle the case against Gunnar unless both sides agreed to arbitration, he could reasonably predict that a three-year exile for Gunnar would not be unlikely, such exiles figuring as a common feature of many arbitrated settlements.[3] What he did not foresee was that Gunnar would violate it, though he is anxious to remind him twice to make sure to adhere to any terms imposed upon him. Such warnings, however, assume Gunnar's will is completely free, and is not fettered in some fatalistic way by the advice Njal had earlier given him.

Again watch the author's cinematography as the second prong is violated. Gunnar and his brother arrange for passage soon after the settlement, and send their wares down to the ship (no trip abroad wastes the opportunity to trade woolens). Gunnar bids farewell, hops on his horse, and as he rides down toward the Markar River the horse trips and Gunnar

> had to leap from the saddle. He looked up towards his home and the slopes of Hlidarend and said, 'How beautiful the slopes are (*hlíðar*, slopes, figure in the name of the farm, *Hlíðarendi*), more beautiful than they have ever seemed to me before, golden cornfields and new-mown hay. I am going back home; I will not go away.' (ch. 75)

Thorgeir Otkelsson is pitched in the air by Gunnar; Gunnar is tossed in the air by his horse. Both airborne journeys end with a bump, the main difference being that the first man flies through the air already dead, while the second is flying to a death brought on by his airborne epiphany. The action in both prongs is perfectly congruent. Magically, the author moves again to

---

3. See Introduction, p. 5.

slow motion, to pan away from Gunnar back up toward his farm, as Gunnar does a voice-over while we look at Hlidarend through his eyes. The author leaves it rather up in the air as to whether Gunnar speaks while in it, or once he hits the ground. But just as Thorgeir bumps against the rock and will not move, so Gunnar hits the ground with an abrupt transformation in his intentional state, and will not move. The author's slow-motion technique—the filmic anachronisms do provide an apt shorthand—has slowed, if not quite suspended, the animation for each airborne violation of Njal's two-point counsel.

It is not the hauntingly surreal vista that Iceland offers that transfixes Gunnar but fertile and productive cropland. Not crevices, jagged rocks, bottomless fissures issuing steam. Nor is it any random domesticated farmland that moves him. This is his farm, his property, his place of defense. Gunnar defies augury, but not without giving reasons for doing so. His reasons do not sound in legality; no mention that the settlement was unjust, that he had an unanswerable defense; no complaint that it should be those who attacked him who should leave rather than he. When the settlement was announced the saga notes in its typically understated way that 'Gunnar said he had no intention of breaking the settlement' (ch. 74).

Some have thought he is thinking of his beautiful and difficult wife now that he is leaving her; that her beauty helps color the beauty of the slopes. The word for slope figures frequently in poetic kennings for women. But the passage says nothing about her, and though she is happy when Gunnar returns, it seems we are not meant to read her happiness as anything more than another instance of her delight in the violation of norms of proper behavior or, as I prefer, her being a stickler about not backing down or moving down. It is the farm that is feminized, hay more than long hair is the attraction, drawing Gunnar in a manner more wistful, more loving, more erotically styled than ever we have seen him with Hallgerd except for their first meeting.[4] True enough, but let us not be moved to tears. This epiphany of love for his land cannot be separated from its underlying motive: defiance.

When Gunnar announces his intention to stay, his brother Kolskegg tries to convince him to honor the settlement. Settlement-breaking, we hear again, is shameful, something Kolskegg could never bring himself to do and something he cannot believe that his honorable brother would

---

4. Cf. Sayers 1994.

contemplate: 'Do not make your enemies happy by breaking the settlement, something that no one would ever expect of you.' Old Norse has a single compound for the pleasure enemies feel at one's expense—*óvinafagnaðr*— literally, 'enemies' joy.' This is a more precise term than *Schadenfreude*, which can be felt by your friends and often is. The Norse term is more biblical in its view: it is restricted to the laughter of your enemies at your discomfiture or defeat. How did English ever manage without these words?

Kolskegg inadvertently stumbles on to some part of Gunnar's motivation. Hallgerd senses it; hence her joy. Gunnar is back to rain mayhem on his enemies rather than letting them experience the satisfaction of his departure. He is back to make them pay for the *óvinafagnaðr* they already feel. If the Icelandic nationalists for whom this scene is so iconic will pardon Gunnar,[5] the allure of his fields and new-mown hay was as much a martial vision as a bucolic one; it was a vision of mowing down fellow Icelanders like hay, the kind of reaping we have seen that Gunnar is very good at. Gunnar gives us textual support from his grave. He means to bring pain to his enemies, 'he would rather die than yield'. This is not about love of country, but about hatred of being seen to flee it, a special kind of leavetaking that Gunnar would rather die than let himself be tainted with. But his utterance from the grave also lets us add another layer to Gunnar's motivation. He is fixin' to die. He does not augment his household better to defend against his enemies; he refuses to take any precautions whatsoever, riding about as if a free man. He does not overpower Hallgerd and take her hair, despite her refusal. He seems to want out of the endless cycle of challenge and riposte with one grand gesture.

Thoughts of vengeance, however, do nothing to improve the allure of home for Gunnar's brother Kolskegg, who seems to have an equal share in the property. Gunnar asks him to stay.

> 'Never,' said Kolskegg, 'I am not going to dishonor my pledge over this nor any other matter I am trusted in. This will be the only thing that will separate us. Tell my kinsmen and my mother that I never mean to see Iceland again; for I shall hear of your death brother, and there will then be nothing to draw me home.'

So strong is the norm against settlement-breaking that even the pull of avenging a brother will not bring him back.

---

5. Jón Karl, 16, 33; Wawn, 158–61.

Kolskegg may be exaggerating in this passage, employing a rhetoric of persuasion, trying to convince Gunnar to adhere to the settlement. He knows no other way to make his point stronger than to announce that he will forsake home, Iceland, and kin, forsake brother and mother, because his brother will be a *griðníðingr*. The passage is moving because of what Kolskegg feels he must renounce, but then a sidekick's pleas, no matter how persuasive, lose some of their force because he is a sidekick.

Kolskegg will get his final scene in chapter 81. He dreams of a man in radiant light who says he will find him a bride and he will be his knight. The author sends him to Denmark, where he gets baptized. Kolskegg's conversion is the first of the saga; it occurs without anything being made of it, and it does not even provide Kolskegg with happiness in Denmark. He heads for Russia, then to Byzantium to serve in the Varangian guard, and gets married, evidently to a Greek woman, not to a figurative bride as we were led to expect for a couple of sentences. We will be better able to judge this as a kind of wry joke, or simple innocence, when we discuss how the author deals with miracles and the expectations more pious literature raises.[6]

Death of Gunnar

Though Gunnar was not outlawed by a court judgment, he became a full outlaw by virtue of the terms of the settlement he agreed to. The law says: 'if a man formally guarantees to accept outlawry on terms clearly stated, there is no need for a judgment. The outlawry is then to be reported at the Law Rock.'[7] Gizur did just that (ch. 75). The agreed terms limited those who could kill Gunnar to the kin of those whom he had killed. Gizur is such kin, but not all the men who accompany him are; they are sheltered by Gizur's privilege. But it does mean that Gunnar need not fear everyone, like a full outlaw normally would.

Within two short chapters Gunnar is killed by a posse of forty men led by Gizur the White. Like Shakespeare with his porters and gravediggers, our saga-writer knows that the tragic is not necessarily undone by the comic.

---

6. On Kolskegg and the trip-abroad motif, see Hieatt, 492.
7. *Grágás* Ia 109.

Take Thorgrim the Norwegian, the first attacker whom Gunnar kills. He faces death with a joke and his story is told fully enough to make him worthy of his cool death, for his is a mini-tragedy too. His story is linked to that of his worthy partner, Thorir, whom Gunnar killed at Knafahills. Thorir had to be goaded into joining the expedition against Gunnar, because he found it contemptible that such a large force needed to be mustered against three brothers. He turned out to be the only member of that pathetic party to make a kill, dispatching Hjort, Gunnar's brother. Before setting out on that hapless expedition, Thorir revealed an admirable soft side, asking his friend and partner Thorgrim not to stay in Iceland to avenge him. Thorgrim, Thorir must know, has valor aplenty, and Thorir urged him to let his discretion get the better part of it. Thorir did not want Thorgrim's conscience to get him killed (nor any weakness of will he might experience in the face of generous offers to seduce him into staying) (ch. 61).

Thorgrim, in the end, could not resist the beseeching of Egil of Sandgil's widow, who lost her husband and her three sons in the battle, no less than his friend Thorir could resist her taunts to fight (and die in) that battle. Both die because they listened to her:

> 'My partner Thorir prophesied that I would be killed by Gunnar if I remained in this country; and he must be right about that, since he was right about his own death.'
> 'But I will give you my daughter Gudrun [she of the beautiful cognomen, Night-Sun] in marriage and the property.' (ch. 64)

So he stayed, but the author felt his death worthy of foreshadowing: why waste famous last words on a nobody? It is he who takes up on Gizur's general request that 'someone' should see if Gunnar is inside his farmhouse. As Thorgrim climbs atop the building he is speared by Gunnar; he topples down and walks over to where Gizur is sitting.

> Gizur asked, 'Is Gunnar at home?'
> 'That's for you to find out,' replied Thorgrim, 'but I know that his halberd certainly is.' And with that he fell down dead. (ch. 77)

Right before Thorgrim's death we get a sadder one, more poignant, and strangely more important. It is the death of the dog Sam, a gift to Gunnar from Hallgerd's brother Olaf, the animal meriting a full conventional introduction accorded a major saga character: lineage (Olaf notes that he got him in Ireland), physical description, and character traits (ch. 70).[8] The author is even moved to provide a circumstantial account of how Sam could be approached, which he took care to foreshadow when Melkolf, the slave, earlier preyed on another dog's kindness to people the animal knew. Sam dies with an eerie yowl, which awakens Gunnar and elicits Gunnar's powerful statement of love for the dog (that is what he declares with 'my fosterling'[9]) far surpassing the love of the woman in his life. It is also perhaps his only statement evincing accurate self-knowledge, as he knows this is the end. The genuineness of his brief eulogy of Sam does more to human-ize Gunnar than any other portion of his biography.

If Gunnar's death chapter begins with an expression of love for his dog, his last living words in it will come close to cursing his wife. Their final colloquy is a request and refusal. Gunnar asks for some plaits of her hair to make a bowstring to replace the one recently slashed:

> 'Does anything depend on it?' asked Hallgerd
> 'My life depends on it,' replied Gunnar, 'for they will never overcome me as long as I can use my bow.'
> 'Then let me remind you,' said Hallgerd, 'of the slap you once gave me. I do not care in the least whether you hold out a long time or not.'

To my mind, this is as artistically fine a revenge as any of the many that history and literature record. So fine that I want to defer my discussion of it until the last three pages of this book, except to raise one point here. Would Hallgerd's hair have made any difference? Is Gunnar's strange lack of self-knowledge reasserting itself? He thinks sending his attackers' arrows back at them will humiliate them; Gizur reads the gesture more accurately as a sign that Gunnar must be running low on ammunition. Hallgerd can

---

8. Sam is not short for Hebrew Samuel; it is ON *sámr*, meaning blackish, dark. On Sam's Irishry, see Sayers, 1997a. Thanks to Kate Abbott JD 2014 for the observation re Sam's introduction.

9. The 'my' is the translators', and it mimics Hrafnkel when he calls the horse Freyfaxi *fostri minn* (ch. 5, ÍF ch. 3). The *Njála* text reads 'Sam fosterling'. But the 'my' is meant correctly to capture the sense of *fostri* as a term of endearment, especially for a beloved animal. It attests to the affective power of the fosterage bond, as witness Njal and Hoskuld, Thorhall and Njal, and the Njalssons and Thord Freedmansson. Ker could not restrain his admiration for how Sam's death is rendered (214): 'Single phrases in the great scenes of the Sagas are full-charged with meaning to a degree hardly surpassed in any literature. . . Half a dozen words will carry all the force of the tragedy of the Sagas. . . with an effect that is like noth-ing so much as the effect of some of the short repressed phrases of Shakespeare in *Hamlet* or *King Lear*.'

hardly think Gunnar can get out of this alive, whatever he might believe.[10] It is now-or-never time for her more than it is for Gunnar. If she is going to even up the score for the slap she had better hurry, before Gizur and his men deprive her of the opportunity.

Gunnar chooses not to overpower her and cut her hair, as we noted before, though that option was available to him. Does that reveal that he too knows her hair does not matter at all? Or did he also realize that she had given him the best gift of all: a way to take no responsibility for his own death, and instead to have history place the blame all on her. His own perfect revenge.

10. KJJ 133 suggests that Gunnar and Hallgerd are putting on a grand play, knowing nothing much hangs on it, because the result is a foregone conclusion; for my view, see the Conclusion (Ch. 22).

10

Revenge for Gunnar:
Chapters 77–81

Hallgerd takes revenge in terms of the balanced-exchange model. A slap demands a return. The problem with Hallgerd is that she sets the price of a slap too high, but she established her price early in the saga. Some, like Gudrun in *Laxdæla saga*, would strike the balance differently, a divorce on humiliating grounds for a slap.[1] But disagreements over price are well within the normal operation of that model. It is why arbitrators, or third parties, are appointed to set the price when the principal parties cannot agree. But chapter 78 shows behaviors that the model cannot explain, for here we see the ethics of revenge and honor being somewhat cynically appropriated for purely political purposes. To the extent that revenge and the feud are mechanisms of justice, we are talking the balanced-exchange model's metaphors of paying back and getting even; to the extent it is about politics, the model is used to provide a legitimating veneer for actions that have nothing to do with justice and everything to do with the competition for power. Sometimes revenge and the feud can fit rather nicely within the law,[2] sometimes they exceed the bounds of the legal, though revenge and feud, even when operating within the law, still can be operating politically.[3]

Gunnar was killed by people who had the right to kill him. He died an outlaw. When Gunnar's uncles, the Sigfussons, ask Njal if there was any basis for bringing a legal action against the killers, Njal correctly tells them that no action lies, but then the man of law, the man of peace, advises

---

1. Gudrun divorces her husband on grounds of cross-dressing. She knit him a low-cut shirt which exposed his nipples; *Laxdæla saga*, chs. 34–5.
2. See *BP* 338–9; as when the law gives the right to kill in serious cases up until the next Althing; *Grágás* Ia 147.
3. On the interconnections of feud, law, and politics in England and the continent, see Hudson 2010 and White 2005.

that they 'dishonor them by killing a few of them off in revenge'. There is obviously no right to such revenge; should they pursue it they would leave themselves open to outlawry for taking it. But Njal believes that they can get away with it because, for one, Gunnar is too grand a man to die unavenged, so that there would be a kind of higher aesthetic justice served by avenging such as he, the law be damned.[4] For another, Njal has some business he wants to take care of; if it is carried out intelligently and ruthlessly there will be no lawsuits against the unlawful avengers of Gunnar.

Thorgeir Starkadarson expects that the killers of Gunnar will be at risk from the Sigfussons. Legal though the killing may have been, it would be imprudent not to expect reprisal. He says:

> 'We won't be safe in our homes with the Sigfussons around unless you, Gizur, or you, Geir, stay here in the south for a while.'
> 'That's true,' said Gizur. They drew lots and it fell to Geir to remain in the district. He went to Oddi and settled there. Geir had an illegitimate son, Hroald. . . he boasted that he had given Gunnar his death blow; he accompanied his father to Oddi. (ch. 77)

First, look at what the Njal–Gunnar alliance was able to achieve in the south between the Markar and Thjors River in the Landeyjar and Fljotshlid district. These two big farmers did not own or have any shares in a *goðorð*, but they have remained free from any domination by big men holding *goðorð*.[5] Who were Njal and Gunnar's chieftains (*goðar*)? No mention is made of whom, according to the laws, they were to have declared themselves to be 'in Thing' with. The author does not even give us a hint. Their local Thing is the one at Thingskalar; Mord is clearly one of the three chieftains who would be responsible for hallowing it. Who else? Runolf? Njal's nephews Holta-Thorir's sons? Do Holta-Thorir's sons even attend the Thingskalar Assembly? This is a case where the author and the lawbooks depart, but it is indicative of how independent Njal and Gunnar have become of the arrangements *Grágás* envisages.[6] Ask who might have claimed Njal and Gunnar as thingmen, and then realize what it means for how far they have risen that the question hardly matters.

---

4. Notice how taking revenge for a justly killed Gunnar maps on to Gunnar having to pay compensation for those he had a right to kill; here some people will have to pay in blood for a man they had a right to kill.
5. See Introduction, n. 17; *goðorð* is also the plural form.
6. See Ch. 15, n. 1.

That has to be part of what Mord finds so frustrating. He holds the formal status of a *goði* but he is less deferred to than Gunnar. Runolf of Dale, another *goði*, hardly makes his presence felt either. Gizur and Geir mostly stay to the other side of the Thjors River until Gunnar's troubles bring them to its east side. Now Geir moves over into the district from his home at Hlid, well on the western side of that river. Njal needs to move quickly to maintain the independence which he and Gunnar forged for themselves, since Gunnar's death creates a crisis for Njal's standing. Njal will do so by commandeering the revenge for Gunnar, directing who is to be hit. Thorgeir expected to be at risk from the Sigfussons. He did not expect to be at risk from Njal and Skarphedin, who simply brushed the Sigfussons aside and took over.

But such overtly political action needs to be clothed in righteousness. Njal and Skarphedin talk 'in private for a long time', which is saga shorthand for discussing weighty matters and planning high-stakes action. They groom Gunnar's son Hogni for the mission, with Gunnar providing some assistance from the grave, chanting vengeful songs that Skarphedin interprets for Hogni: 'there is great significance in such a portent when Gunnar himself appears before us and says that he would rather die than yield to his enemies; and that was his message for us' (ch. 78).

Skarphedin directs the mission, the identity of the targets being no doubt exactly what Njal and Skarphedin had been discussing privately. Odin seems to smile on the enterprise, for two ravens accompany them as they set out for Oddi, the new residence of Geir the Priest. They kill Hroald, his illegitimate son, and another household member there. Then they head for Thrihyrning and dispatch Thorgeir and Starkad, father and son, and then head for Mord, whom they let live on condition that he fund the entire operation. We find out how successful they were and exactly what they accomplished in the next chapter. They get Geir to go back to his main home at Hlid, not only getting that chieftain out of the district but out of the saga as well (ch. 80).[7] Power in this district is now centered at Bergthorsknoll, where before it had been bifocal, shared with Hlidarend, with Hlidarend as the chief partner.

Njal and Skarphedin picked an illegitimate son of Geir's, so as to give Geir himself an out for not pursuing aggressive reprisal. Compensation would take care of it.[8] This son had boasted of giving Gunnar his death

7. See Ch. 18, n. 15.
8. Consider in this light how Njal, but not his sons, is willing to accept compensation for his illegitimate son, Hoskuld (ch. 99). Though illegitimates were postponed to legitimates in

wound, and the laws suggest that boasting can let the avenger take the boaster at his word, or treat his boasting as an actionable insult.[9] They then get rid of the chief local opposition to the former Gunnar–Njal alliance—Starkad and Thorgeir—all at no cost to themselves, the tab picked up by Mord, who does not re-emerge as a serious actor until years after the death of Thrain. Not bad. You can admire Njal all you wish for his peaceful nature, but you can also admire him for looking ruthlessly to his own interests. His special skill is to be able to do so and never have it make a dent in his reputation for being a man of good will.

There is an important lesson here about honor and reputation. Certain people enjoy the benefit of presumptions that get their actions interpreted more favorably than a colder look may warrant; others suffer for negative presumptions applied to them. Reputation has inertia. The honorable can get away with otherwise dishonorable actions, within limits to be sure, but sometimes the limits are rather generous, as the examples of Njal and Flosi in this saga and Snorri the Priest in every saga in which he appears bear witness. Others cannot catch a break, because the presumptions work against them: Mord, to some extent, and Hallgerd, the latter never able to overcome the 'thief's eyes' presumption, even though in one respect she is a model practitioner of talionic reciprocity, of making sure you pay back what you owe, a strict upholder of the moral obligation to settle accounts. Compare, again, Gudrun of *Laxdæla*, who has every Hallgerdian deed of hers accrue to her benefit. Njal gets an enormous benefit from a reputation for having a good reputation, and he is responsible in some important way for making his good reputation durable despite some questionable actions.

Gunnar and Envy Mismanagement

I want to close the story of Gunnar with a discussion of where he went wrong. He can be held to some blame for a fair portion of his troubles; for

inheritance, illegitimacy hardly hurt one's marriage prospects if you had the right father who acknowledged his paternity. Flosi is married to Hall of Sida's illegitimate daughter, and the marriage was self-evidently not disparaging.

9. *Grágás* Ia 149: 'if [the defendant] boasts of having given him a blow, the fact that [the plaintiff] has not prosecuted him for the blow is no defense in the case but the penalty is lesser outlawry and it is to be prosecuted like other malicious speech.'

another portion, there was little he could do if he were to be Gunnar. I have made more than a few points on this issue in asides here and there, but I want to touch on some more directly.

In the honor culture depicted in the sagas, where ranking is fluid, with people's stars on the rise and fall, even given the effect of the presumptions we just discussed, you are playing before very jealous observers who will resent your successes and feel harmed by them. Thus the advice Njal first gives Gunnar when he returns after sterling successes abroad, accoutered in rich clothing and gold rings given him by kings and jarls (ch. 31). The tests Gunnar passed against Vikings and in the presence of nobility in Scandinavia are nothing, says Njal, compared to what awaits him here, 'for there are many who will envy you' (ch. 32). Though the saga says their travels had not made Gunnar or Kolskegg arrogant, Njal urges Gunnar not to attend the Althing for fear of eliciting envy. But Kolskegg wants to attend and Gunnar dismisses the risks Njal tried to alert him to, telling his brother it is not his nature to boast or vaunt himself, but as we saw earlier with his ruefulness about not getting as much pleasure out of killing as he expected to (ch. 54), Gunnar seems to be painting too favorable a picture of himself here. He does not have to boast: he is Gunnar of Hlidarend, the best athlete and the best-looking guy, back in Iceland after having had his act confirmed by royalty abroad. He thinks that if his heart is in the right place, that that is enough. He is remarkably obtuse in this respect. He shows up so well-dressed at the Althing that everyone gawks at him. If it is not in his nature to strut around, what did he think he was doing?

He seems to make a habit of overdressing.[10] When he is sowing grain he brings his fine-woven cloak (ch. 53), when he shows up for the horsefight he is wearing a red tunic with a broad silver belt (ch. 59). This is hardly usual attire for an athletic event. The author feels compelled to note the ostentatious dress, it seems, as a form of obligatory awe for finery that some commentators insist reflects the influence of chivalric romance. This colors Gunnar's portrait in some respects, though these respects are thoroughly Icelandicized, so that they stay within the limits of plausibility imposed by the country's poverty; there are none of the ostentations in this saga that burden the *Nibelungenlied*.[11] One need hardly have recourse to the romance

---

10. KJJ 106 makes this point nicely.
11. What might be somewhat plausible in castles on the continent would not quite work in turf houses. *Grágás* lacks sumptuary provisions, though *Jónsbók* (5.35) includes one.

tradition to explain showing off finery. It is a sociological and psychological commonplace.

Gunnar cannot help his good looks and superior athleticism, but he does not make it as easy for people to endure his successes as it would be wise for him to do. Each legal triumph Njal engineers for him ends with him grabbing all the honor, and makes for more people who would like nothing better than to see this charmed guy stumble. Lest we feel this is just a general human propensity for mean-spiritedness, remember that Gunnar's honor in these cases is funded on the backs of more than a few corpses, and is not going to sit well with their grieving kin and friends:

> Gunnar won great honor from the outcome of this case (ch. 51: self-judgment in the theft case);

> Gunnar rode home from the Althing. . . He gained great honor from all this; and now he stayed at home in high honor (ch. 56: resolution of the killing of Otkel and seven others);

> Gunnar gained great honor from the outcome of this case and everyone agreed that he had no equal in the South Quarter. . . His enemies greatly envied his honor (ch. 66: fourteen dead, Knafahills).[12]

With press like this, is it any wonder that Olaf, his brother-in-law, 'warned Gunnar to be on his guard, and said that there were many who were envious of him—"since you are now considered the most outstanding person in the land"' (ch. 70)? Within four chapters he has moved from having no equal in the South Quarter to Number One in the whole land.

Gunnar is not to blame for a certain paradox in roughly egalitarian honor groupings. No one wants to be inferior to the next guy, but how can you know you are above the other when titles and formal rankings do not exist? There is only the rough measure of honor, as sometimes made vivid when a host has to seat you at his feast, but mostly sustained by talk, by gossip, by who invites you where, by who brags about having talked to you or being a good friend of yours, and whom a host thinks worthy to invite when he invites you. Honor resides in guest-lists, no less than on the battlefield.

But the surest way to know you are doing better than others is when you can see that they are constrained to admit it, *and* that it hurts them to do so. The admission is forced from them against their will, in the form of their

---

12. I rendered *sæmð* in in these passages as 'honor', not as 'credit' or 'esteem' as Magnusson/Pálsson do.

envy. Envy is painful to experience, and thus it is the sincerest form of flattery; it has the magical quality of turning flattery into true praise. Nearly everyone, except those who are not in the game at all, has an interest in seeing you topple, while you have a risky interest in wanting them to envy you because that is the proof of your superiority. Envy is the very mechanism that keeps the honor grouping roughly egalitarian, because its painfulness motivates people to take down people above them, sometimes by killing them, sometimes by competing to surpass them.[13]

People looking to climb could gain prestige points by opposing Gunnar, even at some cost to themselves. An Otkel, a member of a declining branch of a prestigious family, with Skammkel urging him, could have no motive for denying Gunnar hay and food other than to assert himself against someone whom everyone now deferred to. Make Gunnar's expedition a fruitless one, and you get talked about by people who normally would not talk about you; you score points among a whole group of people who feel similarly put out by Gunnar's golden-boy image. Otkel bumbled badly, but it is not hard to see what motivated him.

A young buck like Thorgeir Starkadarson, from a well-heeled family, looking to rise, looking to impress, looking to strut around and wow the women and have the local young men look up to him, nudged by his sister who talks up Gunnar to annoy him, is moved to compete. He thinks first to let his horse do the dirty work and beat Gunnar's horse, which Gunnar says was young and untried, though that could be a standard hedge in case the horse should let Gunnar down. A pretty safe way to make it big among the other young men, who can only dream of playing even at Thorgeir's level, for win or lose, Thorgeir gets credit among them merely for having competed against Gunnar. But not only was Thorgeir's horse not up to it without some help, neither was he when it came to helping his horse.

Even Gizur the White is resented for the status he acquired (to add to the status he had already by virtue of wealth and influence) by felling Gunnar, because apparently he does not wear that achievement lightly in the eyes of some. Says Skapti the Lawspeaker to Gizur and Asgrim, after denying them his support in the Burning case: 'You and I have little in common. You like to think of yourselves as men who have taken part in great events—you Gizur the White for overcoming Gunnar of Hlidarend. . .' (ch. 139). None

---

13. When envy produces productive competition the moralists of the early modern period called it 'emulation', but found it a vice where we now find it a virtue.

of this going after Gunnar should look strange to us. It is the stuff of the westerns I grew up with, in which to be known as the fastest gun in the west spontaneously generated challengers. Academics behave similarly too, though the stakes are rather less lethal. Virtually everyone acts this way: at the workplace, at church, in the cloisters, on the playground.

Gunnar can do little about the fact that he is envied; that comes with success. But he can do much better at playing down these successes, at not strutting them around, at not making others suffer his fancy clothing, even at a horsefight. His pushing his finery in peoples' faces creates enemies like sowing dragon's teeth, which he was also sowing by dressing up to sow his barley field. Cultivating a little false modesty would have helped; though, once one adds to his ostentation the sheer number of people he kills, his acting as if he were above the law and pledged agreements, above being touched by being a *griðníðingr*, he has pretty much compelled even good people to band together to take him out.

Getting false modesty right is not easy; consider Gunnar's lame attempt, if that is what it is, expressed to his brother, that he wonders about his manliness because he fears he is overly reticent about killing. False modesty, not merely lame false modesty, can also be provoking, but people tend to be somewhat assuaged by the effort undertaken to make their envy easier to bear. Were Gunnar to play it down too much though, people might demand he wear his ornate clothes, taunt him for not doing so, call him cheap, even fearful. Compare *Laxdæla saga* (ch. 46), where Hrefna is goaded by her mother-in-law into wearing an ornate headdress that her husband Kjartan had previously ordered her not to wear to avoid provoking envy, the very same Kjartan who makes Gunnar look modest by comparison.

Right after the horsefight the writer provides a brief interlude to the main action by shifting focus to Asgrim Ellida-Grimsson (ch. 60). Why insert this chapter? Asgrim was suing a man named Ulf Uggason over an inheritance claim. Asgrim called the wrong number of jurymen, five instead of nine, a mistake easier to make than one might think because, depending on the amount in dispute, five might be the right number. Ulf was using this error to invalidate the case when Gunnar suddenly appears and challenges him to single combat. He justifies his meddling by alleging that his friends Njal and Helgi Njalsson, Asgrim's son-in-law, would expect him to help Asgrim. Ulf, dismayed, answers:

'But you and I have no quarrel over this claim.'
'That does not matter,' replied Gunnar.

The outcome was that Ulf had to pay the whole claim.

It is plain what Gunnar is up to. Asgrim, though connected by marriage to Njal, is kin to Gizur and he supported Gizur against Gunnar in the Otkel killing cases (ch. 56). Gunnar means to detach Asgrim from Gizur, and it works, but he does so at the cost of making an enemy of Ulf Uggason.[14] The author lets us see a Gunnar that more than a few people are experiencing as a rather highhanded bully, as a different Gunnar from the one Gunnar protests and the narrator also protests he is. But the way chapter 60 conveys its information, its mere insertion in the saga, means that the author is purposely giving us a peek behind the curtain that his narrator has hung up for Gunnar.

14. Compare Gunnar's much smoother neutralizing of Hjalti Skeggjason (chs. 66, 75).

11

The Atlantic Interlude and Hrapp: Chapters 82–9

Hrut and Gunnar had their trips abroad fully depicted; Glum and Sigmund had theirs occur offstage, as they are only mentioned as coming back to Iceland, each to be dispatched, one by Thjostolf, the other by Skarphedin. After Gunnar's death, we have an extended and narratively complex trip abroad not of one character but of four: Thrain, Grim, and Helgi Njalsson, and a newly introduced lowlife who by sheer force of his personality overwhelms the interlude: the rogue Hrapp Orgumleidason, he of boundless energy with the strength of a shot-putter and the running ability of both sprinter and marathoner, witty, and attractive to the ladies, both young and those getting long in the tooth.[1]

Despite the heading of this chapter, the Atlantic interlude does not begin at chapter 82 but in chapter 75, with the brief mention that Thrain, Grim, and Helgi, and with some irony, Gunnar are all setting out for overseas. People were saying that 'the district was being emptied of all its best men'.[2] But when Gunnar refuses his second travel interlude, the author has a small problem at hand. He has just lost his main character, and needs a break before resuming his main story. The saga would not work if it moved right from the killing of Gunnar to the killing of Thrain. Some reading time, and saga time, need to pass. And the author uses the occasion to make a shopping expedition abroad. He needs a replacement for the Gunnar just lost, and finds Kari, a near double, but as we shall see, an exaggerated version

---

1. For the definitive treatment of the structural and formal complexity of this interlude, see Clover 1982: 28–34, 73–5.
2. Michelle Sharpe JD 2008 wrote of the interlude: 'For ten chapters following Gunnar's death, Njal also fades away from his own saga, a sidekick without a hero.' Her provocative thesis was that *Njála* was the saga of a sidekick as hero.

of Gunnar, if that were possible. Kari, though, will have to serve considerable time as a sidekick and grammatical appendage—an apprenticeship Gunnar never had to serve—before he is allowed to take center-stage once Skarphedin and Njal depart the saga.

The crew that does get sent abroad is something of a parody of those worthy of these travel stories that are frequent fare in the sagas. Only one character of appropriate age is left in the saga at this point to merit a non-parodic travel interlude. That is Skarphedin, and he is not to be so favored, nor does he seem to have any desire for the favor, unless it is a frustrated one that he keeps, like most everything else, 'for the most part well under control'.

Thrain openly admits to jarl Hakon that he is no Gunnar, even though he is willing to undertake the obligatory Viking-ridding expedition; he would also have to admit he was no Hrut either. He is only Gunnar's match in one dubious respect, which must be added to our discussion of Gunnar's failure to manage envy very well: ' "You have a taste for the ornate, Thrain," said the jarl, "just like your kinsman Gunnar of Hlidarend" ' (ch. 82). And as a corollary, Thrain was 'bitterly envied' in the Norwegian court. Like Gunnar, he has problems managing prestige, but it is not his shortcomings in envy management that will bring Thrain down. He may be enviable for the favor shown him by a jarl in Norway, but in Iceland he is not that enviable. Thrain is biding time in Norway more than anything else, mimicking the saga itself in that regard. He is waiting, he says, 'for news from Iceland'; part of his motive for going abroad when he did was to avoid the difficult choices that would have afflicted him had he stayed home. He surely did not want to feel pressured into going down with Gunnar.

Grim and Helgi get their one chance to escape being mere sidekicks to Skarphedin. Despite Helgi's prescience and high-status wife, he cannot win, for the two brothers are soon overshadowed by Kari, their rescuer, and by Hrapp, the show-stealer. Though they suffer some cuts and bruises when tied up and show some mettle by not giving up Thrain to jarl Hakon and by resisting Viking pirates, their greatest achievement is to bring back Kari, something better than the curse Hrut brought back. Thrain, meanwhile, brings back Hrapp, and the comparison is meant to be made. Grim and Helgi also bring back a gripe against Thrain, which we will treat in the next chapter.

What is it though that makes the author introduce Hrapp? He is not needed for the plot. He is wholly invented, as is his ancestry. He does provide comic relief at a down moment in the saga; he fills with picaresque liveliness the time the main narrative takes for proper pacing. The author seems, however, to have something else up his sleeve with Hrapp. The key is here:

> Thrain provided [Hrapp] with a farm at Hrappstead. . . but Hrapp spent most of his time at Grjotriver. . . There were some who said that he and Hallgerd were very close, and that he slept with her; but others contradicted this. (ch. 88)

The narrator does not tell us for a fact that Hrapp and Hallgerd are lovers, but he is not about to suppress the local gossip that gives her another slap in the face. He fully had the power to have her and Hrapp unambiguously be lovers. But since he was not really inside the farmhouse himself and it was quite dark, he remains agnostic and thus much nastier, insinuation being more salacious than hard truth. Later, when the Njalssons show up at Thrain's farm at Grjotriver to confront him, the narrator provides this gratuitous detail: 'Hallgerd, who was also standing on the porch *and had been whispering* [lit. talking quietly] *to Hrapp. . .'* Does anyone now doubt that Hrapp and Hallgerd are lovers? With Skarphedin standing hostilely before them she is hardly exchanging sweet nothings with Hrapp. But standing next to Hrapp, the very libido-laden Hrapp, and talking low bespeaks erotic intimacy, no less suggestive than if they were off on a slope and Hrapp asleep with his head in her lap while she searched his hair for lice. The author cannot resist a chance to compromise Hallgerd.

By putting Hrapp in this sneaky way into Hallgerd's bed, the author is inviting us to see exactly what Hrapp's function is in the saga; he is there to fill out the portrait of Gunnar, the Gunnar who rose chanting defiantly from the grave. Had Gunnar gone abroad when he was supposed to, he would surely, like Hrapp in Gunnar's absence, have returned to Hallgerd's bed. Hrapp also fills Gunnar's symbolic space when he makes it to a ship in the nick of time about to embark for Norway, Hrapp leaving, like Gunnar should have, to escape outlawry.

In a different way from the way Thrain replaces Gunnar,[3] taking over his position in the kin-group, Hrapp is meant to be a deeper kind of Gunnar surrogate.[4] No wonder the two men, Thrain and Hrapp, are bonded at

---

3. See Clover (1982: 32) on the Thrain–Gunnar connection.
4. Others have taken Hrapp as an avatar of Thjostolf, e.g. KJJ 144 and Dronke, 26, mostly because both are ruffians who cause a lot of trouble. The author, I think, has more layers to his analogies. One recent attempt to deal with saga characters in *Njála* from a psychiatric perspective diagnoses Hrapp as suffering from '"dyssocial personality disorder" of the

the hip. Thrain, a second-rate Gunnar on the official social side; Hrapp, a parodic Gunnar on Gunnar's natural and physical side. Look how Hrapp and Gunnar match up. Both have near superhuman physical abilities, make out like bandits in Norway, are irresistible to the ladies, are the cause, for one reason or another, of nothing but trouble, and meet their deaths in Iceland with Hallgerd very much in their lives.[5] The more you look, the more you have to stand in awe of the author's talents.

Unlike Gunnar, who seems not to know how to behave so as to assuage people's envy, Hrapp knows exactly how to misbehave, and makes sure he does so with aplomb, fully aware of the comedy generated by violating social norms he fully understands: tricking an amiable sea captain into a free voyage, sleeping with his host's daughter, killing his host's steward, rubbing his host's face in the fact that he slept with his daughter and killed his steward, mortally wounding his host's son, while joking to the dying lad that by virtue of impregnating his sister he is now his in-law: 'I could kill you now if I wanted to, but I'm not going to. I shall show more respect for our family ties than you and your father have' (ch. 88).

If Gunnar is tragic and Hrapp comedic, both cannot quite shake free of certain literary archetypes that run in their blood, and that do not especially help them in Iceland. If Gunnar cannot quite liberate himself from some supposed ostentations of chivalric romance or earlier heroic epic, Hrapp cannot quite shake off some of the folkloric wodewose that lies in his ancestry. In Norwegian woods he is unstoppable, dodging endless ambushes, hiding in thickets. Iceland is less magical and nearly woodless: both Gunnar and he are very mortal in it, though, unlike Gunnar, Hrapp dies with wit. 'Helgi hacked off Hrapp's arm. . . Hrapp said, "What you have done certainly needed doing; that hand has brought harm and death to many"' (ch. 92). Hrapp subscribed deeply to a retributive theory of justice and was absolutely impartial in applying it to himself. In his dying moment he comes to a recognition that one must struggle to accord Gunnar.

ICD-10' [the International Statistical Classification of Diseases, 10th revision] for, among other reasons, showing 'no loyalty to those who have saved his life'; Høyersten. But Hrapp is nothing if not loyal to Thrain, dying in Thrain's and Hallgerd's cause.

5. I am borrowing points made in two student papers: Jake Molland JD 2005; Aaron Singer JD 1999.

12

Setting up
Thrain: Chapters 90–2

Things happen quickly after the Atlantic interlude. With the demise of the Gunnar–Njal alliance the focus returns to the feud that opposed the Sigfussons (Gunnar's kin) and the Bergthorsknoll people. From the perspective of Bergthorsknoll, the exact wrong person emerged as head of the Sigfusson kin-group: Thrain. When he returns 'all Thrain's kinsmen now looked on him as a chieftain (*höfðingi*)' (ch. 88), the head, that is, of his kin-group. There was no hope that the alliance of Gunnar and Njal, which had worked so well to keep the district free of powerful chieftains holding *goðorð*, could be re-established with Thrain occupying Gunnar's slot. Thrain clearly did not want to be a junior partner in such an arrangement, nor did Njal and his sons want Thrain in that position. The qualities that made Gunnar amenable Thrain did not possess. Amenability is what Njal sought in a partner, because he worked by persuasion and counsel. Gunnar was introduced as 'even-tempered, faithful to his friends but careful in his choice of them' (ch. 19). Thrain is anything but: he is impulsive (his divorce), disloyal (to jarl Hakon), and careless in his choice of friends (Hrapp).[1] He is not very bright, as I said before, for he seems oblivious to how he is about to be framed, gamed, and coldly set up by the Bergthorsknoll people.

Had Ketil of Mork emerged as leader of the Sigfussons the saga would stop after the death of Gunnar; we would see the Sigfussons become clients of Njal and his sons, which probably explains why the Sigfussons looked to Thrain as their head. Thrain's emergence as leader is a declaration of Sigfusson independence; Ketil is too compromised by his marriage to Njal's daughter to assume a bigger role.

1. The phrasing of the Gunnar/Thrain contrast is from Megan Lambart Meier JD 2008.

For the Bergthorsknoll people, Thrain is the wrong man for reasons independent of the fact that he wants nothing to do with them. They simply do not like him. He is closely connected to Hallgerd, married as he is to her daughter, and he has never been fully immune to the tone she sets (he was present when the scandalous verses were composed, no doubt enjoying the fun, there being no mention that he tried to put a stop to it). Most importantly, he was complicit in the killing of Thord Freedmansson. What hardly makes a difference to their hostility to Thrain is the spurious claim against him that Grim and Helgi bring back from Norway. Had they not seen Thrain riding around the district like he owned the place when they got back, they would not have thought to bring up such a weak claim as the basis for picking a fight.

Were Thrain smarter, or were he not looking for a way to signal so aggressively that he had no wish to be allied with Njal and sons, he should have given Grim and Helgi gifts as soon as they returned, and said thank you. As Njal says to his sons, 'if you were to kill them now, the killings would be deemed unjustifiable'. It is of some interest that Njal uses the third person plural 'them'. He is not seeing this as just a matter of Thrain, but as a matter of 'them', the entire crew who installed and back Thrain, the Sigfussons. Njal suggests setting them up so that they give his sons grounds that the community will accept as justifying an attack. He advises that his sons keep provoking Thrain and his men until they end up doing exactly what they do: saying the magic banned words—'for they are stupid men' (ch. 91). Njal goes into considerable detail as to what his sons will have to do to justify an attack. They will have to endure humiliation and be patient; we see him reverting to his scriptwriting mode of chapter 22. His speech to his sons anticipates in a not-so-vague way the style of Snorri's wry egging of the anti-Burner faction, suggesting that they disrupt the Althing with battle if they do not get their way (ch. 139). In both Njal's and Snorri's speeches future-tense narration works to goad and prompt, as well as to advise and predict. Both Njal and Snorri can be seen to contrive plots to kill and get away with it.

Nothing shows Njal reluctant to take down Thrain. But then, what to make of this statement inserted in the midst of his plans to set Thrain up? 'If you [Grim and Helgi] had asked for my advice from the beginning you would never have raised the matter.' Had Njal really felt that way, why not come up with a less lethal plan? Or why not have counseled his sons earlier, since it was quite apparent that they wanted to pick a fight with Thrain?

I hazard two explanations. One: Njal is employing a standard hedge so he will have grounds for some 'I told you so's' should the operation fail. Two: Grim and Helgi dug themselves into a public-relations hole by first articulating such a weak claim against Thrain. Not only does the plan have to create arguably justifiable grounds to go after Thrain, it must also over-come the false start of basing a claim on the Norwegian incident. That claim makes the Njalssons seem like they are looking for a fight. Given how stupid Thrain and his men are, and Thrain's own desire to distance himself from Njal, Njal only means to indicate that they could have sat back and waited; Thrain would have given them good grounds without having to contrive them.

Were it not that Thrain and his men had already lost the battle for public opinion by making constant disparaging remarks about the Njalssons, the Njalssons' final provocation is so obvious a set-up one wonders how they get away with it. The Njalssons and Kari decide to confront Thrain by pay-ing him a not-so-friendly visit. Thrain's men and Hallgerd line up on the porch outside. The 'hosts' do not give a greeting, it being clear from other occasions that the first words of welcome are to come from the householder (chs. 9, 13, 47), as it is from the author's statement here that 'there was not a single word of greeting from the group on the porch'. Skarphedin is not about to let a breach in proper etiquette prevent his satirical mockery of good manners by ventriloquizing a welcome: 'we are all welcome.' All the provocation comes from the Njalssons: the visit, the self-welcome, call-ing Hallgerd an old hag and a whore, which gets said before she fires back the banned insults, which trump, it seems, all the overt provocation that prompted her to say them. The Njalssons 'did not leave until the others had all associated themselves with this insult—all except Thrain, who tried to restrain his companions'.

Thrain sees the trap, but only once it had sprung. He did not say the offending words. Neither did Otkel say that Gunnar wept, nor did Thrain strike Thord Freedmansson. Nor did any one of the six men that Gunnar killed in Otkel's band say Gunnar wept. Hearing a culpable insult and not strenuously objecting, not getting up and riding away (see e.g. ch. 98), not offering amends, puts the hearer at risk. Since they know the legal and social world in which they live, they are on notice that they are at risk. If they are too obtuse to figure that out for themselves, well-intentioned people like Runolf of Dale will tell them they are in danger. When a man was put at risk by the culpable sense of humor of his followers or of his mother-in-law, he was to blame for not better controlling such as she or such as Skammkel. If you could not control them, then you had to take positive steps of disassociation, as Gunnar did when he let Sigmund lie uncompensated for, and as Hrut did with Thjostolf when he killed him.

When Skarphedin's axe splits Thrain's skull, Thrain knows why Skarphedin is killing him and for what. It is not because his mother-in-law called Skarphedin 'Little Dungbeard'. That also got said by the puppies Skarphedin refused to kill. Thrain is killed because of what he aspired to be, with no benefits of any doubt to be accorded him by the Njalssons in memory of their foster-father.

Njal's plans are not meant to give full legal immunity to his family for the attack on Thrain. Thrain did not come close to doing anything that merited his being declared *óheilagr* as a corpse.[2] All Njal or Skarphedin needed was to get Thrain's crew to do enough so that there would be no serious public outcry at their deaths. Njal guessed right. There was no public outcry, as there would be at his son's death a decade later. Nonetheless, Njal does not think for a second that Thrain can fall uncompensated for, though he is not so anxious to pay that he offers without first being asked. After all, the magic words 'Old Beardless' did get said, and we know that Njal is not quick with charity when that happens. Ketil Sigfusson, his son-in-law, must raise the matter with him.

Do not think I am blaming Njal. He plays hard, and plays very well; but one must counteract the pieties the narrator heaps on him, even as he takes them away sneakily with his left hand.[3] Njal is a complex character, morally and psychologically. The cost of paying for Thrain surely went into Njal's calculation, but he calls the shots when it is decided that Thrain has to go, not Grim and Helgi. Thus at the end of chapter 91, when the provocateurs come back home, plans are made to kill Thrain: 'Njal and his sons and Kari talked together in undertones for a long time.' That was long before his sons ever took it into their heads to defy their father, who is used to having the say in his own house and in the district. And he is having his say here.

Revisit briefly Skarphedin calling Hallgerd a whore, not using the Germanic form *hóra*, but *púta*. Romance words were entering Skarphedin's world, but where Gunnar may be deemed superlatively 'courteous'

---

2. See Ch. 2, n. 45, Ch. 8, n. 14.
3. Many critics tend to turn a purblind eye to the grayness of Njal's portrait. Not all: Ármann, 211; Helga Kress 1977: 293–5; Dronke, 14.

kurteisastr (ch. 19), Skarphedin learns distinctly uncourteous romance words. Couldn't one imagine an arbitrator reducing any award due Skarphedin for being called Little Dungbeard by offsetting it with *púta*, especially since he started the slanging?[4] Hallgerd might plausibly deserve to be hit harder because the insults she uttered were formally banned at the local Thing (ch. 45), but it is not as if she has not been defamed too. Were this anyone but Hallgerd the case could be plausibly made. This, however, is Hallgerd, and she was whispering to Hrapp, so the author means to back Skarphedin's insult by whispering to us not to concede the feisty lady any virtue at all.

Let me reiterate how action that is purely political must fish around for legal pretexts to sell the legitimacy of that action to a wider public. It gives us a very penetrating and unsentimental look at how politics is played in *Njála*, how law is mobilized to assist political designs, with the Things serving as political as well as legal fora. The whole point of Njal's advice on how to 'cast a wide net'[5] to ensnare Thrain is to make his sons' purely hostile *action* look as if it were nothing more than justified and honorable *reaction* in defense of their honor. Thrain is something of a loser; he is playing a game he does not have the intelligence to play well, nor the character, like Gunnar had, to admit he needed a subtle counselor such as Njal. Thrain is assassinated because of it, and no one quite thinks it was the assassination it was. That shows how important 'spin' was in their day as well as in ours.

Dining with Runolf

One might wish to reconsider accepting invitations to visit the amiable Runolf of Dale. Otkel had his last supper there and so did Thrain. In Otkel's case it was a shepherd who played the messenger of death; here beggarwomen resume that role.[6] Thrain and his companions made the mistake

---

4. *Púta* appears in the Bjarkey laws of Norway, the dating of which is problematic, but they pre-date *Njála* by as many as 50 to 100 years. In them a father or a brother has a right to collect a fine three times from someone fornicating with his daughter or sister before she is deemed a *púta*. The law seems to show concern that her kinsmen might be prostituting her, collecting in effect a double fee for her services; *NGL* 1: 322–3, §102. See Ch. 5, n. 11 for the same anxiety regarding selling out kinsmen.
5. The Old Norse idiom is the same as the English one: *langa nót at at draga*.
6. Poor men can play this role too (ch. 36) or just ordinary men (ch. 42).

of doing these women a favor by ferrying them over the Markar River.
They made their way to Bergthorsknoll, where Bergthora asked them who
helped them cross the river.

> 'The most conceited men alive,' they replied.
> 'Who would they be?' asked Bergthora.
> 'Thrain Sigfusson and his companions,' they replied. 'But we were
> annoyed at all the unpleasant things they were saying about your husband and
> his sons.' (ch. 92)

Bergthora, it should be noted, participates in the active planning of the
attack after she gets the information from the beggarwomen: she and her
sons and Kari 'had a lengthy talk in secret'.

Having beggarwomen play a role that one can easily imagine them playing so as to get a reward tests disbelief less than to have would-be killers
stumble by chance on their prey when the plot demands they meet. The
author is seldom cavalier about how information is conveyed or how people
can get a jump on their enemy. He thus shows them planning attacks and
posting lookouts, as when Sigurd Hoghead spies for the Thrihyrning people; or he shows more elaborate planning, as when Gizur and Flosi organize
their attacks. Though saga scholars might be suspicious and declare such
mean-spirited beggarwomen to be a mere literary device, something about
them strikes me as plausible, rather more so than some of Gunnar's and
Kari's battlefield heroics.

It is a clear, sunny day the day Thrain dies, and such days are not to
be wasted in Iceland. His son will die on one too (chs. 92, 113). Even the
weather in the saga is ironical. I have little to say about the feat of Skarphedin
in killing Thrain, as he jumps the rushing water, slides on the ice, and manages to dodge the blows directed at him without losing his balance. No one
who reads the saga ever forgets it. But it does not even remotely test our
credulity. The distance he leaps, eighteen feet, is an entirely manageable
long jump, even weighed down with weapons. He splits Thrain's skull,
spilling the back teeth on the ice as he slides by, the slippery conditions aiding rather than interfering with his goal.[7] Only many chapters later during
the Burning do we discover that Skarphedin kept at least one, and perhaps
several, of these teeth as souvenirs of his sagaworthy exploit. One scribe
felt it necessary to add a clause here indicating that Skarphedin picked up

---

7. See Ch. 22, n. 3.

a molar and put in his purse.[8] Did Hoskuld Thrainsson ever know what Skarphedin was carrying around all those years? Or are we to assume that Skarphedin put the tooth in an appropriately out-of-the-way place until he thought it might come in handy? Thrain's tooth is suggestively evocative. It is first mentioned on ice, then next and last mentioned in fire, when the tooth takes out an eye.[9] Fire and ice, eye and tooth: the sublimity of this saga.

8. EÓS 1954: 233 n. 4.
9. The contrast of the tooth first appearing on the ice and last seen in the fire I owe to a student whose name I cannot recall; see also Dronke, 3–4.

13

A Tale of Two Hoskulds: Chapters 93–9

Njal pays Thrain's full price, no discount, to Thrain's kin: 'all those who had a legal right to a share accepted it.' A sentence or two later Njal goes to see his son-in-law Ketil Sigfusson to arrange sub rosa that Ketil foster Thrain's young son, Hoskuld. Njal would then in turn take Hoskuld from Ketil. The need for chicanery is self-evident: Thorgerd, Thrain's widow, would never agree to have her boy raised with Skarphedin, his father's killer, nor with Njal, who, she must assume, correctly, counseled her husband's death.

Can children be laundered in such a fashion without the consent of their birth parents? Lehmann argued that Ketil had no power to transfer Hoskuld and that the boy's agreement is beside the point, he not being *sui juris*. To his mind, it is another instance of the author playing fast and loose with the law. I am not sure this is right. The laws do not directly address the matter, but Ketil is now the head of the Sigfusson kin-group.[1] As a matter of practice, he may have the power to do so, if not the right. And one saga case does show a boy, on his own motion, and against his father's wishes, transferring his own fosterage to a different foster-father, one more congenial to the boy than the lowly fosterage his father had previously arranged.[2]

Thorgerd is no fool. She knows Ketil is close to Njal, and is the brother-in-law of her husband's killer, so before she will let Ketil foster Hoskuld she sets certain conditions that Ketil must swear to perform, that

---

1. He may now also be Thorgerd's legal agent, or *lögraðandi*, since women needed one to sue and to enter into certain contracts. On being the chief man of the family, see Helga Kress 1977: 294–6.
2. Lehmann, 92; *Þórðar saga hreðu*, chs. 2–3; though this is a late saga and its author clearly knew *Njála*, such influence could hardly affect whatever independent value its tale of fosterage-shifting has.

will force him to place the boy's interests ahead of any obligation Ketil might feel to Njal. He is to take the boy's side once he is grown, avenge him if he is slain, and fund the *mundr*[3] that he must pay his bride in consideration of marriage (ch. 93). Hoskuld does live with Ketil 'for some time', presumably to let things cool down a bit and make Ketil look less like a mere tool of Njal, before Njal rides over to Mork to take Hoskuld from Ketil.

What could Njal's motives possibly be for undertaking such a risky move? The son would be expected to avenge his father.[4] Having actually to live with and be on friendly terms with the man who cleaved your father's skull does not bode well. This is why Njal questions the boy closely as to his views on the settlement that Njal made for Thrain's death. As I noted earlier, a minor was bound to the terms of a settlement his guardian entered into on his behalf, but it was not wise to trust too completely to the ward agreeing that that had settled the matter. This too is why Njal gives the boy a gift of a gold ring, in order to enter, in effect, into a separate agreement with the boy directly. To make it clear what is being negotiated, Njal asks and Hoskuld answers confirming that he ratifies the earlier settlement:

> 'Do you know what caused your father's death?'
> The boy replied, 'I know that Skarphedin killed him. But there is no need to bring that up again, for it has all been settled with full compensation.'
> 'Your answer is better than my question,' said Njal, 'and you will grow up to be a good man.' (ch. 94)

The boy gave Njal the answer that he hoped he would get. The risk will not come from the boy's quarter, as would be the usual expectation. Hoskuld is fully willing to consider the matter of his father's death closed.

Some have said Njal's motive is to make further amends beyond the compensation payments he paid out for Thrain, but have proffered no evidence.[5] One could perhaps find some in the saying, 'he who fosters another's child is considered the lesser man'. By undertaking to foster Hoskuld, Njal is making a gesture of ritualized abnegation.[6] The fostering would thus work the way a leveling oath does, an oath that elsewhere in Scandinavia

3. See Ch. 2, n. 11.
4. *Vápnfirðinga saga*, ch. 14, is the most horrifying example; a man kills his much-loved foster-father to avenge his father.
5. E.g. Lehmann, 92; Wolf, 76–7.
6. See pp. 35–6. Jon Loftsson took the 4-year-old Snorri to foster to make it up, it seems, to the boy's father after forcing the father, Sturla, to back down in a high-stakes dispute; *Sturlu saga*, ch. 34.

had to be sworn by the payer of compensation to the dead victim's kin, that he too would waive blood revenge and accept compensation were their positions reversed.[7] It could thus be seen as a placatory gesture to the wronged Sigfussons. I doubt it would have been seen that way by Hallgerd or Thorgerd, the boy's grandmother and mother, but something of that does appear to be going on here.

But I suspect Njal is also motivated by more practical matters. First, and most importantly, get the boy away from the women in his family, his mother and, above all, his grandmother, both of whom would goad him mercilessly to avenge his father once he came of age, and would be surely preparing him in the meantime to undertake the mission.

Second, Njal intends to control the boy's future marriage; he does not want the man who will most likely be the head of the Sigfussons in a decade to bring a second Hallgerd into the saga. There is here another irony. Njal does find a high-status marriage for his beloved foster-son, and she, it could be argued, is the chief force behind the Burning of Njal and his sons. Hildigunn, no less than Hallgerd, brought trouble for him and his family when she moved into the district, though Hildigunn had just cause.

Third, the move reflects Njal's deepest, and somewhat fondest, hope for the fostering: restoring the status quo ante to what it was when Gunnar was alive. How? By taking the most promising member of the next generation of Sigfussons (he already has the best of the present generation in Ketil, but that is not enough), the person most likely to emerge as the head of that group, and bind him by fosterage, by love, by forging common interests; in other words, bind him even closer than Gunnar had been bound to him. Njal would play his usual role as advisor and strategist with Hoskuld providing the title and energy. Skarphedin, Kari, Grim, and Helgi would provide the muscle as they had during the previous decade, making up for Hoskuld not being the athlete Gunnar was. This is close to the formula that allowed Njal and Gunnar to maintain a dominant standing in their region without much interference from goðorð-holding chieftains such as Mord, or intruders from the west such as Geir the Priest. And once Njal gets his beloved advisee his own goðorð, all should be more secure than ever. In

---

7. *Laws of Skania* c. 113 (1202 x 15), *DGL* I: 83; *Leis Willemi* c. 10 §2 (Robertson, 258–9): the wrongdoer must swear to his victim that if their situations were reversed and he felt the same promptings of his heart, he nonetheless too would accept compensation.

any event, the Sigfussons (and Thorgerd and Hallgerd) had better behave, because he is holding their most valuable member hostage.

It is a highly risky strategy, as he knows, but if it were to work, as it almost did, then the gains would prove Njal to be the strategic genius he pretty much is. Given two bad options, Njal chose the one that he felt less likely to lead to the violence it ultimately led to. Again we see the naturalistic limits of his prescience. Things did not turn out well, but neither would they have been likely to have turned out well had Hoskuld been left to grow up with his grandmother; they just would have gone bad in a different way. Njal was not being stupid when he fostered Hoskuld. He was aware of the standard risks of raising a boy whose father his son had killed.

The risks he can control he sets about controlling; but there are ones he cannot control, and as to those he has to hope the situations that would generate them do not arise. He probably also trusts himself to solve the problems, anticipated and unanticipated, as they arise. Njal does not lack confidence in his own abilities; he gets tired in the end, but he never doubts the quality of his own counsel (see, for example, his remarks to his sons, chs. 118, 128, and to the Althing, ch. 97).

He may not have foreseen the exact incident that would start things crumbling, but it would not take prescience to have factored in the general kinds of risk that would arise. They inhere in the very structure of Icelandic dispute processing. Here is how. When a servant gets in trouble he will go to his head of household for help; when a middling farmer gets in trouble or needs legal help he will seek out a powerful relative or go to his chieftain for help. If the powerful relative owns a *goðorð*, he will most assuredly run to him with his troubles. The short of it is that Njal's plan seemed to be working fine until Lyting, a man introduced in chapter 98 solely to reveal the kind of risks that could ruin the arrangement, kills Hoskuld Njalsson, Njal's illegitimate son.

Between chapter 94, when Hoskuld Thrainsson is taken in by Njal, and chapter 98, when Lyting is introduced and Hoskuld Njalsson killed, about a decade of time passes silently. The feud has been in remission since the settlement over Thrain's death. Hoskuld grows up and it is time for him to get married. That occurs in chapter 97. In the intervening space the author introduces Flosi and his niece Hildigunn with appropriate genealogies (ch. 95), and does the same for Hall of Sida, Flosi's father-in-law (ch. 96). Nothing else occurs in between the fostering and the marriage proposal other than some peaceful and thus blank years.

Amending the Constitution

But in chapter 97 there is a flurry of action. Just to get Hoskuld married to the woman Njal has picked for him, Njal contrives to bring the country's legal system to a halt by giving advice to litigants that generates gridlock. He creates a crisis which makes the proposal he offers to reform the court system look necessary and reasonable. The particular proposal will require new chieftaincies, one of which will be set aside for Hoskuld. Readers have found this rather hard to accept from a man of such integrity as Njal; commentators sometimes go outside the text to argue that, as a historical matter, Njal really had nothing to do with the creation of the Fifth Court. That was the Lawspeaker Skapti Thoroddsson's doing.[8] Njal is thus to be saved from such openly self-interested duplicity.

The author, however, has taken care to show us that Njal is functioning well within his established character. This is Njal the scriptwriter; it is the same man who wrote the lines for Gunnar to play Hawker-Hedin, who concocted the plot to kill Thrain, and who devised the devious script whereby he wrested Hoskuld away from his mother in order to foster him— so why should we be surprised? Only the scale of the undertaking is surprising. All this scripting was needed to get a chieftaincy for his foster-son if the marriage he had also scripted were going to happen. Njal must revert to scriptwriting because Hildigunn insisted on writing her own: she would marry no one who did not have a chieftaincy.[9]

This interpretation does not violate the rules of realism and plausibility as much as it might seem. Iceland had a complex law, whose experts were rather more than mere local wise men. They were truly lawyers in a non-anachronistic sense. Njal thus had the traits we often associate with lawyers. They plot and plan and write scripts, as I said earlier regarding advisors. They do not just clean up past messes, which also involves writing scripts for their clients; they advise people what to do and what to say in the future too.

---

8. Ari says Skapti introduced the reform in 1004; *Íslendingabók*, ch. 8. The standard English translations of *Njála* note this immediately, the motive of which seems to be to excuse Njal, since the annotations in these translations are few.

9. The word Hildigunn uses is *mannaforráð*, which is generally taken to mean holding a *goðorð*; see Jon Viðar, 48.

The saga-writer could have made it so much easier for Njal by scripting his own plot to have Njal find a chieftaincy to purchase. No constitutional reform would have been needed to get Hoskuld his marriage to Hildigunn if the market in *goðorð* had been more congenial. Yet it was the author's choice to script the condition of the *goðorð* market. He might have seen the opportunity to make Njal 'a founding father' worth the cost imposed on Njal's integrity. Maybe that is exactly a cost he wanted to impose. Or maybe he saw the machinations necessary to create the need for reform commendable in themselves, finding something admirable in the cold calculation it took to advance Njal's political agenda successfully.

It turned out that Njal, more than anyone, paid the price for the reform he engineered, as we shall see. Yet a Fifth Court, operating roughly as an appeals court, was not a bad idea. More people would be made better off by the reform than would be harmed by it. That helps explain why Njal's reputation comes through unscathed. He made sure that his self-interested move could also be understood to be in the community's interest, even if that was hardly his primary motive.

Lyting and the Breach of Father and Sons

No sooner does Hoskuld obtain his chieftaincy and get installed on a farm Njal buys for him, with servants he hires for him, than we are introduced to Lyting. Lyting is married to a sister of the Sigfussons, and is thus a brother-in-law to Thrain and Ketil. Lyting hosts a feast attended by the extended Sigfusson kin-group. This time it is not beggarwomen, but a nameless woman, apparently a servant, who foments strife. She comes in with some news meant to provoke the assembled men:

> 'You men should have been outside just now to see the conceited man riding past the farm.'
> 'What conceited man are you talking about?' asked Lyting.
> 'Hoskuld Njalsson has just ridden past,' replied the woman.
> 'He often rides past the farm,' said Lyting, 'and I find it a constant irritation. I make you an offer here and now, Hoskuld Thrainsson, to ride with you if you want to avenge your father and kill Hoskuld Njalsson.' (ch. 98)

Hoskuld Thrainsson refuses: 'It would be a vile way of repaying my debt to my foster-father. A curse on all your feasts.' He jumps up and rides away.

Even the boastful puppies, Grani Gunnarsson and Gunnar Lambason, insist they will not break a settlement made by good men. All the Sigfussons agree, and the entire guest-list rides away. Another embarrassing Icelandic feast. Lyting is worked up and addresses his household: 'Everyone knows that I received no compensation for the death of my brother-in-law Thrain. I shall never be content until he is avenged.' He and his two brothers then ambush Hoskuld and kill him.

The question that must be answered is this: why does Lyting kill Hoskuld Njalsson now? Why can he all of a sudden not bear the frequent trips Hoskuld has taken past his farm as he goes back and forth from his father Njal's household to his mother Hrodny's? Hoskuld has been riding past Lyting's farm long enough for Hoskuld Thrainsson to enter Njal's household, grow up, and get married. Lyting had never once during those years found that sufficiently annoying to do anything untoward. Only one significant fact has changed in the universe that makes Lyting feel he can act on his griev-ance, or even articulate it.[10] It is the emergence of Hoskuld Hvitanesspriest, as Hoskuld Thrainsson is known after getting his chieftaincy. Finally the Sigfussons again have a big man in their group to whom they can look for protection. His very presence as a chieftain will embolden people like Lyting to assert claims that they would not have dared to press before, claims that have to be embarrassing to Hoskuld Hvitanesspriest, and at times, like this one, a dangerous drag on his alliance with the Bergthorsknoll people. Hoskuld can easily refuse to accept Lyting's invitation to avenge his father, but he cannot so easily refuse Lyting's request to negotiate a settlement that will spare Lyting's life and farm after he kills Hoskuld Njalsson. That is the role Hoskuld Hvitanesspriest has been thrust into now; that is what big men and chieftains do for their kin and other clients.

Lyting's attack is an emblem of the many situations that Hoskuld Hvitanesspriest will find himself in as a *goði* where the duties and demands of his new position will not always coincide with the interests of the

---

10. *Baugatal*, a section of *Grágás* which deals with wergild payments, would have let Lyting receive some compensation as one of five *sakaukar*, 'atonement extras': these are slave-born or *illegitimate sons*, stepfathers, and the *husbands of a sister* or a daughter; Ia 201. Our text says Njal paid everyone who had a legal right to it. *Baugatal* does not ever seem to have been operative; it has the look of a legal training exercise; see also Phillpotts, 27–8, who finds even more grounds for rejecting its applicability. But the author seems to have invested Lyting with knowledge of *Baugatal*. It would have been wise to pay him something, in any event. The issue is taken up again with Amundi who, as an illegitimate son, would qualify for the same payment a sister's husband gets. The author knows what he is doing here.

Bergthorsknoll people. The *goðorð* Njal secured for Hoskuld meant he would have to represent a Sigfusson clientele that he must also keep reasonably satisfied, and they hated his Bergthorsknoll friends. Njal knew this was a risk, and planned around it as much as he could. He picked all Hoskuld's household members, thus keeping out certain more aggressive Sigfusson adherents and making sure too that he had eyes and ears in the residence of the one male in the younger generation that he let move out of Bergthorsknoll. He also seems to have contemplated that the chieftaincy would be partly shared between their households, as when Skarphedin discharged the duties of the office when Hoskuld was absent (ch. 109); and thus too the constant mutual consultation with the Njalssons—they 'were on such intimate terms that no one made any decisions without consulting all the others' (ch. 97)—a chieftaincy by committee. Njal figured, hardly naively, that he could rely on Hoskuld; he also thought he could still control his sons, as he had up until then.

The author shows fissures opening, especially between father and sons, but between sons and foster-son too, when Hoskuld, the foster-son, negotiates a settlement with Njal over Lyting's killing of Hoskuld, the illegitimate son. It calls for a closer look.

Hoskuld's mother, Hrodny, drags his corpse to Njal's farm, props it up in the sheep-shed, its eyes open, and knocks on the door. Pushing past the servant, she orders Njal to 'get up from my rival's bed' and to bring Bergthora and his sons out with him. To Skarphedin she leaves the task of closing Hoskuld's eyes and blocking his nostrils, a standard ritual for the dead, and then formally charges him to avenge his brother's death, indicating she trusts that Hoskuld's illegitimacy would not stand in the way of Skarphedin aggressively undertaking the task. Bergthora, without the least trace of jealousy, goads her sons to hurry up about it (and lets Hrodny stay the night with Njal).[11] As usual with Bergthora, she fully understands the lay of the land; why, that is, there is a need to hurry:

> 'You men amaze me. You kill when killing is scarcely called for, but when something like this happens you chew it over and brood about it until nothing comes of it. Hoskuld Hvitanesspriest will be here as soon as he hears about it; he will ask you to settle the matter peacefully and you will grant his request. So if you really want to do anything you must do it now.' (ch. 98)

---

11. Given their age and the circumstances, coupled with my Puritanism, it seems likely that Bergthora expects that Njal will only be providing Hrodny discursive comforts.

The brothers set out to get Lyting. This is the only time Kari is not part of the group, for reasons not given. Grim and Helgi want Lyting for themselves, but botch it, while Skarphedin kills both Lyting's brothers. Lyting escapes to Hoskuld Hvitanesspriest and the action plays out much the way Bergthora predicted, with one exception: 'they'—Bergthora used the plural 'you' when she predicted they would settle—do not settle; Njal alone does. In a scene meant to recall a similar one fifty-six chapters earlier, Hoskuld Hvitanesspriest, like Gunnar before, asks Njal if his sons should not be present for the settlement. And as before, Njal excludes them, knowing full well they would not settle. He counts on them instead to honor the settlement out of deference and obedience to him.

Njal is remarkably blind when it comes to his sons, overconfident in his ability to continue to command their obedience. Filial obedience can only be asked for a reasonable length of time and Njal is extraordinarily long-lived. Sons are willing to be under their father's *potestas* only so long before they begin to chafe and grow rebellious, especially against a father who kept them on such a tight leash. Even sons given large bailiwicks during their father's lifetime might rebel, as famously was the case with the sons of England's Henry II.

Njal puts a lot of pressure on the father–son bond; eventually it breaks under the stress. He asks his sons to honor settlements that compel them to forgo revenge for people they feel an obligation to avenge in blood: a foster-father, a brother. In each case Njal interposes himself to ensure the continuation of his primary relation with the leader of the Sigfussons, with Gunnar in the case of Thord Freedmansson, with Hoskuld his foster-son in the case of Hoskuld his own son. When the Njalssons, having returned from their killing mission, hear that Hoskuld Hvitanesspriest had already visited as their mother predicted, Skarphedin, echoing his mother, understands that '[Hoskuld] will have been pleading for Lyting'. Grim does not like it and says so, which prompts Njal to express irritation: 'Hoskuld could not have tried to protect him if you had killed Lyting as you were meant to do.' The non-martial Njal blaming his sons for martial failure is too much for even the blandly-portrayed Grim to bear.

Skarphedin, keeping himself well under control, is not about to argue with his father. He mocked Thorkel Hake for having fought with his: 'we will not reproach our father,' says Skarphedin, which cleverly manages to do exactly that, as he admonishes Grim for his bad form by doing so.

I retold so much of the story in order to demonstrate just how substantively important the Lyting episode is. It reveals starkly the fragility of the alliance of Hoskuld Hvitanesspriest and the Bergthorsknoll people and, most importantly, that the stresses on the alliance occur without anyone's ill-will within the alliance. They came about, as I just indicated, because the Sigfussons now have their own big man to protect them, and because that big man would be remiss in his duties if he did not provide them the services a chieftain or head of the family provides his clients. If we are to blame anyone, it is perhaps Njal, his readiness to ask his sons to bear too much in the interests of the 'grand alliance'. But he might feel he took care of that, in this case at least, by giving Lyting about as unfavorable a settlement as he could and still not make Hoskuld, his foster-son, look bad. Lyting's brothers die without compensation, Lyting gets nothing for his wound, and he must pay full compensation for the dead Hoskuld. But conceding him his life and farm is too much for his sons. They might well begin to suspect that Njal will sell them out too, if they get in the way of his affinity to a Sigfusson leader. He already settled for a foster-father, now a half-brother; what is the next step on the ladder: 'I would rather have lost *two* of my own sons' (ch. 111), 'I would rather have lost *all* my sons' (ch. 122)? Add, too, wife and grandson, when he counsels defending from inside the farmhouse (ch. 128).

Are his sons, for instance, aware of a colloquy their father had with Gunnar years earlier? They are not mentioned as having been present. Njal volunteered two of them to die fighting with Gunnar. To Gunnar's great credit, he refused what must have struck him as a rather unseemly offer for a father to make. He says as much:

> 'And now,' said Njal, 'I want Skarphedin and my son Hoskuld to come and stay with you. They will pledge their lives with yours.'
> 'No,' said Gunnar, 'I do not want your sons killed on my account. You deserve better of me than that.'
> 'It makes no difference,' said Njal. 'Once you are dead my sons will become involved in these troubles.' (ch. 75)

This is altogether remarkable, and it displays the amorality of a certain kind of fate-talk. Oh well, my sons will die eventually anyway, we all do, so no big deal. Worth noting is that, to Njal's mind, the causal or associative connections that will arise from Gunnar's death will flow right back into what started when Bergthora ordered Hallgerd to move down. He is not wrong

to see it that way. To his trained eye, *Njáls saga* does not have a unity problem. Feud politics makes for strange plot-lines sometimes.[12]

Did Njal, back then, ask Skarphedin and his son Hoskuld if they were
willing to pledge their lives with Gunnar's? Is he pledging theirs now so
that his foster-son thrives? Father settled for one brother very quickly
already, and then had the temerity to blame his sons for not killing their
brother's killer. Does old dad set too much store by his favorites in the
Sigfusson clan at the expense of his own sons? If there is a fault here, it is
not Hoskuld Hvitanesspriest's. He is just doing his job. Is it Njal's? Not in
as culpable a way as I am probably over-suggesting. The real world unsurprisingly happens to generate problems that do not allow Njal or Hoskuld
to satisfy all their constituencies at once. Nonetheless, it seems that Njal at
times has his own rationality obscured by playing favorites. Not so much
with Gunnar, but with this his one perfect 'son', made in his own image, so
unlike Skarphedin.

Recall Njal questioning the young boy Hoskuld, especially this particular part of the conversation:

> 'Do you know what caused your father's death?'
> The boy replied, 'I know that Skarphedin killed him. But there is no need
> to bring that up again, for it has all been settled with full compensation.'

The usual understanding of this colloquy is that, in Hoskuld Thrainsson,
Njal has found someone like himself in his willingness to pay compensation in preference to taking blood. It is more complex. Njal is hardly averse
to blood when his interests are best served that way or when he himself
is insulted. It is rather, more accurately, that both he and his foster-son
share a strong preference for maintaining their non-blood alliance to taking revenge for those whom the revenge obligation is strongest, a father in
Hoskuld's case, a son in Njal's.

The author hammers certain points home about the importance of the
Lyting episode. One would have to have the skull of Skrýmir not to feel the
force of the blows. First: the repetition, already mentioned, of the request
to have the Njalssons be party to a settlement that Gunnar, in the one case,
Hoskuld, in the other, can see mostly interests the sons, not their father.
In both these cases it is also made clear that the sons honor to a tee the settlements their father binds them to honor. They manage to get Thord's

---

12. Re feud and plot-lines, see Byock; Andersson 1967.

killer on other grounds; and Lyting dies by a miracle without any conniv-
ance of the Njalssons. To make sure we get the point, the narrator ends
chapter 99: 'it should be said that this settlement was never broken.'[13]

A second blow to our heads occurs with the reproduction of namesakes.
Gunnar's enemies unite in two Thorgeirs; here we have two Hoskulds.
The dead man and the man who represents his killer share a name. The
father of one is the foster-father of the other. I had to pepper my exposi-
tion with Hvitanesspriest or foster-son and Njalsson or risk confusing the
reader. I am tempted to attribute to the author a Cervantean kind of jokes-
terism. If we are reluctant to do so it is because, if we cannot quite believe
that something as sophisticated as the sagas got written, we are also unwilling to attribute to the author of a saga such self-conscious gamesmanship.
I would not be the first to suspect him of such gaming.[14] As with the two
Thorgeirs, the author—as far as we know—invented both these Hoskulds,
choosing to give them the same name; no sources that have survived compelled it. Hoskuld Thrainsson's name makes sense, it having been selected
by his grandmother Hallgerd to perpetuate her father's name, though the
boy's mother was not sure it should not have been Glum, after her father.
But to have let Thorgerd name her son Glum would have yielded fewer layers of complexity and irony. That the infant Hoskuld's naming is provided
an explanation and made the subject of a discussion in chapter 59 is itself
reason for the reader to take the name choice seriously; it was not an inad-
vertence by the author, but overtly made part of the narration. Hoskuld
Njalsson's name comes from his maternal grandfather, but that ancestor too
appears in no other source (ch. 116); likewise Glum is apparently invented.
The author went out of his way to make these two Hoskulds namesakes.
If the two Thorgeirs were made to bear a symbolic load, we should also
expect it here.

Some have thought that the whole Lyting episode is an awkward interpolation, not fitting into the story at all, producing merely a needless
tag-along bastard son who never speaks a line in the entire saga and is barely
characterized, if at all.[15] When introduced, Hoskuld Njalsson is given
no description (ch. 25), and we only find in the biased view of Lyting's

13. Mord, however, will suggest (falsely) later that they were in league with Amundi (ch. 109).
14. Andersson 2006: 183.
15. E.g. Finnur Jónsson 1908: p. xx. But the author clearly prepares for Hoskuld Njalsson's
    death as early as ch. 45.

serving-woman that his dress or demeanor is seen as uppity. He is flat in life, but he is important in death. He is paired with his namesake in the mind of his brothers, who feel their father is overvaluing one Hoskuld at the expense of the other. But the saintly Hoskuld Hvitanesspriest is also more symbol than human, though that hardly prevents his death from achieving monstrous importance. He is no less flat than the other Hoskuld;[16] we have much less sense of him as an individualized person than we do of Atli, of Hrapp, of Thjostolf; and it is not merely because he is virtuous. Hall of Sida is virtuous and is a fully rendered character.

Could the author make it any clearer how important the death of the one Hoskuld is in eventually leading to the death of the other? A Hoskuld for a Hoskuld, both bound together as placeholders for the structural stresses in an alliance built to keep an uneasy peace in the feud.

The Lyting episode is so crucial that the author feels it necessary to hammer us a third time. He makes another self-consciously clumsy scene shift, reminiscent of the saga's first chapter. He breaks off the Lyting story right before its natural conclusion wrought by Amundi the Blind on the skull of Lyting, in order to insert the six Conversion chapters. The saga moves from the story of a local feud in one part of the South Quarter to that of a completely transformative national event putting the author's own saga on hold. This move led George Dasent, the first English translator of the saga, to emend the chapter order and place the Conversion chapters directly after the introduction of Hall of Sida (the model Christian in the saga) in chapter 96, and then to postpone the wedding of Hoskuld and the Lyting story, chapters 97–9 until after the Conversion, so that it could directly connect with its 'natural' conclusion, the chapter of Amundi the Blind killing Lyting (ch. 106).[17] Dasent's reordering also worked to fix the saga's misordering of the historical Conversion and the Fifth Court reform, the former preceding that latter by four years. Our author, or some early subtle scribe, gave us the ordering we have because all manuscripts have it.

Much of what we would lose by the Dasent rearrangement can be inferred from what will occupy us in the next couple of chapters. For now, let it stand that we would lose the force of the ominous note struck by interrupting the Lyting episode at the very moment the breach between father and sons has been starkly revealed; lost too will be more subtle

---

16. Accord, Heusler 1922: 11.
17. See Cook 1998.

comparisons and contrasts that the author wishes to connect to the advent of Christianity. And the last line before chapter 100—'It should be said the settlement was never broken'—would sound silly if some time were not to pass before Amundi appeared to take his revenge, which, given his handi-cap, required the introduction of a miracle-working God.

There would be no restoring the status quo ante in which Njal's sons were cast in supporting roles in a play starring father and his favorite Sigfusson. How could Njal have so complacently assumed they would accept that? Hoskuld Thrainsson was no Gunnar, and the 'boys' were now so much older. This breach between father and sons, by the way, occurs without mention of Mord, for he had absolutely nothing to do with it.

14

Conversion and the Genius of the Law: Chapters 100–6

Can it be pure chance that the break for the Conversion begins in chapter 100? Playing number games, especially ones to 100, occupied Dante and the *Pearl* Poet, but did our author care? Are the chapter divisions of the saga his or scribal with an editorial assist? That is not clear. Some of the chapters are so short, and so easily combinable with the one following, that some conscious manipulation of chapter divisions seems to be the case:[1] thus chapters 18, 26, 27, 40, 46, 52, 57, 93, 95, 96, and perhaps a few others.[1] The average number of words per chapter before chapter 100 comes to 553, from chapter 100 to the end the number is 737. Some fiddling seems to have been going on by someone. The answer is not clear, or at least not clear from the two manuscripts I have had access to, but neither is the possibility foreclosed because those short chapters are marked as such very early in the manuscript tradition.

What is in the number 100 even to bother to make the effort? Probably nothing much at all, except to play a numbers game and get the benefit of the vague symbolism that inheres in a number that takes on meanings of completeness or roundedness. The Conversion is dated to anno 1000 (Ari in his *Íslendingabók* used the AD dating). Despite long hundreds of 120 coexisting with decimal hundreds, counting and interest computations in Iceland were decimalized. The laws set the legal rate of interest at ten percent, and the Icelanders were sophisticated enough, when the tithe law was adopted *c.*1097, to prefer to transmute the ten percent income tax the tithe is into a property tax of one per cent. This shows they understood what it meant to

---

1. These are marked as chapters in *Möðruvallabók*. The present chapter division has been maintained in all printed editions since the first one in 1772.

capitalize a yield rate, the computation made considerably easier by setting the legal rate at ten per cent rather than, say, seven.[2] Let us leave it at that.

Concerning Signs and Wonders

The author adapts some of the standard sources of the Conversion story to his needs.[3] He integrates some *Njála* characters into his borrowings. So, for instance, Njal recognizes the superiority of the new faith even before Thangbrand's mission arrives (ch. 100). Hjalti Skeggjason plays a big role in the historical Conversion but has already played a non-trivial role earlier in the saga. One of the first converts, Glum Hildisson, is identified prolepticly as a Burner of Njal, he in fact later identified as the chief incendiary in the lawsuits following the burning (ch. 141) and exiled for life as a result (ch. 145).[4] The Christian tent holds all people; Burners are good Christians. Of the people who play a significant role in the saga, only Mord and his father Valgard strongly oppose the new faith, the son eventually coming to see the light (chs. 102, 107).

Thangbrand is sent by King Olaf Tryggvason as a missionary, and comes selling more than good news; he brings merchandise to trade. When two local chieftains ban trading with him, Hall of Sida invites him and his crew to take lodging at his farm. Hall is impressed when he witnesses Thangbrand sing mass, it being Michaelmas. When Hall asks after the archangel Michael's powers, Thangbrand explains to him that he weighs your good and bad deeds, and such is his mercy that the good weighs more than the bad. A deal this good is almost enough to convince Hall, but he wants to specify even more favorable terms before he commits himself: 'I want to stipulate that you pledge your word on his behalf that he shall become my guardian angel.'[5] Thangbrand promises. Hall and his household are then baptized.

---

2. *Grágás* Ib 140 (legal rate of interest), Ib 205–7 (tithe rate).
3. See EÓS 1954: xliii–xlv: the author drew on Ari's *Íslendingabók*, ch. 7, the sagas of Olaf Tryggvason, and some matter from some version of *Kristni saga*. On the sources for Olaf's Christianizing efforts, see Bagge.
4. This same kind of forward identification also occurs in ch. 96: Kol Thorsteinsson, 'whom Kari was later to kill in Wales' (ch. 158); also in ch. 77, where the killing of Thorvald the Ailing (ch. 102) is mentioned.
5. The guardian angel, *fylgjuengill*, is a Christian's fetch, *fylgja*, the Christian version a male spirit, the pagan one female, at least by grammatical gender.

At no point in *Njáls saga* does theological discussion or orthodox doctrine get dealt with more deeply than at this homely level. There will be allusions to sanctity and martyrdom, there will be miracles of a sort, and then there will be the Battle of Clontarf in the holy land of Ireland, in which most all the rules of saga plausibility give way to the demands of a different literary genre. This writer has no interest in playing Dante, even if he could.

Our author is as fair-minded to the old ways as he can be, and tries to avoid as much anachronism as his knowledge and imagination will allow.[6] Consider the debate Thangbrand has with a woman in the western districts shortly after his ship, the *Bison*, had been wrecked. She, Steinunn, is the mother of Poet-Ref and a poet herself. She tries to argue the merits of paganism with Thangbrand, but he was able to refute her arguments, presumably by pointing to the miserable poverty she endures compared to more southerly and richer Europe.[7] Steinunn gets more specific, trusting in talents her chief god was especially good at: 'Did you ever hear', she asked, 'how Thor challenged Christ to a duel, and Christ did not dare to accept the challenge?' She evinces a not-rare disbelief that a son of God would die in a *passio* without fighting back; thus compensatory poems, like the glorious Old English *Dream of the Rood* in which Christ does victorious battle against the cross; thus too the invention, on the thinnest of scriptural warrant, very early in Christianity's history, of a heroic Saturday on which Christ harrows hell. Some Christians were defensive about a death that was, in the understanding of the times, ignoble, its very ignobility being part of its doctrinal point.

Thangbrand does not answer directly, nor does he deny the existence of Thor: 'I have heard', said Thangbrand, 'that Thor would be nothing but dust and ashes if God did not permit him to live.' Undeterred, Steinunn reaffirms Thor's manifest might:

> 'Do you know who wrecked your ship [the *Bison*]?' she asked.
> 'What do you think?' asked Thangbrand.
> 'I will tell you,' she replied.
> > 'It was Thor's giant-killing hammer
> > That smashed the ocean-striding *Bison*;
> > It was our gods who drove
> > The bell-ringer's boat ashore.

6. See KJJ 143: 'the sagaman does his best so as to make the world pagan before the Conversion and Christian thereafter.'
7. See Fletcher, 242–3.

Your Christ could not save
This buffalo of the sea from destruction;
I do not think your God
Kept guard over him at all.

Thor seized the great ship
Shook its frame
And beat its timbers
And hurled it on the rocks;
That ship will never
Sail the seas again
For Thor's relentless thrashing
Smashed it into fragments.'

With that Steinunn and Thangbrand parted. (ch. 102)

The author gives her the last word in this debate. Does he take some mild delight in making the pious squirm? We are left to believe whatever we wish: that her argument had real force or that her soul is utterly lost, owned by the devil, so that there is no more point arguing with her than Gunnar felt there was arguing with Hallgerd. But Thangbrand's ship, after all, had been wrecked, and Christ did nothing or could do nothing to prevent it. No storm-god he.[8] It is as if the author were gesturing toward the bet-hedging of Helgi the Lean of *Landnámabók*, who was rather 'mixed in matters of faith: he believed in Christ but nonetheless called on Thor during sea voyages and when in great difficulty and for all else he thought most mattered'.[9]

Steinunn is lucky she got out of the argument alive, for the bulk of chapters 101–3 recount how, between them, Thangbrand and his Icelandic bodyguard, Gudleif, kill four men who either insult or oppose them, with one berserk thrown in as a fifth whom no one, pagan nor Christian, wanted to see alive.[10] Another source gives us more (almost certainly fictional) background on Thangbrand. He had bought a beautiful Irish slave-girl, for whom he was challenged to a duel by another claimant. Showing skills he would put to use on his mission to Iceland, Thangbrand killed the challenger. He then took to raiding, converting heathens at swordpoint, gaining more booty than converts. He was sent to convert the Icelanders by

8. On Thor as the god of the sea winds, see Perkins.
9. *Landnámabók*, H 184.
10. *Kristni saga*, chs. 5, 7. Thangbrand's aggressive conversion technique is hardly unusual when considering the Christianizing of the Saxons by Charlemagne or later of the Slavs and Balts in the Northern Crusades; see Christiansen; Bartlett 1993.

King Olaf as penance. Steinunn, we know from other sources, was too well connected to be dispatched as a witch, so she was allowed to fight Thangbrand to something more than a draw.[11]

It seems, though, that the author purposely means to leave matters unresolved between Steinunn and Thangbrand, for he makes a similar move soon after the Conversion, in which he consciously frustrates expectations derived from the genre of Christian literature that he is toying with. After Valgard, Mord's father, comes back to Iceland to see the disarray of Mord's chieftaincy, he hatches the plot to bring down the Njalssons. Father and son agree to put the plan into action, and then the conversation takes a different turn:

> Mord said, 'I would like you to take the new faith, father. You are an old man now.'
> 'No,' said Valgard, 'I would rather have you discard it and see what happens then.'
> Mord refused to do that. Valgard broke all Mord's crosses and sacred symbols. Then [other mss, 'a short time later'] Valgard fell ill and died, and a burial-mound was raised over him. (ch. 107)

The most insightful critic of *Njála*, Ian Maxwell, says Valgard 'dies in an odour of brimstone'.[12] Maxwell is exactly right about the genre the author is gesturing toward, but he misses the author's wry refusal to provide the brimstone. Our writer speaks only of correlation, not causation. Valgard is an old man; he broke some crosses; he died. No black dogs or demons drag him to hell, leaving a sulfurous stench behind. This maps on to the moves the author made with Svan's death when he mocked the pagan credulity of those who thought Svan was welcomed into Kaldbackhorn mountain. We only know that Valgard is dead; as to where he is lodged in death, no opinion is offered. When our author wants to give us an account of God taking or assisting revenge, he knows how to do it, as in Amundi's case. He teases us that Christian genres are supposed to govern, but then leaves it up in the air whether Valgard, an old man, simply died of old age or as a consequence of smashing some crosses.[13]

---

11. Steinunn is mentioned in *Landnámabók*; these are the only two verses attributed to her that have survived, which appear in inverted order in *Flateyjarbók*, 1: 425.
12. Maxwell, 39; also Gottzmann, 315, who sees Valgard's death as a Christian exemplum.
13. Even the variant manuscript readings of *þá*, 'then', or *litlu síðar*, 'a short time later', reproduce the ambivalence, with the former able to suggest consequence in certain constructions, but here both readings refuse to make it a matter of causation, rather than of correlation.

183 CONVERSION AND THE GENIUS OF THE LAW

The author engages in at least two more wry refusals to chalk an event up to an unambivalent miracle when the characters on the spot are more than willing to believe that one took place. First, the miracle of the burning berserk. Gest Oddleifsson, well known for his gift of prophecy across a range of sagas, is holding a feast. Thangbrand is there along with 200 heathens. A berserk named Otrygg was expected to show up too; everyone was afraid of him, but the berserk was afraid of neither blade nor fire. Thangbrand proposes a test of faiths. They were to light three fires. The heathens were to hallow the first, Thangbrand the second, and the third was to remain unhallowed. 'If the berserk is afraid of the fire I hallow,' says Thangbrand, 'but walks through your fire,[14] then you must accept the new faith.' They agree. The berserk comes storming in; strides right through the first fire that the pagans had blessed, and then stops before the second one that Thangbrand had hallowed and said that he was burning all over. I suspect he was not lying. He then 'brandished his sword to strike at the benches, but the sword caught in a crossbeam as he swung it upwards. Thangbrand struck him on the arm with a crucifix and, miraculously, the sword dropped. . .; then Thangbrand plunged a sword into his chest' (ch. 103). The others all join in and make sorry work of the berserk.

These are practical Icelanders. They want the berserk dead by whatever means. If neither God nor the pagan gods are up to it, then the third fire will do the trick. It is not there as an experimental control. I cannot believe someone as wise as Gest let Thangbrand have the second fire, unless Gest was going along with rigging the test so as to make it easier to convince his household to convert, a decision whose inevitability he had foreseen. The 'miraculously' applied to the dropping of the sword, even more overstated in the original (*jartegn svá mikil*, 'a miracle so great') has an almost mocking quality to it.[15] The unlucky berserk was already totally disabled, his sword caught in the accommodatingly and realistically low crossbeams, and he was on fire. We find all manner of miracles or tests this easy to see through in medieval sources, but this author has a track record, as we have already established, of agnosticism on conventional recourse to supernatural claims, whether they be pagan or Christian. No naivety informs his account.

14. Magnusson/Pálsson: 'but walks *unscathed* through your fire'; but there is no unscathed in the original.
15. Cf. the miracle of the berserk in *Kristni saga*, ch. 9, where there is no sign of rigging.

Second, the miracle of Njal's unburned radiant corpse. When Njal and his wife refuse passage out of the burning farmhouse that Flosi offers them, Njal says they should go to bed. They lay down, with their grandson, who refuses to exit the flames, between them. Njal then orders his steward to cover their bodies with an oxhide (ch. 129). Later, when the bodies are dug out, Njal's body is proclaimed by those present to be radiant, miraculously preserved. The author, however, chooses at this moment to supply an unmotivated discrepant detail: 'then they lifted up the boy who had been lying between them; one finger, which he had stretched out from under the hide, had been burned off' (ch. 132).

This is pure mischievousness. Nothing requires mention of the finger, or that the boy stretched out his hand to expose it. Any miracle, it is more than hinted at, was worked by the oxhide and Njal's staging of it.[16] We will return to this scene, because it shows one important way in which Christianity figured in the politics of revenge, of playing for the hearts and minds of the neutrals in the community. It is a story less about God working in strange ways, than how an intelligent man will manage his death so as to secure revenge: by dying as a martyred saint.[17]

'St.' Thorgeir the Lawspeaker

The truly remarkable story about the Christianization of Iceland is also included in the saga. Nothing shows off the Icelandic legal genius better, and it was the Lawspeaker, Thorgeir of Ljosawater, a pagan, who put on the show. He is Thorkel Hake's father no less, the father whom Skarphedin told us Thorkel fought against. *Njáls saga* gives enough of the Conversion story for us to appreciate Thorgeir's intelligence. This story is so oft told I will be brief, and stick to its relevance for the understanding of the saga.[18]

---

16. Commentators piously ignore that finger. For them Njal's preserved body is pure miracle, 'God openly thereby not only showing his direct effect in this earthly realm, but also manifesting his will with regard to a man who already finds himself in the hereafter'; Gottzmann, 318–19.

17. For a discussion of this scene emphasizing issues of memorialization, see Glauser, 18–22.

18. The story is 'too good to be true', according to Fletcher, 398, and he is mostly right, since the earliest source from which the story derives is Ari's little book. But that does not change the tenor of Ari's thought at all, which then is even more surprising for how 'secular' his account is after 125 years of Christianity. See generally Orri 2000; also Berend, 36.

After Thangbrand returned to Norway and complained to King Olaf about the reception the Icelanders gave him, Olaf took hostages from the leading Icelandic families whose sons were in Norway. Gizur and Hjalti undertook to return to Iceland to advance aggressively the Christian cause. The Althing that year put the country on the verge of civil war. Each faction, Christian and heathen, went to the Law Rock and declared themselves out of law with the other. The Althing was in an uproar. This meant Christians refused to be summonable to court by pagans and vice versa. What it meant for the actual substance of the law was pretty much beside the point, because the mutual secession dissolved a single national legal community and in effect personalized the law. Christians would have to set up Christian courts, pagans would have to set up pagan courts; there would be two polities sharing the same space; legal process would not cross the divide. The Christian faction chose Hall of Sida as their Lawspeaker. Hall, to his great credit, made some kind of deal with Thorgeir the Lawspeaker, paying him three marks, so that Thorgeir should speak the laws.[19] 'It was a risk for [Thorgeir] was heathen.'

Thorgeir lay under a cloak all day and spoke to no one; some suggest that he was composing the new section of the laws that he would articulate, others that he was staging, or truly in, a shamanistic trance.[20] In either case Thorgeir is engaging in an ostentatious display of taking his time in the hopes that that would lend more authority to whatever his decision would be. The next day Thorgeir asks for silence and announces his ruling. 'It seems to me that an impossible situation arises if we do not all have one and the same law. If the laws are divided the peace will be divided and we cannot tolerate that' (ch. 105).[21] He asks if they all, Christians and pagans, will accept the law he proclaims. He insists that they swear oaths to that effect. Thorgeir then declares that they shall be Christian. *Njáls saga* has him outlaw worship of idols, exposure of infants, and eating of horseflesh. The penalty for carrying on these practices openly is lesser outlawry, but

---

19. Ari's *Íslendingabók* does not mention a sum paid over by Hall, but uses a more general term, *kaupa*, which could equally encompass that Hall 'made a deal with', 'paid', or 'paid off' Thorgeir; see Grønlie 2006: 25 n. 71.
20. See Jón Hnefill, 103–23.
21. See Ari's version which shows more fully how compelling Thorgeir's arguments were; Miller 1991.

they were not punishable if done in private.[22] The heathens felt betrayed, but they did not go to war or disrupt the peace.

One of the more interesting features of the Icelandic Conversion tale is that the chief story the Icelanders told themselves (or that Ari told for them) was not one of good beliefs driving out bad, of Christ triumphing over Satan or Thor, or of salvation upon the reception of good news, but a story of their respect for their law, of the practical and symbolic importance of its being One. This is a story less about their law becoming Christianized than of Christianity being 'led into [their] law', the metaphor they use to describe the legal process by which an illegitimate child was formally made a member of his paternal family, or by which a manumitted slave was made a free member of the community.[23] Though eventually laws dealing with marriage, burial, tithes, Sabbath and holiday work and travel restrictions would have to be enacted, it was not as if many individual laws would have to change at the beginning. The rules regarding pasturing, pledging, summoning, and so on would stay the same. Baptism would clearly be required and would carry, for some time, most all the meaning of what it meant to have become Christian.[24]

Thorgeir conceived of his decision as an arbitration of a legal dispute brought under the auspices of the old law and old institutions. As is the standard practice with legal claims involving major political stakes in *Njála*, this one ended in the decision of an arbitrator empowered by both parties, not a formal judgment of a court. But this was not the average arbitrator; he was himself a symbol of legal unity. He was the entire body of law, a living compilation of all their laws. He was the Law Rock in human flesh. To be known as a truce-breaker, a *griðníðingr*, of this most solemn settlement in their history turned out to be unthinkable; no general apostasy is recorded, a testimony to the wisdom of allowing private cultic sacrifices. The way this polity handled big cases, by taking them to law or to the Thing and

---

22. The *Njála* author states the compromise in the form of a prohibition and then allowing an exception if the prohibited practices were done in private, while Ari has Thorgeir allow the old laws to stand on these practices but adds a proviso that they must be not carried on publicly.
23. *Grágás* Ia 193, Ib 25.
24. The pagan Norse had an analogous ritual of sprinkling a baby with water and giving the baby its name, to indicate a newborn was to be raised up and not exposed. Thus Hallgerd's daughter, Thorgerd (ch. 14). Magnusson/Pálsson have Thorgerd 'baptized'. That is their anachronism, not the author's, who maintains the distinction between admitting baby Thorgerd into the family—*var vatni ausin*, 'was sprinkled with water'—and ushering Kolskegg and Hall of Sida into the Christian community—*taka skírn* (chs. 81, 100).

then forcing the suit into the hands of arbitrators, was a business they were used to in weighty matters, and it was thus how they became Christian. Thangbrand's mission had little to do with it. No miracles to speak of convinced anyone. It was the admirable flexibility of their law which gave astute political actors enough room to maneuver, to create, in this case, polity-saving legislation which the general population respected because it was 'their law'.[25]

The Christians got the better of Thorgeir's award, although this would have eventually been the case no matter what Thorgeir had decided, now that Norway and Denmark had gone over to the new dispensation. In an argument Gibbon gave its classic form, paganism paid a price for a natural tolerance that came with a pantheon of gods. Paganism was not likely to be jealous of other gods. Why, as a practical matter, would you ever want your enemy praying to your god or God? As Steinunn said, you take Christ, I'll take Thor, and let them fight it out. Belief in the same god got you into a bribing contest with your enemy, which helps explain why saints would step in and play the role the gods used to play. Saints, like the old gods, were supposed to be partial.[26]

Hall of Sida was astute in preferring that Thorgeir announce the law. As a pagan, Thorgeir was more likely to get pagans to accept his ruling than, say, if Hall were to issue the same one. Moreover, Thorgeir was the fully legal Lawspeaker. Hall, no doubt, would have had a harder times getting his own faction to accept the same award Thorgeir issued, because they would see it as Hall conceding, than if they could see that the conceder was the pagan Thorgeir. Thorgeir could more easily allow the two chief features of his compromise: infanticide and, incredibly, the private maintenance of family cults, as long as they kept it unwitnessed. This is a compromise most churchmen would not have been able to make with ease publicly, and it is especially interesting because it shows that a unified law was not meant to

25. While there is no reason to doubt Thangbrand's mission, the conversion would have to be less neat than Ari makes it. We also know that some settlers were already Christian, or at least familiar with the faith, and perhaps picked up some of its customs in Ireland or the Western Isles.

26. Not that some leading Christians did not recognize the need to go slow and make accommodations. The *locus classicus* is Gregory the Great's advice to the Augustine who evangelized in Kent *c.*600; see Bede, *History* I. 30. Though whenever Christianity met a pagan cult Christianity triumphed fairly quickly, at least two pagan cults were well-enough organized and funded to resist for some time: that of the Slavic Wends, during the 10th, 11th, and well into the 12th centuries, and that of the Baltic Lithuanians, whose rulers were powerful enough in the 13th and 14th centuries to hold out even longer before they too entered the fold.

impose a unified system of beliefs or of cultic practices. Thorgeir's compromise, with a little exaggeration and some anachronism, articulated the classic public/private distinction of liberal political theory.

This pagan Lawspeaker, as the last act of any pagan Lawspeaker, declares the new law. The author makes not the barest suggestion that he is playing with the symbolism of the Old Law superseded by the New Law, the new covenant of mercy.[27] What he will show, as I have already suggested, is that the new law in his saga does not work as well as the old law. But he is making a much more nuanced claim than the bald statement of the previous sentence. He is too practically minded to believe that the pre-Christian law of the Things was a feature of some Golden Age. What he shows though is that it made do. It muddled through. Big cases occurred in his saga before the Conversion. They led to arbitrated settlements that bought time, brought peace for a while. That was no mean achievement, given the incessant competition for honor and advantage that made any peace friable. Never, in the pagan period of this saga, had the peace of the Althing or the local Things been violated.[28] The peace of the Althing was even maintained under the single greatest threat that the society had faced until that moment. Thorgeir the Lawspeaker (with Hall's assist) saved the society from fracture, from seeing its law sliced in half.

Before and After Conversion: Compare and Contrast

The author calls heavy-handed attention to the Conversion—by its placement, by the special number of its initial chapter, by the clear signaling of it as a break in the story—so that he almost compels us to undertake a before-and-after exercise. We should not expect such an exercise to yield jarring results; his sensibility is too nuanced. But he does make suggestions.

The author does not depict Christianity as effecting a spiritual transformation of saga and society. Christianity works very little magic in the saga in Iceland outside of Amundi's killing of Lyting, which, if anything, shows that God is not about to interfere with an ethic of revenge, nor with much

27. Allen, 204 n. 16, speculates otherwise.
28. On outbreaks of violence at Things, see Ch. 18, n. 11.

else.[29] Christianity, after all, brought in the Old Testament as well as the New; it could make the accommodations necessary to serve as a religion of warriors, as well as one of shepherds and fishermen. The moment King Brian falls in Ireland, in Iceland some blood appears on a priest's vestments (the good Christian Brian was a warrior), and another priest had a vision of the horrors of the deep, both told with the perfunctoriness of a checklist at the very end of the saga (ch. 157). That is pretty near all the Christian supernaturalism in the saga that occurs in Iceland.[30]

Yet for all his refusal to indulge much miracle-making, heaven or hell, the author recognizes that something has happened which he correlates with the coming of Christianity; that though there may have been an improvement in the quality of the faith that replaced pagan rites (I take it as a given that he believes this), Christianity brought along with it some unintended costs that were not always a change for the better. If you want a quick conclusion, it can somewhat unfairly be boiled down to this: things went from bad, but bearable, before Christianity, to worse and barely bearable after. Some people change their style of dying, but most importantly, it becomes harder to maintain the peace. The rules governing violence seem more under stress afterwards. In both post- and pre-Christian *Njáls saga* revenge thrives, but in the earlier period it adhered better to norms of proportionality than after the Conversion.

An all-too-frequent view voiced by scholars, who should know better, has it that when people waive revenge in the interests of peace, when they compromise and settle claims, even forgive them, that this is a sign of, or due to, Christian influence.[31] As if no society with many gods, or a non-Christian God, or no god, did not have mechanisms for settling disputes, for burying the hatchet, for promoting peace, or for trying to export asocial violent actors. The idea of forgiveness did not need the Gospels, it came quite naturally to any person in a feuding or warring society who

---

29. Andersson 1972: 104: 'when Amundi says "praise be to God" and proceeds to drive his axe into Lyting's skull it is a fair warning not to strain the ethical implication of the Conversion unduly.' See *Prestssaga*, chs. 8-9, for a 'miracle' that allows the future bishop Gudmund to have his outlaw killed in an affray by another man, so Gudmund would not have to lose honor by failing to kill his outlaw or lose his ordination by killing him.

30. See also Ch. 16, n. 3.

31. The most sensible discussion of this issue in *Njála* is Hallberg 1973. Maxwell, as usual, is insightful; so too Andersson 1972. On the other side, see e.g. Lönnroth, 142; Fox; Gottzmann. Even the best of critics fall for a wooden contrast of a so-called heroic code by which pagans supposedly lived without an idea of peace in their heads and a Christian one in which only ideals of peace reigned; e.g. Allen, 90.

was about to suffer grave losses at the hands of an avenger. He was all for his enemy showing a little mercy and forgiveness; he would send emissaries to beg for it.[32] Christianity hardly invented these concepts or even invented seeing practical virtues in them. The pre- or non-Christian would make, or have some others make on his behalf, offers of peace, put forward arguments on its virtues, and so on. People with reputations for being good men, like Njal or Hjalti Skeggjason, in pagan times would intervene and urge, even force, peace on a would-be avenger. People would waive claims if it was sensible to waive them, especially if a way could be arranged to do so honorably. Peace takes work to maintain in any community or society, and it is not clear that *Njáls saga* shows it got easier with the advent of Christianity.

Christianity did, however, give a new diction, a new and powerful way of phrasing peacemaking moves, but it did not invent such moves. When Hall of Sida, in every sense an admirable man (and nobody's fool), waives compensation for his son killed at the Battle at the Althing, everyone is so impressed that they compensate him at the highest rate ever. Was Hall's move really unthinkable in a non-Christian world? Remember, Hall is no weak person. He is a wealthy chieftain and he commands men and respect. For the likes of him forgiveness can be an option, and his being a good Christian probably made it easier for him to avoid some of the taunts of cowardice that might have come his way for being forgiving, to which we can add the privilege of his old age. Compare, say, the kin of that Solvi who got heaved into his cauldron of boiling water (ch. 145).[33] They are not mentioned. They too had to forgive; no other option was available to them, neither in Christian nor in pagan times. Where was the virtue in that?

The Christian ideology of forgiveness makes for grim jokes that suit the Icelandic style very well, some of which could not have been made before, some of which could but would lose their edge. I have to go outside *Njála* for two examples which took place about fifteen years before the saga was written. When King Hakon of Norway asks Thord kakali whether he would still prefer to be in heaven if his enemy, Gizur Thorvaldsson, were also there, Thord answers: 'Most certainly, my lord, as long as there is a lot of distance between us.' Some time later that same Gizur is given his opportunity to make a dark joke. When Gizur is asked by Thord Andreassson,

32. See e.g. Thucydides 4.19.
33. See p. 97.

whom Gizur had just captured, to forgive the wrongs he had done him, Gizur responds: 'Yes I will, the moment you are dead.' Then they kill him.[34]

Those caveats expressed, I still think that the Conversion episode is the pivot or crease on which the saga is to be folded over on itself. The last event before the Conversion is the killing of a man on the grounds that the killer (Lyting) had been excluded from a settlement in which he felt himself entitled to compensation, and in the first death after the Conversion the killer (Amundi) asserts the identical ground when he kills Lyting (chs. 98, 106).[35] If we prefer to attach the Amundi episode to the Conversion story as a concluding miracle story, then observe how the folding of the book brackets a dead Hoskuld with a dead Hoskuld, pagan and Christian namesakes. Moreover, a marriage ends the saga just as one begins it, both involving some suspension of disbelief. Few have failed to notice that Kari is almost a clone of Gunnar,[36] or that the Burning of Njal maps on in numerous ways to the killing of Gunnar, none more starkly than the rejection by Gizur of Mord's suggestion, twice made, to burn Gunnar inside (ch. 77), contrasted with Flosi's decision, after facing some stiff defense, to burn Njal and his family. Skarphedin too participates in the compare-and-contrast exercise: 'The men who attacked Gunnar were chieftains of such character that they would have preferred to turn back rather than burn him in his house. But these people will not hesitate to use fire if they cannot overcome us in any other way. . .' (ch. 128).

Though the author might want to force these comparisons, what conclusions does he mean us to draw from the exercise? One thing we are clearly not entitled to conclude, as I have indicated, is that the Christian society that displaced the pagan one was more peaceful, less perfidious, or more just. But it is surely different in some ways. There can be no doubt that after Christianity the story gets progressively bleaker, and that can only be denied if you think that the killing of Hoskuld Thrainsson, the Burning, the Battle at the Althing, and Kari rejecting all the old limits governing revenge is an improvement over the state of affairs that brought Gunnar down.

After Christianity is led into the law, it is downhill for the law in *Njáls saga*. The norms of feud become stressed, as again the Burning, the outright

---

34. *Íslendinga saga*, chs. 192, 200 (the triple s in 'Andreassson' is the proper form).
35. Also rightly noted by Maxwell, 38–9; see Ch. 13, n. 10.
36. Both are also able to jump *backwards* over beams; Allen, 59. But see Ch. 20, n. 15, for Bolton's rather different and nuanced view.

rejection of settlements (by Flosi, Kari, Thorgeir), the Battle at the Althing, and Kari's excessive revenge reveal. Gunnar stays home and violates the law and he is justly killed on account of it; Kari goes abroad to hunt down people who went abroad fulfilling a ruling that required them to go abroad, and who are hunted down nonetheless.[37] And Kari, unlike Gunnar, is never sanctioned. No innocent parties die along with Gunnar, as they will in the Burning. Kari rejects the old principle of justice as balanced exchange, not in the service of forgiveness, which also purports to reject the principle of balance, but in the service of a revenge ethic unhinged from community controls and the taking of counsel. Did Christianity undo the ideology of evenness, of balance? Ideas like the plenitude of grace, eternal damnation, or, for that matter, eternal reward reject proportionality unapologetically. But the author does not take that line.

The writer was a child, perhaps a young man, during the endemic civil strife that ended with Norwegian-imposed laws replacing the laws of *Grágás* that captured his imagination. He saw disputes grow much greater than the ones he might have known from sagas other than the one he would write; he saw them become organized and defined territorially, with big men acting more like exploitive lords than mere local big men. In these disputes bishops took a prominent role and, as we shall see, a bishop could even justify burning as a permissible tactic.

Might the author be suggesting that Christianity brought with it institutional changes which a fragile older order could not survive? The institutional structure of saga Iceland—Thing meetings lasting a couple of weeks a year, local ad hoc meetings of the poor-law administrative units, a Lawspeaker and a Law Rock—was minimal. Consider what a sophisticated institutionalized religion would bring with it: the Church with its bishops, eventually non-native Norwegian ones, the claims of a Norwegian archbishopric, tithes and thus taxation (and of course writing and thus record-keeping, among which records the sagas take first rank). Even individually-owned church buildings, which sprouted up widely, would effect changes in the landscape, the places where people would meet, and

---

37. It is a nice legal question whether Kari is not violating the law by killing them abroad. While Flosi defends Kari when he kills Gunnar Lambason by asserting that Kari 'is not in any settlement with us' (ch. 155), *Grágás* provides a plausible argument to the contrary. Those Burners who were exiled for life are under a sentence which could be classified as outlawry 'with mitigation', the mitigation being precisely that they are allowed passage abroad and are immune there; see *Grágás* Ia 95–6.

under what terms.[38] But the author cannot make the institutional argument directly without engaging in anachronisms much greater than he allows himself, for institutionalization of Christianity in any serious way did not take place for almost a century after the final events in his saga had occurred.

The author does *not* say that Christianity caused the breakdown in social order we see in the second half of the saga. Christianity had absolutely nothing to do with Kari's excesses or the Battle at the Althing. It is not as if disputes did not expand before the Conversion. Bergthora and Hallgerd knew how to do that. The author hardly makes the pre-Christian period golden. He must have had access to the body-count given for the battle at Knafahills where Hjort dies in *Landnámabók*: four plus Hjort.[39] He triples the number. High casualty counts were in his saga not something that occur only after the Conversion, though the size of hostile musters increases: forty to attack Gunnar, 100 or 120 to attack Njal. Presumably he wanted to embellish Gunnar's martial talents, but he also knew that he was doing more. Pre-Conversion Iceland could discipline an excessive Gunnar whose disproportionate killing took place mostly (with the exception of the attack on Otkel) in self-defense, but post-Conversion Iceland neither had the will nor ability to discipline a Kari. Our author sees pluses and minuses before, and fewer pluses and more minuses after. One would think he would make a stronger statement, because he so clearly invites the expectation of one with the obviousness of the placement of the Conversion episode, but he is too subtle a political and social thinker, so given to grays rather than blacks and whites, even when he wants to go black and white: white knights like Njal, Gunnar, and Kari, end up noticeably grayed; and he gives the reader the grounds to gray blackened souls like Mord and Hallgerd too. He might be concluding nothing more than that, after nearly 300 years, it may still be too early to evaluate the benefits and costs of the presence of the Church.

38. Orri 2000: 90–1; see also Jón Viðar, 106–15.
39. *Landnámabók*, S 354, H 312.

15

Valgard 'the Wise' and Hoskuld's Blood: Chapters 107–16

Valgard, Mord's father, is nobody's fool. He does not spend much time in Iceland or in the saga, but when he makes his occasional trips back he casts a cold eye, consults his own or his son's interests, and then puts what his eye discerns to work. His cognomen—*grai*, 'gray'—means spiteful, but I am not sure that that is fair. He just plays the game hard. Valgard notes the falling off in the family chieftaincy; Mord tells his father he is losing thingmen to Hoskuld, a new chieftain.[1] Valgard then comes up with a plan to restore Mord's fortunes to such as they were before Skarphedin forced Mord to fund the costs that Skarphedin and Hogni Gunnarsson ran up avenging Gunnar. Valgard wants Mord to divide Hoskuld and the Njalssons by slander; make the Njalssons kill Hoskuld and 'the death of the Njalssons would follow as a consequence'. He then tells him how to go about it. Take your time, give gifts, develop a friendship, and then start the backbiting: 'you will only regain your authority when they are all dead' (ch. 107).

Valgard's advice depends on two things. He, like everyone else, can see the obvious. The alliance of the Njalssons and Hoskuld is held together with a string and a prayer, and is already unraveling. Flosi had made the same observation several years earlier when he questioned the wisdom of

---

1. On the mostly-hollow right of thingmen to choose their chieftain in the 13th century, see Orri 2007. Valgard's remarks also seem to indicate that a new Thing has been established at Hvitaness, and that people are going there, whereas the laws would contemplate a thing-man still attending the same local Thing but declaring himself to be 'in Thing' with one of the other two chieftains who were responsible for that local Thing. This is another instance where the saga varies from the structure that *Grágás* delineates.

marrying his niece to Hoskuld: 'this is a good offer,' said Flosi, 'on the other hand there are grave dangers in your family relationships' (ch. 97).[2] We have discussed the various fixes Njal undertook to control the centrifugal forces undermining the fosterage alliance: the constant mutual consultation of the Njalssons and Hoskuld, a formal friendship between sons and foster-son, the servants in Hoskuld's household all chosen by Njal (ch. 97, last paragraph). That was before Lyting appeared.

Valgard does not think dividing them will be impossible; he does not even think it will be all that difficult. Neither does the author, who thinks it so easy that he devotes merely two perfunctory and dissatisfying chapters to Mord's 'tricking' the Njalssons into killing Hoskuld. The author could have shown the Njalssons more reluctant to admit Mord into their midst, but then that would be no less false, because when the saga-writer broke off in chapter 99 for the Conversion, the unraveling of the relations between Njal and sons, between sons and foster-son, was well under way.

Valgard can also see that in the underlying Sigfusson–Bergthorsknoll feud, it is the Njalssons' turn to kill. True, a settlement was concluded for their brother Hoskuld Njalsson. But so was one for Svart, Kol, Atli, Brynjolf, Thord, Sigmund, and Thrain. Sometimes these settlements were openly violated, sometimes the next killing found different grounds, as in the case of Sigmund, but the model set forth in the Bergthora–Hallgerd feud showed that each move was balanced twice, once by money, once by blood. The Njalssons are out a Hoskuld and one is right there for the taking. Mord need only play on what is by now obvious to the brothers: their father's favoritism, a father who sold his flesh-and-blood Hoskuld, carrying him in his purse, to this foster-son Hoskuld, moved heaven and earth on behalf of this stranger Hoskuld to get him a chieftaincy and thus a great marriage, bought him his own farm, even let him live in it, and quite simply loves him like no one else since Gunnar. Cain killed Abel for considerably less. That hardly makes the killing justifiable, for it is not. It will be murder, pure and simple, in our sense of murder. But it is understandable, and to the likes of Valgard not one bit surprising.

---

2. See too Njal's remarks to the Althing in which it is assumed that the conditions giving rise to these 'grave dangers' are matters of general knowledge: 'Most people know of the trouble there was between the Grjotriver men [Thrain and company] and my sons. . .' (ch. 97).

The second point that underpins Valgard's advice is that he is able to predict—his astuteness matches Njal's—that even if Mord is complicit in the plot to kill Hoskuld, even if he stabs Hoskuld, even if he is legally culpable as his killer, that it will not be Mord whom anyone responding to the assassination will go after. It will be the Njalssons and Njal. Valgard correctly believes that politics will trump justice. He sees how the lines of force are drawn in the South Quarter, that the forces have been skewed by the marriage out of the quarter Njal made for Hoskuld; that Flosi is a new factor to be considered; that in the scramble to fill the vacuum left by Hoskuld's death Mord will not matter, because no one really sees him as a dangerous new man on the rise: those are the Bergthorsknoll people. Whom would you rather have to defend against once you had taken your turn and avenged Hoskuld Hvitanesspriest, if you were, say, Flosi? Mord, or Skarphedin and Njal?

Easy: Mord. While probably portrayed as more inept than he really is, Mord keeps his ambitions within conventional limits. His ambitions are quite predictable. He just wants to be a leading chieftain in his district. The Bergthorsknoll crew is another matter. They are to be reckoned with, and if one of them can rewrite the constitution to pursue his own interests, and his son can leap twelve ells over Markar River and kill his newly-emerged competitor in the district, whom would you take out if the opportunity arose? Because they are a family who have been on the rise, and they still seem to have ambitions to keep rising, no one can be quite sure of the limits of their ambitions. Like Gunnar generating enmity because he got too big, so too it might be argued that the Burning at Bergthorsknoll, as our author sees it, is about clipping the wings of a very able family of unprepossessing origins that insists on rising and rising.

Valgard can predict that it is the Njalssons who will be targeted. Valgard can see this without any prescience being attributed to him. Njal knows this too and even more: '[the killing of Hoskuld] will lead to my death and the death of my wife and all my sons' (ch. 111). The irony is that by getting Hoskuld his chieftaincy he brings a Lyting out of the woods, who forces Hoskuld into an independence Hoskuld does not even seek. And by marrying Hoskuld to Hildigunn, Njal ends up bringing Flosi into the Sigfusson orbit, a man of position and authority to whom the Sigfussons can turn once Hoskuld is dead. The best-laid plans. . .

Hoskuld Martyr

Perhaps the most obvious effect Christianity wrought on *Njáls saga* was to elevate the moral standing of a new way of dying a violent death: passively rather than actively. Only two characters take 'advantage' of the new style: Hoskuld and Njal. We might add Bergthora and Thord Karason, but they do not consciously mobilize this new *ars moriendi* in the way Hoskuld and Njal do. The forgiveness Hoskuld offers his assassins, even the blow to his head, are all signs that Hoskuld has been familiarizing himself with stories of martyrdoms. His death mimics Thomas Becket's. Becket was set on by four, not five, but the first blow was to the top of his head.[3]

All five attackers agreed to strike Hoskuld, who when he sees them emerge from behind the turf-and-stone fence turns to escape. That is too much for Skarphedin to resist mocking his flight: 'don't trouble yourself to run away, Hvitanesspriest.' Skarphedin overloads his statement with alliteration, which the author joins in after Skarphedin finishes speaking: '*Hirð eigi þú að hopa á hæl, Hvítanessgoðinn' ok höggur til hans ok kom í höfuðit ok féll Höskuldr á knéin* (ch. 111). But it is calling him by his title—Hvitanesspriest—that stands out. There lurks in it a confession of resentment, because Hvitanesspriest is what his father made him. The epithet also means to mock his victim, because to Skarphedin Hoskuld should be addressed as 'Hoskuld', yet at this moment that name is solely the property of their dead half-brother.

Despite Skarphedin's insinuation that Hoskuld is fleeing in cowardice, Hoskuld is no coward. He would not be a worthy martyr if he were, nor would his death elicit much sympathy. Once even the pretense of good relations has broken down between the Njalssons and Hoskuld, he refuses Flosi's offer to move east out of harm's way: 'Then people would say that I was fleeing from Ossaby because I was afraid, and I do not want that' (ch. 109). He is armed with a sword while sowing seed, a concession to his own evaluation of the risks he is now assuming merely sowing grain. The action seems to take place in an abstracted world. The half-allegorical Hoskuld is sowing that sunny day in a field Njal gave him, in a cloak Flosi gave him.[4]

---

3. If the author is deliberately evoking Becket's martyrdom, he is not taking any of his phrasing from *Thomas saga erkibiskups* I. 542.
4. The phrase is from Gavin Kentch JD 2011.

The author has shifted his style: where before significant symbols are barely discernible in the narration of hard fact, here the facts seem to be tagging along on a primarily symbolic ride. Symbolic, though, of what? The poison, *das Gift*, in the gift (of field and cloak)? Certain things seem to carry a symbolic load and no one is supposed to ask too closely what is represented, other than to infuse the air with a waft of the 'symbolic'. Sowing, and in this saga, cloaks, spring, and sunshine, will do that.[5]

More than thirty years ago I wrote an article entitled 'Justifying Skarpheðinn'. It had something of the form of a legal brief on his behalf, showing some of what I have already shown here: that Mord did not need to dupe the Njalssons, that they had more than enough reason to want to kill Hoskuld. But the article was mistitled. It would have been more accurate to de-polemicize it and call it 'Excusing Skarpheðinn', or 'Putting in a Word for Skarpheðinn', because anyway you cut it the killing of Hoskuld Hvitanesspriest is unjustifiable. The entire community agrees: 'The killing of Hoskuld was talked about and condemned throughout the land' (ch. 112). Runolf of Dale is direct: 'Hoskuld was killed for less than no cause; all men mourn his death' (ch. 115).

Nothing the Njalssons could ever allege in court would give them an answer to a prosecution for the killing; nothing could be alleged in mitigation. That does not mean they did not have grievances and reasons. They are those I have set forth. The deed is not inexplicable; people understand it to be part of the feud that started with the disagreement over seating arrangements years earlier. It is not Freudianizing the story to point out that their deep motivation lies against their father. The participation of all the sons against one foster-son further confirms that this was about their father, not about Hoskuld. They do not hate their father because they want to sleep with Bergthora, but because he favors his pet Sigfusson—whether it be Gunnar or Hoskuld—against his sons' interests; and the Njalssons do not like the Sigfussons for reasons independent of their father's favoring their best man in subsequent generations. Njal simply will not grant his sons the freedom to act independently, ever. His counsel is understood by his sons to harbor commands. Notice, in this regard, Njal's explicit complaint to Bergthora, right before the killing of Hoskuld (ch. 110), that his sons are excluding him from their consultations. The exclusion is for

5. Hallberg 1962: 112: 'the entire situation of the peaceful sowing of grain in the early morning affords a touching contrast to the blackness of the atrocious deed.'

obvious reasons, but the author's taking care to have Njal note it brings home Njal's own understanding that his counsel is meant to command, not merely to share in deliberations.[6]

Still, as a literary matter, and partly as a political one too, the killing of Hoskuld is Skarphedin's original sin and his alone. He who took on Thrain's men five on eight has no reluctance in not giving Hoskuld a fighting chance. As Hildigunn says when she first sees the body: 'It would have been man's work if only one man had done it' (ch. 112). Skarphedin announces himself as the killer near the field of action (ch. 112), and then at the Althing to Gudmund the Powerful: 'I stand condemned, as is understandable, for the killing of Hoskuld Hvitanesspriest' (ch. 119).[7]

Valgard was right; no one considers Mord a killer of Hoskuld. Grim and Helgi die, one in the fire, one in women's clothing trying to escape,[8] but their actions receive no special comment by people at the Althing as Skarphedin's do; they are sidekicks, who are asked to do little more than take one trip abroad, and marry so as to bring property in one case and connections in the other into the family.

And Kari? He suffers not the least taint for striking a blow against a man whom he cannot even complain was inordinately favored by his father. Njal is only his father-in-law, a good one too, not stinting Kari the way he stinted his sons, for Kari was given a farm when he took Njal's daughter to wife, though Njal must have made it clear that the couple were to live as his married sons do: at Bergthorsknoll. Kari only stabs Hoskuld because at this stage he too is a tag-along, a sidekick who by a nearly inviolable literary law is not allowed a will of his own, though a sidekick with a flamingly bright future, but who must wait until that fine head of hair he was introduced with gets burned off and his blade blued. At that time he will undergo his sea change in the form of a baptism by fire, which allows him to re-enter the community of saga heroes, after having been shelved following his first appearance as a conventional hero rescuing Grim and Helgi from Vikings.

---

6. Thus too Njal's 'counsel' to defend against Flosi from inside the farmhouse.
7. When confronting Thorkel Hake he calls himself 'an innocent man', *saklaus* (ch. 120). The claims of guilt and innocence are mostly meant to set up the insults that follow. Even less weight should be given to the sincerity of his claim of innocence, because he is playing on words: *Ek heiti Skarphéðinn, ok er þér skuldlaust at velja mér hæðiyrði, saklausum manni.* Thorkel is *skuldlaust*, literally, free of debt, and so 'innocent', that is, without an obligation to pay Skarphedin with hateful words, and since Skarphedin is a man not owed by Thorkel, he is an innocent man as to him. The play is a clever one on *skuldlaust/saklauss*.
8. O'Donoghue, 92, notes Helgi's stark contrast with his mother.

Hoskuld Hvitanesspriest dies in the spring for the sins of others, a scape-goat of sorts. But Skarphedin will bear the full moral burden for killing this Christlike Hoskuld, he bearing the sins of the others who stabbed Hoskuld, though guilty in his own right. The community seems to see the two, victim and killer, in some sense as moral and social equivalents. In the settlement reached after the Battle at the Althing, the arbitrators, the price-setters, value Skarphedin in death as equal to the Hoskuld he killed: 600 ounces, the equivalent of three high-standing men, one balanced against the other. That should give Christianizing critics pause, unless they wish to halluci-nate a symbol of the Trinity. And that 'man-evening' gives us the final line to our balanced-exchange model of the feud. To the 12-ounce, 100-ounce, and 200-ounce paired men, we now have our 600-ounce pair.

The Cloak and Holy Relics

Hildigunn finds her husband's body, gathers up his blood and folds it into the cloak he had been wearing, the one Flosi gave him, and puts it away in a chest. Mord convinces Ketil to assign him the killing case—Ketil, together with the other Sigfussons as nearest male kin, owns the legal right (and duty) to bring the killing case.[9] The saga takes a short breath to introduce two new characters—Gudmund the Powerful and Snorri the Priest (chs. 113–14)—who will play purely political roles; neither will be seen nor heard outside the Althing. Gudmund gains the honor in the saga of dragging in more names with him than any other character. He gets twenty-nine named ancestors, while Thorlaug, his wife, brings in another nineteen. No one else comes close, but Mord beats him and everyone else in one genealogical dimension. He is given the longest patriline, ten generations, though it is not presented as Mord's but as Valgard's (ch. 25). Gudmund's patriline stops at six generations. To Mord, even someone such as Gudmund looks like a parvenu, so when Mord looks at Njal, who cannot be traced beyond his grandfather on his father's or mother's side, what must he think?[10]

---

9. Mord transfers the case back to the Sigfussons in ch. 121.
10. The saga-writer truncates Njal's lineage by one generation from the one given in *Landnámabók*, S 342, H 301.

The fanfare for Snorri and Gudmund concluded, we turn to Flosi. Flosi is perhaps the most difficult character to fathom in the saga. He is something of a proto-Hamlet—cursing the spite that put him in the role as avenger of his niece's husband. At times he seems to overplay his role, at times he appears mystified as to why he is even in the saga. His sensibility parallels the more famous Dane too, in that for much of his time onstage he appears to be afflicted with what a sixteenth-century physician would diagnose as melancholia.

When Flosi hears the news he was 'deeply disturbed and angered'. He sends to Hall of Sida, his father-in-law, asking him to attend the Althing in force. He immediately contacts other important East Quarter people, asking the same of them. One of these men notes, in typical Icelandic phrasing, that 'he has often seen Flosi more cheerful than now'. Answers Flosi: 'I would give all I possess for this never to have happened.' He does not know that he is understating the price that he should have volunteered for it never to have happened. He seeks out the good man Runolf of Dale to get an exact account of the events, for 'you are a truthful man, and you are close to the source' (ch. 115). Flosi cares to verify his information, to get the facts right. The criteria he gives for the quality of information are nearness in space to the events, which maps on to the law's requirement that panel membership be selected on the basis of proximity to the incident,[11] and the informant's reputation for truthfulness. The stakes are too high here for Flosi not to care to get the best information he can.

Here is the question that should trouble us—it troubles Flosi. Why is it that everyone looks to him as the man who will be responsible for taking action over the death of Hoskuld? Flosi is not related by blood to Hoskuld; the right to sue or take revenge falls to blood relatives.[12] Yet everyone, including the Sigfussons, who are of the blood, look to Flosi, who has yet to do much of anything in the saga except give Hildigunn in marriage to Hoskuld at Njal's solicitation and give Hoskuld a cloak. The general answer lies in the structure of feud politics. The higher the social level of a person who plausibly can be identified with a group, the more likely that he will eventually assume a leading position, even though his obligation and interest in the affair will at first be rather attenuated and indirect. Giving

---

11. E.g. *Grágás* Ia 157.
12. The right to prosecute a killing case follows the ordering of the inheritance law except that women are excluded.

Hildigunn away was sufficient. Flosi thus expects things might come his way. And that is why he mobilizes forces on first hearing the news.

Flosi might also have an inkling of what awaits him when he visits the grieving widow, his niece. He can guess that she will not be urging a peaceful response. Others would suspect the same, which is probably why Runolf counsels him, before he leaves his farm on his way to Hildigunn's, to 'take the course that will lead to the least trouble' (ch. 115).

Flosi is to be treated to one of the best-known scenes in the saga corpus.[13] The author depicts Flosi's nervous defensiveness perfectly, no less than he has Hildigunn overplay her part with cold, calculating brilliance. Thus the words of welcome—'My heart rejoices in your coming'—the high-seat, the faux icy laugh, the towel with holes, the promise literally to get in his face—'we shall get closer yet before we part'—and then to approach Flosi closely, push her hair back from her eyes and weep.

Hildigunn is embarked on a ritual with a big R, a bloody-token ritual, common to many cultures in which revenge is a moral and legal duty. Its purpose is to have the corpse itself, through an intermediary, such as the corpse's widow, formally charge the person at whom the ritual is directed, in this case Flosi, to act on behalf of the corpse. The understanding made explicit in the charge to take revenge is that the corpse would have done the same for the living person were their roles reversed. It thus purports to mutuality, to brotherhood, to being a mutual vengeance-taking pact, contracted between the dead and the living: 'Hoskuld would have taken blood revenge if he were in your place now.' That this does not comport very well with the Hoskuld we knew is beside the point, for the dead man, so to speak, has changed his mind to accord with the demands of the ritual in which he or his body-parts have been cast in a starring role.

At least three other performances or references to this ritual or variants of it in can be found in *Njála* alone. These reveal that it was subject to much improvisation. Crucial was some Real Presence of the corpse; a relic was an indispensable actor. Thus Hrodny drags her son Hoskuld to the sheep-shed, props him up, staring ahead, and charges Skarphedin to avenge him (ch. 98); later Hrodny uses Hoskuld's bloodstained cap to get her brother Ingjald of Keldur to dissociate himself from Flosi's party (ch. 124), and recall Hallgerd's remark to the shepherd who couldn't bear to

---

13. On the bloody-token ritual, see Miller 1983*b* and Clover 1986*a*, who places the ritual in the context of Germanic women's poetic laments.

hold Sigmund's head once Skarphedin and his brothers left the scene: 'It's a pity you didn't [bring me the head]. I could then have taken it to Gunnar, and he would have had to avenge his kinsman or else be despised by all men (*hvers manns ámæli*)' (ch. 45). The formula she uses tracks Hildigunn's to Flosi, though not word for word: 'or be the vilest creature to all men (*hvers manns níðingr*).'

The ritual has as ancient a pedigree as any. It is performed in Genesis 4, when Abel's blood cries out to God. Abel has no Hildigunn to do the work for him, because not only is he unmarried but his parents are as obliged to his killer as to him, so his own blood undertakes the task. Judges 19 tells an appalling tale that leads to a performance of the ritual, when a Levite cuts up his gang-raped and murdered concubine into twelve pieces and sends her parts out to all Israel to summon them to exterminate the tribe of the perpetrators. Apparently drawing from the model of Judges 19, Jesus cuts up his figurative body into twelve pieces and hands it out to his disciples, charging them to do what? To avenge his most foul murther; and by subsequently converting half the world, some might think they were rather successful.[14] Hamlet *père* must journey up from the purgatorial fire to charge his son to avenge him, no one but his murderer knowing there was anything to avenge, and no blood to sop up or body-parts to cut up to perform the ritual, so the reality of his Real Presence becomes an issue in the play. Saints' relics, their blood and bits of body or clothing, can be used in this same way.

Hildigunn has a special prop to add even more power to the force that is already inherent in this gruesome ceremony: the cloak Flosi gave Hoskuld. In Old Norse, gifts from notable givers are specified with the form X*nautr*, where X is the genitive of the giver's name. To designate an artifact in this form only makes sense when the name of the giver is seen to add value to the artifact, to make it special by giving it a noble ancestry. When Hoskuld sows grain the day of his death he is said to be wearing the cloak 'Flosi's Gift', *Flosanautr*.[15] Hildigunn will squeeze every drop of meaning she can out of that gift.

---

14. On cutting up bodies in rituals of contract formation, see Faraone; also Miller 2006: 44–5, 80. One referee for the press resists my claim that Jesus at his last supper was urging his disciples to avenge him, and suggests, quite plausibly, that Jesus was subverting an existing vengeance ritual to redirect it to other ends. That Jesus was loading the ritual with ironies and several layers of meaning is something we both agree on; Jesus cleverly merges the Passover sacrificial ritual with the bloody-token ritual of Judges .

15. For *Skarpheðinsnautr*, see p. 274.

Once Flosi does not give the answer she wants regarding the redress she can look to him for—he talks about an arbitrated settlement and compensation—blood will be her argument. How does a reader not thrill to Hildigunn going to the locked chest, retrieving the cloak, walking back over to Flosi, and throwing it over him with the clotted blood pouring down on him?

> 'This is the cloak you gave to Hoskuld, Flosi, and now I give it back to you. He was wearing it when he was killed. I call upon God and all good men to witness that I charge you in the name of all the powers of your Christ and in the name of your courage and your manhood, to avenge every one of the wounds that marked his body—or be an object of contempt to all men.' (ch. 116)

Flosi, not surprisingly, is rather upset, so upset that his face turns into a light-show, 'one moment as red as blood, then pale as withered grass, then black as death'. Even suspecting something like this might happen did not inure him to the force of the grisly ritual. That is the power of Ritual; it gets you in spite of yourself or your better judgment.

The layers of meaning pile up. Hildigunn mobilizes not only the significance of blood to effect a posthumous blood-brotherhood ceremony, but also the meaning of gifts. Hildigunn is arguing that the gift of the cloak imposes more than an obligation on the recipient to make a proper return; it also continually obliges the giver to warrant his gift, to ratify it, to defend the possessor of it in his right to wear it, especially a gift that bears his name. By giving it back she can claim either that Hoskuld is now refusing the gift from such a poltroon as Flosi, or more poignantly, that he is satisfying his obligation to make a return gift. If Flosi's body and soul inhered symbolically in the cloak when he gave it to Hoskuld, when Hildigunn now makes Hoskuld's return gift she is not returning quite the same cloak as Flosi gave, because now it has been somewhat transformed by Hoskuld's blood and soul. Hoskuld's gift of this cloak, transfigured by his blood, demands a return in blood. She even manages to imply that somehow the mere wearing of the cloak when he died could be seen as a proper return to Flosi by honoring the gift, with the suggestion also that it somehow failed to protect her husband. The layered meanings are a tour de force, and the author generously makes it a function of Hildigunn's genius, not his own.

Hildigunn calls God and good men as witnesses, to charge Flosi in the name of 'your Christ, your courage, and your manhood'. This is like invoking the pantheon, and the force of it flows from its inclusiveness. She invokes everything that matters in their social world, everything that matters to Flosi: his personal god—*his* Christ—and his courage and manhood, the condition of which she is scorning. Hildigunn's God, as well as Flosi's Christ, as she understands them, are, or should be, fully on the side of revenge. She invokes the Golden Rule: 'Hoskuld would have taken blood revenge if he were in your place now.'

Hildigunn performs this ritual because she knows full well that Flosi is not strictly obliged to take revenge for Hoskuld. She wants to clarify for him, as starkly as possible, that he owes *her*, not just the corpse; that it is not the corpse who is the chief party of interest, but she herself: 'What redress, what help shall *I* now get from you?' Hoskuld is only someone he should avenge as a second-order matter, because Flosi gave *her* to him. She is the primary source of the obligation that Flosi is on the hook for. If the cloak can work to oblige him in some way to Hoskuld, then surely the fact that he gave her in marriage also obliges him to warrant *that* gift. (The Old Norse for marriage, when used of a woman, recall, is *gipt*, the same word as English *gift*.) He is now in any case her legal guardian, her agent at law, and she is making clear, as a client would to her lawyer, the outcome she desires, by using this ritual to force upon Flosi a contract that binds him the moment the blood touches him; it is a handshake with the dead man to whom he gave her. The ritual is meant to generate strong feelings, to suspend its object's rationality, and that it got to Flosi emotionally is a good part of what makes it work for *her*.

One small detail remains, that may be of no great significance. Right after Hildigunn says 'we shall get closer yet before we part', they both talk 'in undertones for a long time'. The content of their conversation is neither for us nor for the narrator to hear, and thus not for those present in the hall. Could it be that she is making her demands for blood first, to see if she needs go through with the ceremony? That she is threatening to continue a ritual that he can see she has already started? Or more perversely, are the two of them colluding, Flosi, in effect, wanting her to perform the ritual, so that he has a cover for his own aggressive actions should he decide to take them?[16] He would thus be able to say to those men of standing urging him

---

16. See *BP* 213, showing such collusion was possible but we would have a hard time accounting then for Flosi's changes of color. Blushes and sudden paleness, changes of blood-flow to the face, are nearly impossible to fake.

to settle, that he has been bound to pursue a more aggressive course. I do not know. Nor does the narrator, because he could not hear what they were saying either. But he does make us wonder what the substance of that conversation was so that they felt the need to conceal it.

More than this ceremony, or the fear of its being performed, brings Flosi on to the scene, because he is already considered a member of the class of eligible avengers whom Hildigunn could reasonably call upon. Something else makes everyone look his way, as I noted earlier. The author, from chapter 115 until well after the Burning, skillfully keeps moving back and forth from the Sigfusson–Flosi party to the Njalssons and their party, keeping us posted on what each side is doing at the same time. But whenever it is the turn of the Sigfusson–Flosi party to be the focus, the author makes Flosi the center of attention. The Sigfussons are yet again reduced to mere passing significance, now that their leading man has been killed. The author follows Flosi from the moment he gets the news; he follows him on his various stopping-points on his way to the Althing. At the Althing his state of mind is everyone's chief concern, though it is not until chapter 124, after Flosi has rejected the settlement that the community had its hopes set on, that the Sigfussons formally ask Flosi to lead them, despite that having been a fait accompli for nine chapters. Says Ketil of Mork then what has been obvious for some time:

> 'If it were up to us brothers to decide, we would all choose you to lead us. There are many good reasons for this; you are descended from a great family, and you are a great chieftain yourself, shrewd and resolute. We also think that you would take best care of our interests in this.' (ch. 124)

The full explanation for the shift of focus to Flosi must await further developments, but it has to do with the rapid transmogrification, expansion, and redefinition of the underlying dispute. The politics of it have changed. It is no longer just a feud between two families located in one subsection of the South Quarter; it has expanded despite itself. Flosi is a symptom, not the cause of that expansion.

16

Skarphedin *Ascendans*, Flosi's Ninth Nights: Chapters 117–23

In the meantime, at Bergthorsknoll, the breach between father and sons could not be more open. Njal, as we saw, had earlier complained to his wife about no longer being consulted by his sons and Kari (ch. 110); after the killing he is reduced to asking them: 'What plans have you in mind now, you brothers, and Kari?' The 'you brothers', not 'my sons', takes on a pointedness. Skarphedin's openly hostile answer confirms it, which elicits an equally unloving response:

> 'We do not follow dreams for much of anything. But if you want to know we are going to ride to Tongue to meet Asgrim . . . Are you going yourself, father?'
>
> 'I shall ride to the Althing, for honor demands that I do not abandon you while I am still alive. . .' (ch. 118)

Neither will their former allies abandon them. Asgrim sticks with them, indeed he will be the spokesman for the support-mustering; with him comes Gizur the White. Hjalti Skeggjason is of their party too, along with Njal's nephews, the sons of Holta-Thorir.

The killing of Hoskuld Hvitanesspriest is a universally unpopular act, the kind of deed that would alienate the uninvolved, or give allies an excuse to break with you. Flosi says exactly that when he hears from Runolf the truth about Hoskuld's death: 'then they will find it hard to get support' (ch. 115). That turns out to be only roughly true. None of their prior allies abandon them, and Skarphedin's purposefully aggressive insulting of those people who deny them support ends up perversely getting them the support of the chieftain controlling the most numerous body of followers. Gudmund the Powerful decides to back the Njalssons after his initial refusal when he hears of Skarphedin's devastating insult of Thorkel Hake,

Gudmund's arch-enemy. Again the principle 'the enemies of my enemies are my friends' works its charms.

Reintroducing Skarphedin

Skarphedin at the Althing is a grand story, and his sheer presence, the uneasiness he inspires in those who see him, his ominousness, his wit, his drive for self-destruction, make him operate within two or more literary genres at the same time. At one level he is the cool, mouthy, imposing character he has always been, but now he is something more. He takes over the saga. He comes to dominate it by sheer force of character. The author indicates the modal shift in two ways: one is the compulsive questioning regarding the man fifth in line whom everyone knows at first sight yet feels compelled to ask his identity, for they see it has in some way shifted. The action in part has transcended the practical world of support-mustering and is now operating in a parallel symbolic universe, almost as if coming to us from the innermost depths of Kaldbakhorn Mountain. The genre-shift, as noted earlier, suborns the will of those whose support they seek: they *must* ask after the man fifth in line; it is the only place in the saga where the author deprives his otherwise naturalistic characters of free will.[1]

Rare the character treated to a reintroduction in which he gets a second physical description.[2] The author in effect reintroduces Skarphedin *after* he has already insulted Skapti, Haf, Snorri, and Gudmund. It means he is about to ascend to yet another level of 'beyond'. They are now heading for Thorkel Hake's booth, and though I have discussed the substance of the insult with which Skarphedin gelds Thorkel to explicate what was so insulting about Dungbeards, the scene is too rich not to revisit for its other features. Asgrim asks Skarphedin, please, to refrain from sabotaging their support-mustering with his insults and then we get:

> Skarphedin grinned. He was wearing a blue tunic with a silver belt, blue-striped trousers, and black top-boots. He was carrying a small round

---

1. See p. 64. The successive character-destruction of the insultees recalls *Lokasenna*, and similar enactments of serial insults delivered in *Bandamanna saga* and *Ölkofra þáttr*.
2. Compare the deferred description of Egil: *Egils saga*, ch. 55; but his has to be deferred because we first meet him as a boy; likewise Thorhall Asgrimsson, for which see p. 273.

shield and the axe with which he had killed Thrain Sigfusson and which he called 'Battle-Troll'. He wore a silk headband, his hair combed back behind his ears. He looked every inch a warrior, and everyone knew him at first sight. He kept exactly to his position in the line. (ch. 120)

This reprises in some respects his introductory description (ch. 25). In both he is every inch a warrior (*hermannligastr*); the mouth is featured by the grin this time, instead of by description as the first time. The sense of him as 'for the most part under control' (*longum vel stilltr*) is recast by his hair combed and held in place by his headband, and by his will to hold precisely to his position, fifth in line, the Icelandic getting the idea of willed control more vividly: *Hann gekk sem honum var skipat, hvárki fyrr né síðar*: 'he kept to his appointed order, moving neither forward nor back.' His self-restraint is not effortless, and yet it is seldom not perfectly cool. By this time his axe, too, which was not part of his original introduction, has earned the right to have its history reiterated—that Skarphedin named it himself and that it split Thrain's skull. By the time of this reintroduction Skarphedin's axe is attached to him as if it embodied his biography; it is somewhat differently attached to him than Gunnar to his halberd, for some thought Gunnar vitally lacking without it. Thus Skammkel's remarks on the non-threateningness of Gunnar *sans* halberd (chs. 50, 53) and Gunnar's response (ch. 54). Would anyone think Skarphedin less threatening without his axe? The grin is more than enough.

The grin unnerves everyone, as well it should; it is the embodiment of the ironic principle that threatens purpose with ultimate meaninglessness, it is a kind of grimmer version of the moralist invoking 'the vanity of human wishes', or a precocious child's tearful question of 'what's the point?' when he first understands that he too is mortal or that the sun will burn out. Strange that Skarphedin really only emerges as the dominating, unforgettable character he is once the Conversion takes place. Before that he was given to localized acerbic comments, black-humored in a bantering way familiar to us all. Now the grin precedes the comments, and the grin itself is the message: Christianizing critics might see it as a doom-laden pagan leer, aware that its world has been superseded, while Skarphedin might think that their view merits more grinning. Nothing has changed; the moral demand for a saga character is the same. Live a sagaworthy life and die a sagaworthy death. Let us just say that, for the moment anyway, he is beyond good and evil.

That he has moved the saga briefly to a meta-level is what makes people ask him his name in repetitive formulaic patterns, unconsciously often punning on it; it is almost a way of each of them asking: 'Excuse me, would you tell me please whose saga we are cast in right now?' One can almost see Njal's decision to take his family inside, the way father and son will compete in the art of dying, as a struggle to the death over which one of them gets to own this saga, because Skarphedin is never, in the hard, factual world of the saga at its most material and practical, going to own Bergthorsknoll, until it burns him in it within an hour of his father's death. It will be Njal's house that is burned, even though it came to him from Bergthora Skarphedinsdottir. If I am overreaching by overreading I will try to prove up these claims more fully when we deal with the Burning, when both father and son become miracle-workers of a sort.

Backing Down Thorkel Hake

Thorkel Hake gets an extensive introduction right before Skarphedin is re-described. It needs quoting in full for it to reveal its ironies:

> Thorkel Hake had been abroad and won fame in foreign lands. He had killed a robber east in Jamtland Forest, and then travelled east to Sweden, where he joined forces with Sorkvir the Old. Together they harried in the Baltic. One evening, on the coast of Finland, it was Thorkel's turn to fetch water for the crew; he encountered a monster and was only able to kill it after a long struggle. From there he traveled south to Estonia, where he killed a flying dragon. After that he returned to Sweden, then to Norway, and then to Iceland, where he had these feats carved above his bed-closet . . . Thorkel claimed that there was no one in Iceland whom he would not meet in single combat or before whom he would yield ground. He was called Thorkel Hake because no one with whom he had to deal escaped the weight of his tongue or his arm. (ch. 119)

Unless your name is Grettir, few kill monsters in Iceland, dealings with occasional afterwalkers excepted. You have to go to places sufficiently far away so that no one can falsify any of the tall tales you bring home to carve on your bed-closet. The authorial deadpan of Thorkel's killing a flying dragon as well as another monster, neither event meriting more than a sentence, the multiplication of improbabilities, presents us, with a wink, the inverse correlation between veracity and the distance from home.[3] No wonder one of Flosi's stated criteria for quality of information was spatial proximity to the events.

This paragraph describing Thorkel is meant to set him up for the brutal deflating he is going to receive in short space. One can argue that Skarphedin at this moment shares some blood with monsters, but never without losing one ounce of his enviable humanity. The passage is in keeping with the negative twist the saga-writer gives to the standard travel-abroad theme of the sagas. In his saga, instead of the traveler coming back to triumph, he comes back to deflation, to bad marriage, or to death.[4] Thorkel was of the opinion that his trip to the continent was of the standard type: great feats abroad leading to fame, glory, and fancy woodwork back home. He is about to discover that his foreign successes succumb to the *Njáls saga* travel syndrome.

Move to Thorkel's reaction right after he is accused of picking bits of mare's ass out of his teeth. Thorkel jumps up in fury, draws his sword:

'This is the sword I got in Sweden. I killed a great warrior to get it, and since then I have killed many more with it. And when I get at you I shall run you through and pay you back for your obscene insults.'

Skarphedin stood there grinning, with his axe raised, and said, 'This is the axe I had in my hand when I leapt twelve ells over Markar River and killed Thrain Sigfusson while eight men stood by and couldn't touch me. And I have never raised weapon against anyone and missed my mark.'

He burst past his brothers and Kari and charged up to Thorkel. 'And now, Thorkel Hake, you have a choice,' he said, 'put away your sword and sit down, or I shall drive my axe into your head and split you to the shoulders.'

Thorkel sheathed his sword and sat down promptly. It was the only time in his life that such a thing happened.

---

3. See Bartlett (2008: 101–6) on dogheads, noting that people believed that the fabulous lived very far away and kept receding as one got nearer to what before had been far. I think here our author is quite tongue-in-cheek about stories of the fabulous far away, consistent with his general agnosticism on such matters. Note too how the perfunctoriness of the telling of Thorkel's monster-killings matches the tone of the miracles occurring in Iceland simultaneously with Brian's fall at Clontarf (ch. 157); see p. 189. To Thorkel Hake's credit, his carved bedposts are mentioned in *Moby Dick*, ch. 16. But how did Melville know of them? Thorkel's bedposts appear only in *Njála*; *Moby Dick* (1851) was published a decade before Dasent's English translation (1861). A Latin translation dates from 1809 and Melville read Latin, but a copy would not have been easy to find. There was an Icelander on the *Pequod* (ch.40). Perhaps he is Ishmael's source.

4. See Ch. 2, n. 1.

Thorkel has to go to Sweden to tell the story of the sword he just drew; he believes the tale of its origins makes him more intimidating. Not to Skarphedin, who just keeps grinning, knowing that he has the perfect response to the story of the Swedish sword, as he retells the events we have ourselves witnessed twenty-eight chapters earlier. He did split Thrain's skull while eight (seven?) men could not touch him; he will gladly match the story of his axe with Thorkel's story of his Swedish sword. And Thorkel knows Skarphedin is not exaggerating, for those events took place in Iceland and were witnessed by living people who can confirm the account. No need to carve them on his bed-post. Moreover, Skarphedin is employing another black-humored saga trope of the Hobson's choice type: you pick, friend Thorkel, whether to sheathe your sword and sit down or to have your skull split to your shoulders. It is wholly up to you. Thorkel had given Skarphedin no choice, but Skarphedin generously gives him two.

The Struggle for Settlement

The next chapter is a new day in which the lawsuit against the Njalssons and Kari is scuttled (ch. 121). The tricksterism of the sort Mord and Thorhall engage in to invalidate the case has no basis in law. We will return to such tactics when Eyjolf Bolverksson dies without compensation for his law-yerly moves, no less devious than Thorhall's advice here. The low trick is considered a credit to Thorhall's genius, but a discredit to Eyjolf's char-acter: thus the presumptions in reputation (with an assist from authorial partiality).[5] The author is here playing to the amateur lover of legal stories in his culture, of which there seems to be no shortage among us either, who wants his prejudices about the law's perversity confirmed.

The author needs a device to get the plaintiffs to agree to settle and not pursue their outlawry claim to judgment. In Gunnar's cases he could arrange this with ease, because Gunnar had perfect defenses to the charges brought against him. No plausible defense exists in the case against the Njalssons to provide leverage to force the plaintiffs into settlement. But we

5. For the legal errors, see Lehmann, 96–9. One of them might trouble a general reader: aren't the neighbors that Thorhall says the plaintiffs could go back to the scene of the crime to cite already at the Althing? They are the same neighbors Mord cited for the named wounds. There is no need for a fruitless trip home.

have seen before how legal cases that are just too big to go to judgment end
up being put over to a panel of arbitrators, even when one side has a winning case (ch. 74). Men of good will step forward begging the parties to take
the road that offers the best chance of peace. If lucky, a partial resolution of
the underlying conflict by some sort of compromise may result, involving
something less than either non-suiting the plaintiff, or giving him, as in
this case, his outlawry judgment. This killing case is of such magnitude
that 'many people tried to bring about a reconciliation'. In fact, this is what
the author has happen in the very next chapter.

Flosi thus faces near-irresistible pressure to settle; dramatic arguments
are put to him by Njal and Hall of Sida, both speeches made before large
audiences. Njal's is especially remarkable:

> 'I want you all to know that I loved Hoskuld more dearly than my own sons;
> and when I learnt that he had been killed, it was as if the sweetest light of my
> eyes[6] had been extinguished. I would rather have lost all my sons, to have
> Hoskuld alive. . . and now I beg you, Hall of Sida, Runolf of Dale, Gizur
> the White. . . give me a chance to settle this killing on behalf of my sons.'
> (ch. 122)[7]

What must Skarphedin, Grim, and Helgi have thought when they heard
their father profess this to the most important people in the polity? Would
they have said, 'Oh, dad is merely making one of his rhetorical moves to
spare us outlawry; he has got to make a dramatic gesture of this sort, in
order to convince Flosi and the Sigfussons to agree to a settlement'? Or
would they have had their beliefs about their father's preferences confirmed? If they had any doubts that their own self-interest was clouding
their judgment about their father's inner states, they could erase them now.
Surely the assembled auditors must have found this speech rather shocking,
even if the more astute ones would suspect that there had been serious ten-
sions between father and sons long before.

Recall the earlier mention of *Thorstein the Staffstruck*, in which Thorstein,
having killed three of Bjarni's servants, is adjudged to pay himself over to
Bjarni as a settlement of the claim. Thorstein was said to have worked as
hard as any three men at the story's start. The exchange of three men for
one was not hypothetical. It was a true measure of their different values.

---

6. On the clerical source of this metaphor, see Lönnroth, 114.
7. Notice the direct appeal to other big men to add a whiff of force to the moral suasion
directed at Flosi, whom Njal had called on to hear him out.

Njal is making such a hypothetical three-for-one exchange right now. He can still pay his three remaining sons over. He already sold one to Hoskuld Hvitanesspriest for 200 ounces; might it be that Njal's statement of wishing away three sons for his foster-son works to suggest the 600-ounce price the arbitrators put on Hoskuld?

A suspicious soul might think that some such dark wish, perhaps unconscious, made Njal put that cloak and boots on top of the 600 ounces of silver. An even more paranoid soul might think that such a wish informed his advice to defend against Flosi and his men from inside the farmhouse. The reader must come to some conclusion about the extent of Njal's ability to discern the future. I think that any suspicion with regard to the gift of the cloak is unfounded, but it still requires some explanation, of which more anon; the advice to defend from inside requires considerably more. Whatever position one takes on these matters, the author surely intends us to debate Njal's motives, forcing the issue upon us, even if they cannot be ascertained with certainty.

Yet Njal must make some powerful profession to convince Flosi, and to energize others to keep pressuring him. Njal is claiming that, even though he is the father of the killers and bound to make good for them, he is the most wronged person present (Hildigunn does not appear to be there). No one loved Hoskuld more; and he is relying on the good will he has generated in the community to beg others to do this for *him*. There is considerable presumption in his rhetorical move, but his sons will vouch for the fact that he is sincere. Those assembled in court must see that this is no phony rhetorical ploy, that Njal really is spilling his guts out before them. Among people whose culture is governed by strong norms of reticence, imagine the force of such a profession.[8] People can see that he favored Hoskuld, treated him better than he treated his own sons, moved heaven and earth for him; one imagines that it was a topic of gossip. Nonetheless, the assembled multitude must have been quite taken aback by such an overt declaration of love.

---

8. See Vésteinn, 114, who notes the speech as example of unrestrained saga emotionalism. Regarding the culture's strong norms of reticence, consider Allen's observation (xiv): 'One cannot help but wonder at times at a society which produced and admired extensive narratives in which so many people have so much trouble talking to one another.' The saga at times threatens to shut down in silence as one character after another refuses to talk; see e.g. ch. 37 (reaction of Gunnar and Njal to death of Kol).

Hall of Sida, on the other hand, makes not the obliquest reference to anything that invokes the new Christian dispensation, and he is the person, given his piety, we would most expect to do so. He speaks to Flosi as someone who owes him for past favors. 'Will you now keep your word, and grant me the favor you once promised me when I helped your kinsman Thorgrim Digr-Ketilsson to escape from the country after killing Halli the Red?'[9]

Flosi accedes to Hall's request; twelve men, six by each side, are selected as arbitrators. The author allows us a rare opportunity to listen in on how the arbitrators arrive at their decision. Snorri the Priest excludes any district outlawry or banishment, citing as a reason that they are often disobeyed and give rise to further killings.[10] They decide to award what Snorri calls 'triple man-payment', 600 ounces, to be paid at the Althing, so pricey, he says, that no man 'should ever be so costly as Hoskuld'. Since such a sum is impossible for Njal to have or even to raise, the arbitrators agree to fund half of it themselves.

When Hall announces the award at the Law Rock he asks everyone to contribute, 'for the sake of God', using the example of the arbitrators' own generosity to set an honorable example. Hall then names witnesses, formalizes the ruling, and proclaims its inviolability. Skarphedin stands nearby quietly and grins. Everyone goes back to his booth to get his money and bear it to the church at the Althing: Njal and his sons add 200 and the rest is supplied in response to Hall's plea, not a penny short. Njal then places a silk cloak and a pair of boots on top of the pile.

Njal's gift of the cloak gets its share of blame for the disaster about to happen, but the arbitration award itself must bear some of the blame. Not because the Njal party has to pay only a third of it, but because the award is not as strict as it could or should have been, despite Snorri's concern that there might be enforcement problems were exile part of the sanction. Gunnar's case surely shows that such sentences might not be obeyed, but it also shows that one should not disobey them cavalierly. The sanction imposed on the Njalssons and Kari is too soft. A more plausible settlement

---

9. It is highly probable that Hall made himself liable for lesser outlawry for assisting Thorgrim; *Grágás* Ia 149, II 342–3.

10. These forms of outlawry are to be distinguished from full outlawry or *skóggangr*; the laws make no provision for district outlawry; any such limited outlawry is imposed as a term in an arbitrated settlement, not by a formal judgment of a court. As to mitigated outlawries that allow for passage abroad, see Ch. 14, n. 37.

would mimic the one dealt out to the Osvifrssons in *Laxdæla saga* for killing Kjartan Olafsson, Hallgerd's nephew, which for all practical purposes was exile for life, or like the one that was imposed on Flosi and other Burners, with exiles of three years in Flosi's case and for life in some others; moreover, these were adhered to (ch. 145).[11] The arbitrators' rejection of even three-year exiles for the killers could not make the settlement any easier for Flosi to accept.

Flosi *Furioso*

We are about to experience another uncomfortable 'scene'. The whys and wherefores are hard to pin down. Before leaving for the final ceremony Njal asks his sons not to ruin it. 'Skarphedin stroked his brow and grinned in reply.' These grins occur now in quicker succession—five of his nine grins occur during this session of the Althing. The talent for discerning present probabilities of future events seems to have passed from father to son. Njal does not appear to have a clue what effect his well-intentioned gift of the cloak will have.[12] Does Skarphedin have an inkling? I am not sure; his behavior would be more than enough to ruin things had the cloak not beat him to it.

This particular grin of Skarphedin seems to register bemused contempt for anyone who would allow himself the imbecility of optimism at such a moment. That 'anyone' happens to be his father: 'now our case has a happy solution.' But Njal's statement could more generously be read as a prayer or a hope, even one he might know is a fond one. Njal's optimism does not run very deep. Is not his warning to his sons not to ruin it an admission of his knowledge of the fragility of the settlement? Something, though, has happened. Njal is still trying to write scripts, but people no longer are saying the lines he wants them to say. Before the death of Thrain, or even before the death of his foster-son, his 'desiring' coincided almost exactly with 'knowing'. No longer, unless we want to attribute to him a wish to ruin the settlement, and that I think is without any warrant whatsoever.

11. See *Laxdæla saga*, ch. 51: the Osvifrssons were not to return before the last of Kjartan's brothers and son had died, effectively exiling them for life.
12. Some commentators believe that Njal knows what the consequences of the cloak will be; Dronke, 14; cf. Lehmann, 102.

His acute sense of probabilities is no longer as reliable. He is now more resigned to accept that his role is at best to help clean up the messes as they arise, rather than to prevent them from happening in the first place.

Did the loss of Hoskuld, the dashing of his highest hopes for a knowingly risky fostering, reduce him to such despair that he lost his confidence in his own talent to get the odds right? He lost a bet into fairly long odds, but he was under no illusion about the risks, as we discussed earlier. Something happened in the intervening time. He perhaps hoped more than it was healthy to. Or was it not hope at all, but love that muddled his normally keen and cool rationality?

Grief and sorrow for the loss of a loved one can trouble rationality, especially when it ends in despair, where actions are undertaken without thinking much about consequences, for why bother? Does Njal feel that he cost Hoskuld his life? Reconsider the metaphor that Njal employed to describe the loss of Hoskuld: 'it was as if the sweetest light of my eyes had been extinguished.' Take away the 'as if' and Hoskuld's death cost Njal his eyes. Lines from *Lear* pop into my head, not from *Oedipus*. The metaphor of the extinguishment of sweet light, of blindness, also suggests an unconscious verdict by Njal on his own prescience, only to be restored, as we will conjecture, by the glare emitted by the flames that will engulf his family and home.

Njal and his sons approach from the west; Flosi and the Sigfussons from the east. In a lawsuit the plaintiff is on the south side, the defendant on the north (chs. 56, 73, 121, 142), a settlement moves the parties a quarter-turn withershins.

> Skarphedin moved over to the middle-bench and stood there.
> Flosi entered the Court of Legislature to look at the money, and said, 'This is a great sum of good money, and handsomely paid, as was to be expected.'
> Then he picked up the cloak and asked whose contribution that might be. No one answered him. Again he waved the cloak and asked who had given it, and laughed; but still no one answered. Then he said, 'Does none of you really know who owned this garment? Or does none of you dare to tell me?'
> 'Who do you think gave it?' asked Skarphedin.
> 'If you want to know,' said Flosi, 'I will tell you what I think. I think it was your father who gave it, "Old Beardless", for few can tell just by looking at him whether he is a man or woman.' (ch. 123)

As soon as Flosi picks up the cloak, if not before, it is all over. That is why Njal does not answer. His silence has to register his demoralization, his

sense of having blown it, his own deflation of knowing that he had not even
so much as anticipated this consequence of his well-intentioned gift. We
know Flosi's picking up the cloak and asking after its giver was not uttered
in a tone that showed genuine interest in an answer. The tone was con-
temptuous right from the start. Njal's silence tells us so, but so does Flosi's
gesture: *'again he waved* the cloak...'[13] He did not pick it up with the care
worthy an expensive garment, or worthy a gift, or even in a way indicative
of mere curiosity. Notice the narrator's reticence in informing us about
Flosi waving the cloak the first time. He delays; he waits discreetly, as if
allowing Flosi a second chance, a chance to backtrack and reconsider his
tone and his gesture. He thus waits for Flosi to confirm his hostility a second time before reporting to us what occurred the first time. Masterful.[14]

Cloaks are often given as an added generous gesture of good will to conclude a settlement; for example, Hrut to Osvifr (ch. 12). But a cloak was the
exact wrong gift to have given Flosi on this occasion. He did not pick up
the boots and wave them. The cloak reminds him of another gift of a cloak,
a return gift, he had received some two weeks earlier.

There is a small but surmountable problem. The cloak Flosi gave
Hoskuld was a *skikkja*; Njal gives Flosi a *slæðr*, each rendered in English as
'cloak'.[15] Various commentators have suggested that a *slæðr* is more ornate,
ambiguous as to whether it is appropriately a male or a female garment.[16]
But Egil's best friend Arinbjorn gave Egil a silk *slæðr*, and if Egil can handle
a silk *slæðr* so can Flosi. Egil even composed a verse about his *slæðr*, he was
so taken with it. Years later Egil thought his son Thorstein not man enough
to presume to wear it, and considered it a betrayal when his son did wear
it at his mother's suggestion without Egil's permission. The misuse of the
slæðr merited another verse. Egil was not a cross-dresser, and woe to the
academic who might suggest his prized garment was effeminate.[17]

One would love to know how far away Skarphedin stands from Flosi,
whether he is arrayed in front of him, directly in his line of vision. I have no
idea how far Skarphedin's position at the middle bench is from where the

13. The Icelandic is more explicit, literally, 'A second time, he waved it. . .'.
14. Contrast Allen, 226 n. 28.
15. The one Hrut gave Osvifr was a *skikkja*.
16. EÓS 1954: 312–13 n. 4.
17. *Egils saga*, chs. 68, 82; see Dronke, 13; Ármann, 199. Moreover, it is clear that Flosi knows
    who gave the cloak and thus he must understand that it was only meant as a conciliatory
    gesture, not as a mocking one.

money is piled up. The suggestion, however, is that Skarphedin is prominently situated. That too cannot have exerted any calming influence on a
Flosi already on edge. Skarphedin's presence would test any person's ability
to maintain cool reason.

Why though does Flosi direct his insult at Njal? Njal did not kill Hoskuld.
Njal has meant well throughout this whole proceeding. Flosi's own chief
advisors invoke Njal's merit as a reason for Flosi to choose a peaceful course
(Runolf, ch.115). When he accedes to Hall's request that he agree to a settlement, Flosi himself invokes Njal as the reason he will do so: 'Njal fully
deserves that I grant him this' (ch. 122). Perhaps Flosi constructs a causal
chain in which Njal could plausibly be seen as the first cause of all his troubles. Whose idea was it to marry Hoskuld to Hildigunn? Who sought out
whom to propose the marriage (ch. 97)? Maybe he sees Njal, as indeed he so
often is, as the author of these events. But what is to be gained by insulting
the respected old Njal? Could it be that Flosi is playing to an audience not
all of which is as well disposed toward Njal as the narrator would have us
believe? As a realistic matter it would be impossible for someone as politically involved as Njal not to have made enemies along the way, but if he
has, only Hallgerd and Flosi give such un-nuanced voice to it.

Even were that so, going after Njal harkens back to Hrut challenging an
old Mord, and though Mord got jeered at, Hrut knew he had done nothing
to be proud of. Njal is now so old he must be lifted off the horse he rides and
'borne' indoors (ch. 118).[18] And it is precisely on the issue of mocking an old
man that Skarphedin first hits back at Flosi: 'It is wrong to mock him in his
old age and no worthy man has ever done that before. You can be quite sure
he is a man, for he has fathered sons on his wife; and we[19] have let few of our
kinsmen lie unavenged at our doors.' Skarphedin's answer does not require
much explication except to note something of an 'anti-leveling oath' in it.
You, Flosi, were about to accept compensation, I swear we would never
have done so were our situations reversed. In an indirect way he is thus
indicating that they did not leave their own Hoskuld unavenged, for whom
Hoskuld Hvitanesspriest was marked for death by the deep logic of the
balanced-exchange model of the feud and homophonic attraction. I do not

---

18. Cf. the treatment of old Hall of Sida (ch. 147), who also is taken off his horse, kissed, but
instead of being borne into the house is led into the house between Kari and Thorgeir, no
carrying implied.

19. Skarphedin is also contrasting Njal's sons, the 'we', with their father who was too willing in
the sons' minds to leave his kinsmen unavenged.

want to push that very far, but Hoskuld Njalsson is the only kinsman he could be referring to that could be considered unavenged, the benefit of Amundi having killed Lyting not accruing to the Njalssons.

We are asked to suspend some minor disbelief and not question too closely where Skarphedin got the blue trousers to fling, or why Flosi should be so willing to play the straight man by asking Skarphedin why he should need pants more than a cloak:[20] 'you certainly will [need them] if you are, as I have heard, the mistress of the Svinafell Troll, who uses you as a woman every ninth night.' Remarkably, to claim a man is a woman every *ninth* night is specifically banned by the Norwegian Gulathing law.[21] Skarphedin is insulting Flosi with a *níð* of ancient vintage.

As noted, Flosi is a strange mixture, a complex character, his native intelligence and capacity for cool rationality marred by virulent eruptions of irrationality. His irrationality looks almost contrived at times, as if he decides to misbehave and be stupid for the hell of it, or because his bad angel whispered some enticement in his ear—as when he later pays Asgrim an unwelcome visit and more. But he also has the Njal-like ability to predict the exact consequences of strategies advocated by the hotheads in his entourage. Several chapters *before* he kicked over the pile of silver and insulted Njal he had this to say to the hotheads Grani Gunnarsson and Gunnar Lambason:

> 'I feel that you and many others are now demanding something that you would later give much never to have taken part in. I realize only too well that even though we kill Njal *or* his sons, they are men of such family and standing that we shall be faced with such consequences that we shall be forced to grovel at the feet of many men and beg them for help before we get clear of trouble. And you can also be sure that many who now are rich would be stripped of wealth, and some would lose their lives as well.' (ch. 117)

That summarizes much of the plot of the remainder of the saga. But it also includes one very unsettling phrase, even before the 600 ounces is assembled and rejected amidst insults hurled at Njal. What do we make of

20. It is not clear as to whether the blue breeches are women's wear or men's. They are called *brœkr* here (*brók* sg.; *brœkr* pl). Hallgerd's nickname rendered Long-Legs is in fact *langbrók*, long breech (where it refers not to trousers, but rather to her height), but then Skarphedin is wearing partly-blue *brœkr* too (ch. 120). Whether the breeches are a kind of female underwear, 'bloomers', which Flosi needs every ninth night to allure his demon lover, or whether he needs them better to play the man, the insult is the same. EÓS 1954: 314 n. 2; Helga Kress 1977: 312–13.
21. NGL I: 57.

'though we kill Njal *or* his sons'—which suggests the possibility of target-ing Njal alone to avenge the killing of Hoskuld? Can this be? Magnusson/ Pálsson, and Cook too, try to take some of the sting away by translating 'Njal *and* his sons', but the Icelandic has the adversative conjunction *eða*, 'or'.

The difficulty largely disappears when we remember who and what Flosi is responding to. Grani had just stated his desire to hit 'them' hard, not just for killing Hoskuld but for killing Thrain too. ' "When they killed Thrain at Markar River," said Grani, "and then his son Hoskuld, I made up my mind that I would never be reconciled with them. I would gladly be present when they are all killed." ' Grani is carrying a grudge against all Bergthorsknoll for actions in which Njal was clearly a participant that long pre-date Flosi's concern with the Sigfusson–Bergthorsknoll feud. Avenging Thrain is not even remotely a concern of Flosi's. Flosi is in effect quoting Grani's desire to hit any or all of them so as to dismiss it coldly and rationally. The irony is that Flosi becomes the hothead, attacks Njal indi-vidually with words as just discussed, and then indiscriminately, yet quite coldly, burns even innocent people by summer's end.

An enormous sum of 600 ounces of silver still remains. Some of the people wanted to reclaim their contribution, but Gudmund the Powerful staked out the moral high ground, saying he would never shame himself by taking back that which he had already given. He shamed the others into following his example. Snorri suggests that Gizur and Hjalti be charged with keeping the money. Says Snorri: 'I have a feeling that it will not be long before it is needed.' Again we see certain people playing banker, and though this particular fund is not specifically mentioned again, it does not need to be. Much of the funding of the award settling the Battle at the Althing the next year would have drawn on this sum. Its existence meant there was enough money available at the assembly to fund much of the 800 ounces that was paid over to Hall of Sida for waiving any claim for his son Ljot. I must reinvoke the perversity of incentives that such a fund created. It meant, as we saw with the purse Njal handed back to Gunnar, that should a debacle occur at the following Althing it was already substantially paid for. The saga will now move swiftly to the Burning, which is little more than a month away.

17

The Burning: Chapters 124–32

Flosi wastes no time. No sooner has his exchange with Skarphedin taken place than he summons his supporters, a hundred strong. They pledge their property and lives to the enterprise and swear oaths to that effect.[1] The thought of any compromise is rejected from the start: 'I will give my promise to the Sigfussons never to abandon this cause until one side or the other is destroyed.' Flosi more than fulfills his promise; both sides are destroyed.

Flosi gives instructions as to when and where they are to meet for the attack. Fire is already in the picture, at least figuratively: 'we shall. . . attack the Njalssons with fire and sword and not withdraw until they are all dead' (ch. 124). The people who are to ride west with Flosi meet at his farm; after matins they eat, and Flosi assigns the servants their tasks while he is gone. These men run farms, and provisioning the household comes first, which is why the attack is set after the haymaking is finished (ch. 124). The author's attention to detail matches Flosi's.

Flosi rides to Surt at Kirkby,[2] one of his allies, and prays there. Flosi would hardly take care, or the author take care for him, to mention mass, matins, and prayer unless to mark that Flosi was taking all the proper ritual precautions before a big enterprise. Not a hint of satire or of taking Christianity lightly is to be found in Flosi's pious preparations.[3]

'Burning inside' (*brenna inni*) is a term of art, a phrase meaning to kill by setting fire to a building housing people. This saga marks it as an especially egregious tactic, beyond the rules of fair play, something close to what we would designate a war crime. Fire does not discriminate among its victims;

1. Compare the oath of Kari, Mord, and Thorgeir Skorargeir to pledge their lives to their cause until Kari releases them (ch. 135).
2. This is not Otkel's farm; they merely share a name.
3. Orri 2000: 44: 'Flosi was entirely conscious of the wrong he was about to do, and he resented having to do it'; Flosi might have known he would resort to fire if he had to, but he hardly knew if he would have to until he saw whether a conventional attack would first fail.

it kills women and children. Fire saves having to draw on much courage, by sparing having to go hand-to-hand as long. It bears a heavy symbolic load, as it is one of the chief bases the author presents for distinguishing the moral order before the Conversion with the one that replaced it.

In 1255 a certain Finnbjorn Helgason, a retainer of King Hakon, in a shouting match with Bishop Heinrek (bishop of the northern Icelandic diocese, 1247–61), says: 'all know that burners are deemed the most abhorrent outcasts in both God's law and man's.'[4] But Bishop Heinrek concedes nothing to Finnbjorn; he claims that the burners of Flugumýr were justified,[5] considering the killings and humiliations that they had suffered before. Burning is thus not so unthinkable in the Sturlung Age that it is not part of the toolkit of the big power players; nor is a churchman reticent about making arguments in its defense. Our author, not given to easy moralizing, can be seen to split some of the difference between Finnbjorn and the Bishop, though he tilts the balance much more toward Finnbjorn. He believes that the Burning was an evil deed and shows little sympathy for most of the Burners, yet he does not paint their leader, the man who alone made the decision, as an evil man. Flosi in *Njála's* view is a victim of circumstance and perhaps of his times.[6]

---

4. *Þorgils saga skarða*, ch. 57; 'abhorrent outcasts' renders *brennuvargar*; the reference is not to mere arsonists but to those who burn people inside; in *Jónsbók* (7.30) the term is expanded to include burners of ships, haystacks, and shielings. In *Erik's Law of Zealand*, (c.1300) II §xv (DGL 5: 90–1) re *morthbrand* (arson murder), the burner is to be punished capitally, burned himself or broken on the wheel. *Morthbrand* is the only offense punished by death in the Danish provincial laws. (Finnbjorn, by the way, was married to Oddny, illegitimate daughter of Orm of Svinafell, Flosi's niece, eight generations removed.)

5. There are three famous examples of 'burning in' from the Sturlung period, the burning at Flugumýr in 1253 most likely occuring in the author's lifetime: burning of Langahlid, 1197, burning of Thorvald Vatnsfirðing, 1228; *Guðmundar saga dýra*, chs. 14–15; *Íslendinga saga*, chs. 67, 172–4.

6. Sagaworthy burnings are somewhat harder to find in the pre-Christian period. Ari Thorgilsson records one in c.962, which formed the basis of *Hænsa-Þóris saga; Íslendingabók*, ch. 5. There are no other classic examples of burning inside in Iceland in the family sagas. There are cases of burning farms to destroy property, not to kill people, though two women burn when they refuse to leave in one such case; *Harðar saga Grímkelssonar*, ch. 21. One scoundrel who is about to be outlawed burns all his property and his household members lest anyone get anything from him; *Reykdæla saga*, ch. 3. There are attempts: *Ljósvetninga saga*, ch. 20 (post Conversion). For a comparison of the burnings in *Njála* and *Hænsa-Þóris saga*, see Müller. Cf. Bennett. If *Njáls saga* raises serious moral concerns about burning as a tactic, it should be noted that other sagas, when dealing with events in Norway, seem rather blasé about 'burning in', and likewise *Landnámabók* about events during the settlement period; e.g. *Egils saga*, chs. 22, 46; *Gísla saga*, ch. 3, *Óláfs saga Tryggvasonar*, ch. 34, A ms (tr. Andersson 2003): ch. 32; *Landnámabók*: S 42, H 31; S 125, H 97 (slave's work); S 348 (those inside surrender, no loss of life). In Norway, buildings were made of wood and were easy to fire. It was easier to resist evil in Iceland where it was harder to get a fire going. Old Sæunn

The scene now shifts to Bergthorsknoll, and the next four chapters, dense with sustained power, replete with motivational difficulties, raise a multitude of interpretive possibilities, the ambiguities not signs of authorial incompetence but of his psychological and dramatic powers at their best.

Grim and Helgi are off visiting their children, who are being fostered at a farm about four miles away. They said they would not be home that evening. Some beggarwomen show up with the news that they saw the Sigfussons all armed heading toward Thrihyrning Ridge. Helgi and Grim realize that Flosi has come from the east and that they had better hurry home to be with Skarphedin. Back at Bergthorsknoll, Bergthora asks everyone to choose their favorite food, because it is the last she will serve. If Grim and Helgi, she says, arrive this evening that will prove her prediction true. Bergthora is feeling augury in the air, as so many saga characters do, but this is not like the portentous vision Hjalti needed to interpret in chapter 125; the meaning of this one is clear. They all know from Ingjald of Keldur to expect an attack this summer. That must be why they have apparently increased the size of their household so that it includes about thirty men (ch. 128), up from the nearly twenty-five mentioned earlier in the summer (ch. 124), although these could be mere approximations indicating the same number of people.

Njal involuntarily confirms his wife's prediction; he has a vision of the gable walls collapsing and blood all over the food. When Njal sees augury, given his reputation, it has a greater effect on the household than when Bergthora makes ominous predictions: 'Everyone was greatly perturbed except Skarphedin, who told them that they must not wail or do anything disgraceful that people would talk about, "for our behavior will be judged by stricter standards than that of others, and that is as it should be"' (ch. 127). Skarphedin in his own way is a stickler for propriety. He keeps exactly to his place fifth in line; his hair is carefully combed; and now that they have a good chance of dying, they must behave with sagaworthy impeccability. There is a cold aestheticism to Skarphedin's style that is almost dandyish in its commitment to proper forms.

He is also ever-so-slightly owning up. If Flosi seeks the blessings of the Christian God before he embarks on this major mission, then Skarphedin

---

was not being wholly foolish to want Skarphedin to get rid of the chickweed; we must assume that Melkolf had plenty of hay to set Otkel's storehouse on fire.

accepts a certain justice in their being thus sought out. Because kill-ing Hoskuld was an evil deed, no one will cut us any slack. We must act grandly from now on; style points are everything. The demand to comport themselves well is also made of the women and servants, another minor but telling mark of the inclusivity of all household members in household repu-tation and fortunes. The little people's performances matter too.

Grim and Helgi then arrive, and people are unnerved that they do. They tell the news, and Njal issues an order, still *pater familias*: no one is to go to bed that night. The irony is that he will purposely take to bed himself, and in grand style.

The Decision to Go Inside

The Njal forces array themselves in front of the house; Flosi and his men approach. They are still out of firing range and we listen to discussions on both sides. Flosi comes to a halt, lamenting having to attack if the enemy stays outside: 'I suspect we will never get the better of them if they stay out of doors.' Flosi outnumbers his opposition by perhaps four to one, if we make his hundred men a long hundred. But this is more than mere autho-rial lionization of the fighting prowess of Skarphedin and Kari, or deni-gration of some of Flosi's troops. Flosi is aware of an important social and military truth. First, the Njalssons have the house to cover their rear. But that hardly matters, because Flosi can still flank them.

The point is that Flosi knows that very few of his supporters have any personal stake in the outcome. They are there because they have debts they owe Flosi or the Sigfussons, or were recruited by kin and friends of the principal parties. They are just bodies, and mostly do not give much of a damn. They can be relied on only to fight enough so as not to disgrace themselves. There can be little doubt that they will not fight as hard as the Bergthorsknoll crew, who know they are fighting for their lives.

This is one of the paradoxes of the support-mustering process, when bodies are recruited either to attend the Thing to keep cases from being railroaded, or for combat. The more men you recruit, the farther away from close kin and close friends and the personally aggrieved you get, the less committed to your cause the people you recruit are. Flosi is explicit about the problem: 'there are many here who are showing less fight than

they said they would.' These are the people who will be the first to take
time-outs, the last to go forward, the first to flee, and they are the ones who
are most eager to talk to their friends on the other side with equally small
stakes in the matter about stopping any fighting. Were it mercenaries Flosi
had in tow, who have to fight at least well enough to get hired on for the
next affray, he would get a better performance. Nor are there any specially-
armed retainers, except for a very few household men who owe Flosi their
position and hopes for advancement.

Given the lack of élan of many of his men, Flosi will now find it prudent
and necessary to use fire. It is Skarphedin who provides the reason: 'They
will assume, and quite rightly, that it will cost them their lives if we escape.'
One must be impressed with Skarphedin's cold confidence, but when he
makes that statement I believe him. So does Flosi, who does not even have
to hear it to have already factored it in to his decision tree. With a muster
of a hundred (recall that the largest pre-Conversion muster in the saga was
forty) this is, measured on an Icelandic scale, beginning to look like war,
not feud, yet the feuding rules still exert considerable force. The notion
of turn-taking survives. If Flosi botches his turn, then it is Skarphedin's
turn to play offense. When it was Thorgeir Skorargeir's and Kari's turn it is
rather revealing what havoc one or two gifted killers could cause. Imagine
if one of them were Skarphedin. Flosi knows he cannot leave without
killing them.

Then the scene shifts to Njal and his sons and Kari. The scene recalls
Njal's blunder with the gift of the cloak. But unlike that scene, this time we
get a discussion; reasons are set forth for the positions advanced. The passage requires full quotation:

> Njal said to his men, 'How many do you think they are?'
>
> 'They are a tightly knit force,' said Skarphedin, 'and strong in numbers,
> too; but they suspect that they will have a hard task to overcome us, and this
> is why they have halted.'
>
> 'I do not think so,' said Njal. 'I want everyone to go inside, for they found
> it hard to overcome Gunnar of Hlidarend, even though he was only one
> against many. This house is just as strongly built as his was and they will never
> be able to overcome us.'
>
> 'That is the wrong way to look at it,' said Skarphedin. 'The men who
> attacked Gunnar were chieftains of such character that they would have pre-
> ferred to turn back rather than burn him in his house. But these people will
> not hesitate to use fire if they cannot overcome us in any other way, for they
> will resort to any means to destroy us. They will assume, and quite rightly,

that it will cost them their lives if we escape. And I for one am reluctant to be suffocated like a fox in its den.'

Njal said, 'Now you are going to override my advice and show me disrespect, my sons—and not for the first time. But when you were younger you did not do so, and things went better for you then.'

'Let us do as our father wishes,' said Helgi. 'That will be best for all of us.'

'I am not so sure of that,' said Skarphedin, 'for he is a doomed man now. But still I do not mind pleasing my father by burning inside with him, for I am not afraid of dying.' (ch. 128)

Njal's son Helgi, remember, is prescient also. He too seems to have lost it. Neither Njal nor Helgi talk the language of prophecy, omen, or portent at all. In fact, Njal talks tactics, and military history, specifically about Gunnar's last stand. He notes the quality of Gunnar's house and how well his own compares; he invokes the success that Gunnar had—outnumbered forty to one—against much greater odds than they face now. His bringing up Gunnar's last stand is also something of an unconscious subsuming of his friend's saga into his own, and indicates a like desire to have his own death resound throughout the land as Gunnar's did.[7] There may even be a bit of wistfulness in recalling the 'glory years' of his alliance with Gunnar.

Whether Njal has lost it, or more nefariously still has it and means to take his family down with him, his ability to draw on his knowledge of law, the politics of feuding, and his astute assessment of character to construct very good probabilistic assessments of future behavior and events seems to have deteriorated. To be fair, Njal was never portrayed as an expert in combat or military tactics. He was good at handling the legal phases of the feud, good at counseling and plotting killing when that was necessary to maintain his position in the district, but he left the killing tactics to those, mainly his sons, whom he commissioned to carry out that kind of work. This feud, however, has metastasized into something he has never seen before.

He is at this last moment facing a hundred armed men or more, and wholly out of his element. He even fails at judging character, something at which he was without equal. Skarphedin is right in every respect, on tactics, the character of the enemy, reading exactly why they have pulled up. He also knows he is right, and does not press the matter unduly, though

7. For a detailed comparison of the attack on Gunnar and the Burning, see Bolton.

he makes clear to everyone the grounds of his views.[8] He defers to counsel he knows is suicidal out of a sense of decorum, because, as he ordered a few hours earlier, they must all hold themselves to the strictest standards of behavior. It would be unseemly to argue with his father now, even when the old man is dead wrong.

The chief interpretive quandary in this passage revolves around this question: if Njal is still prescient can we excuse him sending his sons, grandson, wife, and himself knowingly to death? Unless his prescience has shifted its proper terrain to mean it allows him no choice but that it must adhere to the plot of *Njáls saga*; and yet even in that case he is imposing his will against Skarphedin's. But why does the author make him out to be so wrong and Skarphedin so right? The author is not taking the Burning as a cheap fait accompli; there were choices to be made that could have averted it. His entire saga has shown that people make choices, some smart, some stupid, that affect outcomes. People choose how to respond to challenges, and their responses are not dictated, except by an occasional saga topos which seems to require a guest to announce which day he is returning from a feast so he can be conveniently ambushed. The Burning may be an historical event that had to take place, but the author invented characters like Skarphedin, and he has used as much of his own free will in telling this story as he generously grants his characters. No, it is not that Njal knows it is his saga and it is called *Brennu-Njáls saga*. The action, the conversation before entering the house, everything the characters do, bespeaks choices argued for and made knowingly after a deliberative vetting of views.

Is it that Njal is just old and tired? He is a very old man now and he is ready to retire. His grandest strategy, the fostering of Hoskuld, undertaken to put the feud back into remission, failed. Skarphedin's sense of his father being doomed, *feigr*, may mean nothing more than that he is old and failing. His going to bed early, as Skarphedin remarks as his father lies down under the oxhide to die, is entirely to be expected, 'for he is an old man.' Even perhaps more revealing is the reading in the Reykjabók manuscript which adds, when Njal says to Bergthora, 'Let us go to our bed and lie down',

---

8. See the burning of Langahlid for a dispute on whether to defend from inside or outside; *Guðmundar saga dýra*, chs. 14–15.

this: 'for I have long been fond of ease and comfort.'[9] In short, he is indicating with some self-directed mockery that he has had enough.

His prescience, as I tried to show very early on, rarely, in fact only once, exceeded the naturalistic bounds that come with being a very cagey counselor who partly sets about creating the events that he predicts. Though old and tired, he has more than enough energy left to orchestrate his death such that his final taking to bed works to enact three separate rituals simultaneously. How he does this will require further explication below. In dying he knows exactly what he is up to. He will greatly influence events after his death by dying as he arranged to do; he can reasonably predict this. The interpretive problem is that for every fact we can allege for Njal having lost it, we can show one that cuts the other way. That means we have hardly disposed of the niggling suspicion that he knows his advice to go inside is bad and that he desires the results that obtain.

Let me rephrase the problem as we have developed it so far. The state of his prescience is almost a red herring. We are thus left with the need to ascertain Njal's motives for advising to defend from within. He has heard Skarphedin's apt analysis and persists in the face of it. Nothing in the remainder of the Burning will show that Njal has lost IQ; so it is not far-fetched to believe that he desires exactly what Skarphedin says he does, that he die and that he require his sons to obey him as they used to do, so that they will die too. Helgi says that it is best to follow their father's advice, but look closely at Skarphedin's reply: 'I am not so sure of that, for he is a doomed man now. But still I do not mind pleasing my father by burning in the house with him, for I am not afraid of dying.' Skarphedin is hardly being dutiful for the reasons Njal sets forth: that when they obeyed him things went better for them. He knows that following Njal's advice means they will burn to death, and that, as he rather pointedly indicates, is what he believes his father intends. His last dutiful act of obedience is coldly undertaken: 'for I am not afraid of dying.'

Njal does not answer this sardonic acceptance of his counsel, but he is not silent because he is offended, or because he is despairing, as when he remained silent in the face of Flosi's repeated questions as to who gave the cloak, but because in this case he has gotten his way. Skarphedin fully

---

9. *Hefi ek lengi værugjarn verit; værr + gjarn*, to be eager for tranquility, comfort, snugness. There may also be a reference here to his good relations with his wife, as well as to the warmth of the fire.

understands that. Father wants them all to die. He will obey because his
dominant motive is to maintain decorum in this climactic act of his play—
he will do nothing to mar going out in style. His statement means he will
face his death knowingly, without illusions. He is also in a very small way
making amends to his father for killing Hoskuld. Very small indeed.

Why is Njal doing this? To avenge Hoskuld? Is his advice meant as
filicide by proxy? Is he repudiating his sons as Hallgerd and Hrut did to
Thjostolf? Njal cannot very well kill his own sons, but he can order them to
obey him in such a way that others will do the work. Balderdash, you say.
This is Njal, the man of good will, beardless, a loving husband, friend, and
foster-father. Let the author tell his story; stop trying to psychologize this.
But Skarphedin has already psychologized it. It is not me, but Skarphedin
who gives psychological reasons for Njal's suicidal advice. He is doomed,
he is old, and he is our old imperious father, demanding obedience one last
time, because that's the way he likes it. And how better to prove obedience
than by following a lethal order? Obedience is not tested if you want to do
what you are ordered, or even if it is smart to do what is ordered; it is tested
when it is observed in the face of knowing the command is misguided.

When Flosi offers passage to Njal he refuses: 'I have no wish to go outside, for I am an old man now and ill-equipped to avenge my sons, and
I do not want to live in shame.' He is too old to avenge them by his own
hand, but avenging with his own hands was not his style when younger
either. Is he too old to hire, or to advise those with enough muscle to do so?
Does he not *want* them avenged? No, that cannot be it. When Thorhalla
Asgrimsdottir says, as she takes passage outside the flaming house, 'I shall
urge my father and my brothers to avenge the killings that are committed
here,' Njal answers, 'You will do well, for you are a good woman.' Her
father and brother will play lead roles in taking action against the Burners.
Asgrim takes all the survivors of the fire into his own household, a testament not just to how astute Njal had been years earlier in allying himself
with that family via marriage, but also to Asgrim's wealth, which he would
need in order to make such a generous offer (ch. 132).

As we will see, Njal arranges to die a very Christian death, Christian in
the form his body will take at least. Absolutely no forgiveness is asked or
offered.[10] So yet again, and not surprisingly, we find that human motivation

---

10. Cf. the pious motive given by Vésteinn 1998: 200: 'there lies a more profound impulse. He
    wants to die with his sons in the hope that they will all receive forgiveness for their sins. His
    death signals a rejection of the old order and marks a step into the new one.' The view finds

is hard to discern, that various motives operate at the same time, not always consistently, that those that motivate the commencement of an action may not be those that motivate its continuance. Njal wants his sons dead, he wants them obedient as they had always been except for one rebellious deed, and he wants them avenged; or more precisely, he wants his own and Bergthora's deaths avenged, and knows that it will be impossible not to have those vengeances also accrue to his sons. He will do all he can to make sure the cause of avenging himself and even them will be popular.

Njal's Virtuoso Going to Bed for the Last Time

The sagas depict a strange retirement ritual, specifically a retirement from the harsh demands of the honor game and the duty of revenge. A man becomes too old, too weak, too frustrated, too despairing, and so takes himself out of the game. The classic cases saga readers know well: old Kveld-Ulf takes to bed when he hears of his son Thorolf's death in *Egils saga*; Havard takes to bed for three years at the killing of his son in the saga bearing his name; and Sturla consciously parodies the ritual in his saga when he 'mourns' the passing of his enemy Thorbjorg, for now that she is dead he no longer will have any fun avenging himself on her sons.[11] The elements of the ritual are quite simple: an ostentatious taking to bed, alleging old age and grief as the reason. This taking-to-bed functions also as a plea for help, that the old man alone is not up to doing his duty unaided. Should help not be forthcoming then one is to read the bed-taking as a formal announcement that he is no longer a player in the game; he has retired. Njal is performing this ritual when he takes to bed, and in case we miss the point that he is enacting it, he first states that he is too old to avenge his sons. And Skarphedin seems to understand the purport—'Father is going to bed ['retiring'] early. . . and that is only natural for he is an old man.'

scant textual support (absolutely no mention of forgiveness or of sin). Moreover, if 'the old order' is rejected it is an order that in this saga at least would not have sunk to the level of burning one's opponents.

11. *Egils saga*, ch. 24; Egil is also performing it before he composes *Sonatorrek*; see *Havarðar saga Ísfirðings* generally, and *Sturlu saga*, ch. 36; I treat this ritual quite fully in Miller 2011: 127–54. The ritual also appears in *Beowulf*, vv. 2444–71.

He combines the retirement ritual with a second ritual when Bergthora refuses Flosi's offer of passage, citing her marriage to Njal as her reason for refusing. She turns to her husband, asking what they should do now. Njal says, 'Let us go to our bed and lie down.' They are re-enacting the marriage ritual, with great wit, by following the precise letter of the law which requires that a valid marriage be sealed by going to bed 'in light',[12] that is, illuminated by firelight, visibly, and witnessed. This time the light is somewhat brighter and warmer than when they were first married, and this time we are all witnesses to the consummation, in the double sense that that word takes in this setting.

To the rituals of retirement and of marriage, add a third: martyrdom. We already touched on this when we discussed the author's penchant for undermining the miraculous, in this case by the arbitrary insertion of the detail of little Thord Karason's finger being burned off because he had stretched it outside the protection of the covering oxhide. But there is more to this miracle martyrdom; it attests to Njal's intelligent management of the new faith's proclivity to look to corpses for miracles to make sure that he, and his sons, to the extent he cares about them, will be avenged.

Njal is also deploying the taking-to-bed ritual as an old man's plea for aid in revenge-taking. Njal wants a ritualized death that can mobilize people on his behalf, and that is partly why he means to die as a saint, in the new Christian style of passive martyrdom. He ironically goes down fighting by lying down, a *passio*.[13] But not before he has prepared the miracle, ordering the steward to cover them with an oxhide and take note of exactly where they are. This is heroic death in the new style. The three cross themselves, commend their souls to God. The steward exits the burning building and tells his tale. Skarphedin too is not unimpressed: 'My father must be dead now, and not a groan or a cough has been heard from him.' But Njal needs to be able to count on others to direct the miracle. He can only do so much. Shift ahead now to see how well the people of his party know their parts, for everything depends on their putting on the proper show.[14]

---

12. *Grágás* II 66: *gangi brúðgumi í ljósi í sama sæing konu*, 'a bridegroom goes in light [with torches] into the same bed with a woman', which is a necessary condition of a valid marriage.

13. This kind of irony figures in many of the early martyrdom stories, the classic instance being St. Perpetua, who sees her passive endurance of torture as active gladiatorial combat with the devil.

14. Contrast how the congregation of Father Zossima mismanages assuring that his body met the requirements of sainthood in *The Brothers Karamazov* (vii.1). And note also the analogue to the bloody-token ceremony in mobilizing Njal's corpse to aid his own revenge.

Kari knows, or has been instructed, just what to do. He asks Hjalti to accompany him to look for Njal's bones, 'for everyone will accept your account and your impressions' (ch. 132). Hjalti is thus given the role that mimics exactly that of the judge in ordeals of hot iron: he is to declare the state of the body, whether it passed the test of fire. They start out with a party of fifteen; they summon others along with Njal's neighbors until the group numbers a hundred. Hjalti asks Kari where to look: 'They dug through a deep layer of ashes, and underneath they found the oxhide; the flames had shriveled it. They lifted it up, and found Njal and Bergthora lying there, quite unmarked by the flames. They all gave praise to God for this, and thought it a great miracle.' So far it could not be better managed. The large audience is already proclaiming a miracle. Then follows, lest we too start proclaiming, or blaming medieval credulity, the detail about the boy's finger. The bodies are carried out and everyone approaches to look at them.

> 'How do these bodies impress you?' asked Hjalti.
> 'We would rather hear your verdict first,' they replied.
> 'I shall put it into plain words,' said Hjalti. . . 'Njal's countenance and body appear to have a radiance which I have never seen on a dead man before.'
> They all agreed.

One must admire the political acumen evident in the account. Kari does not solicit any random man to officiate, and 'officiate' is the proper term, at this unveiling and quasi-canonization. He seeks out Hjalti Skeggjason to play the key role in finding and declaring the facts. Hjalti, along with Gizur and Hall of Sida,[15] were the leaders of the Christian party at the Althing. Hjalti, in a country as yet without a clerical hierarchy, is about as high-ranking a Christian as there is. In this regard too it is noteworthy that Hjalti is sought out by people with troublesome visions for their inter-pretation, and he is also a healer, who heals Ingjald of Keldur's leg-wound (chs. 125, 132). His healing of Ingjald occurs right after the 'miracle of the preserved body', completing the miracle story with the standard healing that proves Njal's holiness, though this healing, in yet another mark of saga

---

15. Each side is blessed by the presence of Christian leaders: Gizur and Hjalti, on behalf of Njal, and Hall of Sida with Flosi. Bolton, 205, notes that the opposing groups in the second half of the saga are not in any way divided by religion, both sides making about an equivalent number of gestures in the proper direction.

realism, still leaves Ingjald with a limp.[16] Hjalti is something of the resident Christian holy man, just the right person for dealing with the otherworldly and magical. It is certainly not for Kari to make the judgment about Njal's corpse; his judgment would be dismissed as marred by interest.

Njal got his wish, for having his body be the object of a miracle before a large audience is to take a big step toward recruiting people to the anti-Burner cause. Like his foster-son, Njal will die in the style of a martyred saint, and people will flock to his cause because of it. Njal has already intuited the politics of sanctity and how important saints were to politics, not infrequently to the politics of revenge.

Credit Njal with having his cake and eating it too. He gets to take down his sons by demanding that they obey him and die with him. And then, because of the perfect way he manages his death, he makes sure that he will be avenged. Does he also mean for his sons to be avenged? That is a harder question, but it is the Burning that will be avenged, not just the Burning of Njal. He cannot exclude the other victims of the flames from being included by the avengers; that is indeed beyond his control. Yet neither Kari nor Skarphedin are willing to trust that they will be properly avenged by Njal's miracle-making. Kari will thus specifically dedicate his last ten killings to his son. Skarphedin, not unlike his father, will prepare from inside the burning building to make sure they are *all* avenged, preparations only slightly less deliberate than his father's.

Skarphedin's Miracle

After the radiance of Njal's body has been proclaimed, another miracle awaits to be witnessed. It too is man-made, but not contrived in any suspect sense. The miracle is wrought by Skarphedin. Compare the miracles of father and son. Father lies down, and makes use of a prop, the oxhide. Skarphedin dies on his feet, except he has pretty near no legs to stand on. He never goes down; he never falls, even with his legs beneath the knee burnt to the bone. Now that is a miracle. It is as if he means to construct an emblem of contrast with his father; both are fearless in the face of death, but

16. Contrast Thorhall Asgrimsson's violent self-healing of the infection on his leg which immediately cures him completely; no limp at all (ch. 145).

one insists on being horizontal, the other on being vertical. The latter orientation is somewhat more difficult to manage. Skarphedin, like his father, needs a prop to carry this off, and so he manages to get wedged between the gable and a fallen beam. But father and son do not come by their props in the same way. One observes a level of calculation in Njal's staging of events that one does not see in Skarphedin's. Dying right, in Skarphedin's moral system, cannot be achieved by lying down or even by going down. But lucky for him the gable and roof collapsed in such a way as to pin him upright. Still, though the fire got him from the knees down, the rest of him, with no oxhide to assist, remains *óbrunnit*, unburned, that adjective being only elsewhere applied to those under the oxhide. The other victims of the fire are evidenced by their bones; nothing else of them remains.

Yet Skarphedin is no less ingenious about using his death to ensure revenge than was his father. So fiercely competitive is this world of precedence and honor (son vs. father) that we can see yet another competition for who can act best under fire (brother-in-law vs. brother-in-law). Kari loses an implicit *mannjafnaðr*, a man-comparing, with Skarphedin over who should try to escape first, the better man being the one who is less eager to leave the flames. You go first; no, you go first. OK, I will go first, says Kari, for 'it is every man's instinct to save his own life' (ch. 129). Skarphedin will never let himself lose that contest, a variant of the game of chicken, with the only other man still alive who could possibly challenge him. Kari had even conceded earlier that Skarphedin is without peer. That compliment, coming from Kari, led to Skarphedin's ninth and final grin, perhaps the only one indicating satisfaction, mixing the pleasure of a compliment from a man whose compliments matter, with the pleasure of the action that elicited it: catching Hroald Ozurarson flush in the face with the upper horn of his axe, killing him instantly. Says Kari: 'There is no escaping you, Skarphedin; you are the bravest of us all' (ch. 128).

Getting Kari out of the burning building is Skarphedin's version of the oxhide. He thus arranges that Kari leave the flames, and he knows that Kari will take revenge. He in fact charges Kari to avenge them as he launches him forth: 'I shall laugh, brother-in-law, if you escape, for you will avenge us all.' Kari is an extension of Skarphedin's will, and this is confirmed by an unnamed Burner with inadvertent insight when he mistakes Kari escaping with clothes and hair on fire for a flaming brand that he believes Skarphedin has thrown at them:

Kari took hold of a blazing brand and ran up the sloping cross-beam; he hurled the brand down from the wall at those who were in his way outside, and they scattered. Kari's clothes and hair were on fire by now, as he threw himself down off the wall and dodged away in the thick of the smoke.

Someone said, 'Was that a man jumping down from the roof?'

'Far from it,' said someone else. 'It was Skarphedin throwing another brand at us.' (ch. 129)

That 'someone else' had no idea of how precisely right he was. The impeccable artistry of the writer is again on display.[17]

Return to the corpse-unveiling, and look at it from the viewpoint the narrator gives us, which is that of the people gathered at the scene. Skarphedin's eyes are open; he has bitten down on his lip. They take him out and strip his body. They gaze upon his mutilated corpse as it stares back at them. This had to be unsettling, given whose eyes they were, but no: 'they all agreed that they found it less uncomfortable to see Skarphedin dead than they had expected: for no one felt any fear of him.' And this group is mostly made up of people partial to him, some of them are his friends. What an homage! People he has never harmed, nor sought to harm, can finally relax in his presence.

I am hard-pressed to find a more succinct, and thus greater, testament to the anxiety that filled the air when he was present. Surely others had the same eerie capacity to instill fear and unease, without being perversely cruel and insane like Nero, Caligula, or Caracalla, but neither Achilles, David, Caesar, Sulla (who comes close), Wallenstein, Frederick the Great, nor Genghis, all of whom had that force in their sheer presence, ever had it expressed in such a powerful way. An aura of threat radiated from him. He killed many fewer men than Gunnar, than Kari, than Flosi. It was a mélange of the grins, the ugly mouth, the pallor, the devastating wit, but I think it must have mostly been the effort that people could discern it took for him to keep himself *löngum vel stilltr*, for the most part well under control, that unnerved everyone around him. The irony is that it was his good behavior that was so unnerving. He did not throw tantrums, but you knew that he leapt through the air, cleft Thrain's skull, and could not

---

17. Clover (1982: 69) perfectly sums up the compositional tour de force of the Burning thus: 'the narrative marshals through the tragic scenes no fewer than thirty-one named men and women. . . at least twelve of whom are distinct personalities with a particular set of reasons for being in that place at that time. The picture bears little resemblance to the mediaeval artist's depiction of a crowd as identical people acting in unison.'

be bothered to kill the little whelps in Thrain's party. His very restraint was more menacing than reassuring. The non-fakeable leakages are the key: the paleness, the teeth. Though grins are fakeable, it is clear his were not faked, though more than a few of them were performed with a sense that they were unnerving and not quite appropriate. They were, quite simply, threatening.

Gunnar's dominance and popularity, his being the best fighter, the handsomest guy, the best athlete, created challengers as if by spontaneous generation. Skarphedin's reputation was as a man absolutely not to be messed with. No challengers, no one was looking to gain reputation by having beaten Skarphedin. Thorkel Hake thinks to answer the insult of having disgusted his shepherd, the insult inviting revenge as an answer, and soon wishes he had not presumed. Only one person seems unintimidated by Skarphedin, and that person is almost otherworldly in his refusal to abide by social norms—Hrapp. And even he is only responding to Skarphedin's death-threat to him: 'Hold your tongue, Skarphedin; I won't hesitate to apply my axe to your skull' (ch. 91). But the author intervenes to punish Hrapp for having dared to show no fear in the face of Skarphedin by treating him to death by sidekick, a pair of them. Grim and Helgi kill him, though the author repents enough to give Hrapp one last wonderful line.

And Skarphedin's will? The smoke could not get him to close his eyes, nor could the fire nor near-leglessness get him to fall. He made sure his axe did not melt either, it being imbued with some of his personhood—one imagines its edge mimicking his grin as it assists the fallen beam to hold him upright—for the axe would pass to his avenger. And those crosses burned onto his chest and back? Those looking at him thought he had branded himself with them, but they are in a pious mood at the moment and are anxious to see him making a visible concession to the new spiritual order.[18] The narrator takes no position on the matter. He describes in his own voice only that there were two 'marks' on him in the shape of a cross, but then shifts to the people in the scene to have them make the judgment that Skarphedin had intentionally branded himself. It is not clear he did anything of the sort.

18. See discussion on pp. 303–4.

Flosi's Flinch

After Kari's escape the action is rapid and the details reveal that mundane logistics are seldom beneath the author's sight lines and must be accounted for. Thus when Thorgeir Skorargeir, Njal's nephew, invites Kari to stay with him, he indicates that he will take care of managing Kari's farm out in Dyrholm, which is rather close to Flosi's region of control (ch. 131). Mord offers good advice not to plunder the Sigfusson farms, so as to give the Sigfussons reason to travel there to visit their women, to help manage their farms, thus rendering themselves vulnerable to attack as they travel to and fro. Flosi must now lodge and feed a large band. For this reason he sends men throughout the district to increase his stocks. It is homely stuff like this, the *Stofffreude*, the details like those noted at the start of this chapter, that makes me credit the author as having a special claim to be taken seriously as a political and social theorist, precisely because he stays away from high abstraction and, like Thucydides, builds his theory of his society from the ground up. Nor is it just about heroics; the mundane matters just as much.

At the Burning we see an effective Flosi, smart, authoritative. He correctly understands the meaning for them of Kari's escape. Flosi makes another of the author's mandatory before-and-after-the-Conversion comparisons by declaring Kari the second coming of Gunnar (ch. 130). The Burners' response to the news of Kari's escape, which they received from a certain Geirmund,[19] is handled with astute psychological realism, as one sees the Burners' sense of accomplishment and relief change to disbelief, then to the sickening feeling of realizing what they are now in for. Flosi invites all the Sigfussons to live with him. Some people still given to glorying in their feat poetize; Flosi, more ambivalent about the greatness of their deed—*stórvirki ok illvirki*, 'great [extreme?] and evil action'—mocks the boasting. One of the men wants to make sure Skarphedin is dead, probably because they also had thought Kari was, and had been sadly mistaken. Then we get a hauntingly evocative pre-Dantesque image: 'The fire burned fitfully, at times flaring up then sinking again.' Skarphedin's spirit

---

19. See Clover (2012: 115–21) on Geirmund's function as a provider of proof of facts, otherwise hard to prove, given the narrator's reluctance to report things he claims no special authority as narrator to know.

seems somehow to be present in those struggling flames, for he, alive or dead, utters a verse invoking a weeping woman. Dead, he can allow himself to express a hint of Eros, unless we credit him with that when he called Hallgerd *púta*. Flosi orders the stupid men who still want to gawk to move quickly; they have business to settle with Ingjald of Keldur, who broke faith with them.

'Flosi never boasted about the deed, no one ever saw any fear in him' (ch. 131). That statement comes one chapter after Flosi played a game of chicken with Ingjald of Keldur who, recall, had forfeited life and property by not showing up for the attack, as the oath they all swore at the Althing a couple of months earlier stipulated. They meet on opposite sides of the Rangriver. Ingjald defiantly rejects Flosi's demand that he give him self-judgment— actually a mitigation, because Flosi recognizes Ingjald was in a difficult situation with obligations to both sides. Flosi says if Ingjald is not *ragr* he will sit still while he sends him a little present. Ingjald says he will not move. Flosi hurls a spear at Ingjald which hits him in his thigh and sticks in his saddle-tree. Ingjald yanks the spear out. Now it is your turn not to move 'if you are not *blauðr* ('soft,' doing the same work as *ragr*)'. When Flosi sees Ingjald's return gift heading straight for him, he yanks his horse back and the spear goes right through Thorstein Kolbeinsson, Flosi's brother's son.

What do we make of the judgment regarding Flosi's fearlessness? One can imagine some would not have flinched. Ingjald did not (and with no one behind him to suffer the consequences if he did). I cannot imagine any of these flinching: Thjostolf, Hrut, Hrapp, Skarphedin, Gunnar, Kari, Otkel's brother Hallbjorn, Thorgeir Skorargeir, or the two Norwegians lodged at Sandgil; nor, if they could be put to the test, Bergthora, Hallgerd, or Hildigunn. These people, we guess—and know in the case of Ingjald—would be able to suppress their flinch reflex when put to the test. Flosi comes up short in comparison. The author will continue this ambivalent presentation of Flosi, but let us take the narrator at his word, which is actually not his but the view he attributes to other people in the community, that 'no one saw any fear in him'. Are we seeing here some concession to the local theory of courage that certain failures in what we might call stupid tests of courage, like games of chicken, are discounted? But the reader does not discount for Flosi here. His inability to suppress his flinch reflex cost him his nephew. Thorstein thought it safe to be located right behind his uncle; I guess that attests that Flosi's *reputation* for courage was seamless, though perhaps the real game of chicken was to see if you were man enough to stand behind Flosi in a game of chicken and not flinch. Suppressing the flinch reflex is connected with something we think of as courage, even if not being able to do so would not necessarily make you a coward. Flinching is exactly the reflex any person who plays contact sports must learn to suppress when necessary, or be deemed a failure. But whether you were able to suppress it would hardly determine whether you could face up to many kinds of danger that did not require its suppression.

This would all be beside the thirteenth-century-Icelandic point if within pages the author were not about to make an issue of Thorhall Asgrimsson's purely involuntary somatic responses precisely because they test local theories of courage and manliness too. We will also see Flosi behave not just courageously but almost affectlessly in many dangerous and tense situations. But we also saw him flinch, when the ability not to flinch was specifically the game being played. Perhaps that is why the author makes it up to Flosi for his flinch by showing him purposely invite death before jarl Sigurd (ch. 153). If I may employ a phrase I loathe: the author 'feels Flosi's pain' of being cast in the role he must play in this saga, and does him the favor of showing how much he suffers in the role; he also does him an even grander favor of making him as fully articulated and believable a character as any in the saga corpus.

Thorhall Asgrimsson Hears of Njal's Death

Before we leave these rich chapters we must deal with one more vignette: Thorhall's fainting. Thorhall is one of the more attractive characters in the saga. The good man cannot disguise how deeply he takes things to heart, and take them to heart he does. He means to be as cool as the next reticent Icelander, but his body keeps betraying him. Later he will burst into tears as large as hailstones (ch. 142). When his calf gets infected, it swells to the thickness 'of a woman's thigh'. Even with a real infection his leg seems to overreact, perhaps to fill the symbolic responsibilities that have been imposed upon it (ch. 135).

> Thorhall Asgrimsson was so shocked when he heard that his foster-father, Njal, had been burned to death that his whole body swelled up; a stream of blood spouted from his ears and could not be staunched, until he fell down

unconscious and the flow ceased of its own accord. Then he got up and said that he had not behaved like a man. 'My only wish now is to take vengeance for what has just happened to me upon those who burned Njal to death.'

The others said that no one would call his behavior shameful; but Thorhall replied that no one could stop people talking. (ch. 132)

Being laughed at for seizures or pratfalls such as slipping on the ice can prompt as much shame as embarrassment, and shame, if not embarrassment, can prompt murderous and vengeful impulses as well.[20] What Thorhall's friends are telling him is that as a matter of objective truth there was nothing enduringly shameful in his behavior, though he may not feel that way now. They are telling him that his swelling, bleeding, and fainting are the stuff of mere 'embarrassment', not shame, even if they have to use phrases instead of a single word to make the distinction.[21]

But Thorhall knows the agonistic world in which he lives, a world of highly competitive honor and shame. People, not even enemies, will use his swelling and seizure to make jokes at his expense. Friends are allowed some latitude to tease, as when the Njalssons laugh at Thorhall for the unstylish cloak he was wearing, though even then Thorhall was not amused. Instead of laughing along with them he took to dire prophecy: 'I shall have discarded it by the time I have to take redress for the death of my foster-father' (ch. 118). Rest assured that Thorhall will *never* find anything funny about his fainting. So powerful is his mortification at his body's reaction that he displaces the claim he has against the Burners. He now wants to take revenge on them, not for burning Njal, but for the reaction that his body had to the news.

Thorhall feels shame; his companions feel it incumbent upon themselves to assure him he is being too hard on himself. They behave with exquisite tact, for it must have been awkward to witness his seizure. How sweet their response; they try to calm him down, console him, let him know that he has nothing to feel ashamed of or to blame himself for. Considerable refinement is possible in this world, considerable sweetness of soul, sustained by noteworthy psychological acuity.

20. E.g. *Eyrbyggja saga* ch. 41; *Þorsteins saga hvíta*, ch. 4.
21. On embarrassment becoming lexically distinguished from shame, see Miller 1993: ch. 5.

Cleaning Up Some Leftovers

Some details in these chapters still require comment; I will deal with the more important ones, and let others fend for themselves.

Thorgerd Njalsdottir; Skarphedin's and Grim's wives: Thorhild and Astrid. What is the case with Ketil of Mork's wife, Thorgerd Njalsdottir, unless the author has been nodding? He reminds us (and it seems himself too) that Ketil is married to Njal's daughter (ch. 93), but they are never seen together, and Thorgerd only appears onstage once: at the Burning. She is inside the flames and she exits with her brother Helgi disguised as a woman. Would the decent-souled Ketil allow fire to be borne to a building his wife was in? He is one of the Burners, and it is he who helps Njal's steward exit the flames, at which moment he laments: 'Great sorrow has been allotted us, that we should all share such terrible ill luck' (ch. 129). We do have several saga examples of burners having their kin, wives, and fathers inside. One of the cases involves Gudmund the Powerful, in a saga that makes him considerably less appealing than *Njáls saga* does.[22] But Ketil is not such a person. Thorgerd's presence inside, though probably an authorial oversight, suggests that Njal not only does not let his sons set up independently, but he keeps his married daughters at home (as hostages?) too.[23]

Thorhalla, the only woman of her generation who seems to matter in Njal's household, for reasons already adduced, is allowed a dignified farewell from her husband Helgi, who is about to be degraded into cross-dressing, though he remonstrates some. At the suggestion of Astrid, the wife of Grim, Helgi is decked out by her and Thorhild, Skarpedin's wife, an idea and perhaps a task that did not occur to his high-minded wife Thorhalla. Helgi exits between his sisters-in-law, along with his sisters, Thorgerd and Helga, Kari's wife. This is the only time Astrid and Helga appear onstage, Astrid at least given a speaking part, something Helga never gets. In a scene remarkable for exits refused—Njal's and Bergthora's—or made in flames—Kari's—or in drag—Helgi's, these other woman simply

---

22. *Ljósvetninga saga*, ch. 20 (wife inside); *Guðmundar saga dýra*, ch. 14 (says that his daughter's being inside would not have stopped him); *Þorgils saga skarða*, ch. 32 (father inside).
23. On the forgotten daughter Thorgerd, and on Njal's refusal to release his grown children from his control, see Helga Kress 1977: 295ff.

walk out the door, most of them never even to be mentioned again. That Astrid makes the offer to Helgi and not to her husband Grim is perhaps not to be pushed too far, the members of this large household being 'one big happy family', but one careful reader suggested this: when the sons of Njal are introduced (ch. 25), Skarphedin and Grim are both tall (*mikill*) and strong, while Helgi, though strong, is not said to be *mikill*. He is the only one, in other words, whose height might let him pass for a woman.[24] Add that he shares with Njal, not beardlessness, but prescience, that being enough to feminize Helgi somewhat by association.

Mord. I have given Mord short shrift, and will do so again here, leaving him for a larger discussion of morals and villainy at the very end. Let us say that he now is on the side of the good guys, and, more than that, the good guys want him on their side. They know that he is not always to be trusted when he is on your side, but that is a risk more than a few are willing to take.[25] Mord is the first person, after a farmer nearby named Bard lends Kari a horse, that Kari seeks out after he escapes the flames (chs. 130–1). Mord immediately gathers forces and is active in the hunt for the Burners. The Mord as constructed by the narrator and the critics, compared to the one the people in the district know, live with, and seek marriage alliances with, does not seem to be quite the same person.

Coda: Exit Skarphedin and his Grins, *Obit* Njal

Grins can mean many things, depending on when they appear, depending on the type of grin, depending on who is grinning. Though grins are usually thought to show the teeth, only two of Skarphedin's nine grins indicate his teeth bared (chs. 119, 128 less directly), but given the prominence of his teeth, it might be quite difficult for him not to show them when he grinned. His grins have the power to represent him; they signature him. Try to imagine Skarphedin as the dominant presence he is if he

24. Thanks to Ingrid Hedström.
25. Statements that allying with him leads to more ill than good are not rare—Ketil (ch. 112), Runolf (ch. 115), Hall of Sida (ch. 119)—but no one calls him an *illmenni*.

did not grin. From the first grin, his grins mark him out. They capture an unsettling threateningness in his character, that uncomfortably exceeds the low-level *Schadenfreude* that gets normal people through the day. Only one other person in the saga grins, and that one too is ominous—Thjostolf, as he walks off after Hallgerd has ordered him not to avenge the slap her beloved husband Glum gave her (ch. 16).[26]

Skarphedin's grins mostly register contempt, sometimes bemused, some-times malevolent. The contempt refuses to differentiate between slaves and those who are players in the honor game; there is a fundamental egalitari-anism to it. He acts as if others bored him, or only slightly better, as if he found them trivially amusing. What a nice threat advantage he gains by having a tic-like grin that is unreadable as benign even when it may be; a person witnessing it cannot relax.

The grin hardly indicates that he does not give a damn. Probably no one in the saga is more concerned to look good in that heroic way that matters so much to him. No fear, no whining, no arguing with father, taking care that everyone else in the household does their best to act well in the face of danger and death. The final performance is judged on aesthetic grounds so powerful that they become moral grounds too. He even insists on the high-est demands of style when he deals death to Sigmund and to Thrain. No easy killing by raking Viking ships abroad, no cannon-fodder to fling off halberds by the dozens. Implausible body-counts and slicing bodies in half are allowed Gunnar and Kari who, as Heusler noted, seem to be playing by Continental conventions in their fights, but not Skarphedin. When it comes to killing, he, whom we might find the stranger man as a literary and psychological matter, is a pure Icelander who never picked up any improb-abilities from abroad.

He failed once, and that was because he felt the normal resentments of a normal man. Only once did he not play his part with the style with which he insisted that he play it at all other times. In the end, he was not above the politics of the district, any more than Gunnar, Hoskuld Hvitanesspriest, or his father was. He too was entangled in the causal chain that started when Hallgerd came south and Bergthora ordered her out of Thorhalla's seat. And

26. 'Grin' works quite accurately to capture ON *glotta*, and *glotta við tönn* (with the teeth show-ing). The gesture indicated by the word has never escaped the anxiety that a certain hostil-ity and uncanniness may well reside in it; see e.g. *OED* s.v. grin, v. 2. It is used for the rictus, both in English and in ON; e.g. *Fóstbræðra saga*, ch. 23.

despite his cultivated bemused contempt, he seemed to care for the victims his mother and Hallgerd offered up more than anyone, which probably supplies the deep reason behind the cultivation of that contempt. He liked Atli, who played his walk-on part so exquisitely; he loved his foster-father; he got impatient with having to wait until his father said he could come off the bench and start playing in that feud (ch. 43): 'how far must matters go before we can take things into our own hands?' Thus Sigmund, and then Thrain, and then Hoskuld die. His victims are all killed within the context of a feud between two households that started over 'a straw'. Father ran the show and Skarphedin deferred, except once; he did his bidding, except once. Njal quite simply asked too much of him, too often. The remarkable thing was that he accepted such limiting of his career as long as he did. One thinks of other dutiful but eerily forceful souls who accepted second billing with only one or two rare lapses: Joab, Hagen.

Skarphedin is married, but his wife barely appears, and never in dialogue with Skarphedin, nor did he have sons or daughters, or if he did, they were not thought worth mentioning. We thus do not get to see Skarphedin henpecked, dominated, outwitted, in the way Gunnar, Njal, and Flosi (by his niece) are. Skarphedin does get goaded by his mother, but she does so in a way that shows that he and she are in perfect accord. He is insulted by Hallgerd, but that is avenged. He is detached from female influence and only seems to hint at some phantom attachment in a garbled poetic reference uttered when dead. He is absolutely never free from paternal influence, which was much of the motive informing a garish and failed act of severance—the killing of Hoskuld Hvitanesspriest.

Let me qualify my Skarphedin-philia, not retract it, but admit some modulation. This is, after all, *Njáls saga, Brennu-Njáls saga.* Skarphedin made a move to take over the saga; he had one glorious killing to his credit; he dominated completely one Althing, and then competed with his father as to which of them could die most impressively. But Skarphedin could no more wrest the saga from his father than he could the family farm, or even his wife's farm at Thorolfsfell.[27] Father called the shots. He determined who in his house married whom, and where they lived after they got married, which either was at Bergthorsknoll or within a stone's throw of it. The alliances his sons forged, their friends and allies, were of Njal's choosing and his alone, except for their one act of rebellion. Though beardless

27. See Ch. 6, n. 5.

and rather disembodied, and eventually so slight that he could be lifted off his horse and carried into the house by a man who could not have been much younger than he was, he nevertheless had so much mass that no one in the area could escape his gravitational field, try as he or she might. Not his sons, especially Skarphedin, except once. Even after that attempted escape father called the shots, because none of his sons was ever going to leave Bergthorsknoll, if father had anything to say about it. And he had everything to say about it. No male that we know of, who was born at Bergthorsknoll, ever got out of it alive. Helgi had to dress as a woman to try, and he died in the attempt. The household's orientation to the out-side world was in Njal's sole control. Grim and Helgi, even when married, needed father's permission to go abroad, and their attempt to start things up with Thrain when they returned had to be taken over by Njal, for they did not know how to manage getting rid of Thrain intelligently on their own.

The author consciously makes Njal a composer of scripts, for Gunnar, for his household, for the entire polity. But Njal could not script everything to his own liking, because the author placed him in an objective political and social world that generated too many variables for one man to control. Njal did have sufficient control over his household, though, to make sure no one in it was going to take his saga away from him. This was no easy feat for him, because he had one son who was fully sagaworthy (and a wife with a mind of her own too). Nonetheless, Njal made sure to keep the saga his. Because of his decision Skarphedin would not survive him by more than a handful of minutes, during which brief interval, as I noted briefly earlier, in a kind of bad joke, Skarphedin had, by operation of law, come to own Bergthorksnoll, which then collapsed upon him.

Njal does quite well, despite losing some aptitude in old age; he rises up the social scale, becoming respected and prominent; he manages a long-lived local feud so that he can live until old age, with only his last year being one of sorrow and despair. He negotiated messy situations with skill, sometimes eliciting a bit of a wink at what were less than fair dealings. He was for a long time a very skillful operator. His gravest fault, as suggested earlier, was that he lived too long. His strong will and his sons' acquies-cence produced a solid familial power-base; his way worked quite well for a long time, which has to be part of the explanation why the sons did not chafe earlier. It was hard to argue with success.

People were not about to go out of their way to incur the enmity of the extended family lodged at Bergthorsknoll, for it had brains and muscle.

But at least one of the men of muscle also had brains, and though he kept his ambitions subordinated to the group enterprise, finally grew frustrated when it was clear that father was defying all the mortality tables and had selected an heir-apparent not of the blood to whom he already had gifted a significant amount of power. Either Njal should have died younger or should have ceded more authority to his sons. Because he did not, they rebelled.

18

Preparation for the Next Althing: Chapters 132–7

In the same chapter in which the bodies are dug out of the ashes, planning starts immediately for how to respond to the Burning. Asgrim enlists his mother's brother Gizur, and the two of them now emerge as the leaders of the anti-Burner faction. Gizur's trajectory is one of several that reveal the permeability and fluidity of faction in the Icelandic blood-feud. He was Gunnar's executioner and now succeeds to the leadership of the pro-Njal faction, Gunnar's avengers.

I called Gizur Gunnar's executioner, but the author stays clear of saying that. Gunnar is said to die of exhaustion mostly, and from many wounds. The boaster who claims to have given him his death-wound would get killed for his big mouth, but mostly because he happened to be a convenient target for other reasons, as we saw (chs. 77, 79). Gunnar's death was portrayed as a fully communal killing of an outlaw, much like a biblical stoning, in which individual responsibility for the killing is explicitly avoided. The author wanted Gizur's hands to stay clean and so they did. He had to prosecute Gunnar for the killing of Thorgeir Otkelsson (ch. 73), it being his turn after Geir had 'won' the lottery to prosecute Gunnar for killing Otkel; that supplies the reason why Gizur would lead the posse enforcing any violation of the settlement that came out of the claim that he had prosecuted. His excellence of character is proved by his response to Otkel's prosecution of Gunnar in the theft case, by his refusal, twice given, to burn Gunnar inside, by his forbearance regarding Rannveig's remarks after her son Gunnar's death, by his praise of Gunnar in death (ch. 77), and by his leading, along with Hjalti and Hall, the Christian faction to victory without violence at the Althing (ch. 104). The author even cares to have

Skarphedin give him his imprimatur: 'the men who attacked Gunnar were chieftains of such character. . .' (ch. 128).

Gizur's reorientation toward the underlying feud means that Mord will have to reorient himself whether he likes it or not, for Mord is married to Gizur's daughter and he loves her like his eyes. Gizur determines that between Kari and himself they will pressure Mord to undertake the most prominent part in the prosecution of the Burners: the case against Flosi.[1] Should Mord refuse, Gizur will collect his daughter and take her back home. One critic was horrified at the perversity that would require us to imagine Mord as 'a pleader for the "innocent side"'.[2] To his mind, it was a sign of the moral decay depicted in the saga. But that is to hold Mord, or the author, to standards that did not govern political action in the medieval or the ancient world. Side-switching was not surprising; it was business as usual, especially given how unclear it was at the margins exactly how to draw a line around any one side.[3] A group would define itself differently depending on the precise occasion. Outsiders too would see it as having a varying membership depending on the outsider's specific alignments and the point of view he was taking. Who exactly 'we' are and who exactly 'they' are were very seldom clear once a minor dispute expanded into full-fledged feud. The claims on others to align themselves either for or against, or to insist that they should not get involved at all, made for messy situations, in which ideas like loyalty, which are still considered virtues, are quite hard to get a fix on.[4] The people you fought today might be your in-laws next year, or had been the year before. Thus the Icelandic saying: 'everyone has a friend among his enemies.'[5]

Flosi and Support-mustering

Because *Njála* is the Thing saga par excellence, it also ends up as *the* support-mustering saga. The author is not very circumstantial about

---

1. A father does not have the formal authority to take his married daughter home, but given the assumptions of near on-demand divorce, or the power of this particular father, there is nothing in the threat that is not credible.
2. Bolton, 208.
3. On side-switching, see White 2007; in the 12th-century Danish context, see Hermanson.
4. On Icelandic group formations, see *BP*, chs. 4–5.
5. *Hallfreðar saga*, ch. 6.

support-mustering before the Conversion but thereafter it comes to bear a good portion of the narrative.[6] The two chapters featuring Skarphedin fifth in line is the first of several iterations which, if not quite as entertaining, are no less important politically. A reprise occurs at the next Althing in which the prosecution of the Burners takes place (ch. 119–20; 139–40); we also get a detailed account of Flosi recruiting his lead lawyer, Eyjolf Bolverksson (ch. 138), but before that we follow Flosi on his long trek to beg support in the East Quarter (ch. 134).

Support-mustering is quasi-ritualized in some of its forms. When Asgrim leads his party from booth to booth in chapters 119–20 the group includes eight, and the author takes care to specify the order in which they entered each booth, with the fifth position made memorable. In chapter 139 the important members of the party are enumerated up to the fifth position, which was occupied by Thorgeir Skorargeir, 'the outstanding member of the family now' and thus the one to whom fell Skarphedin's axe, as well as, evidently, his position in the support-mustering line. Skarphedin, with Battle-Troll as his surrogate, is 'after-walking' in some fashion, still fifth in line.

I suspect, though I cannot prove, that the author is preserving a ritualized protocol for making formal requests for support. Some ritual would be needed to smooth the way for making requests of people who are not bound to you by kinship, friendship, or neighborhood. (Remember what asking to buy hay and food from someone not bound to you led to.) When Flosi makes his support-mustering trek (ch. 134), the ritual form must vary because he is not going booth to booth, but from farm to farm, some separated by significant distances. Flosi intentionally makes his support-mustering a humiliation ritual, which asking for favors often is anyway, but his will take on the trappings of an express humiliation ritual. He predicts before the Althing that they will be reduced to groveling if they take blood revenge—'we shall be forced to grovel before many men and beg them for help' (ch. 117)—and quotes himself later as they are about to set out to ask for help: 'Let us go in search of support; and you will now learn the truth of what I once said, that we should be forced to grovel before many men before all this is ended' (ch. 133).

---

6. See too *Hænsa-Þóris saga*, where mustering support takes the form of an extended trickster tale.

With the fires still flickering at the Burning, he says that many will call it *illvirki*, an evil deed. He seems to be in accord with the negative judgment, though that will not keep him from asking people to help him defend against the just consequences of that evil deed. He does, though, want people to see that he is not glorying in the Burning; he walks, he does not ride. Such is the moral egregiousness of 'burning inside', at least the way this saga presents it, that it would allow people to use the badness of the deed as a convenient excuse to deny requests for help. Hence his need to engage in acts of self-abnegation, to play a version of Henry walking to Canossa in hopes of making it more awkward for those whose aid he seeks to say no.[7]

Flosi and those accompanying him must have been very footsore at the end of their expedition: the distance from Svinafell to Hall of Sida's is roughly 150 km; the distance covered to visit the seven others another 400 km. The return, on which they could ride, would be a good deal shorter, since they could take a more direct route back to Hall's which would more than halve the distance. But Flosi did rather well for himself. The support of the first person he visits, Hall of Sida, is a foregone conclusion; Hall advises him whom to seek out. Of the seven people he then visits only Sorli Brodd-Helgason refuses, because he is married to Gudmund the Powerful's daughter; he will back Gudmund and so will not commit. Flosi does not accept the refusal graciously: 'I can see from your replies that you are under woman's rule here' (ch. 134). Ritualized humility is meant to get yeses; when it fails of its purpose the humility gives way to anger and cursing, as many a rejecter of a panhandler has experienced.

Two of the six who agree to assist Flosi accept payment; four give their support without it. One of those accepting payment, Hallbjorn the Strong, and one who does not, Bjarni Brodd-Helgason—'I have never bartered my manhood or my support for bribes'—both insist they will stand by Flosi as if he were their brother, as strong a statement of commitment as one can make.[8] Bjarni ends up instrumental in recruiting Eyjolf Bolverksson to Flosi's cause. Hallbjorn loses a big toe that Kari slices off in the Battle at the Althing, which nonetheless does not prevent him from fast flight along with the rest of Flosi's forces. Hallbjorn, as mentioned earlier, does

---

7. Compare the more lurid ritual of abnegation Hrapp employs to force Thrain's hand (ch. 88). See discussion of rituals of self-abnegation in Miller 2011: chs. 9–11.
8. Gudmund the Powerful's thumb does not reach that extra link to Sorli's brother, Bjarni, or two extra links to Sorli's sister's husband, Hallbjorn, to keep them from committing to Flosi. Neither Hallbjorn nor his wife appear in other sagas or genealogies.

get some relief from his pain by pitching the lowly meat-vendor into his boiling cauldron (ch. 145).

Bjarni's remarks about forgoing payment for support should not be read to paint Hallbjorn as ignoble for accepting payment. Flosi will eventually have to repay Bjarni anyway. Flosi does not begrudge Hallbjorn his payment, nor did Hallbjorn barter for it. The transaction is rather delicately handled for reasons that are deducible from the interaction. Flosi initiated it by taking a purse of silver from his belt, saying that 'he wished to give it to him'.

> Hallbjorn took it, but said he that he had no cause to expect gifts from Flosi—'I would, however, like to know how you want me to repay this.'
> 'I have no need of money,' said Flosi, 'but I would like you to ride to the Althing with me and give me your support—even though I have no claims on you through blood or marriage ties.'
> 'I give you my promise,' said Hallbjorn. 'I shall ride to the Althing and give you my support, as if you were my own brother.'
> Flosi thanked him. (ch. 134)

We may assume Bjarni and Flosi have already well-established relations. That makes Bjarni's willingness to grant his support without prior payment or a gift exactly right, just as the lack of any ties or basis for gift-giving between Hallbjorn and Flosi makes the way that Hallbjorn behaves appropriate. Though it is a purse of money that is transferred, the transaction is euphemized by using the diction of gift-exchange. Hallbjorn's receiving the gift and agreeing to be bound to make repayment is generous, for the very reason Flosi states: Hallbjorn owes Flosi nothing. The author provides much social information in these interactions, where we can construct some of the smallest of social rituals and how their forms vary given the particulars of the situation. We can trust that these three actors in these negotiations followed the normative script.

If the saga-writer seems almost to fetishize the mustering of support in the post-Conversion period, it is to show how integral it was to the expansion of the feud that Bergthora would claim Hallgerd started, so that it now involves half the country, with enough involvement of people located in the North and some few in the West to have effectively nationalized the dispute. But why do people engage in these support-mustering efforts? There is only one fairly routine court case in *Njáls saga*—suing to recover a dowry, the saga's first lawsuit—and it went haywire for reasons we saw. Still, it was not a case arising from feud, nor was it politics by other means.

Other routine claims lie beneath the surface of the saga: a paternity claim, an illicit cutting of wood; but these are banked by Njal to use as offsets. Had those cases been brought they would have been routinely disposed of by judgment or settlement. Assuming they are one-off cases without prior enmity playing a role in them, no one would be mustering multitudes to attend the court in those cases.[9] This is the stuff of routine matters in any community: paternity claims, divorce settlements, debt-collection, illicit joyriding on someone else's horse, land-encroachments. Small claims, or even larger claims but between small people, tend to be processed by handing the claim over to one's chieftain, or to the head of one's kin-group. As long as these big men were not using these claims to harass another big man it was the routine business of the Things to process claims such as these.

But the cases that make up the storyline of this saga are not routine cases. They are surface phenomena of deeper underlying competitions and divisions. The core issue in them is not a killing or a theft—the legal issue—but competition for precedence and power, political struggle. Sometimes the law can handle these competitions reasonably well, keeping them in compensable bounds; sometimes, however, the enmity gets too big for the law to handle, as in the fallout from the killing of Hoskuld Hvitanesspriest. That in a nutshell is one of the chief themes of the storyline of post-Conversion *Njáls saga*.

For routine cases, with negligible political components, no one has to go booth to booth, or farm to farm, mustering support. The chieftains' thing-men already in attendance provide the necessary backing to keep the peace if the losing party loses his temper and decides to fight or break up the court by threatening the judges and empaneled neighbors. Among us, we take for granted that people will somehow just sit quietly as they receive a death sentence. But an armed bailiff or two stands there. When the stakes go up, and the cases pass beyond the routine, pitting powerful groups against each other, then each group believed it prudent to make sure to attend in force. They expect the other side will do so, and it would be imprudent in the extreme to be caught short-handed.

The dominant motive for support-mustering in highly contentious cases was prudence, more to make sure you were not routed than to rout. It

---

9. Even for the dowry case Hrut and Hoskuld show up at the Althing with a large company (ch. 8). They did not want to get caught off guard lest Mord showed up in force.

was about maintaining order in the court.[10] Actual disruption of legal proceedings was fairly rare, but that was largely because the parties took care
to defend against the possibility, and the greater number of uninvolved
wanted the peace kept. The Battle at the Althing is an exceptional case.[11]
Support-mustering also serves other functions. It is a way of canvassing as if
for an election. The more people willing to back you, the more such backing serves as a verdict of the community as to what justice demands; the
judges might find it harder to rule against a cause they see is popular, with
crowds cheering one side and booing the other.

Compare the ways Flosi and Asgrim organize their groups and muster
their support. The anti-Burner party secures their core group of kin and
affines, Asgrim, Mord, Gizur, Holta-Thorir's sons, before the Thing. Once
at the Althing, Gudmund the Powerful joins them, and because he has such
a large force they need look no further; they also gain Snorri's assurance that
if it comes to a fight he will have his men assist them. The only recruitment
back on their home turf is making sure Mord agrees to take on the prosecution of Flosi. This group still has Njal's blood kin in it, but they take orders
from Gizur who never had any connection with Njal. Except for Thorgeir
Skorargeir, who acts later in a smaller unit of Kari and himself as pure blood
avengers, Njal's blood kin are there to confer legitimacy on the enterprise,
and little more. This is a group formed by South Quarter power-brokers—
Gizur and Asgrim—to meet East Quarter intruders—Flosi and Hall of
Sida—with men of an equal dignity, even though it is ostensibly a group
formed to bring an action on behalf of Njal and those burned with him,
an action owned by Njal's nephews, the sons of Holta-Thorir. It is a more
complex version of Njal's commandeering revenge for Gunnar, but making sure Hogni Gunnarsson went along for the ride to provide a legiti-
mizing veneer to the action. Since Mord on big matters takes orders from

10. *Grágás* Ia 53 purports to limit to ten the number allowed the moving party in an action at the
    Althing, a stricture the sagas do not confirm as more than a pipe-dream; courts convened
    on location to settle rights in a meadow limited each party to twenty; Ib 85, II 456.
11. Several sagas show fighting at local Things, but recorded outbreaks are infrequent; and
    no battles take place at the Althing of the sort described in *Njála*. An affray takes place in
    Hænsa-Þóris saga, ch. 14, but it is outside the Thing grounds and does not succeed in disrupt-
    ing the Thing. That incident led to the reform that divided the country into quarters, yet it
    does not merit an entry in the annals as does the battle in *Njála*, anno 1011: *Lögmansannáll*.
    See further *BP* 234, 234 n. 25, and Heusler 1911: 104–5 (cases of railroading judgments,
    threatening judges).

Gizur, he is now an active member of that core group. Mord is not where he is because he stabbed Hoskuld Hvitanesspriest.

I do not want to exaggerate: the lawsuits against the Burners are not mere pretext. No killing of Hoskuld, no Burning, and there is nothing else in the saga one could point to that would have opposed Gizur and Asgrim to Flosi and Hall. But once those events happen the response to them cannot be explained by a simple balanced-exchange model of feud primarily based on kinship or household organization. That model, with its attendant ethic of revenge, still holds some in its thrall who feel truly aggrieved—Thorgeir and Kari; but that is only part of the story, and not the part that explains why it is Gizur and Asgrim now running the main show.

If South Quarter affiliation is mostly what unites the anti-Burner party, Flosi's group is fully an East Quarter array. Flosi's adherents are not the people one would expect to be natural allies, but who rather would be feuding amongst themselves for local dominance. Why are they not squabbling like the people living in Njal's and Gunnar's region of the South Quarter the generation before, or like Thorkel Hake and Gudmund the Powerful in the North?[12] Something has changed, and this tracks very much the author's knowledge of what happened during the Sturlung period of the thirteenth century, where basically one family dominated the East Quarter: the Svinfellings, Flosi's family, who take their name from Flosi's farm.[13]

The feud has changed its form in *Njála*, and is moving toward something looking more like war, pitting regions against each other. We now, with caution, can shade in some more of the picture that made Flosi take the lead in following up on Hoskuld's death. Though the text is obscure on some of the matters to be discussed in this and the next paragraph, I think it better to offer reasons for these largely political issues than to dismiss them as mere givens of the story that we must concede the author. This is an author who cares to have his narration make political and psychological sense; he devotes so much space to detailing why the dispute takes the form it does, why its opposed groupings align the way they do and then undergo realignments, that I am not willing to believe he was casual about

---

12. See *Ljósvetninga saga* detailing Gudmund's ultimate victory over Thorkel. Kari confirms that some Northern chieftains have joined Flosi's cause.
13. See Jón Viðar, 66.

such matters. Caveats and excuses thus made, let us proceed: Ask yourself what there was for Njal in seeking Hildigunn for Hoskuld? Why look for a marriage outside the quarter? From Njal's point of view this is another marriage upward, though now that he is established it is not very much up. He is expanding politically in a new direction:[14] literally, eastward. Could it be that he does not want to be caught without having planned ahead, should those close kinsmen Asgrim and Gizur, who are the powers on the west side of the South Quarter, and much more powerful than he is himself, reduce him to nothing more than a mere client? It looks like Njal may be playing balance-of-power politics lest he be swallowed up by his own stronger allies.[15]

Suppose that that to be part of Njal's motive, but then what was in it for Flosi? Might it not be this? He, by virtue of Hoskuld, gets some modest say in a new quarter. His own sense of what a wife's father means comes from his relationship with Hall of Sida: chief advisor, even power behind the throne. He perhaps means to make Hoskuld his creature as much as he is already Njal's, or at least confuse Hoskuld's loyalties by making him something less than Njal's total creature. Hoskuld purely aligned with Njal and sons would create too powerful a presence on Flosi's western border, especially given Njal's affiliation with Asgrim, and through Asgrim to Gizur. This is conjectural, but makes sense, and maybe would be so apparent to an audience who had recently suffered from this kind of power politics that it would not need much more clarification than the author chooses to give it.

14. He already has some interests in property in an eastward direction. There is Kari's farm at Dyrholm, and if Astrid brought Diupriverbank with her, that farm is located in the East Quarter some 25 miles to the west of Svinafell.
15. The actual locus of power in the Rangriver plains during the 12th and early 13th centuries radiated from a farm mentioned only twice in *Njála*: Oddi. Geir the Priest establishes himself there when he moves into the district after Gunnar's death, and it is where the two ravens accompany Skarphedin and Hogni when they kill Geir's son and drive Geir back to the other side of the Thjors River (chs. 77–9). A good portion of *Íslendinga saga* details the decline of the people of Oddi (the Oddaverjar, mentioned in *Njála* as descended from Ulf Aur-priest, brother of Valgard the Gray (ch. 25)), ultimately to be displaced by the descendants of Gizur the White. The saga surely reflects that reality even as it constructs a fantasy with the help of Odin's ravens to let Njal hold his own against the big family to the West and the big family to the East, the Svinfellings. On the rise of the Oddaverjar and their control of the Rangriver district, see Helgi Þorláksson's careful treatment; also Jón Viðar, 64–6.

Flosi Visits Asgrim, Chapter 136

Flosi, a man of extremes, has evidently had enough of groveling for support; he is now up for blowing off some steam. On the way to the Althing, accompanied by the Burners, he pays Asgrim 'an unwelcome visit' (*troða illsakar við hann*, lit., to tread hostilely upon). The Norse phrase bears some of the markings of a quasi-legal term of art for a type of ritualized imposition, overtly hostile.[16] In this way it is comparable to terms like *brenna inni*, to burn people inside, or *dreita inni*, to make people defecate inside their houses, as when you surround their home, block the doors, and deny them access to the privy.[17] Asgrim meets a ritualized hostile visit with ritualized hospitality, fulfilling all the forms of graciousness except for the accompanying gracious mental state.[18] He prepares his house, as Hildigunn did for Flosi, so the 'guest' will see that special labors were undertaken to welcome him.

Asgrim's servants think the band approaching must be Thorgeir Skorargeir and his men, but Asgrim sees that they are laughing and in good cheer: 'the kin of Njal, especially the likes of Thorgeir, will never laugh until he is avenged' (ch. 136). Not laughing when the vengeance obligation hangs over you is a saga trope, but probably mirrors actual ritualized propriety, indicating that the unfulfilled obligation is still in the mind of the avenger, also serving as a kind of mourning 'dress'.[19] Remember that Gunnar Lambason claimed he had not laughed from the time of Thrain's death until the Burning (ch. 130). That was about ten years. Lord Chesterfield insisted that he was never heard to laugh since he had his reason, which I suppose he put at age 12. The same was said of Charlemagne's son Louis the Pious.[20] Such self-control is possible.

16. The visit of the Njalssons and Kari to Thrain in ch. 92 shares some features with Flosi's visit to Asgrim, but it is much less ritualized.
17. *Laxdœla saga*, ch. 47, also *Íslendinga saga*, ch. 7, where because the expression is used without further elaboration it bears all the marks of term of art, a well-known move to humiliate an opponent.
18. One was generally required to board up to five people on the way to weddings, spring Things, etc. *Grágás* Ia 27, II 31.
19. See e.g. *Droplaugarsona saga*, ch. 13.
20. *Letters*, 9 Mar. 1748; smiling was acceptable for Chesterfield and perhaps for Louis as long as the teeth were not shown nor sounds made; see Thegan of Trier, *Deeds of the Emperor Louis*, ch. 19, Noble trans., 203.

The vignette shows us another form of a highly stylized competitive shaming, this one mapping perfectly onto the norms of hospitality, with the 'guest' playing a sophisticated philological joke without knowing it. The word *guest* and the word *host* come from the same Indo-European root, as do other opposite senses such as hostile, hospitable, and host, as in army.[21] The guest arrives with a host of men, in a hostile imposition of hospitality, all those words clones or cousins of each other. The ritual strips bare the norms of hospitality and shows them to be a kind of protection payment, unless you, as the host, really have the power to put an axe in the head of your guest, which Asgrim finally loses enough patience to try. Asgrim wins the moral encounter, his magnanimity and his lack of cowardice besting Flosi's rude intrusion.

After they depart Asgrim's, Flosi and his men travel on and meet Hall of Sida, some of his people praising the display of hostility, while Hall condemns it as plain stupid. Asgrim is a voice of relative reason among his enemies; Flosi has now pushed him into full accord with the bloodiest-minded in his group: Kari and Thorgeir. Flosi's erratic behavior is fully convincing psychologically. He bounces between lethargy, in-your-face hostility, suicidal stupidity, strategic competence and intelligence, showing himself capable of both atrocity and generosity of spirit. The author cites the received opinion of him: 'it has been said of [Flosi] that he had nearly all the qualities of a true chieftain (*höfðingi*)' (ch. 146). In some bizarre way he is no more in control of his inner roil than Thorhall Asgrimsson is, though both roils are differently constituted, one manifesting itself somatically, the other characterologically. We will have more than one occasion to return to Flosi in the pages that follow.

21. See Pokorny I. 453, s.v. ghosti-s; *OED* s.v., guest, n.

19

The Trial of Flosi and the
Battle: Chapters 135, 141–5

The trial of Flosi, the battle of Mord and Thorhall versus Eyjolf, with the cheers and jeers, show all the signs of a spectator sport. Or to switch metaphors: trials were great theater for the men attending the Thing, no less than they were theater for the children back home once people returned from the Althing (ch. 8). That certain aspects of the law provide such fertile grounds for entertainment still draws people to law school, or at least to movies and television programs.

Our author may not be an expert in the law of the Commonwealth period, though he surely has more than a passing interest in it. He understands rather well the role that the law plays in his society; he also knows that some of the legal mumbo-jumbo and technicality of formal pleading will entertain or impress enough of his readers/listeners to lose nothing for including it. The author may demand that we suspend disbelief when neither Mord nor Eyjolf know what the basic qualifications for panel membership are—something Njal would have surely covered in his first-year curriculum for the boy Thorhall. Yet it works anyway. Even for those who are not drawn to legal technicality, even if sometimes the details are not quite accurate as a legal-historical matter, the literary effect is to generate suspense and retard the action that has been moving at breakneck speed since the Conversion.

My law students' reactions to these chapters do not make a bell-curve but a Bactrian camel, with one hump at the positive side made up of those who find it fascinating. At last they can justify taking this course as part of their legal education. At the opposite end, the other hump, are lumped those who if they read them at all are bored and eager to get back to the killing. But none at the positive end can match the enthusiasm of Ian Maxwell, a barrister before becoming an English professor. He makes a spirited and typically perspicacious defense of the author's commitment to legal technicality, especially in the chapters that we are presently dealing with:

> Then there are the legal technicalities, which are not always right, and which Einar Ólafur [EÓS] admits to be excessive. Perhaps my young days at the bar disable my judgment, but again my impression is different. How could anyone deny. . . the superbly dramatic use of legal formulae in the last great suit, where the dry battle of forms reins in the passions of men, obscures the merits, and leads to the battle of arms. (This author knows what he is doing: Eyjolf's final objection is stated in the curtest summary.) If we are to have this scene we must also have a graduated course of legal instruction earlier in the saga; and surely we must admire the judgment with which his material is gradually fed into a long succession of suits. . .[1]

Law and its Limits

A significant number of other commentators, it being almost the received wisdom, take the saga to be an indictment of the law, some of them thinking that this is the message delivered early in the saga when Njal writes the script to reopen Unn's dowry claim by tricking Hrut, or even earlier when Hrut resorts to trial by combat, despite it being a perfectly legal defense at the time. The law of *Njála*, in their eyes, is little more than a bag of tricks and manipulations, and one of the main themes of the saga is specifically the law's failure to constrain violence.[2] The saga-writer's critique is subtler. For starters, notice that Njal must intentionally throw a wrench in the works of the legal system to bring about support for the reform that leads to Hoskuld getting his chieftaincy (ch. 97). Up to then people felt the legal system had been working quite well for them. Njal had to grind it to a halt; it was not grinding itself to one. It is not until after the Conversion that we see the law run up against its limits. And what is the chief substantive point about the Conversion episode? Can it be anything other than to show how well the Althing and its law could work to maintain the peace, when blessed with

---

1. Maxwell, 24; see too Burrows, 37–43.
2. E.g. Fox, 301; Allen, 129; Andersson 2006: 200.

THE TRIAL OF FLOSI AND THE BATTLE

the political and legal imagination of Thorgeir the Lawspeaker? From that peak it will decline to battle in eleven years.

The author clearly loves law as a generator of stories, as a domain that he finds fascinating for a multitude of reasons: the intelligence it demands, the drama it provides, the good things that flow from it when it is working reasonably well. He is captivated by legal process and legal technicality. He cares to apprise us of the rankings or standing of lawyers. In the saga's first generation the best is Mord Fiddle, title then passes to Njal, and finally to the latter's prize student, Thorhall. He forces us into the kind of argument sports fans have over who the best player is at a given position. At the time of the trial of Flosi, we know that Eyjolf and Thorhall are two of the three greatest lawyers in Iceland. But who is the unnamed third? Surely it is Skapti the Lawspeaker, to whom our author is not all that kind—he makes him one of Skarphedin's insultees and humiliates him in the Battle at the Althing. But Skapti never shows himself as anything but knowledgeable and able as Lawspeaker.

The tricksterism? To the layman the law seems like nothing but a slough of tricks and traps—filled with loopholes, gaps, uncertainties, ambiguities, in which the 'true' meaning of a text is the one that would never occur to the average person (hence the average person's need to hire a lawyer). This is the standard indictment of the law featured in folktales of equivocal oaths, of letter triumphing over spirit, of form over substance, of the letter not meaning what it says, and so on. *Plus ça change.* It is these features of the law that inform much of present popular culture's view of it, as well as that of satirists throughout the ages.[3] That does not mean that people do not understand that law is preferable to anarchy; the medieval Scandinavians generated a proverb that Njal invokes: 'with laws shall our land be built up but with lawlessness laid waste' (ch. 70).

Our author adds another point that goes beyond the folk critique. In the trial of Flosi, after Mord and Asgrim send to Thorhall for the third time to come up with an answer to Eyjolf's challenges, Thorhall, unsurprisingly, has an answer. Eyjolf is uncertain that Thorhall is right and sends to Skapti the Lawspeaker to settle the point:

'There are more great lawyers alive today than I thought,' replied Skapti. 'I can tell you that this is so precisely correct that not a single objection can be

3. See Miller 1998.

raised against it. But I had thought that I was the only person who knew this specialty of the law now that Njal is dead, for to the best of my knowledge he was the only other man who knew it.' (ch. 142)

What is the state of a law if only one person knows it? If Skapti is the only person who knows a law, then that law can be whatever he says it is for whatever party he favors or that pays him the most. Nor is this merely a quirk of oral law. It is no less a problem with written law, if there are no indexes, if there is no authoritative copy of the text, or if people do not know where to look; or if, as in the modern regulatory state, there are so many laws and administrative rulings issued by different rule-making bodies that even computerized searches cannot track down every relevant provision or decision with some claim to authority on a particular point. The point the author is making is not really a worrisome one in their legal culture because the law drew many people to it, smart people. These were the people the laws contemplate whose responsibility it is to correct or teach the Lawspeaker when his knowledge fails him:

> The Lawspeaker shall recite all the sections so extensively that no one knows them much more extensively. And if his knowledge does not stretch so far, then before reciting each section he is to arrange a meeting in the preceding twenty-four hours with five or more legal experts, those from whom he can learn most.....[4]

Skapti and the author are mostly joking, we might suppose, about the nature of expertise. Systems grow so complex that they must generate a class of experts to function; nor is it quite certain that the class of experts are not the ones helping generate the complexity, not only for mere self-interested reasons of putting one over on the laity, but also because they have a genuine passion for trying to come up with proper answers either to the inexhaustible problems that the real world presents, or to win a case for their client, or because they find it entertaining to pose hypotheticals and compete among themselves to see who can come up with the most elegant solution. The culture of legal expertise can begin to take on a life of its own, but as this saga indicates, refined expertise has real consequences for how certain claims will be argued and who will win or lose them. This

---

4. *Grágás* Ia 209. Thus the group that met at Hafliði's in 1117 to put the laws into writing, emending them, and suggesting new ones; see *Íslendingabók*, ch. 10. One might even discern a budding legal professionalization in early 12th-century Iceland. That such incipient professionalism should occur in non-urban, very poor Iceland is remarkable. See Foote 1977.

is all rather trite, but our author is there at ground zero, seeing matters quite clearly. He recognizes the attraction of legal expertise; he admires it. He named his saga after the most talented of the experts.[5]

Tricksterism and cunning are not signs of law's failure; they come with the territory. The problem for a legal system is to keep the perception of tricksterism and actual tricksterism within acceptable bounds so that the law still maintains a certain level of respect among most actors. It is predictable in sports, no less than in games like trials, that the loser will claim that the winner cheated, or that the referees were biased. To Eyjolf, Thorhall is simply superior in cunning, and to Thorhall, Eyjolf is a cheat who does not know his law well enough to pull it off. The cleanest law cannot get rid of the perception that makes expertise a cause for mistrust, the expert an object of fear, awe, compensatory contempt, and loathing.

There are tricks of the trade that any competent lawyer should know and it would be malpractice not to employ; and there are low or cheap tricks, as we noted when discussing Thorhall's tactics in chapter 121, that even the professional would consider cheating or unprofessional. The low trick and the clever trick that is not quite so low have always made for good stories; and sometimes we make heroes of those like Reynard the Fox or the Njal of chapter 22 (reviving Unn's dowry), if not quite the Njal of chapter 97 (the Fifth Court), where though the first trick may be low, the latter is rather ingenious. In any event we are mostly meant to admire Njal for outsmarting his adversaries.

When Thorhall rises from his sickbed, it is not because of Eyjolf's tricks, which he was more than capable of counteracting within the bounds of the law, but because his own man screwed up, and Thorhall lost all patience for continuing to play the law game. Note too that tricksterism, or cunning moves, are no more or less apparent at the beginning of the saga than at its end. It is only an issue of whether your side is gaining more than losing by them. The highest triumph of the law, Thorgeir's decision making Christianity the official public religion, may have been helped along by some greasing of his palm by the most decent man in the saga, Hall of Sida.[6]

---

5. What Chris Wickham, 1–5, calls the 'disjuncture between legal sophistication and institutional weakness' that characterized the communes of early 12th-century Tuscany was not quite as rare a phenomenon as political and legal theorists tend to assume.

6. See Ch. 14, n. 19.

Those who want to see the saga as indicting the law from the start must not only account for the inclusion of the Conversion, a triumph of their law ways, but they must also account for the fact that up until the Conversion disputes got settled at the Althing, and these settlements depended on legal process getting the parties to the bargaining table. I think the author may have misled readers into thinking the saga condemns the law as a whole by overwhelming them with the sheer brilliance of the symbolic role he gives Thorhall Asgrimsson and his swollen lower leg, thick as a woman's thigh. The polity is swollen with infection; their world is in the process of being turned upside-down, as when the upper part of a woman's leg becomes the lower part of a man's: a gender-bending image of disorder and disease. When the greatest lawyer in Iceland feels the law has reached its limits and starts killing, well, what can that mean but the law has failed (at least in this case)? Or that the sickness in the system, the pressure of the violence that the law can no longer channel, needs aggressive surgical intervention: the lancet. And whose spear is it that pierces the leg in a pressure-relieving ejaculation of pus, and then impales the first of the Burners?

> Thorhall snatched with both hands the spear that Skarphedin had given him, and drove it deep into his own leg. The flesh and the core of the boil clung to the blade as he gouged it out of his leg, and a torrent of blood and matter gushed across the floor like a stream. Then he strode from the booth without a limp, walking so fast that the messenger could not keep pace with him, and hurried to the Fifth Court. There he encountered Grim the Red, one of Flosi's kinsmen. As soon as they met, Thorhall lunged at him with the spear. (ch. 145)

That was the first killing of the battle, the act of the best lawyer in Iceland. The symbolism is as obvious as our author is likely to make it. But the law has failed in the trial of the Burners not because the problem is one with the law, or because the law is corrupt, or because the law is stupid, but because the problem is political and institutional (or more precisely the absence of institutions) more than it is legal. Remember too that many people are itching for battle, the hot-tempered Thorhall included, who has his seizure to avenge.[7] An ominous sign of how generally pessimistic the entire mood of the assembly is about maintaining the peace of the Thing is that everyone armed themselves to attend the trial and 'put battle emblems on their helmets' before the case was pleaded (ch. 142). How can we tell

---

7. Thorgeir Skorargeir (ch. 137); Asgrim (ch. 136).

'us' from 'them' in an age before uniforms and when helmets obscured the identity of the fighter? These men are making sure that they do not die by friendly fire, because 'fire' is expected. The detail is ominous and telling.

There is another irony: the straw that breaks Thorhall's back is Mord's failure to get the most recent innovations in the law under control. Who was it that proposed the rule excluding judges from the panel of forty-eight in the Fifth Court because only thirty-six could issue a judgment? Njal at his most self-interested (chs. 97, 144). Were we to extend Njal's prescience beyond the limited bounds within which the author lets it roam, we might see not only the Burning but also the Battle at the Althing as scripted by this lawyer acting as a legislator. The basis for doing so is weak, but the irony still persists that Njal's reform not only got Hoskuld his chieftaincy, but that the extra chieftaincies so created necessitated procedural innovations that made it easier for battle to replace pleading as a way of resolving the claim against the Burners of Njal. The Battle at the Althing is no casual affray: it is a kind of sacrilege, a polluting of the people's most sacred space with blood.[8]

Some Procedural Matters, Chapters 135, 142

After Mord is bullied into taking up the prosecution of Flosi, he instantly takes over the action. Thorgeir Skorargeir, as next of kin to Njal and his sons, owns the case and he is present to assign it to Mord. I will list a few mistakes the author makes here and some technical matters of interest as an aid to the reader in the order the issues arise.[9]

Mord needed to dig up Helgi Njalsson and classify the wounds on the corpse, and have the procedure witnessed by the neighbors, as we saw earlier (ch. 55). He would then determine whether it was a 'brain wound, internal wound, or marrow wound' that killed Helgi. He would thus not need to repeat the three types of wound throughout his pleadings, but would have the knowledge to plead the type of wound it was that Flosi had inflicted when he severed Helgi's head.[10]

8. See text at Ch. 14, n. 28.
9. On the deviations from *Grágás* in the trial of Flosi consult Lehmann, 103–27.
10. He is to state 'what the injuries are, whether brain wound, internal wound, or marrow wound'; *Grágás* Ia 157.

But why does the saga focus on the case of Flosi's killing Helgi when the most egregious wrong for which Flosi is responsible is the Burning? Lehmann, more than a century ago, gave the most plausible answer.[11] Many formulae for pleading a killing case are preserved in *Grágás* and the procedure is laid out fully, a good portion of which finds its way into the saga. *Grágás*, however, has only a few short lines on burning cases. Thorgeir Skorargeir does plead the case against Glum Hildisson for torching the building, but we get no account of that proceeding except for its publication at the Law Rock. By prosecuting for the killing of Helgi the author could copy an authoritative text from a lawbook.

Most mystifying to readers is the doubling of each stage of the proceedings, all the formulae repeated verbatim except to vary the actual grounds of the claim: in one form it is the assault that led to the wound that killed Helgi that is in issue, in the other it is the wound that resulted from the assault that is prosecuted. According to *Grágás*, the pleader has the choice to make two independent cases out of a killing; he can plead it as a single cause of action or as a double action. Each case of the double action—for the assault and for the wound—goes forward at the same time. The duplication that follows in Mord's pleading, in which each stage is repeated only reversing the order of assault and wound, is good law. The author could have chosen a single action or a double action for Mord; he chose the one that would lengthen the text, and further retard the action.[12]

Mord reserves the right to correct any mistakes he makes in his pleadings (ch. 142). There is no evidence for this 'right to correct' in *Grágás*, but this strikes me as such a serious substantive legal innovation that the author would be chary of inventing it. Historians of medieval law still dispute how true it was that one slip of the tongue, or later one slip of the pen, destroyed a case.[13] One cannot deny that a high level of formalism characterizes procedures for commencing and pleading cases at the Things, but there is precious little in the sources suggesting that to misspeak a single word is to lose the case. *Grágás*, in fact, establishes a harmless-error standard in matters of witness testimony. If words were mistakenly added or dropped, as long as they did not 'affect the case' there were no consequences.[14] The stricter

---

11. Lehmann, 9.
12. Lehmann, 105–6; *Grágás* Ia 156–7.
13. E.g. Brand, 3, Hudson 2012: 313, 828, re *miskenning* in 12th-century England.
14. *Grágás* Ia 57. Procedural errors deemed of consequence, such as calling five neighbors when the case required nine or vice versa, as Asgrim did in ch. 60, void the case; Ia 143.

standard, demanding not even the smallest slip, would make more sense in oaths or ordeals or in a later period when pleadings and writs were in writing. It may in fact be that hyper-formalism of the sort that to slip in a syllable is to lose the case is as much a creature of written law as it is reputed to have been of oral law.[15]

Mord is perhaps being somewhat more expansive in his right to correct errors than the practice was. Some errors, obviously, are more serious than others, and would kill the case or force the complainant to start again from the beginning; other mistakes would not be fatal, if he made a timely correction of them, or if he paid the fine that was assessed, or if the mistake, as with witness testimony, met a certain triviality test.

As to the hapless Eyjolf, he is not guilty of anything in accepting a gift from Flosi to act as his defense lawyer. The relevant *Grágás* provision refers to bribing judges or panel members, but not to paying someone to represent a claimant or defendant in court, which is standard fare in the sagas.[16] But as to Eyjolf's jurisdictional ruse of having Flosi transfer his chieftaincy to his brother and then declare himself to be in-Thing with Askel, a North Quarter chieftain, this is too low a trick for the law to countenance. Such a switch would have to be announced at three Things, the local spring Thing, the Althing, and the fall meeting, before it could become effective.[17]

The author is not writing for lawyers, but for people who enjoy trial drama. It is remarkable how well the *Njála* author anticipated modern courtroom dramas.[18] I will stop my own pettifogging and concede him

15. The only 'strong' proof alleged for requiring the pleader to get every word right is a line in *Hrafnkels saga* saying that Sam presented his case 'without misspeaking', where the Icelandic word *miskivðalaust* has the look of a technical term, it occurring rarely, and confirmed as a technical term by Mord: *ek tek miskviðu alla ór máli mínu, hvárt sem mér verðr ofmælt or vanmælt*, 'I except all misspeaking from my pleading, whether I say too much or not enough.' One could argue whether *of-* or *van-mælt* means one extra word or wanting merely one word, but a more serious standard of error seems indicated, as the prefixes *of-* and *van-* tend to have a strong effect on the noun or adjective they are attached to, and as the allowances in the provision on witness testimony would also indicate. Cf. Heusler 1911: 108; in the English context Hudson (2012: 828) argues sensibly that the strict rule was an excuse for exacting a fine, and then one could proceed; thus Mord's being fined for the procedural error of failing to cite the nearest neighbors (ch. 142).
16. *Grágás* Ia 78; but this is not the author nodding. He had planned to get Eyjolf on these grounds 47 chapters earlier, for in his otherwise reasonably accurate reproduction of the *Grágás* text on the Fifth Court, he deviates to add a prohibition on paying 'for support' to the general prohibition relating to bribery of decision-makers; see EÓS 1954: 244 n. 3.
17. *Grágás* Ia 140–1, which also only allows a person to attach himself to a chieftain outside his quarter under limited circumstances.
18. See Clover 1998, 2012.

his druthers, for in fact they do not get in the way of the story. His errors would only bother a legal historian and, as I have indicated, the legal historian who clings only to *Grágás* is not always right; our author is mostly very astute about what the law in action must have looked like.

Three Lawmen

These chapters also invite us to look at three men of law—Mord, Eyjolf, and Thorhall—each of whom plays a different role in this part of the story, and to compare them implicitly to another man of law whose burning puts them all to work in these chapters.

Eyjolf is easily dealt with. As he suspected, he was being offered a position as cannon-fodder, to be, in his words, *forhleypi*, literally a 'before-leap man', a one-man forlorn hope. Bjarni would not let his cousin Thorkel Geitisson represent Flosi: 'it will mean death for the man who undertakes the defense of the Burners' (ch. 138). The risk is not that Thorkel will be killed in court, but that by being the central actor in court representing an unpopular cause, he will become a focal point for all the resentments the Burning and the frustrated legal action generate. Eyjolf is thus recruited by Flosi and Bjarni, who are as casual about his life as the nameless people who directed Atli to Kol earlier in the saga were about Kol's. In the interests of plausibility, the author introduced him as fond of money; and if that were not enough, Flosi makes sure he brings along some muscle to make Eyjolf an offer he cannot refuse. Eyjolf is called one of the three greatest lawyers in Iceland as a foil to Thorhall, to show that Thorhall is really playing in a league of his own. Eyjolf is the last man killed in the Battle at the Althing, and we are meant to delight in his death:

> Thorgeir Skorargeir said: 'There's Eyjolf Bolverksson, Kari. Reward him for that ring.' Kari grabbed a spear from someone and hurled it at Eyjolf. It struck him in the waist and went right through him; Eyjolf fell down dead at once. Now there was a slight lull in the fighting. (ch. 145)

It is as if the fighting can now stop because by killing Eyjolf some kind of symbolic justice was done. Kill the lawyer. The final judgment this supposedly-gifted lawyer will participate in (as a corpse) is one that declares him to be of zero value. Lumped with Skammkel and Sigmund's Swedish companion Skjold as not worth one ounce dead, he dies for having done his best for his client, who held an axe to his head to force him to take up a case that he knew was hopeless. Eyjolf is offered up to appease the anti-lawyer and anti-Burner sentiment—though he was not himself a Burner—of both the audience at the Althing and those reading the saga centuries later.

Mord is understood by readers to be a classic villain, motivated meanly, who opposes characters we like.[19] I have downplayed his causal role in events considerably. His envy of Gunnar is not unnatural, nor unique to him; Mord's envy is evident to other enviers of Gunnar, who ask for Mord's counsel and employ him in various capacities. He is not as inept as the narrator makes him out to be, for there are hints provided by the author that he is not without abilities. He is a *goði*, wealthy, well-connected by marriage. Gizur would not select Mord to plead the most important case against the Burners if he did not think Mord an able pleader. He could thus more than competently handle the routine legal work of a chieftain, which involved pleading many of his thingmen's claims. We should hardly be surprised that 'Mord was an extremely fine speaker' (ch. 141), or that he might be fairly charming. Ketil of Mork, despite having 'the impression that Mord does more harm than good', cannot withstand the charm: 'but as soon as Mord talked to him, Ketil, like so many others, believed Mord would be reliable' (ch. 112).

Mord is no Iago. He mostly reacts. Ian Maxwell gets it right: 'Mord takes advantage of openings created by others.'[20] That is true whether he is advising Gunnar's enemies, or 'tricking' the Njalssons into killing Hoskuld. In neither case did he initiate the situations he tries to exploit. Gunnar-haters come to him, not he to them. As was clear, he did not have to work very hard to get the Njalssons to do something they, at some level, were hankering to do.

He is no hero, but he, no less tha\n Njal, does not hold himself out as a warrior; he is not engaging in any pretenses on that score. If one wanted to risk blasphemy, there is much of Njal in Mord and of Mord in Njal. Both are operators, unmartial, and suspected of trickery by those who oppose

<hr/>

19. Andersson 2006: 196: 'villains. . . stud this saga.' Allen, 106: 'Mord is an embodiment of an evil-seeking agency.' I disagree. Only Thorgeir Starkadarson and Skammkel seem to have no redeeming virtues, but even these characters make social and psychological sense as to why they would find Gunnar unbearable; we only get pure, and flat, villains once we get to Brodir and Kormlod of the Clontarf episode.
20. Maxwell, 31.

them (e.g. chs. 23, 65). One is much more skilled, and rather more ambitious, and that is not Mord. Mord does, however, lead men into combat in the Battle at the Althing. The most reprehensible thing he does is not an act but an omission that we discussed: when he fails to break up the battle between Gunnar and Otkel. A close second is the cold ruthlessness with which he and Thorgeir Starkadarson plan to expose Thorgeir Otkelsson to Gunnar's halberd, so that Gunnar will have killed twice in the same lineage, picking very astutely which lineage that was to be—one that would remobilize Gizur the White, who would then be forced to go after Gunnar yet again. This is not motiveless malignity; this is politics, rather smart politics. Gunnar, not Mord, generated anti-Gunnar sentiment. Mord merely played the hand that was dealt him reasonably well against Gunnar.

Were we to see things from his side we would see a local chieftain of ancient lineage, accustomed to deference in the district, but finding himself unable to get as much as his kinsman Gunnar or as the talented lawyer Njal. Probably more than anyone, he (we do not know about Runolf of Dale) is the person losing most by the rise of Gunnar and Njal. At least that is how Mord and his father see it. He is coming out on the short end of a zero-sum game. That is surely the case after Skarphedin impoverished him to fund, literally, Njal's illicit revenge for Gunnar. Mord goes into remission for a decade. No one could be unhappier than he is (nor more disgusted than his father is) at seeing Njal's young protégé threaten to keep him in remission forever, a protégé who got his chieftaincy under rather dubious circumstances. Hoskuld is now the most popular chieftain in the area, and Mord is losing his thingmen to Hoskuld. Truly zero-sum. Is it villainy to want to win a game you have to play because you were to the manner born, born a chieftain who must hold his own or fail an implicit trust to your ancestors from whom you inherited your *goðorð*?

Mord is something of a poor man's Snorri the Priest, as we briefly suggested earlier, who foments strife (Snorri much more so than Mord), keeps himself out of harm's way, and comes in either to steal the prize or to watch his enemies and competitors exhaust themselves warring against each other. This is the Snorri who is consistently portrayed from saga to saga as an operator, as cunning, as self-interested in the extreme, and as ruthless about pursuing his interests as anyone in the family sagas. Who is it that pretty much goads the anti-Burner faction into turning the Althing into a battleground not by mere words, but by mobilizing his forces, at very little risk to those forces, to aid its cause should a battle occur (ch. 139)? Snorri gets a pass from our author, because he either remains neutral or feigns neutrality, and manifestly does not oppose the golden boys of the saga. When it comes down to it, does not most of Mord's villainy reside in his daring to oppose Gunnar and Njal in their saga? Were Mord as cunning and able as Snorri, able to cash in better on the problems of others, he would be a very good villain, but in the pragmatic world of the sagas he would then be too respected as a winner to be cast in that role.

The claim could be made that Mord, not unlike Hallgerd, can catch no break from the author. But that is not quite true with Mord, who gets some small rehabilitation. The author softens on him once the vagaries of the feud force him to affiliate with the anti-Burners. He mostly comes through. And he loves his wife 'like the eyes in his own head' (ch. 135). The threat of losing her makes him amenable to undertake the prosecution of Flosi. Must we really understand Mord's love for his wife the way any saga scholar would tell us we have to? Does the writer only intend to show Mord as uxorious, and thus as contemptibly unmanly?[21] Probably, but the knowledge that it is not all cold self-interest with Mord ends up complicating his portrait by having the author choose to unman him in this particular way, rather than have him whimper and cower before an angry Kari threatening to kill him or flee from battle.

Mord ranks third in the number of words spoken in the saga, behind Njal by nearly two thousand, a mere twenty-five behind Flosi, but he is ninth in the number of separate speeches.[22] The reason is easy to discern. Mord pleads the killing case against Flosi in direct discourse, these speeches being considerably longer than the usual conversational turn. Recall Bergthora blasting Njal for talking too much when he lamented the decline of public morals for more than one sentence (ch. 47). Mord is the person the saga fronts to provide us with the specialized grammar and diction of the law. Geir and Gizur gave us hints of it earlier (chs. 56, 73), but as Maxwell says, only to offer us 'a graduated course of legal instruction' so we can make sense of these chapters in which Mord prosecutes Flosi.

The language of law is formalized in statutes, in pleadings, in boilerplate, some of Mord's locutions qualifying as boilerplate, representing the accrued care of lawyers over decades to avoid a specific pitfall that caught someone else up short a century before. Make sure repetition clarifies what

21. KJJ 204 notes the difficulty in how to read this passage.
22. For the figures, see Hallberg 1966: 149.

the antecedents are; that pronouns, if used at all, given their inherent ambiguity, are disambiguated as to their referent. There is a certain universality in the diction and formalization of what we now call boilerplate, and it is surely in evidence in Mord's pleading. Would anyone mistake Mord's pleading for normal discourse? It has lawspeak written all over it. It is also rather remarkable how quickly laymen learn that lawspeak takes this form, and tune out, to the great advantage of one party to a transaction.[23]

Mord cannot be a villain if he is only saying lines that the law has scripted for him, saying them well, in a proceeding in which he represents the wronged party. The author, however, cannot find it in his heart not to have him blunder, though his intentions were hardly villainous, unless we want to impute to Mord a level of nefariousness nothing he had previously done would prepare us for. No, he does not blunder on purpose. The proof: we last see him leading troops into combat, something he surely would have preferred to spare himself.

Thorhall is the legal scholar. We do not see him plead or represent anyone in court. Nor did we see his tutor, Njal, as a pleader. These men, Njal and Thorhall, are legal counselors, the experts in law, who, as we noted, were expected to instruct and correct the Lawspeaker, and from whose ranks the Lawspeakers would be selected. With Njal and Thorhall we might be catching a glimpse of a separation of legal expertise into pleaders on one hand and jurists on the other, these latter coming to play a central role as legislators as well as advisors in litigation, as is the case with Njal and the Lawspeakers Skapti and Thorgeir of Ljosawater.[24]

I have already spoken rather fully about Thorhall, in every respect an inspired authorial creation. We see him as a boy fostered out to get instructed in law, the culture passing on legal knowledge from generation to generation by tutoring, in which certain obviously intelligent youngsters are earmarked to be so trained. We see him as passionate, emotional, his body swelling and nearly exploding with fluids. He fears that his body makes him a laughing-stock; his taste in clothing elicits teasing from the Njalssons, as we noted in another context, but no one thinks him a joke. They respect him to the core.

---

23. For a masterful treatment of the diction of law, see Daube 1981, also 1969.
24. Mord Fiddle, the legal expert two generations earlier, pleaded his own case to his manifest detriment.

Compare his 'defect' with Njal's. One's body cannot extrude facial hair, the other's cannot help but vomit forth fluids. Both are abnormal, but despite his fear that he will be ridiculed, no one makes mocking verses about Thorhall's fainting, seizures, and gushings. Unlike Njal, but like Odysseus, Thorhall is big and strong. He is hot-tempered, and when provoked, he will kill. Being physically imposing will do wonders for making others suppress their desire to mock a somewhat strange man with a very high IQ. Thorhall is endearing. I am not indulging in ahistorical sentimentality to think so, for the author feels the same way about him, as did those people concerned to comfort this sensitive soul when he lost consciousness on hearing of Njal's death.

Thorhall, in his modest way, captures the saga from the moment he faints until the moment he impales Grim the Red on his purulent spear. Thorhall gets special treatment. Because he first appeared as a boy that Njal took in to foster, he never received a conventional introduction. But now that Thorhall is an adult, his character and body fully formed, he is playing too important a role not to be properly introduced. His body is again misbehaving, and since the narrator feels called on to describe the swollen leg of the bedridden Thorhall, why not use the occasion to give the audience a sense of what his body looks like when it is not misbehaving, as well as a summary of his most telling character traits?[25]

> And now the time for the Althing drew near. Thorhall Asgrimsson developed an inflammation of the leg, so acute that above the ankle his leg was as thick and swollen as a woman's thigh, and he could only walk with the help of a stick. Thorhall was a tall, powerful man, dark-haired and sallow-complexioned, as quiet-spoken as he was hot-tempered. He was one of the three greatest lawyers in Iceland. (ch. 135)

When the trial itself is about to begin and the men have put markings on their helmets, Thorhall, from his sickbed, gives his father and other members of their party advice on how to proceed. Take it slow, he tells them, and if things go wrong let me know. Without a word about internal states, the author packs the scene with an array of sentiments. He does not describe Thorhall from some omniscient narrative plane; rather we see Thorhall through the eyes of his father and through our own as we are put into the scene amongst the 'others': 'Asgrim and the others looked at him; his face

---

25. See Ch. 16, n. 2.

was as red as blood, and tears like hailstones burst from his eyes. He asked
them to bring him his spear, the one that Skarphedin had given him; it was
a most valuable weapon' (ch. 142). We start positioned as Asgrim and those
looking at Thorhall; we then follow their sightlines to Thorhall's face, right
after he had just given his advice to go slow and stay calm. That face is
not calm at all, not its natural sallow color, but red as the blood he will
soon cause to flow. A hailstorm of tears breaks out and no one, we can bet,
would dare mock him for weeping. We hear him, via indirect discourse,
request a spear, for he senses, as everyone else does, that another storm is
about to erupt. The spear is not just any spear but one that brings with it the
ghost of Skarphedin—*Skarpheðinsnautr*.[26] Then a small digression about the
weapon,[27] which tells us that Skarphedin thought well of Thorhall as a warrior, as he had thought well of Atli. Finally, back to Asgrim, whose looking
at his son started the passage, to sum up with typical understatement what
we have just seen: 'My kinsman Thorhall was not easy in his mind when we
left him behind in the booth and I do not know what he will do.'

Thorhall has a body that behaves allegorically, while retaining all its natural mixture of humors: he is as real as a fictional character can get, more
fully embodied in flesh, pus, blood, tears, than those surreal bodies owned
by Gunnar and Kari. Thorhall is meant not only to be himself, which he so
perfectly is, but also to embody the entire polity. He is the microcosm, the
little world, of his society at this precise moment, as it is about to burst the
seams of its limited institutionalized restraints. One might also see in him
the embodiment of the land itself for all times: eruptions, hail, gushing tor-
rents, fire and ice; and learned in law.

Eyjolf, Mord, and Thorhall all have their last appearance at the Battle at
the Althing; they depart the saga in the same chapter. Of them, only Eyjolf
gets a formal leave-taking, because Kari hurls a spear through him. In the
standard Icelandic edition we last see or hear of Mord and Thorhall on the
same page: Thorhall is attacking with his father, together with Gizur and
Hjalti, where Flosi and the Sigfussons are arrayed, while Mord, Gudmund
the Powerful, and Thorgeir Skorargeir head for those North Quarter and
Eastfjord chieftains whom Flosi recruited to his cause. Eyjolf lasts a few
pages longer as he waits to be dispatched by Kari, and is finally dismissed

26. On gifts being designated by the name of their giver, see p. 203.
27. The digression on the weapon mimics the style of the digression on the place-name where
    Thorgeir Otkelsson's body came to a sudden halt as it floated downstream; see p. 136.

as *ógildr*, uncompensated for, in the settlement toward the chapter's end. The three men of law who played their part in the big trial of the Burners are no longer needed, as the saga shifts to those who refuse to settle and prefer blood: Thorgeir Skorargeir and Kari. We have seen the last lawsuit in *Njáls saga*, the only one that goes to judgment (and the judgment was a divided one to boot), and the last of its lawyers. The saga, like the feud itself, changes focus, and those who mattered greatly at one time matter not at all the next.

20

Kari and Friends: Chapters 145–55

In the battle the Burners got the worst of it. After the death of Eyjolf there is a lull, both sides evidently wanting some way to bring matters to a halt. That is the cue for Snorri and Skapti to intervene with forces to separate the sides. Men look to the dead and wounded, and the next day they gather at the Law Rock to talk settlement, compose insulting verses, and bring some closure to most of the outstanding claims.

Hall of Sida, whose good will no one has ever doubted, proposes 'a settlement on even terms', rendering *jafnsætti*, literally 'even-settlement'.[1] Without Kari's gloss to guide us it is not easy to know exactly what Hall is proposing. Kari refuses to join the settlement, for he reads Hall as asking that the Burners' losses in the battle—they were sorely beaten, losing six dead to one, and many more wounded—should satisfy their liability for the Burning: 'You are trying to equate the Burning with these killings, and that we could never tolerate.' Hall is asking them to call it even. Remember he has lost his son, so though the deal sounds risible to Kari, to Hall it represents a real concession.

Amidst the high seriousness and genuine sorrow of Hall, others cannot resist composing verses that mock the injuries or less-than-heroic fighting of some. Given that situations calling for obligatory piety seem to provoke mockery to this very day, I find this mix of mockery and gravity not implausible. The mocking verses, as far as we know, are not forced on the author because they might have been preserved in other sources so that he felt obliged to work them in. This saga's commitment to realism is also

---

1. *Jafnsætti*, the word Hall uses, can also a refer to a settlement determined by a panel with each side picking an equal number of arbitrators, or more generally it can mean a fair, impartial settlement as when employed by Osvifr (ch. 12).

revealed in its refusal to interject as much verse as was customary in many sagas. For our author, a verse seems more suited to a corpse or to Valkyries in a vision than to be recited by a character in the midst of social action. The few verses a character might be allowed to speak are thus mostly made part of the action and have consequences: ask Thorhild the Poetess or Sigmund, and Sigmund's are only reported; we do not get to hear them. Kari alone gets away with more than a stanza, and his poeticizing marks him as something of the *sui generis* outsider he is, of which more later.[2]

A quite comprehensive settlement is reached. The battle seemed to scare everyone into shaping up, except Kari and Thorgeir Skorargeir, who feel too much is being buried in the interests of some kind of finality; they are still in blood-lust mode. In the end, Hall of Sida's original proposal is rejected as being too soft. Kari was right about that. Gudmund the Powerful offers another, stiffer compromise: he is willing to guarantee the compensation for the killings in the battle if the claims for the Burning still stand, which is soon clarified as costing the Burners considerably more than Hall's original proposal: triple compensation for Njal, double for Bergthora and her sons, and single compensation for the other victims, as well as exile for the Burners, Flosi and some others for three years, others for life.

Hall of Sida had waived compensation for his son Ljot as a gesture to shame everyone into coming to a settlement. So grateful was the assembly to Hall that people contributed to compensate him nonetheless, and it came to quadruple compensation. Could we see a more powerful indication that, despite the violence that captures the reader's imagination and makes events sagaworthy, most people want peace, and feel that its chief spokesman, Hall, earns sincere and thus pocketable gratitude? Hall could not have expected or even have fantasized that he would be rewarded so greatly for his humility and unselfishness. But there is no mention that he refused the money. From that point on, were someone to make a public-spirited waiver of compensation, he would find it psychologically harder not to suspect his own motives; would people snigger that the purse holding his kinsman was quite heavy?[3]

2. Guðrún Nordal, 199: 'Kari [is]. . . the only proper poet of the saga in *Möðruvallabók.*' *Möðruvallabók* is the manuscript that EÓS uses for his edition and upon which modern translations are based. It represents a line of manuscripts in which there is very little verse. Some manuscripts of the saga contain substantially more verses, which are by common agreement non-authorial.

3. For all his decency of spirit Hall is no pushover: consider his reasons for why Flosi should settle with Thorgeir and let the Sigfussons, Flosi's clients, worry about themselves (ch. 146).

Recall the 600 ounces raised the year before and kept in reserve (ch. 123). At that time Snorri indicated the money would soon be needed. We are not told that it helped fund these settlements, but we must assume it did. A considerable amount needs to be paid for the victims of the Burning, for the victims of the battle—even though the wounded among the Burners were not compensated, those on the other side were—and to fund Hall's generosity of spirit. Gudmund must have looked to that sum to assist him in meeting the guarantee he made for any compensation awarded. It was important for that money to have been available to sweeten the settlement pot. If those entitled to compensation could walk away with the money they were due, or at least a non-trivial portion of it, then the settlement was more likely to hold than if they had to take an IOU and sureties had to be found, unless the surety was as well-heeled as Gudmund.

Even as the saga wants to give a sense of decline, showing the failure of certain institutions that are no longer up to the stresses put upon them, one must admire how quickly and efficiently the breakdown at the Althing was accounted for, and I mean 'accounted' in its bookkeeping sense. Though the trend in the saga is to show disputes outrunning the capacities of all but the biggest and wealthiest to play the game, because only they could afford to play, we still see someone like Snorri watching the battle and interfering to stop it once the limits of compensability had been reached: 'as soon as I estimate that you have killed off as many of them as you can afford to pay compensation for without exile or loss of your chieftaincies, I shall intervene with all my men to stop the fighting' (ch. 139). This is rather remarkable. Imagine, for instance, a bar fight in which the brawlers check their wallets to see how many teeth they can knock out or noses they can break before they have to call a halt, as Gunnar did when he kept a running tally of how many he could afford to kill (ch. 72). As long as the victor still figures he might have to pay the loser for his losses, we have not fully abandoned the world of feud for that of war, even though the saga shows things moving in that direction.

The arbitrators are not without their artistic side; consider the layers of meaning in equating the value of Skarphedin and Hoskuld Hvitanesspriest, the latter's price having been declared the year before to be treble compensation—600 ounces. Skarphedin is thus worth his father and worth his father's foster-son, and that those three are worth more than anyone else, in the saga's terms, the highest compensation ever awarded (ch. 123). It was left to the community to add its own ironical comment by upping the ante for

Hall's son Ljot to 800 ounces, but that was a gift, not an adjudged amount, and manifestly a measure not of Ljot's value but rather his father's.

The arbitrators invite us too to play the game of what it means to balance Skarphedin against Hoskuld. Is it pagan against Christian, violence against peace, nature against culture? Hardly. This author is less given to easy reductionism than we are inclined to be. His arbitrators make no statement other than one of equivalence, recognizing, it seems, that greatness comes in a variety of styles that for some purposes must be equated. Skarphedin was a Christian, because everyone was. Hoskuld was praised for his skill in arms, just as Skarphedin was. Even if we insist, which we should not, that Skarphedin was meant to represent the old values and that Hoskuld was some aspirational representative of the new, then the community was more capable of dealing with irony and ambiguity than we are. Whatever symbolism might lurk in the arbitrators' award, it was meant mostly to do practical work, to make as many people accept the rightness of the decision as they could, given how limited the stocks of hard cash were. It mattered who was chosen to balance against whom at what price, even if no one had to back it up with silver or sheep or land, because each corpse was the money used to pay for the other.

Kari and Thorgeir

Two necessary participants refuse to be party to the settlement. They do not like the way the arbitrators struck the balance. Eleven members of Njal's family and household died in the fire. It would take five more corpses before Thorgeir could accept that he was quit, and fifteen more before Kari thought himself quit. They have a case, if blood is the specie. Not enough Burners died in the Battle at the Althing or were killed in the attack on Bergthorsknoll. Kari divides his unsatisfied claim into two parts. Once Thorgeir and he take on the Sigfussons, two on fifteen, killing five of them, Kari considers the Burning avenged. Adding those killed at the Althing brings the total to eleven, though I doubt he is merely counting corpses. Nonetheless, it strikes a better balance than the settlement terms accepted at the Althing.

Hall of Sida, on behalf of Flosi, then seeks out Thorgeir and Kari to see if they will settle. Kari refuses and Thorgeir is reluctant to abandon

Kari. Kari has to threaten Thorgeir to make peace, but gives cogent reasons too: 'you will never be in a stronger position than this' (ch. 147). Kari is right. If Thorgeir were to continue killing he would not be acting within the limits of the license his grievances give him. He can now settle in good conscience: he will not be judged to have taken excessive, and hence unjustifiable, revenge, nor can he be accused of carrying his kin in his purse. Kari grants himself, though, a continuing license to kill because he claims that he has not yet specifically avenged his son Thord who died in the flames.

One of Thorgeir's conditions for settling is that Kari have sanctuary at Thorgeir's home, which is conceded. Kari, however, refuses to take advantage of the safe home: 'No, *mágr* (in-law), that must not be, for if I kill someone, they will immediately accuse you of being in league with me' (ch. 148). This is apt. 'Former' enemies are not likely to put the kindest gloss on each other's actions. Suspicions will tend to bias their perception of perfectly legitimate dealings, subjecting them to unfavorable or ungenerous interpretation. Thus, as we saw, when Kolskegg tried to recover Moeidarknoll for his mother and pay cash instead, it was claimed to be a violation of a settlement (chs. 67–8, 70); so too after the settlement of the Burning case, Thorgeir and Kari stay well clear of Thorgeir's brothers at the family farm at Holt, 'for Thorgeir did not want his brothers to be implicated in anything that might happen', and then after he and Kari attack the Sigfussons, 'Thorgeir sent his brothers east to Skogar, where they owned another farm, for he did not want them to be called *griðníðingar* (truce-breakers)' (ch. 146).[4]

How are we to understand Kari's motives for urging Thorgeir to come to terms? On the positive side, he does not want to put Thorgeir at more risk, nor, to take him at his word, does he want to see Thorgeir waste his optimal time for an advantageous settlement; nor does he wish to humiliate Hall of Sida by turning his peacemaking journey into a fool's errand. He wants Hall to have something to bring back to Flosi. Kari may lack measure when it comes to his own grievances, but not when it comes to Thorgeir's. I am, however, mistrustful of Kari. I am not sure that Kari wants to share his moment in the saga sun with someone like Thorgeir, who is too much cut in Kari's mold. That is why Kari recruits the likes of Bjorn of Mork. Though, with some irony, Bjorn ends up upstaging Kari, Kari at least does not have to share his kill-count with Bjorn, or anyone else, as he had to,

---

4. Kari's and Thorgeir's care in these matters is the flipside of Thrain's and Otkel's lack of care in dissociating themselves from liability-generators in their own group.

or would continue to have to, if Thorgeir insisted on coming along for the ride.

Kari does ask one favor of Thorgeir. He conveys his property to Thorgeir in something resembling a trust, to insulate it from confiscation should he be outlawed and/or from claims for compensation that he expects will be made by the kin of the people he means to kill. As Njal sheltered some of Gunnar's assets, so does Thorgeir Kari's: 'I should like you to take over my property and let it be assigned to you and to my wife, Helga Njalsdottir, and my daughters. Then it can never be confiscated by my adversaries' (ch. 148). Like many a prudent wrongdoer, Kari makes sure to render himself judgment-proof.

Bjorn of Mork and Kari

Bjorn is obviously comic, but not obvious is why the author is so merciful to him. The standard comic braggart soldier, the *miles gloriosus*, like Falstaff, conventionally comes to a hard end. But not Bjorn. W. P. Ker devoted almost a page to Bjorn; even if you might not fully be in accord, you will lament the passing of the day when critics like Ker held sway:

> The comedy of Bjorn is that he proves to be something different both from his own Bjorn and his wife's Bjorn. He is the idealist of his own heroism, and believes in himself as a hero. His wife knows better; but the beauty of it all is that his wife is wrong. His courage, it is true, is not quite certain, but he stands his ground; there is a small particle of a hero in him, enough to save him.[5]

Bjorn, to whom I have referred several times in passing, is married to Valgerd, who is a first cousin of Gunnar, which one would think would make her someone whom Kari would stay clear of, she being connected by blood to the Sigfussons, and living, it seems, close by Ketil of Mork. Some people get reputations for being willing to provide help to outlaws and outcasts, though Valgerd hardly seems like one of these,[6] but given Valgerd's kinship to the Sigfussons her farm is the last place anyone would suspect

---

5. Ker, 228.
6. E.g. Thorgerd, mother of Gest Oddleifsson (*Gísla saga*, ch. 23); Helgi Hardbeinsson (*Laxdæla saga*, ch. 62); also see *Bjarnar saga*, ch. 22.

Kari to head to for aid, so the move makes sense from Kari's perspective should Valgerd, for whatever reason, be unwilling to betray him.

The author is practical enough to know that not even Kari can kill as much as he wants to if he is alone. His targets ride in convoys for defense. He needs to have someone keep watch so he can sleep; he needs someone to cover his back, even if it is only to stop an axe. Bjorn is keen-sighted, a real virtue in a world of no corrective lenses. Kari toys with Bjorn for his own amusement, but then so does everyone, including the author. Yet when it comes time to report to Bjorn's wife what Bjorn accomplished there is no mockery in Kari's voice, no exaggeration, just fact. Kari does right by Bjorn in a practical Icelandic way, not in romance/heroic vein; Kari shows that his moral clock is ticking perfectly on this occasion. He knows that Bjorn cannot trust to literary conventions to keep him from getting killed. Kari therefore arranges for Thorgeir Skorargeir to take Bjorn under his protection and exchange Bjorn's farm for a new one right next to Thorgeir's (ch. 152). To Kari's credit, he recognizes when a debt is due for favors rendered. He repays gifts of positive value in proper measure; it is 'gifts' of negative value he has problems pricing appropriately.

Bjorn plays the age-old literary type when 'one moment [he] was all for fleeing as fast as possible, and the next moment he was all for staying to deal with [the enemy]. Kari found it all most entertaining.' If Kari ever enjoyed himself in the saga, it was with Bjorn and Thorgeir, but that was probably because their company was a prelude to blood, which we find Kari enjoys more than banter (ch. 150).[7] Bjorn is mocked for his obvious fearfulness. But if he did not fear, would his delivering in the crunch, not once but twice, mean much? He also had to keep a cool exterior when he got information out of the Sigfussons about their itinerary. A Bjorn whose fantasy life was impermeable to all aspects of reality, and thus to fear, would be merely psychotic. He would be as one-dimensional as Kari might have been had he not found Bjorn to humanize him.

The scenes with Bjorn are superbly wrought. When Kari and he ride to Skal to announce their killings, one of the dead being the head of the

7. Kari is not violating the ritualized refusal to laugh until revenge is taken, for he is in the process of taking it, and like Gunnar Lambason when he breaks his laugh-fast, he can acknowledge he is enjoying the process. We can excuse Kari's poetic riposte to Skapti that provoked loud laughter at the Althing as its own revenge upon Skapti (ch. 145). There is no indication that Kari was laughing at his own verses.

household there, Gunnar of Skal, Kari says to them that they had better get the badly injured Grani inside and look to his wound if he were to live. Grani is in some sense Bjorn's counterpart. Bjorn is Gunnar of Hlidarend's in-law, Grani is his son. Grani, pinned to the ground like a bug to a board by a spear in the thigh right below his groin, is himself a cowardly boaster and has been coldly called on it by Flosi (ch. 117) and by Ketil of Mork (ch. 149). Life could not have been easy for Grani Gunnarsson. Imagine having a father like Gunnar to have to live up to. Or would it be worse to be the grandson of a slave, as Bjorn was? Both Bjorn and Grani are trying to compensate for problems that lineage stuck them with; one of them is endearing, the other only a mother could love[8]—Grani's father certainly did not (ch. 75).

Bjorn adds his comments after Kari announces the killings:

> Bjorn said he was unwilling to kill [Grani],[9] although he richly deserved it. The [people at Skal] replied that few men were rotting in their graves on account of Bjorn. Bjorn retorted that he was now in a position to make as many of the men of Sida rot in their graves as he chose. That would be just terrible, was their reply. (ch. 150)

The servants' drollery requires that making men rot in their graves be a virtue, because that is what Bjorn in his fantasy life thinks it is. Whether they sincerely subscribe to the belief is beside the point, but recall Bergthora's casual response to Atli when she heard he had injured or killed a lot of men. Bjorn, nonplussed, expands on his fantasies. They, without missing a beat, in a tone of voice still heard perfectly eight centuries later: yeah right, you sure scare us.

When Bjorn returns from his mission with typical braggadocio, he must face his wife:

> 'Our troubles have certainly increased, woman.'[10]
> She made no reply but smiled a little. Then she said, 'How useful did you find Bjorn?' (ch. 152)

---

8. Grani and Hallgerd live together after Gunnar's death with Thrain and Thorgerd (ch. 78).
9. One scribe, c.1400, added 'for the sake of his being connected to him by marriage', apparently feeling that Valgerd and Bjorn's kinship connection to the Sigfusson's needed some further confirmation, given their willingness to aid Kari; see EÓS 1954: 432 n. 2.
10. Judd notes that Bjorn takes an opportunity to get even with his wife by calling her the 'pejorative' *kerling*, when before he had addressed her respectfully as *husfreyja*. I think this misreads the tone. *Kerling* can be pejorative, but it can also carry the tone of 'old gal', almost a term of endearment, as when Skarphedin calls his mother that as he tries to keep himself under control when the red spots appeared on his cheeks.

Smiles of amiability are not all that uncommon in the sagas, though lethal ones are surely more salient; but Valgerd's is neither. Her smile is one of presumed complicity with Kari, one of knowing contempt, waiting for the expected confirmation, so she can finally walk out on Bjorn. We can only guess whether Kari's matter-of-fact response generated more satisfaction in Bjorn than disappointment in Valgerd.

That Bjorn lands on his feet is genius. He saves the saga from sinking us into the depths of gloom. Mord, it seems, lands on his too. In each case our expectations have been toyed with. But Bjorn transcends the saga in a way Mord does not. Bjorn, long before Don Quixote, reminds us that the sagas generated fantasy lives back then as fictional heroes still do for us today. The difference between Bjorn's fantasy and ours is that he actually was called on to play a part in a saga not of his own imagining, after having fantasized being in real ones all along to everyone's eye-rolling mockery and to his wife's impatience and contempt.

Were the opportunity given us, would I, you, would we, do as well as Bjorn did? We would not have to do as Thorgeir did, axe two attackers with one blow, catching one on the back swing, the other on the forward stroke, with Skarphedin's axe no less. We would only have to cover Kari's back, keep other fighters at bay, succeed in injuring several of them, get wounded ourselves. Bjorn did well enough to have earned the stature of mattering enough to have enemies: '[Thorgeir] arranged a full settlement on Bjorn's behalf and effected a reconciliation for him with all his enemies. Thereafter Bjorn was considered much more a man than he had been before' (ch. 152). If any redemption can be found in this saga, that is it. Bjorn is introduced as a failed character, a buffoon, and exits having earned some modicum of respect from those who had always thought him nothing but a joke. He does not manage this by any special heroics, nor by any god descending from a machine, nor by magical transformations, but simply by doing better than our low expectations, expectations wrought by both literary convention and by Bjorn himself, would predict. No one reading this book can realistically see himself as Skarphedin or Hildigunn. But as Bjorn? And yet would our own uncertain courage do as well?

Kari vs. Gunnar

Kari might have all the athletic virtues of Gunnar, and like him be something of a killing machine. To some, like Flosi, he is the second coming of Gunnar, as a warrior and as a man with a handsome head of hair. Unlike Gunnar, Kari is pure, unadulterated avenger. Except for Otkel, none of Gunnar's killings are in revenge. But neither the balanced-exchange ideology nor actual feuding practice would allow for Kari's personalized and idiosyncratic measures of evaluation. Little Thord Karason? No child who chose his death and was accommodated in his wish by his ever-doting grandmother, Bergthora, would be judged the equivalent of ten adults from good families, some of whom it appears might not even have been Burners, like Gunnar of Skal, a worthy farmer (ch. 150). Kari finds Iceland too small to sate his blood-lust; he heads for the British Isles to hunt down two more before he feels the balance is struck.

Examine any of the arbitration awards in the saga to see if Kari is playing in the same moral world, or by the same exchange-rates, as others. The entire community believes that the Burning is settled on reasonable terms; even Thorgeir Skorargeir, with a little pushing, accepts that. Kari feels himself bound by nothing but his own grief, unhinged from community norms, and about which we see him poetize. Grief in people like Kari 'must not unwatched go'. 'Grief' is something of a term of art, not merely an emotion term. Grief often bears with it a claim to take revenge. The Norse word rendered grief in English is *harmr*, self-evidently cognate with English *harm*. The variation in the primary meaning the same root took in the two languages reveals the claim for revenge lying at the core of grief. Kari informs his partners, David and Kolbein, that he means to head for Wales to hunt down another Burner, 'for he would not conceal from anyone the fact that he felt he had not yet fully avenged his grief (*harma*) on the Burners' (ch. 158). *Harma*, a plural form, drives the meaning more toward *wrongs* here; it is not working as an emotion term, for which the singular would be expected. Even today grief makes us curse God. The life-insurance industry arose partly to fill an emotional need to make sure that we get handed our purse of silver in compensation for the 'grievous' harm done us by God taking our loved one.

To put the disproportion of Kari's revenge in broader perspective consider this: the rules of balance in revenge contemplated less death than the law for the same wrong. Every man who participated in or furthered the Burning was liable for full outlawry. As an outlaw, as we saw in the Introduction, he could be killed with impunity by anyone, and indeed the person who got him outlawed was obliged to kill him. Revenge, on the other hand, was measured not against the culpability of the wrongdoer but against the wrong suffered. So no avenger would be within his rights killing one hundred men for eleven who died in the fire; somewhere between three and eleven would be within the proper limits, depending on the status of the people killed in revenge and that of the victims being avenged. Revenge, unlike outlawry, does not have to target a wrongdoer. A nephew of any Sigfusson would be a permissible vengeance target even if he had not been a Burner. The law, in other words, at least officially, contemplated a hundred corpses, the feud or vengeance system about one-tenth that number, but the corpses need not have been culpable as a matter of law.

Kari is playing the vengeance game by his own accounting rules.[11] Then too, remember that though the law was clear that these hundred men should be outlawed, the community was not about to let that happen either. As we know from today, great wrongs, committed by a great number claiming many victims, are dealt with, if at all, not with harsh criminal sanctions, except for an exemplary few, but by truth-and-reconciliation commissions and some form of amnesty. To deliver actual justice, justice that the law itself legitimates, to all who had it coming would be only a mite less horrific than the horror of the original wrongs.

Gunnar was killed for flouting a settlement; Kari avoids the issue by refusing settlements and is allowed to flout norms as foundational as the one Gunnar flouted. One way of explaining Kari is that he is playing in a different genre, a romance genre,[12] while Gunnar, though he was influenced by romance motifs that showed in his dress and his killing acumen, still operated in a functional Icelandic social order. Gunnar is never not embedded in the community which brings him down; his refusal to dis-embed himself for three years killed him. Kari rarely descends from that romance unreality. And that is part of the reason why Kari, unlike Gunnar, does not seem to elicit the toxic envy that Gunnar does. He just is not really part of this Icelandic world. No wonder he ends up traveling abroad to a world that goes supernatural, with heads reattaching, boiling blood raining from the

---

11. Cf. Hjalti Skeggjason, who, when he hears of the Burning, was 'appalled at the news, and said that it was imperative to pursue them and kill every one of them' (ch. 131). That is said in the heat of the moment and reflects how angry and upset he is, but killing them all is neither morally nor politically feasible, nor was it militarily possible.

12. Heusler 1922: 8.

sky, weapons unsheathing themselves and warring with each other, and Valkyries weaving gut-cloth.

Gunnar is of this world in the most common way; we see him engaged with his wife in connubial unbliss. Kari's wife Helga speaks no words, though she is given his property; she is mentioned taking passage out of the fire, but that is it. No interactions between husband and wife are depicted. Gunnar was still committed to law and order; he enters into settlements, even the one that he eventually violated. Kari finally settles when there is only one person left to settle with.

Unlike Gunnar, too, Kari has a style of humor that condescends to the person he talks to, especially when these are his partners. It is not reserved for his enemies. He patronizes Thorgeir Skorargeir, of all people, a person about whom there might well have been a lost saga to which Kari refers: 'But I know what you have set yourself; you are planning to take on eight of them. And even that is an easier task than when you killed seven men in a gorge after lowering yourself down to them by rope' (ch. 146). Or when Thorgeir asks if Kari wants first to wake a band of sleeping Sigfussons that some people in the countryside have obligingly directed them to before attacking them: 'Need you ask,' replied Kari, 'when you must already have made up your mind not to attack men in their sleep and thus kill dishonorably?' This way of imputing intentions to his interlocutor is also how he talks down to Bjorn of Mork (ch. 151), but Thorgeir Skorargeir is not Bjorn. Though the author may be setting Thorgeir up by having him ask those questions to the greater glory of Kari, it is also possible to think that Thorgeir harbors doubts about Kari, whose prowess and virtue within Iceland, we need to remind ourselves, has not been greatly tested yet. Thorgeir may well be uncertain whether Kari would not, like Odysseus and Diomedes, take a perverse delight in killing sleeping enemies.

Once Kari starts killing it is strangely without Gunnar's level of battle-fury. In the set-up of Thrain, recall, Njal plans that Kari discuss matters with Thrain, 'for Kari can control his temper' (ch. 91), although since he was not implicated in the Dungbeard insult there was less to provoke his temper. He will prove himself a colder killer than most, one whom Thorgeir might well imagine sinking to Diomedean levels for a little cold fun.[13]

---

13. Perhaps this is what Fox means when he refers incomprehensibly to Kari's 'complete lack of bloodthirstiness' (306).

It is of some symbolic import that Kari makes himself judgment-proof by transferring his assets to Thorgeir. He becomes, if not Gunnar reborn, then Thjostolf reborn. When Thjostolf is introduced he is accompanied with the standard saga trope of the *ójafnaðarmaðr* ('uneven-man', an unjust man), the man who does not recognize the principle of paying for his wrongs, whose sense of equivalence is out of whack: 'he had killed many men and paid compensation for none of them' (ch. 9). Should we be surprised that Thjostolf has a past in the Hebrides as does Kari, kills abroad and in Iceland, as Kari will soon kill in Wales and the Orkneys? As an aside of some interest: Thjostolf is not specifically called an *ójafnaðarmaðr*, though he more than meets the test. In *Njála* only Thorgeir Starkadarson's cousins, the Egilssons, are introduced as *ójafnaðarmenn*, where the meaning is probably best captured by 'jerks', or more vulgarly, 'assholes'. Kari, interestingly, first appears in the saga as a person who evens things up; he corrects imbalance: 'who are the players in this uneven game (*leik svá ójafnan*)' (ch. 84). He still thinks that is what he is doing hunting down Burners, but he is blind to his own heavy thumb on the scale.

If I have been too hard on Kari, accused the author of giving him less depth than he could have, there are leakages in Kari's behavior that hint of deeper motive, if not quite reason, to his excessive revenges. Kari is not at ease over surviving the Burning. He was not only outmanned by Skarphedin (who isn't?), as we saw, but also tellingly by his little boy Thord, who chose not to flee the flames, much in the way Helgi Njalsson, dressed as a woman, is outmanned by his mother who stays. That Kari is troubled by doubts of his own motives is given good warrant in the text. It is reflected both in the substance of some of his verses and by the fact he is given to versifying in the first place; he is not at ease in his mind. When Gizur says it was great fortune that Kari escaped, Kari responds with a verse, perhaps a bit defensively, and puts a rather self-serving gloss on his own mental state when he left the burning farmhouse. He left, he says, *ófúss*, that is, 'constrained, compelled, unwillingly' (ch. 135); but little Thord felt no such compulsion. That it is not overreading to suggest that Kari might be motivated to overkill in order to kill his shame (or in modern jargon, his 'survivor's guilt') is that others accuse him of flight and cowardice. Thus Skapti: 'You would be better not to have deserted your kinsmen, Kari, and not to except yourself from a settlement now' (ch. 145). Might it be that Skapti has hit on exactly what drives Kari's excesses? Kari responds to Skapti with his longest poetic effort, not by denying Skapti's claim, but by argument ad hominem, that is, by accusing Skapti of what Skapti had just accused him, of martial failings.[14]

Flosi and Kari

If it takes some work and verse to keep Kari from being one-dimensional once he escapes his role as sidekick, Flosi needs work to reduce the welter of his complex character. Flosi has a strange relationship to the idea of Kari, if not to Kari himself. They have never been interlocutors in any face-to-face interaction until the very last chapter. Kari was never more than a tagalong in the marriage negotiations between Flosi and Njal, or at the wedding that followed. After the killing of Hoskuld they are separated by the mandatory avoidance of open enmity. But once Kari escapes the Burning he becomes something of an icon that Flosi venerates: 'The man who has escaped comes nearest to being the equal of Gunnar of Hlidarend in everything' (ch. 130).[15] ' "There are few men like Kari," said Flosi. "He is the man I would most like to resemble in character" ' (ch. 147)—this after Kari had convinced Thorgeir to settle, but still refused to settle himself. Later, Ketil arrives to tell Flosi of yet another attack by Kari in which three more of Flosi's adherents were killed. 'Flosi showed little concern, but said that he was not convinced that would be the end of it—"for there is no one now in all the land like Kari" ' (ch. 151). When Kari beheads Gunnar Lambason in jarl Sigurd's hall, Flosi defends him: 'Kari has not done this without cause. He is not in any settlement with us, and he only did what was his duty' (ch. 155). One might also translate this last clause, no less faithfully to the original: 'he only did what he had to do' or 'a man's gotta do what a man's gotta do', the statement qualifying as something of a proverb across more than one culture. And when he beheads Kol Thorsteinsson in Wales, Flosi 'never uttered a word against Kari' (ch. 158).

14. Thanks to Chris Ting JD 2013 on Kari's shame for being bested by his son. On Kari and versifying, see this chapter, n. 2.
15. See Bolton, 196, who takes Flosi's remark as one of several false inferences characters make in the attack both on Gunnar and Bergthorsknoll: 'it is Skarphedin, and not his brother-in-law, who is the true successor to the master of Hlidarend, as shown by the authorship of the second poem in each pair [i.e. their death verses], by their similar defiance in the face of death, and by Skarphedin's own references to the parallels between them.'

There are several ways to explain Flosi's admiration for Kari. One can be dismissed fairly quickly. Flosi understands that Kari is not targeting him, nor is he about to. Why should this be clear to Flosi? Is he not the leader of the Burners? The fact is that Flosi is too big for the likes of Kari to target. Geir the Priest can thus know that when he moves into the district to protect Gunnar's enemies after Gunnar's death, he is safe even if his illegitimate son is not. Skarphedin and Hogni threaten to kill Mord in their revenge of Gunnar, but that threat was not so serious that Mord could not buy his way out instead. One of the reasons the world of the saga comes near to crumbling completely is that once Hoskuld Thrainsson is made a chieftain, he is supposed to be off limits to anyone except another chieftain. Big guys do get killed, but that is a last option, or a sign the game is bursting beyond its unofficial rules.[16] It is still something of a sign of Gunnar's being a *novus homo* that he is killed for violating a settlement, and why Mord waltzes right through the saga, hated by the reader but by no one else. Some people might not deem it wise to trust him, but no formal hatred is directed his way, as there is against another upstart: Thrain. Or again, against the Njalssons, *novi homines*. Flosi, the leader of the Burners, the man who made the decision to use fire, thus gets a three-year exile, while some other lesser Burners are exiled for life. Flosi, in other words, is not thanking Kari for letting him off the hook, nor currying favor by praising him so as to be spared being targeted.

If Njal sinks into apathy after the collapse of the settlement with Flosi right up until he remobilizes his energy to die with style in the fire, then after the Battle at the Althing (but not after the Burning) Flosi sinks into it too and never seems to resurface. His is a special kind of apathy. He is a good leader to his men, tries to counsel them wisely so that they do not come to grief, and provides generously for them at Svinafell. He goes out of his way to fulfill punctiliously the terms of the settlement for the Burning. He is above setting his men up for death, but when they die at Kari's hands he is completely unmoved, except to express admiration for their scourge and minister.[17] Flosi must feel that Kari's victims have it coming; that their

16. On the laxer sanctions meted out to the powerful as opposed to their followers at law and in arbitration, if not always in matters of blood revenge, see Heusler 1911: 141–3. The turmoils of the Sturlung Age did not spare big men from assassination, but as before they were spared harsh legal sanction.
17. That he and Ketil decided not to inform those marked for death in Flosi's dream (ch. 133) is no less cold than kind, given the high rate in the real world, if not in sagas, of false dreams, and given the demoralization it would have led to in those who set store by such things.

deaths are just, and that he, their leader, vicariously dies a little bit with each one of them, because he knows that he has grave wrongs to expiate. Hence his compulsion to engage in a variety of behaviors with a penitential cast to them: he refuses to make a claim for compensation for his injuries at the Althing (ch. 145); he bizarrely covers himself in moss after his shipwreck in the Orkneys, it meaning something more than a mere means of keeping warm (ch. 153);[18] he confesses to killing Helgi Njalsson to jarl Sigurd in a manner meant to invite death; and finally he makes a pilgrimage to Rome, which he undertakes as soon as he hears, with typical phlegm, the news about his men falling at Clontarf (ch. 157).

The author also employs Flosi on a different plane, entrusting him to seduce the reader into excusing Kari's excesses, for if Flosi is not complaining about Kari killing his men in and out of Iceland, and pleads on his behalf in Orkney, then how can a twenty-first-century student of blood-feud complain? The author even adds testimony from disinterested parties to suggest that Flosi is moved by something other than morbid self-flagellation when he defends Kari. Thus after the tables are wiped clean of the blood spurting from Gunnar Lambason's headless neck, King Sigtrygg and jarl Sigurd act as a chorus. Says Sigtrygg:

> 'That was a resolute man, to act so boldly and give no thought to his safety.'
> 'There is no one like Kari for courage,' replied jarl Sigurd. (ch. 155)

That exchange has the look of special pleading, an editorial comment inserted into the text to make sure we continue to accept the burnished image of Kari that Flosi has subverted somewhat by praising him excessively; Flosi has been protesting too much. Kari is Flosi's fantasy of an *unconflicted* man of action, as Fortinbras was to Hamlet.

It has been noted that if anyone should be the villain in this saga it is not Hallgerd, nor Mord, but Flosi. Yet he is spared, dying at sea full of years and reconciled to the fact that his time has come. The sensitive and complex treatment that Flosi receives has been attributed to the author being a kinsman, or in some way affiliated with the Svinfellings of the thirteenth

---

18. The warrant for this interpretation of lying under moss is Skarphedin's insult of Skapti for his abject behavior after he had killed Ketil of Elda: 'you shaved your head and smeared it with tar, and bribed some slaves to cut you a strip of turf to cower under for the night' (ch. 119). See also Miller 1988: 209–10.

century. We will never know.[19] I am more inclined to credit an author who is ever willing to accept moral and social complexity, at every level of his story, except perhaps in Kari's case. When he tries to turn Mord into something like Iago, not only is Mord not up to it, but the author is not willing to let his other characters treat him as if he were an Iago. The author surely has his pets and whipping-girls. Hallgerd can do no right, Kari can do no wrong. Yet even with Hallgerd, he gives us enough material to construct a story that could compete with his own. The author is too honest an analyst of political, moral, and social action to be consistently judgmental, even against Mord, and certainly not against Flosi. Though he burned the author's main characters, there are, as Njal says, two sides to the story, even when revenge is the necessary outcome (ch. 44).

Kari and the Author

The authorial pessimism revealed by scenes of social breakdown which occupy the post-Conversion saga—the killing of Hoskuld, the collapse of the settlement for his death, the Burning, the Battle at the Althing—is displaced after the settlement for the Burning and the Battle by a bout of authorial cynicism. The cynicism comes attractively packaged in a Kari outfit. That is, in fact, what makes it cynical. We might accuse him of gilding disorder and dysfunction with a bit of Hollywood dash; an unmeasured man, unconstrained by the rules, makes us cheer for the very anomie that informs the pessimism of the saga. We can accuse the author of doing a genre-shift, in which he moves from a story of constrained political realism to one of escapist fantasy once the Battle at the Althing ends.

Compare Skarphedin, a fantasy figure of sorts too, but utterly devoid of escapes or escapism. He cannot escape the flames, he cannot escape Iceland, he cannot escape his father's home, and he pays dearly for his one excess.

---

19. People have long tried to prove that the author was a Svinfelling. See the discussion in Lönnroth, 174–87. See EÓS 1954: lxxxiv–c, on the author's geographical knowledge and sense of direction, showing much less familiarity with the region of Njal and Gunnar than with Flosi's region; see also cvii–cxii.

Kari escapes the flames and culpability for killing Hoskuld into escapism, into computer-game battles in Iceland, and then the entire saga escapes to Ireland and the Western Isles for some magic, and on to Rome for pro forma absolution, and then back home cynically to an improbable marriage. Can we account for this?

21

How Not to End a Saga,
Unless...: Chapters 146–59

The author seems to have trouble figuring out how to end his saga. The marriage of Hildigunn to Kari is improbable and perfunctory, as if he were throwing up his hands in despair at how to bring his story to a close.[1] Can the Hildigunn we know accept that marriage? Moreover, such a marriage does nothing to settle the feud. It has already been settled de facto by mutual extermination and exhaustion. Only one Sigfusson of any standing remains, if he indeed remains: Ketil of Mork, who must be very old. No one from Bergthorsknoll survives that we know of except Kari, and he is not a blood member of that group.[2] A formal peace still remains to be concluded between Kari and Flosi, yet even Kari by this time has decided it is over. He has made a ritualized gesture squarely to indicate that.

1. Fox refers to 'the final, masterful touch' of Flosi giving Hildigunn to Kari. So too Vésteinn, 204. I must confess to marveling at the number of critics I admire who do not evince any puzzlement by that marriage, not even Allen, 131, or Maxwell, 21–2. A welcome exception is Dronke, 4–5. The cleverest reading of Flosi's gift of Hildigunn to Kari comes from a student paper on Gunnar, Skarphedin, and Kari, as metonymized by their signature weapons. The claim is that Kari is his sword in a way that neither Gunnar nor Skarphedin can be reduced to halberd and axe. Kari, in his reading, is a pure instrument of some disembodied will: 'Perhaps this is why Kari can get away with breaking the rules of the feud, ending the old order of body counting and turn-taking: he's not the one controlling his actions. And perhaps this is the only explanation for why Hildigunn. . . could possibly agree to marry Kari, recognizing his passivity, acknowledging his transformation, and putting aside her resentment to become his sheath': Daniel Hulme JD 2013, 'A Measure of their Metal: Saga Weapons and Character Traits'.

2. The children of Grim and Helgi fostered at Holar are not worth counting as players or successors in the saga's terms; they are not even named (ch. 127). Nor are the daughters of Kari and Helga Njalsdottir considered successors to the feud, and though they are named, it is only in the concluding lines of the saga. Except for Thord Karason, burned between his grandparents, the author seems not to want to give life to the generation of Njal's grandchildren. Nor was any life granted to succeeding generations of Sigfussons. To have done so would make ending the saga even harder.

If Flosi undertakes a pilgrimage to Rome for genuine penitential (and legal)[3] motives, Kari's pilgrimage does different work. By going to Rome he makes a public statement that, as far as he is concerned, this feud is finished; how better to publicize such a strong, unilateral commitment than by undertaking that pilgrimage? That has to be his primary motive, for Kari has never been troubled by killing, nor doubted his right to do so, quite differently from Flosi's troubled sense before, during, and after the Burning. That is why I called Kari's absolution pro forma at the end of the last chapter. Showing up shipwrecked at Flosi's and being offered a hospitable welcome ritually ends any de jure state of enmity, no marriage needed.

If the author is not writing a morality play, neither is he writing a novel. A saga, given its political themes, bears some of the features of a chronicle. Characters you love die and the story goes on. Consider the problems the author faced along the way and resolved competently. One main character after another gets killed: Gunnar, then Njal, Bergthora, and Skarphedin. Wouldn't any storyteller close up shop soon after the Burning, when all the readers' favorites are dead and gone? Not this author: Hrapp, Flosi, Bjorn, Kari, and Thorhall come to the rescue. He even shifts genres several times over the final seventeen chapters, from legal trial, to heroic romance, to comedy, to miracle story. Still, he must be thinking what must I do to end this, if the Burning did not, if the trial of the Burners and Battle at the Althing did not? How do I bring the curtain down?

As brilliant as this writer consistently is at landing on his feet after the loss of yet another character who has dominated the saga, what prompts him to sail off to the Orkneys and then to Ireland for what has been called *Brjáns saga*? Is this the same man who wrote the sublime composition we have just read? How could his taste lapse like this? Some have claimed the Clontarf episode to be an interpolation, but there is no justification for that. If it is an interpolation it seems to be the author's own.[4] We are unable to blame it on a scribe or some later redactor, as one is tempted to do when offended by ancient or medieval aesthetics. The author's own attempt to justify his ending by sending Kari to the British Isles strikes me as something of a reach, for he could have had Kari kill Gunnar Lambason and Kol Thorsteinsson before letting them get out of Iceland. To transport Flosi and the Burners

---

3. Flosi's pilgrimage is not stipulated in the terms of his exile in ch. 145, but it can be inferred from his remarks at the end of ch. 157 that such a stipulation had been imposed.
4. See EÓS 1954: xlv–xlvix.

abroad makes sense to the extent they are meeting the conditions of the settlement at the Althing. To justify a full description of the Battle of Clontarf because fifteen Burners happened to die there smacks of desperation or distraction or both. Do we need to follow them there to be told that? He could simply say the Burners went abroad and fifteen fell at the Battle of Clontarf, and here I end the saga of the Burning of Njal.

I have always been at a loss to explain the ending to my own satisfaction. Here are some attempts I have made out of desperation, until several years ago one student came up with the best I have seen, but even his explanation still leaves the end dissatisfying. The weakest first. Sometimes saga-writers cannot resist adding a full scene to a saga because they love a story, a joke, or a poem too much to leave it out, even though it does no work whatsoever in their saga.[5] This is the case with Thorstein Sidu-Hallsson in our saga, a Burner, the son of the benevolent Hall of Sida. Thorstein, like the other Burners who join up with jarl Sigurd, find themselves yet again on the wrong side and are routed by King Brian's forces. Sigurd's men begin to flee, leaving him to die holding his own banner:

> Thorstein Hallsson stopped running while the others were fleeing, and tied up his shoe-thong. Kerthjalfad [Brian's foster-son in command of his forces in the center] asked him why he was not running.
>
> 'Because,' said Thorstein, 'I cannot reach home tonight, for my home is out in Iceland.'
>
> Kerthjalfad granted him quarter. (ch. 157)

I would have used any excuse to get this story in too. Thorstein's answer is both heroic and mock-heroic. Mock because he is fleeing, heroic because he stops fleeing and wants to get in a clever line before he is killed. The line was good enough to save his life, swelling the hearts of Icelanders, because part of what tickles his would-be killer is that he lives in Iceland. Iceland and his wit saved his life. Had he said that he could not get back that night to England or Francia he would probably have been killed. The joke should figure in any story of Icelandic ethnic pride. Thorstein has his own saga in which this story is told, but not as well. He says he cannot make it home by fleeing.[6] No mention of his home being in Iceland. Our author has

---

5. A good example occurs in *Laxdæla saga* (ch. 28), on which see Miller 2011: 102–6.
6. *Þorsteins saga Síðu-Hallssonar*, ch. 2: 'then a man said, "Why are you not fleeing, Thorstein?" He answers, "Because I could not make it home tonight if I fled."'

confidence that he can tell the story better. He does so and thus extends his saga unnecessarily for the purpose of getting it in.

Second theory. It is not infrequent to find medieval writers employing a palinode—a retraction or recanting of the content of the work it concludes. The most famous for English speakers is Chaucer's retraction of the best of his Canterbury tales. Suppose we read the Clontarf episode, with its Passion Week miracles, its visions of hell, as our author's retraction. He might be hedging his bets for having been rather ungenerous in his earlier wry accounts of Christian miracle-making—the miracle of the burning berserk, the miracle of Njal's radiant body, the non-miracle of Valgard the Gray's death—and for having made the pagan past look, if not perfect, then more functional than his post-Conversion society. He could even have had Brian's head reattaching itself work as a pious visual palinode, retracting the detached heads that he sent rolling to the delight and sometimes to the sorrow of his readers up until then.[7] Surely taking his two surviving main characters and sending them to Rome and back in the last chapter has palinodic qualities to it. He is not sneering at these pilgrimages, even if Kari is taking his for something other than penitential motives. Kari is still taking it for a good motive: to bring his (Kari's) own saga of revenge to a conclusion. This view has its problems: *Darraðarljóð*, the Valkyries' weaving song, for one, might be seen to compromise the piety of the end, though we could still assimilate it into northern Christian syncretism. Even if there is some plausibility to the palinodic theory, it is not very satisfying.[8]

But now a third theory I owe to a student whose core idea I will expand upon.[9] Here is his basic idea. Consider the Trojan War: you have pro-Greek accounts and pro-Trojan accounts. The war inspired many storytellers, each with variations on the theme or with wholly invented side-stories featuring different characters. This is just what the *Njála*-author wants to prevent. The saga proper, in this theory, ends with the settlement at the Althing and with a few mop-up killings for Kari and Thorgeir. The rest of the saga serves no other purpose than to send Kari out to kill off competing

7. Brian's head reattaching is not in the source the author draws from, which makes his reattachment bear more of a palinodic sense than it would otherwise have.
8. A Christianizing critic would find no need for a palinode, because he would see nothing impious to retract, having already constrained and cramped the saga by figuration and allegory into a pious mode long before its conclusion. See Lönnroth for the best-known of this kind of interpretation of the saga; see Ch. 14, n. 31.
9. Jason Thomas JD 2007; unfortunately I have lost his paper, but I can resume its chief points without it.

versions of the saga of the Burning. This argument explains why Kari has
to hunt down Gunnar Lambason and Kol Thorsteinsson.

Repair to the Orkneys, where King Sigtrygg and jarl Gilli have been
invited, jarl Sigurd hosting.

> The hall was so arranged that King Sigtrygg sat on the center high-seat
> with the jarls on either side of him. The followers of King Sigtrygg and jarl
> Gilli sat on one side, and on jarl Sigurd's side sat Flosi and Thorstein Hallsson.
> Every seat in the hall was occupied.
>
> King Sigtrygg and jarl Gilli wanted to hear all about the Burning and what
> had happened since. Gunnar Lambason was chosen to tell the story, and a
> chair was placed for him to sit on.

In the meantime Kari and his comrades have landed in Orkney and Kari
goes right to the hall while Gunnar is reciting his saga of the Burning.

> Kari and the others stood outside, listening. It was Christmas Day.
>
> King Sigtrygg asked, 'How did Skarphedin bear the burning?'
>
> 'Well enough to start with,' replied Gunnar. 'But in the end he wept.'
>
> His whole account had been extremely biased, and riddled with lies. But
> this was too much for Kari. He burst into the hall with his sword drawn. . .
> He ran the length of the hall and struck Gunnar Lambason on the neck with
> such violence that his head flew off on to the table in front of the king and
> jarls. (chs. 154–5)

Remember how quickly children could make theater out of events at the
Althing (ch. 8); this scene shows that a version of *Brennu-Njáls saga* is already
extant within three years of the Burning, and we can suppose it begins
a little before the killing of Thrain. Gunnar Lambason, the saga-teller,
is the person who mocked Skarphedin during the Burning, asking him
if he were crying. The question prompted Thrain's tooth, with an assist
from Skarphedin, to bite out Gunnar Lambason's eye. Gunnar Lambason
is a half-blind saga-teller, a squinting Homer, who deserves no pity. It was
unwise to accuse the living Gunnar and Skarphedin of weeping, unwise to
claim it of the dead Skarphedin.[10] But the key point is that Kari's mission
is no longer about avenging his son, but about repressing alternate versions
of the saga. After the tables are cleaned up, the company finds the saga too

10. See *Íslendinga saga*, ch. 192, where Thord kakali, in Bergen, overhears the burning at
    Flugumýr narrated to the discredit of the Burners and very favorably to his enemy Gizur
    jarl; he knocks the teller unconscious with his axe; see also *Óláfs saga helga*, ch. 118; Hermann
    Pálsson 1983: 50.

good not to continue and it falls to Flosi to tell the saga of the Burning: 'he gave every man his proper due and this account of it was believed.'

The saga-telling at Sigurd's has been marshaled by literary historians to show that sagas were told, how they were told, and the audience they commanded.[11] This account shows also that my fascination with Skarphedin has a long pedigree, for he is the character about whom King Sigtrygg wants to hear more. Even the biased version of Gunnar Lambason cannot obscure Skarphedin's charisma—or are other sagas of Skarphedin making the rounds of the North Atlantic?

Kari has one more man to kill, Kol Thorsteinsson, Hall of Sida's nephew. Unlike Gunnar Lambason, who loses his head telling a false version of *Njáls saga*, Kol loses his while counting silver. Kol's head, though, has one more word left in it as it flies off his shoulders: 'ten.' He said his own number: he is the tenth of Kari's victims that Kari claimed were dedicated to his son. It is harder to make Kol's death fit the theory that Kari is repressing false versions of the saga, though with a small stretch Kol fits too: he is described as delivering *mest hæðiyrði*, the most taunts, the most slanders, of the Burners, that is, he tells lies about the Bergthorsknoll bunch. Also fitting is that Kari's last two killings stop people in the midst of talking, a special kind of talking. Both victims are *counting* or *telling*, both words—one Romance, the other Germanic—covering the same semantic ranges in the history of their sense development: counting numbers and telling tales,[12] as still today we have bank *tellers* who must give an *account* of their actions if they juggle the *account* books by counting wrong.

The argument can be simply stated: from chapter 146 until the end the saga-writer is not writing *Njáls saga*, but writing the proof that his *Njáls saga*, already finished, is the true one, because anyone who might claim the authority to tell another version, favoring other parties, has been or will be killed. That is why we go to Clontarf, to kill off more Burners, possible anti-Bergthorsknoll tale-tellers.

11. See Andersson 2006: 7–9, who anticipates Jason Thomas: '[Gunnar Lambason losing his head] may be an indirect way for the saga author to vouch for his own truthfulness, although it is hard to believe that there was much residual truth to be had 280 years after the events described.' Thomas's point is not directed to the issue of the saga's historical reliability, but to the question of what *Njáls saga* is doing after the real story has ended shortly after ch. 145.
12. ON *telja* has the same senses as English 'tell', meaning both to count numbers and to tell a tale. Kol is 'telling' when he loses his head, Gunnar is 'saying' (*segja*) the saga when he loses his.

Who are the chief spokesmen left alive who know the inside and outside of the story of the Burning? Flosi can cover the outside; he was there. Moreover, he made all the decisions leading up to the Burning. His veracity has been proven and has been given Kari's and the author's imprimatur. And on the inside? Until he escapes, Kari was there. We have our two eyewitnesses.[13] There is only one *true Njáls saga*, and it turns out to be the one we have. Those who would tell an alternate version the author had either Kari or Brian's forces kill off. Yet it would not be too hard to read this ending as the author's admission that there are indeed other oral, or perhaps even other written, versions out there (that have not survived), like so many false Don Quixotes in Part II of the *Quixote*, that the true Don Quixote must combat.

This theory works better than any other, but it still leaves me bewildered at the marriage of Kari and Hildigunn. Had Njal himself been alive to author his saga after the Burning, he would never have concluded it with such a marriage. The one marriage he authored involving Hildigunn turned out to be the death of him.

I am left with the one true theory: sometimes some of the greatest writers are not good at writing endings. There is no point in exercising one's interpretive skills, such as they are, to save it. The end just is not of a quality with what went before it. In this our author finds himself in the company of other gifted writers such as Stendhal, George Eliot of *The Mill on the Floss*, Tolstoy stumbling around at the end of *War and Peace*, among a host of others. Let it stand at that.

---

13. This view jells nicely with Clover's thesis (2012) about the author's concern to prove up the facts asserted in the narration.

22

A Conclusion: Justice and Exits

There are a number of ways a character can exit a saga, though only one is certain: the fourth. First, he can be formally dismissed, declared 'out of the saga'. Six people in *Njála* exit this way.[1] But the declaration is not foolproof. By authorial oversight one of these, Hogni Gunnarsson, appears again accompanying Ketil, his uncle (ch. 93), and is mentioned by Mord as attending a feast at Hoskuld Hvitanesspriest's (ch. 109).

The second way is to die or to be killed. But that too is not foolproof, though less so in this saga than in some others. Gunnar makes a brief re-appearance singing in his grave after he dies. Nor is it certain Skarphedin does not speak a verse while dead. Some people find it strange that Svan, sorcerer that he was, did not reappear as an afterwalker, but he did not. Had he found himself in *Laxdœla saga* or *Eyrbyggja saga* he probably would have. We see no one in *Njáls saga* taking care to lay the ghost, that is, engaging in some ritualized practice to make sure a corpse does not pay unwelcome visits. The closest we come is that Gunnar is perhaps threatening that he will continue to reappear unless revenge is taken for him.[2] The subsequent revenge puts his body permanently to rest, closing up his grave-mound for-ever. Gunnar and Skarphedin might be understood to afterwalk by proxy; their weapons, quasi-avatars of their departed owners, still do lethal work. More mundanely, people continue to be mentioned by other characters after they have died, from minor actors like Thorir the Norwegian to the main character, Njal.

---

1. Osvifr (ch. 12), Thorarin the Lawspeaker (ch. 17), Geir the Priest and Hogni Gunnarsson (ch. 80), Kolskegg (ch. 81), and Gudmund the Powerful (ch. 145).
2. Heusler (1911:35) notes that the unavenged dead do not tend to appear as afterwalkers and that Gunnar is exceptional. True, but the bloody-token ritual is a form of a return of the dead, evincing the power of body parts or relics of the unavenged dead to compel revenge.

The third way is to wrap up a clearly designated bit-part. We can read such wrap-ups as implying X is now out of the saga, even when that tag is not employed. Many exit this way, such as the children playing on the floor acting out Hrut vs. Mord. Bjorn of Mork provides as good an example as any. He moves under Thorgeir's protection, and as we quoted earlier: 'Thereafter Bjorn was considered much more of a man than he had been before' (ch. 152). That comes close to: 'and he lived happily ever after.' Equally final, but the inverse of Bjorn's exit, is that of Thorhild the Poetess, Thrain's first wife, unceremoniously kicked out of the wedding feast; her painful exit seems more final than had she exited with the tag: 'and now she is out of the saga.' But these exits are not quite foolproof, for as with Hogni, the character might reappear or be mentioned again.

Finally there is the foolproof exit. The character simply never appears or is mentioned again, even indirectly. This differs from the previous types only in that the character is important enough that we expect him or her to be accounted for, to be formally dismissed. Theirs are exits de facto. This kind of exit can have a benign explanation, as when Thorhall Asgrimsson is last seen charging ahead in the Battle at the Althing, his part finished when the saga no longer includes a scene at a Thing. Some of these exits can seem to be a lucky break, as in Mord's case, or a dishonorable discharge, as in Hallgerd's, whose last words are to repeat the lethal insults: 'Go home, Little Dungbeards' (ch. 91), never to be heard from again, after having been rather more than a mere supporting actress. Having spewed the venom that the Njalssons sought to provoke, she is last mentioned in the next chapter intending to ride to Runolf's with Thrain, her daughter, and others. It is not clear that either she or Thorgerd did go, but if they had gone presumably they would have departed with Thrain and thus witnessed his death. But nothing is said on that score. It would be unlike this author to let an intention to visit Runolf's be sufficient to mean they did not go without a more explicit accounting, since the presumption would be otherwise.[3] It seems the author really did forget that he had left Hallgerd unaccounted for, a greater insult than had it been advertent.

<hr />

3. After Thrain asked certain named men to accompany him we have: *Þær skyldu ok fara Þorgerðr ok Hallgerðr*. Given the two women are mentioned neither departing Runolf's nor being present at Thrain's death, we can let *skyldu* allow for the possibility that the future action it indicates did not take place and translate it, a little tendentiously, as 'intended to go', or as implying the conditional as both Cook and Magnusson/Pálsson do with 'were to go'.

What of Mord's disappearance? He departs with Thorhall, as we saw, when the saga's law- and Thing-work is done. Some would like to see Mord dragged back onstage, bound and gagged. I said earlier that he is standing at the end, but that is an assumption, though a defensible one. His death would have been noteworthy. Mord's last appearance, though, is not the first time he disappeared from the saga; he took a long hiatus, as measured in years and activity, between Njal and Skarphedin's revenge for Gunnar and his father Valgard's return to Iceland to set the plans to kill Hoskuld in motion, only punctuated by a brief mention of his initial opposition to Christianity. This hiatus is not the author nodding, or having too many characters on his hands so that he forgets about some for a while, but an astute commentary on survival in the political and social world of this saga. One lays low when one has to; one bides one's time; one goes about one's business but accepts being relegated, in the sense that that term has in English football. There is something to be said for resilience, the ability to absorb hits and bide one's time, the ability not to become so demoralized as to grow reckless, or just to quit. Mord, I suspect, lands on his feet, not to dominate but to do all right for himself, because types like him tend to land on their feet, even if they may break a foot from the fall and have to nurse it for a few years. It is rare to find a politically successful person who does not possess the virtue of living to fight another day.

Njáls saga is better as history and politics, better as truth, better as a story, because Mord does not get dragged back onstage for a good beating. The author does not even imply he is in or wish him to hell. Except for the excursus to Ireland, the prospect of hell only arises by disappointed implication when it is pointedly not mentioned at Valgard's death and when Njal tries to calm his panicked household as the flames engulf them by denying its prospect: '. . . this is just a passing storm and it will be long before another like it comes. Put your faith in the mercy of God, for He will not let us burn both in this world and the next.' Nothing obliges God to activate his mercy in the next world because one happens to burn to death in this one. Njal's concern here is not about the afterlife or theological accuracy, but that, no differently from Skarphedin, he wants everyone to play his and her final part upon this stage with dignity and courage.

To the credit of our author, he also makes no comment about Skarphedin's damnation or salvation. The closest he comes even to raising the issue is to have the people who see his corpse be rather charitable in their view that he branded cross-like marks on himself. But consistent with the author's

psychological acuity, one wonders if these people are not wishfully thinking that the crosses will prevent Skarphedin from reappearing. They were
hoping that he had thereby laid his own ghost.[4]

And Mord gets away, as does Kari, with stabbing Hoskuld
Hvitanesspriest. They both get away with the saga's second greatest crime
after the Burning. We may ask no less of Kari than we do of Mord: that
he get his just deserts. Readers are more likely to ask it of Mord, and give
Killer-Kari a free pass; the author thus exposes our own failures of impar-
tiality, and that our own morals might be rigged. Why are both living
at the end and neither has been treated as culpable in that crime? Justice
gives way to political realities in Mord's case and to some vague heroic
dispensation in Kari's. Who takes the blame, in any case, is only partly
a moral consideration, only partly a legal consideration. It is, in this saga
as in life, also a matter of politics, and of the accommodations, the moral
compromises, humans make as they muddle through to the next generation. That so much of that muddling in this saga is accompanied with wit
and panache reveals that our author, though pessimistic about the changes
in the political and social order he depicts, is no misanthrope. In the end,
it may be rather more surprising that Bjorn of Mork gets no comeuppance
than that Mord escapes his.

Let me conclude with Hallgerd, because the saga starts with her. The
author may be no misanthrope but one can perhaps argue that he is a
misogynist. The argument should fail merely upon its statement. Only
respect and admiration is shown for the ruthless and intelligent Bergthora,
for her better-looking younger counterpart Hildigunn, for Thorhalla
Asgrimsdottir when she leaves the flames, promising to urge her father and
brother to take revenge. Not even Gunnhild is an object of loathing. She
is a colorful fact of Norwegian political life, not to be crossed. At the other
end of the social register, the women servants and travelling beggarwomen
are no less tough than Gunnhild, Hildigunn, or Bergthora. They do not
kowtow to men or masters; they avoid all shows of deference in conversation, and the men take it, except when, in an unwise moment, a husband
attempts a dull assertion of an authority not admitted and slaps one down.

I have already shown how Hallgerd's theft is a little less than a theft; she
thought she was avenging a wrong done her husband with the only means
at her disposal, and proudly indicated as much. She is crushed that he does

4. Cf. Allen, 218 n. 20.

not see it that way. Why show her in a good marriage to a good man, Glum, whom she takes revenge for by sending Thjostolf, her foster-father, to his death? Is this to bless with rectitude our blaming her because she has shown she can behave properly if she wants to?[5]

Recall when Gunnar's bowstring breaks:

> 'Let me have two locks of your hair, and help my mother plait them into a bow-string for me.'
>
> 'Does anything depend on it?' asked Hallgerd.
>
> 'My life depends on it,' replied Gunnar, 'for they will never overcome me as long as I can use my bow.'
>
> 'Then let me remind you', said Hallgerd, 'of the slap you once gave me. I do not care in the least whether you hold out a long time or not.'
>
> 'To each his own way of earning fame,' said Gunnar. 'You shall not be asked again.' (ch. 77)

How many readers, when they first read the saga, had by this time forgotten that there was a third, unavenged slap of Hallgerd some twenty-nine chapters earlier? I confess I had, if my memory is serving me correctly. How perfect of the author to be patient, to make Hallgerd be patient, to make her something more than a mere spoiled, impulsive actor, whose impulses overcome her intelligence more often than not. She bided her time. It was not the meanness of her refusal that awed me on first reading, but that she had not forgotten, like I had, that she had a debt to repay. When a forgotten obligation rises up again in memory it bears with it a chastisement for having been forgotten. The reader is reminded of his inattentiveness as well as of the unrequited slap, his own dimwitted failure to count up to the epic three.

When Skarphedin, his eyes smarting from the smoke, is mocked by Gunnar Lambason, who says he has not laughed since Thrain's death, Skarphedin digs into his purse to extract Thrain's tooth. He kept it as a souvenir, something to remind him of his most spectacular feat, and now he wants to make it a *minjagripr*, a souvenir, a concrete reminder for Gunnar Lambason too, who hardly needs one, especially this one. Gruesome as it is, Skarphedin's linking memory and justice, memory and getting even, operates in the comic mode, grimly comic to be sure; when Hallgerd denies her hair, is that meant to be tragic? It is not clear, is it? It lacks all the overt comedy of Gunnar Lambason's dangling eye and Skarphedin's hard joking, but

5. Wolf, 67.

simply to classify it as tragic is to take sides—Gunnar's side. The poetry of
Hallgerd's denying her husband her hair is from her point of view classically
comic: she is setting her world back to even, setting things aright, which is
the conventional form of comic closure.[6] Instead of hating Hallgerd, at that
moment I stand in awe and admiration.

The author is not doing her a disfavor. He is doing her the grandest of favors. He knows he did, and he is sorry he did it. For he makes
amends immediately by trying to correct his misgauged generosity. He
has Rannveig,[7] Gunnar's mother, threaten her with infamous memorabil-
ity: 'you are an evil woman, and your shame will long be remembered.'
This is uncharacteristically heavy-handed for the author. Rannveig's
remarks have the look of instructions delivered to the reader, a gloss
inserted into the text, because Gunnar's last words are subtler—*hefir hverr til
sins ágætis nökkut*, literally, 'each has something for his own renown', which
could serve almost as a mantra for the American self-esteem movement,
but Magnusson/Pálsson get its pejorative sense right: 'to each his own way
of earning fame.' Yet the sense is not easy. Gunnar's statement has the form
of a proverb, and mimics proverbs in the way that, though one knows by
a kind of cultural fiat what it praises or blames, it is often the case that one
is not quite sure how the words generate the meaning everyone attributes
to the saying. Moreover, Rannveig's speech—'you are an evil woman, and
your shame will long be remembered'—has none of the naturalism that
marks everyone else's speech. The author must fear there are too many
readers/hearers bearing my moral and aesthetic sentiments who needed
some coaching. He keeps it up; he has Hallgerd talking soft and low to
Hrapp fourteen chapters later, confirming the whispering of others about
her relations with him. She will then stupidly utter her scurrilous insults,
decide (perhaps) not to ride off to Runolf's, and disappear without a trace.

The author needs to have Rannveig editorialize because at some level
we know that Hallgerd's hair only buys a hair's breadth of time before the
inevitable outcome, that her refusal makes very little practical difference.
But her revenge is more grandly artful and hence, strangely, more blame-
worthy for having no appreciable practical effect; it is pure revenge. There

---

6. See Burnett, xvi–xviii, 36.
7. Rannveig is on more than one occasion given the role of the chorus; see e.g. chs. 39, 74. In
any event Thorkel Elfara-Poet's verse on Gunnar's last stand (ch. 77) makes no mention of
Hallgerd; it may well have been this saga-writer who made her shame long-remembered.

is not a shred of the political or practical in it. It is revenge devoted wholly to the aesthetics of getting even. And because Hallgerd takes special care to remember, the author has his revenge upon her by forgetting her, by dropping her from the story with nary a word of farewell.

Against Hallgerd, so rudely dismissed, let us place Mord, who never gets paid back. Why are his doings the special object of no one's moral memory? Remember the balanced-exchange model of the feud that Skarphedin was in part grinning about. It had gaps and inconsistencies; it was at times incoherent, but it still declared a powerful moral norm: pay back what you owe, settle your debts. In that sense the model voiced an aspiration. But returning like for like is not a self-activating principle. If no one thought it worthwhile (or lacked the courage) to take justifiable revenge for a wrong of sufficient gravity, then the wrong-doer won a kind of amoral lottery, the harms he caused officially forgotten. That may not make for a satisfying ending. That is the problem with being honest about the limits of law, justice, and feud, where everyone must deal with a world of probabilities, not certainties. No wonder this talented writer had Kari, like Mord a lottery-winner, and Flosi, a lottery-loser, make up and have their different allotments of luck balance out at zero. Flosi can then drown, he not being a lucky man in the role he was called on to play in this saga; nor were a good number of people who accompanied Flosi to Bergthorsknoll lucky, to say nothing of the crew of the ship on his final voyage.[8] The author can now end his saga by naming it and taking full responsibility for his wondrous creation by his first and only explicit self-reference in the entire saga:

ok lýk *ek* þar Brennu-Njáls sögu.
And there *I* end the saga of the Burning of Njal.

Sublime.[9]

---

8. See Foote 1979: 56.
9. Only one other family saga in the Íslenzk Fornrit editions—*Finnboga saga*—ends with the narrator employing the first person singular. Generally the formula in a last sentence is an impersonal construction: 'now here closes. . .'; or less frequently, but not uncommon, is 'now we end (close) the saga. . .', with the first person plural. If it were a scribe who thought to end *Njála* thus, then we must thank him for contriving the sublimity of the ending.

Works Cited

PRIMARY SOURCES AND TRANSLATIONS

Ö is ordered as if it were O, thorn (Þ) as if it were Th; Icelandic authors
appear under their given name.

Andersson, Theodore M., and Kari Ellen Gade, trans. and commentary. 2000.
Morkinskinna: The Earliest Icelandic Chronicle of the Norwegian Kings (1030–1157).
Islandica 51. Ithaca, NY: Cornell University Press.
Auðunar þáttr Vestfirzka. ÍF 6: 359–68 (M version). Trans. Andersson and Gade,
211–15; F version *Flateyjarbók* 3: 410–5. Trans. Miller 2008: 7–12; Hermann
Pálsson 1971: 121–8.
Bandamanna saga. ÍF 7: 291–363. Trans. *CSI* 5: 283–312.
Beowulf. Klaeber's Beowulf. 4th edn. 2008. Edited by R. D. Fulk, Robert E. Bjork,
and John D. Niles. Toronto: University of Toronto Press.
Bjarnar saga Hítdælakappa. ÍF 3:109–211. Trans. *CSI* 1: 255–304.
Brennu-Njáls saga. ÍF 12. Trans. Bayerschmidt/Hollander; Cook; Dasent;
Magnusson/Pálsson. See under Secondary Works.
Droplaugarsona saga. ÍF 11: 135–80. Trans. *CSI* 4: 355–78.
Edda: die Lieder des Codex Regius, 3rd edn. 1962. Edited by Hans Kuhn.
Heidelberg: Carl Winter. Trans. Terry.
Egils saga. ÍF 2. Trans. *CSI* 1: 33–177.
Eyrbyggja saga. ÍF 4: 1–184. Trans. *CSI* 5: 131–230.
Finnboga saga. ÍF 14: 251–340. Trans. *CSI* 3: 221–70.
Flateyjarbók. 1860–8. 3 vols. Edited by Guðbrandur Vigfússon and C. R. Unger.
Christiania [Oslo].
Fóstbrœðra saga. ÍF 6: 119–276. Trans. *CSI* 2: 329–402.
Gísla saga Súrssonar. ÍF 6: 1–118. Trans. *CSI* 2: 1–48.
Grágás: Islændernes Lovbog i fristatens Tid. 3 vols. Edited by Vilhjálmur Finsen.1852
(Konungsbók), 1879 (Staðarhólsbók), 1883. Copenhagen. Repr. Odense, 1974.
Translation of Konungsbók with selections from Staðarhólsbók and other
mss: *Laws of Early Iceland: Grágás. The Codex Regius of Grágás with Material from
other Manuscripts*. 2 vols. 1980, 2000. Trans. Andrew Dennis, Peter Foote, and
Richard Perkins. Winnipeg: University of Manitoba Press. Vol. 1 contains
Grágás Ia 1–Ia 217; vol. 2, *Grágás* Ia 218–Ib 218 in Finsen's pagination.

Grettis saga Ásmundarsonar. ÍF 7: 1–290. Trans. *CSI* 2: 49–191.

Grønlie, Siân, ed. and trans. 2006. *Íslendingabók, Kristni saga: The Book of the Icelanders, The Story of the Conversion.* London: Viking Society for Northern Research.

Guðmundar saga dýra. ST 1: 160–212. Trans. MT 2: 145–206.

Hallfreðar saga. ÍF 8: 133–200. Trans. *CSI* 1: 225–53.

Harðar saga Grímkelssonar. ÍF 13: 1–97. Trans. *CSI* 2: 193–236.

Hávamál. In *Edda* 17–44. Trans. Terry, 11–35.

Hávarðar saga Ísfirðings. ÍF 6: 289–358. Trans. *CSI* 5: 313–47.

Hermann Pálsson. 1971. *Hrafnkel's Saga and Other Stories.* Harmondsworth: Penguin.

Hrafnkels saga Freysgoða. ÍF 11: 95–133. Trans. Hermann Pálsson. 1971. 35–71.

Íslendingabók. ÍF 1: 1–28. Trans. Grønlie, 1–32.

Íslendinga saga. ST 1: 229–534. Trans. MT 1: 115–447.

Jónsbók: Kong Magnus Hakonssons Lovbog for Island. 1904. Edited by Ólafur Halldórsson. Repr. 1974: Odense Universitetsforlag.

Kristni saga. ÍF 15.2: 1–48. Trans. Grønlie, 33–74.

Landnámabók. ÍF 1: 29–397. Trans. Hermann Pálsson and Paul Edwards. 1972. *The Book of Settlements: Landnámabók.* Winnipeg: University of Manitoba Press.

Larson, Laurence M. ed. and trans. 1935. *The Earliest Norwegian Laws, being the Gulathing Law and the Frostathing Law.* New York: Columbia University Press.

Laxdæla saga. ÍF 5. Trans. Magnus Magnusson and Hermann Pálsson. 1969. Harmondsworth: Penguin. *CSI* 5:1–120.

Ljósvetninga saga. ÍF 10: 1–139. Trans. Andersson and Miller; *CSI* 4: 193–255.

Lögmansannáll. In *Annálar og Nafnaskrá.* 1953. Edited by Guðni Jónsson. Reykjavík. 75–158.

Lokasenna. In *Edda* 96–110. Trans. Terry, 72–84.

Magnússona saga. ÍF 28. *Heimskringla.* Trans. http://omacl.org/Heimskringla/.

Morkinskinna. ÍF 23–4. Trans. Andersson and Gade based on earlier editions with different chapter divisions.

Njáls saga. See *Brennu-Njáls saga.*

Óláfs saga helga. ÍF 27. *Heimskringla.* Trans. http://omacl.org/Heimskringla/.

Óláfs saga Tryggvasonar (Odd's version). ÍF 25: 123–362. Trans. Theodore M. Andersson. 2003. *The Saga of Olaf Tryggvason by Oddr Snorrason.* Ithaca, NY: Cornell University Press.

Ölkofra þáttr. ÍF 11: 81–94. Trans. Hermann Pálsson 1971: 82–93. *CSI* 5: 231–37.

Prestssaga Guðmundar góða. ST 1: 116–59. MT 2: 91–143.

Reykdæla saga. ÍF 10: 149–243. *CSI* 4: 257–311.

Sneglu-Halla þáttr. ÍF 9: 261–95 (M and F versions). Trans. *CSI* 1: 342–57 (F version); Andersson and Gade, 243–52 (M version).

Sturlu saga. ST 1: 63–114. Trans. MT 1: 59–113.

Terry, Patricia. 1990. *Poems of the Elder Edda.* Philadelphia: University of Pennsylvania Press.

Thómas saga erkibiskups. A Life of Archbishop Thomas Becket. 2 vols. 1875–83. Edited with English translation by Eiríkr Magnússon. London: Longman.

Þorðar saga hreðu. ÍF 14: 161–226. *CSI* 3: 361–96.

Þorgils saga ok Hafliða. ST 1: 12–50. Trans. MT 2: 25–70.

Þorgils saga skarða. ST 2: 104–226. Trans. MT 2: 345–485.

Þorsteins saga hvíta. ÍF 11: 1–19. Trans. *CSI* 4: 303–13.

Þorsteins saga Síðu-Hallssonar. ÍF 11: 297–326. *CSI* 4: 447–59.

Þorsteins þáttr stangarhöggs "Thorstein the Staffstruck." ÍF 11: 67–79. Trans. Hermann Pálsson. 1971: 72–81; BP 52–8.

Vápnfirðinga saga. ÍF 11: 21–65. Trans. *CSI* 4: 313–34.

Víga-Glúms saga. ÍF 9: 1–98. Trans. *CSI* 2: 267–314.

SECONDARY WORKS

Agnes Arnórsdóttir. 2010. *Property and Virginity: The Christianization of Marriage in Medieval Iceland, 1200–1600.* Aarhus: Aarhus Universitetsforlag.

Allen, Richard F. 1971. *Fire and Iron: Critical Approaches to Njáls Saga.* Pittsburgh: University of Pittsburgh Press.

von Amira, Karl. 1895. *Nordgermanisches Obligationenrecht,* vol. 2: *Westnordisches Obligationenrecht.* Leipzig: von Veit.

Andersson, Theodore M. 1964. *The Problem of Icelandic Saga Origins: A Historical Survey.* New Haven: Yale University Press.

Andersson, Theodore M. 1967. *The Icelandic Family Saga: An Analytic Reading.* Cambridge, Mass.: Harvard University Press.

Andersson, Theodore M. 1972. Rev. of Einar Ól. Sveinsson. *Njáls saga: A Literary Masterpiece* and of Richard F. Allen. *Fire and Iron: Critical Approaches to Njáls saga.* *JEGP* 71: 100–4.

Andersson, Theodore M. 2003. Rev. of Robert Cook, trans. *Njal's Saga. JEGP* 102: 567–9.

Andersson, Theodore M. 2006. *The Growth of the Medieval Icelandic Sagas (1180–1280).* Ithaca, NY: Cornell University Press.

Andersson, Theodore M. 2012a. *The Partisan Muse in the Early Icelandic Sagas (1200–1250).* Islandica 55. Ithaca, NY: Cornell University Press.

Andersson, Theodore M. 2012b. 'Sea Traffic in the Sagas: Quantitative Reflections.' In Melve and Sønnesyn, 156–75.

Andersson, Theodore M. and William Ian Miller. 1989. *Law and Literature in Medieval Iceland: Ljósvetninga saga and Valla-Ljóts saga.* Stanford: Stanford University Press.

Ármann Jakobsson. 2007. 'Masculinity and Politics in *Njáls saga.*' *Viator,* 38: 191–214.

Bååth, A. U. 1885. *Studier öfver Kompositionen i några isländska Ättsagor.* Lund: Gleerup.

Bagge, Sverre. 2006. 'The Making of a Missionary King: The Medieval Accounts of Olaf Tryggvason and the Conversion of Norway.' *JEGP* 105: 473–513.

Bandle, Oskar. 1972. 'Strukturprobleme in der *Njáls saga.*' In *Festschrift für Siegfried Gutenbrunner*. Edited by Oskar Bandel, Heinz Klingenberg, and Friedrich Maurer. Heidelberg: Winter.

Bandlien, Bjørn. 2005. *Strategies of Passion: Love and Marriage in Medieval Iceland and Norway.* Turnhout: Brepols.

Bartlett, Robert. 1993. *The Making of Europe: Conquest, Colonization, and Cultural Change, 950–1350.* Princeton: Princeton University Press.

Bartlett, Robert. 2008. *The Natural and Supernatural in the Middle Ages.* Cambridge: Cambridge University Press.

Bayerschmidt, Carl F. and Lee M. Hollander, trans. 1998. *Njáls Saga.* Wordsworth Classics. Ware: Wordsworth.

Bennett, Lisa. 2007. '"The Most Important of Events": The "Burning-In" Motif as a Site of Cultural Memory in Icelandic Sagas.' *Journal of the Australian Early Medieval Association*, 3: 69–86.

Berend, Nora. 2007. 'Introduction.' *Christianization and the Rise of Christian Monarchy: Scandinavia, Central Europe and Rus' c. 900–1200.* Cambridge: Cambridge University Press.

Bolton, W. F. 1972. 'The *Njála* Narrator and the Picture Plane.' *SS* 44: 186–209.

Boulhosa, Patricia Pires. 2005. *Icelanders and the Kings of Norway: Mediaeval Sagas and Legal Texts.* Leiden: Brill.

Brand, Paul. 1992. *The Origins of the English Legal Profession.* Oxford: Blackwells.

Bryce, James. 1901. 'Primitive Iceland.' In *Studies in History and Jurisprudence.* Oxford: Clarendon Press. 312–58.

Burnett, Anne Pippin. 1998. *Revenge in Attic and Later Tragedy.* Berkeley: University of California Press.

Burrows, Hannah. 2009. 'Cold Cases: Law and Legal Detail in the Íslendingasögur.' *Parergon*, 26.1: 35–56.

Byock, Jesse L. 1982. *Feud in the Icelandic Saga.* Berkeley: University of California Press.

Christiansen, Eric. 1997. *The Northern Crusades.* 2nd edn. London: Penguin.

Ciklamini, Marlene. 1963. 'The Old Icelandic Duel.' *SS* 35: 175–94.

Clover, Carol J. 1974. 'Scene in Saga Composition.' *Arkiv för nordisk filologi*, 89: 57–83.

Clover, Carol J. 1982. *The Medieval Saga.* Ithaca, NY: Cornell University Press.

Clover, Carol J. 1985. 'Icelandic Family Sagas (*Íslendingasögur*).' In *Old Norse-Icelandic Literature: A Critical Guide.* Edited by Clover and John Lindow. Ithaca, NY: Cornell University Press. 239–315.

Clover, Carol J. 1986a. 'Hildigunnr's Lament.' In *Structure and Meaning in Old Norse Literature: New Approaches to Textual Analysis and Literary Criticism.* Edited by John Lindow, Lars Lönnroth, and Gerd Wolfgang Weber. Odense: Odense University Press. 141–83.

Clover, Carol J. 1986b. 'The Long Prose Form.' *Arkiv för nordisk filologi*, 101: 10–39.

Clover, Carol J. 1993. 'Regardless of Sex: Men, Women, and Power in Early Northern Europe.' *Speculum*, 68: 363–88.

Clover, Carol J. 1998. 'Law and the Order of Popular Culture.' In Sarat and Kearns, 97–119.

Clover, Carol J. 2012. 'Composing Facts: Evidence and Narrative in *Njáls Saga*.' In *News from Other Worlds, Tíðendi ór öðrum heimum: Studies in Nordic Folklore, Mythology and Culture*. Edited by Merrill Kaplan and Timothy R. Tangherlini. Berkeley: North Pinehurst Press. 109–33.

Clover, Carol, and John Lindow, eds. 1985. *Old Norse-Icelandic Literature: A Critical Guide*. Ithaca, NY: Cornell University Press.

Cochrane, Jamie. 2012. 'Gossips, Beggars, Assassins and Tramps: Vagrants and Other Itinerants in the Sagas of Icelanders.' *Saga-Book of the Viking Society*, 36: 43–78.

Cook, Robert. 1998. 'The Dasent Shift.' In *Guðrúnhvöt kveðin Guðrúnu Ásu Grímsdóttir*. Reykjavík. 83–5.

Cook, Robert, trans. 2001. *Njal's Saga*. London: Penguin.

Cook, Robert. 2002. 'On Translating Sagas.' *Gripla*, 13: 107–45.

Cormack, Margaret. 2007. 'Fact and Fiction in the Icelandic Sagas.' *History Compass*, 5/1: 201–17.

Dasent, George Webbe, trans. 1861. *The Story of Burnt Njal or Life in Iceland at the End of the Tenth Century*. 2 vols. Edinburgh: Edmonston & Douglas.

Daube, David. 1969. *Roman Law: Linguistic, Social and Philosophical Aspects*. Edinburgh: Edinburgh University Press.

Daube, David 1981. 'The Forms of the Message.' In his *Ancient Jewish Law*. Leiden: Brill.

Dronke, Ursula. 1981. *The Role of Sexual Themes in Njáls saga*. London: Viking Society for Northern Research.

Einar Ól. Sveinsson. 1933. *Um Njálu*. Reykjavík: Bókadeild Menningarsjóðs.

Einar Ól. Sveinsson. 1953. *Studies in the Manuscript Tradition of Njálssaga*. Studia Islandica 13. Reykjavík.

Einar Ól. Sveinsson. 1954. Introduction and textual and explanatory notes. *Brennu-Njáls saga*. ÍF 12.

Einar Ól. Sveinsson. 1971. *Njáls Saga: A Literary Masterpiece*. Translated by Paul Schach. Lincoln, Nebr.: University of Nebraska Press.

Esmark, Kim, Lars Hermanson, Hans Jacob Orning, and Helle Vogt. 2013. *Disputing Strategies in Medieval Scandinavia*. Leiden: Brill.

Falk, Oren. 2005. 'Beardless Wonder: "Gaman vas Söxu (The Sex was Great)".' In *Verbal Encounters: Anglo-Saxon and Old Norse Studies for Roberta Frank*. Edited by Antonina Harbus and Russell Poole. Toronto: University of Toronto Press. 223–46.

Faraone, Christopher. 1993. 'Molten Wax, Spilt Wine and Mutilated Animals: Sympathetic Magic in Early Greek and Near Eastern Oath Ceremonies.' *Journal of Hellenic Studies*, 113: 60–80.

Finnur Jónsson. 1908. '*Einleitung.*' *Brennu-Njálssaga (Njála)*. Edited by Finnur Jónsson. Altnordische Saga-Bibliothek 13. Halle a. S. xiii–xlvi.

Firth, Hugh. 2012. 'Coercion, Vengeance, Feud and Accommodation: Homicide in Medieval Iceland.' *Early Medieval Europe*, 20: 139–75.

Fletcher, Richard. 1997. *The Barbarian Conversion: From Paganism to Christianity*. Berkeley: University of California Press.

Foote, Peter. 1977. 'Oral and Literary Tradition in Early Scandinavian Law: Aspects of a Problem.' In *Oral Tradition, Literary Tradition: A Symposium*. Edited by H. Bekker-Nielsen, P. Foote, A. Haarder, and H. F. Nielsen. Odense: Odense University Press. 47–55.

Foote, Peter. 1979. 'Review Article: New Dimensions in *Njáls saga*.' *Scandinavica*, 18: 49–58.

Fox, Denton. 1963. '*Njáls saga* and the Western Literary Tradition.' *Comparative Literature*, 15: 289–310.

Gade, Kari Ellen. 1985. 'Homosexuality and Rape of Males in Old Norse Law and Literature.' *SS* 58: 124–41.

Gísli Sigurðsson. 2004. *The Medieval Icelandic Saga and Oral Tradition: A Discourse on Method*. Translated by Nicholas Jones. Publications of the Milman Parry Collection of Oral Literature, No. 2. Cambridge, Mass.: Harvard University Press.

Glauser, Jürg. 2007. 'The Speaking Bodies of Saga Texts.' In *Learning and Understanding in the Old Norse World: Essays in Honor of Margaret Clunies Ross*. Edited by Judy Quinn, Kate Heslop, and Tarrin Wills. Turnhout: Brepols. 13–26.

Gottzmann, Carola L. 1982. *Njáls Saga: Rechtsproplematik im dienste sozio-kultureller Deutung*. Frankfurt am Main: P. Lang.

Grønlie, Siân. 2012. 'Saint's Life and Saga Narrative.' *Saga-Book of the Viking Society*, 36: 5–26.

Guðrún Nordal. 2008. 'The Dialogue between Audience and Text: The Variants in Verse Citations in *Njáls saga*'s Manuscripts.' In *Oral Art Forms and their Passage into Writing*. Edited by Else Mundal and Jonas Wellendorf. Copenhagen: Museum Tusculanum Press. 185–202.

Hallberg, Peter. 1962. *The Icelandic Saga*. Translated by Paul Schach. Lincoln, Nebr.: University of Nebraska Press.

Hallberg, Peter. 1966. 'Några Anteckningar om Replik och Dialog i Njals Saga.' In *Festschrift Walter Baetke dargebracht zu seinem 80. Geburtstag am 28. März 1964*. Edited by Kurt Rudolph, Rolf Heller, and Ernst Walter, Weimar: Hermann Böhlaus Nachfolger. 130–50.

Hallberg, Peter. 1973. 'Njála miðaldahelgisaga?' *Andvari*, 98: 60–9.

Heinrichs, Anne. 1994. 'Hallgerðr's saga in der *Njála*: der doppelte Blick.' In *Studien zum Altgermanischen, festschrift für Heinrich Beck*. Edited by Heiko Uecker. Berlin: Walter de Gruytur. 327–53.

Helga Kress. 1977. 'Ekki höfu vér kvennaskap: nokkrar laustengdar athuganir um karlmennsku og kvenhatur í *Njálu.*' *Sjötíu ritgerðir helgaðar Jakobi Benediktssyni 20. júlí 1977.* Edited by Jónas Kristjánsson and Einar Gunnar Pétursson. 2 vols. Reykjavík: Stofnun Árna Magnússonar. 1: 293–313.

Helga Kress. 1991. 'Staðlausir stafir: um slúður sem uppsprettu frásagnar í Íslendingasögum.' *Skírnir* 165: 130–56.

Helgi Þorláksson. 1989. *Gamlar götur og goðavald. Um fornar leiðir og völd Oddaverja í Rangárþingi.* Reykjavík: Ritsafn Sagnfræðistofnunar 25.

Hermann Pálsson. 1983. 'Eftir Njálsbrennu.' *Andvari,* 108: 47–50.

Hermanson, Lars. 2013. 'How to Legitimate Rebellion and Condemn Usurpation of the Crown: Discourses of Fidelity and Treason in the *Gesta Danorum* of Saxo Grammaticus.' In Esmark *et al.* 107–40.

Herzog, Don. 2012. *Household Politics: Conflict in Early Modern England.* New Haven, CT: Yale University Press. http://deepblue.lib.umich.edu/handle/2027.42/90021

Heusler, Andreas. 1911. *Das Strafrecht der Isländersagas.* Leipzig: Duncker & Humblot.

Heusler, Andreas. 1922. 'Einleitung.' *Die Geschichte vom weisen Njal.* Jena: Eugen Diederichs. 1–20.

Hieatt, Constance B. 1979. 'Hrút's Voyage to Norway and the Structure of *Njála*.' *JEGP* 77: 489–94.

Hines, John and Desmond Slay, eds. 1992. *Introductory Essays on Egils saga and Njáls saga.* London: Viking Society for Northern Research.

Høyersten, Jon Geir. 2001. 'The Icelandic Sagas and the Idea of Personality and Deviant Personalities in the Middle Ages.' *History of Psychiatry,* 12: 199–212.

Hudson, John G. H. 2010. 'Feud, Vengeance, and Violence in England from the Tenth to the Twelfth Centuries.' In Tuten and Billado. 29–53.

Hudson, John G. H. 2012. *The Oxford History of the Laws of England:* Vol. II, *871–1216.* Oxford: Oxford University Press.

Ibn Fadlān. 2012. *Ibn Fadlān and the Land of Darkness: Arab Travellers in the Far North.* Translated with an Introduction by Paul Lunde and Caroline Stone. London: Penguin.

Jesch, Judith. 1992. ' "Good men" and Peace in *Njáls saga.*' In Hines and Slay. 64–82.

Jochens, Jenny. 1995. *Women in Old Norse Society.* Ithaca, NY: Cornell University Press, 1995.

Jón Hnefill Aðalsteinsson. 1999. *Under the Cloak: A Pagan Ritual Turning Point in the Conversion of Iceland.* 2nd edn. Jakob S. Jónsson. Reykjavík: Háskólaútgáfan.

Jón Karl Helgason. 1999. *The Rewriting of Njáls saga: Translation, Politics, and Icelandic Sagas.* Clevedon: Multilingual Matters.

Jón Viðar Sigurðsson. 1999. *Chieftains and Power in Commonwealth Iceland.* Viking Collection 12. Odense: Odense University Press.

Judd, William E. 1984. 'Valgerðr's Smile.' *SS* 56: 203–12.

Karras, Ruth Mazo. 1988. *Slavery and Society in Medieval Scandinavia.* New Haven: Yale University Press.

Ker, W. P. *Epic and Romance*. London: Macmillan, 1897.

Kristján Jóhann Jónsson. 1998. *Lykillinn að Njálu*. Reykjavík: Vaka-Helgafell.

Lehmann, Karl, and Hans Schnorr von Carolsfeld. 1883. *Die Njálssage insbesondere in ihren juristischen Bestandtheilen: ein kritischer Beitrag zur altnordischen Rechts- und Literaturgeschichte*. Berlin: R. L. Prager.

Lönnroth, Lars. 1976. *Njáls Saga: A Critical Introduction*. Berkeley: University of California Press.

Louis-Jensen, Jonna. 1979. 'En nidstrofe.' *Opuscula*, 6: 104–7.

Mack, Maynard. 1960. 'The Jacobean Shakespeare: Some Observations on the Construction of the Tragedies.' In *Jacobean Theatre*. Edited by John Russell Brown and Bernard Harris. London: Edward Arnold. 11–42.

Magnusson, Magnus, and Hermann Pálsson, trans. 1960. *Njal's Saga*. Harmondworth: Penguin.

Maxwell, Ian R. 1957-9. 'Pattern in *Njáls saga*.' *Saga-Book of the Viking Society*, 15: 17–47.

McTurk, Rory. 1992. 'The Supernatural in *Njáls saga*: A Narratological Approach.' In Hines and Slay. 102–24.

McTurk, Rory. 2005. *A Companion to Old Norse-Icelandic Literature and Culture*. Malden, Mass.: Blackwell.

Melve, Leidulf, and Sigbjørn Sønnesyn, eds. 2012. *The Creation of Medieval Northern Europe: Essays in Honor of Sverre Bagge*. Oslo: Dreyer Forlag.

Meulengracht Sørensen, Preben. 1983. *The Unmanly Man: Concepts of Sexual Defamation in Early Northern Society*. Translated by Joan Turville-Petre. Odense: Odense University Press.

Miller, William Ian. 1983*a*. 'Justifying Skarpheðinn: Of Pretext and Politics in the Icelandic Bloodfeud.' *SS* 55: 316–44.

Miller, William Ian. 1983*b*. 'Choosing the Avenger: Some Aspects of the Bloodfeud in Medieval Iceland and England.' *Law and History Review*, 1: 159–204.

Miller, William Ian. 1984. 'Avoiding Legal Judgment: the Submission of Disputes to Arbitration in Medieval Iceland.' *American Journal of Legal History*, 28: 95–134.

Miller, William Ian. 1986. 'Dreams, Prophecy, and Sorcery: Blaming the Secret Offender in Medieval Iceland.' *SS* 58: 101–23.

Miller, William Ian. 1988. 'Ordeal in Iceland.' *SS* 60: 189–218.

Miller, William Ian. 1990. *Bloodtaking and Peacemaking: Feud, Law, and Society in Saga Iceland*. Chicago: University of Chicago Press.

Miller, William Ian. 1991. 'Of Outlaws, Christians, Horsemeat, and Writing: Uniform Laws and Saga Iceland.' *Michigan Law Review*, 89: 2081–95.

Miller, William Ian. 1993. *Humiliation: And Other Essays on Honor, Social Discomfort, and Violence*. Ithaca, NY: Cornell University Press.

Miller, William Ian. 1995. 'Deep Inner Lives, Individualism, and People of Honour.' *History of Political Thought*, 16: 190–207.

Miller, William Ian. 1998. 'Clint Eastwood and Equity: The Virtues of Revenge and the Shortcomings of Law in Popular Culture.' In Sarat and Kearns. 161–202.

Miller, William Ian. 2003. *Faking It*. Cambridge: Cambridge University Press.

Miller, William Ian. 2006. *Eye for an Eye*. Cambridge: Cambridge University Press.

Miller, William Ian. 2008. *Audun and the Polar Bear: Luck, Law, and Largesse in a Medieval Tale of Risky Business*. Leiden: Brill.

Miller, William Ian. 2010. 'Threat.' In Tuten and Billado. 9–28.

Miller, William Ian. 2011. *Losing It, in which an aging professor laments his shrinking brain, which he flatters himself formerly did him noble service: a plaint, tragic-comical, historical, vengeful, sometimes satirical and thankful in six parts, if his memory does yet serve*. New Haven: Yale University Press.

Miller, William Ian. 2012. 'Conscience, Interest, Side-Switching and *Laxdæla saga*: chapters 59 and 61.' In Melve and Sønnesyn. 373–88.

Müller, Harald. 2000. '". . . und gut is keines von beiden": Gedanken zur Akzeptanz der Brenna in der *Njáls Saga*.' In *Studien zur Isländersaga: Festschrift für Rolf Heller*. Edited by Heinrich Beck and Else Ebel. Berlin: Walter de Gruyter. 198–207.

Noble, Thomas F. X. trans. 2009. *Charlemagne and Louis the Pious: Lives by Einhard, Notker, Ermoldus, Thegan, and the Astronomer*. University Park, Pa.: Penn State University Press.

O'Donoghue, Heather. 1992. 'Women in *Njáls saga*.' In Hines and Slay. 83–101.

O'Donoghue, Heather. 2004. *Old Norse-Icelandic Literature: A Short Introduction*. Oxford: Blackwell.

Orning, Hans Jacob. 2008. *Unpredictability and Presence: Norwegian Kingship in the High Middle Ages*. Translated by Alan Crozier. Leiden: Brill.

Orri Vésteinsson. 2000. *The Christianization of Iceland: Priests, Power, and Social Change, 1000–1300*. Oxford: Oxford University Press.

Orri Vésteinsson. 2007. 'A Divided Society: Peasants and the Aristocracy in Medieval Iceland.' *Viking and Medieval Scandinavia*, 3: 117–39.

Perkins, Richard. 2001. *Thor the Wind-Raiser and the Eyrarland Image*. London: Viking Society. http://www.vsnrweb-publications.org.uk/Text%20Series/Thor_the_Windraiser/Thor.pdf.

Phillpotts, Bertha Surtees. 1913. *Kindred and Clan in the Middle Ages and After*. Cambridge: Cambridge University Press.

Pokorny, Julius. 2002. *Indogermanisches etymologisches Wörterbuch*, 4th edn. Tübingen: A. Francke.

Reynolds, Susan. 1991. 'Social Mentalities and the Case of Medieval Scepticism.' *Transactions of the Royal Historical Society*, 6th ser. 1: 21–41.

Robertson, A. J. ed. and trans. 1925. *The Laws of the Kings of England from Edmund to Henry I*. Cambridge: Cambridge University Press.

Roth, Martha T. 1997. *Law Collections from Mesopotamia and Asia Minor*. 2nd edn. Atlanta, Ga.: Scholar's Press.

Samson, Ross. 1992. 'Goðar: Democrats or Despots.' In *From Sagas to Society*. Edited by Gísli Pálsson. Middlesex: Hisarlik. 167–88.

Sarat, Austin, and Thomas Kearns, eds. 1998. *Law in the Domains of Culture*. Ann Arbor, Mich.: University of Michigan Press.

Sayers, William. 1994. 'Njáll's Beard, Hallgerðr's Hair and Gunnarr's Hay: Homological Patterning in *Njáls saga*.' *TijdSchrift voor Skandinavistiek*, 15: 5–31.

Sayers, William. 1997a. 'Gunnarr, his Irish Wolfhound Sámr, and the Passing of the Old Heroic Order in *Njáls saga*.' *Arkiv för nordisk filologi*, 112: 43–66.

Sayers, William. 1997b. 'Sexual Defamation in Medieval Iceland: Gera Meri ór einum, "Make a Mare of Someone."' *North-western European Language Evolution*, NOWELE 30: 27–37.

Sigurður Nordal. 1940. *Hrafnkatla*. Studia Islandica 7. Reykjavík: Ísafoldarprent smiðja. Translated by R. George Thomas as *Hrafnkels saga freysgoða: A Study*. Cardiff: University of Wales Press, 1958.

Thorstein Gylfason. 1998. 'Introduction.' *Njál's Saga*. Wordsworth Classics Edition. Ware: Wordsworth. xi–xxx.

Tuten, Belle S., and Tracey L. Billado, eds. 2010. *Feud, Violence and Practice: Essays in Medieval Studies in Honor of Stephen D. White*. Aldershot: Ashgate.

Vésteinn Ólason. 1998. *Dialogues with the Viking Age: Narration and Representation in the Sagas of the Icelanders*. Translated by Andrew Wawn. Reykjavík: Heimskringla, Mál og Menning Academic Division.

Vésteinn Ólason and Sverrir Tómasson. 2006. 'The Middle Ages.' In *A History of Icelandic Literature*. Edited by Daisy Neijmann. Lincoln, Nebr.: University of Nebraska Press. 1–173.

Vilhjálmur Árnason. 2009. 'An Ethos in Transformation: Conflicting Values in the Sagas.' *Gripla*, 20: 217–40.

Wawn, Andrew. 2000. *The Vikings and the Victorians: Inventing the Old North in Nineteenth-Century Britain*. Cambridge: D. S. Brewer.

White, Stephen D. 2005. *Feuding and Peacemaking in Eleventh-Century France*. Aldershot: Ashgate.

White, Stephen D. 2007. 'Alternative Constructions of Treason in the Angevin Political World: *Traïson* in the *History of William Marshal*', *e-Spania*. http://e-spania.revues.org/2233. 4: 1–47.

White, Stephen D. 2013. 'The Feelings in the Feud: the Emotional Turn in the Study of Medieval Vengeance.' In Esmark *et al.* 281–311.

Wickham, Chris. 2003. *Courts and Conflict in Twelfth-Century Tuscany*. Oxford: Oxford University Press.

Wolf, Alois. 1982. 'Zur Stellung der *Njála* in der isländischen Sagaliteratur.' In *Tradition und Entwicklung: Festschrift für Eugen Thurnher zum 60. Geburtstag*. Edited by Werner M. Bauer, Achim Masser, and Guntram A. Plangg. Innsbruck. 61–85.

Maps

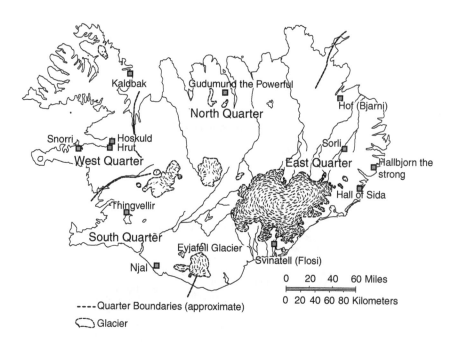

Kaldbak

Gudumund the Powerful

Hof (Bjarni)

North Quarter

Snorri

Hoskuld
Hrut

Sorli

West Quarter

East Quarter

Hallbjorn the
strong

Hall of Sida

Thingvellir

South Quarter

Eyjafell Glacier

Svinatell (Flosi)

Njal

0   20   40   60 Miles

0 20 40 60 80 Kilometers

----Quarter Boundaries (approximate)

Glacier

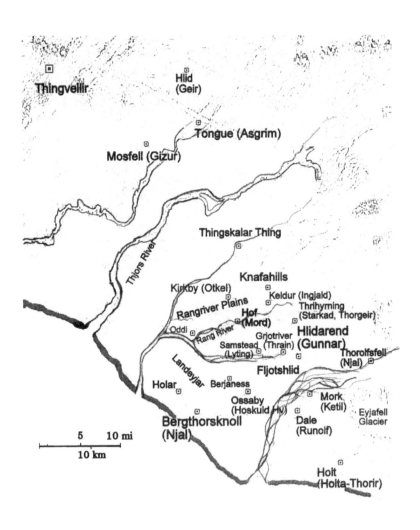

Thingvellir

Hlid
(Geir)

Tongue (Asgrim)

Mosfell (Gizur)

Thjors River

Thingskalar Thing

Knafahills

Kirkby (Otkel)   Keldur (Ingjald)
                                                      Thrihyrning
Rangriver Plains   (Starkad, Thorgeir)
                          Hof
Oddi   (Mord)
           Rang River   Grjotriver   Hlidarend
                    Samstead (Thrain)   (Gunnar)
                    (Lyting)   Thorolfsfell
       Landeyjar   (Njal)
                              Fljotshlid
Holar   Berjaness
                                              Mork
                    Ossaby   (Ketil)
                    (Hoskuld Hv)   Eyjafell
Bergthorsknoll   Dale   Glacier
(Njal)   (Runolf)

5   10 mi   Holt
                                              (Holta-Thorir)
    10 km

Genealogies

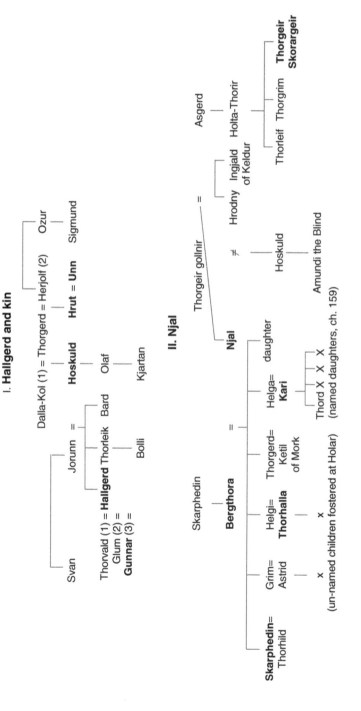

I. Hallgerd and kin

```
                    Dalla-Kol (1) = Thorgerd = Herjolf (2)      Ozur

                    Hoskuld        Hrut = Unn               Sigmund
                                              |
         |                         Olaf
         Jorunn  =                  |
                                  Kjartan
    |           |
Thorald (1) = Hallgerd  Thorleik  Bard
Glum (2) =              |
Gunnar (3) =           Bolli
    |
  Svan
```

II. Njal

```
                                      Thorgeir gollnir  =        Asgerd
                                                          |
                                        Hrodny  Ingjald  Holta-Thorir
                                                of Keldur
                                            |
                          ≠                Thorleif  Thorgrim  Thorgeir
                          |                                    Skorargeir
              Njal      Hoskuld
               |
Skarphedin  Bergthora  =
                                    Amundi the Blind

                        Helga = daughter
                        Kari
                              |
                        Thord X  X  X
                        (named daughters, ch. 159)

Helgi =  Thorgerd =
Thorhalla  Ketil
           of Mork

Grim =
Astrid

Skarphedin =
Thorhild

(un-named children fostered at Holar)
```

IIIa. Descendants of Sighvat the Red: Mord & Gunnar

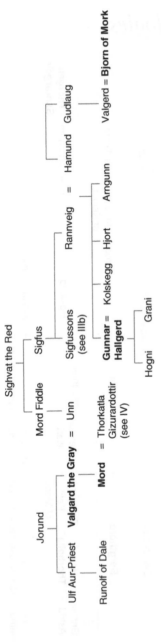

IIIb. Descendants of Sighvat the Red: the Sigfussons

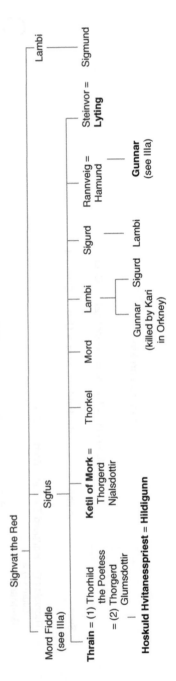

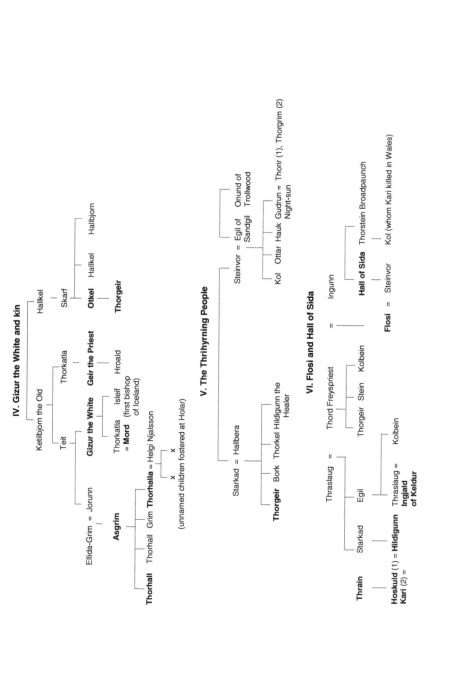

IV. Gizur the White and kin

Ketilbjorn the Old
- Teit
  - Thorkatla
  - Ketilbjorn the Old — Thorkatla — **Geir the Priest**
    - **Gizur the White** Thorkatla
      - Isleif (first bishop of Iceland)
    - = **Mord**
  - Hroald
- Hallkel
  - Skarf
  - **Otkel**
- Hal1kel
  - Hallkel
  - **Thorgeir**
- Hallbjorn

Ellida-Grim = Jorunn
- **Thorhall**
- **Asgrim**
  - Thorhall Grim **Thorhalla** = Helgi Njalsson
    - x   x
    - x   x
  - (unnamed children fostered at Holar)

V. The Thrihyrning People

Starkad = Hallbera
- **Thorgeir** Bork Thorkel Hildigunn the Healer

Steinvor = Egil of Sandgil
- Onund of Trollwood
- Kol Ottar Hauk Gudrun = Thorir (1), Thorgrim (2) Night-sun

VI. Flosi and Hall of Sida

Thrain
- Thraslaug =
  - Starkad Egil
- Thord Freyspriest
  - Thorgeir Stein Kolbein
- Ingunn

Hoskuld (1) = **Hildigunn** Thraslaug = **Ingjald of Keldur**
- Kolbein

Kari (2) =

Flosi = Steinvor
- **Hall of Sida** Thorstein Broadpaunch
  - Kol (whom Kari killed in Wales)

Index